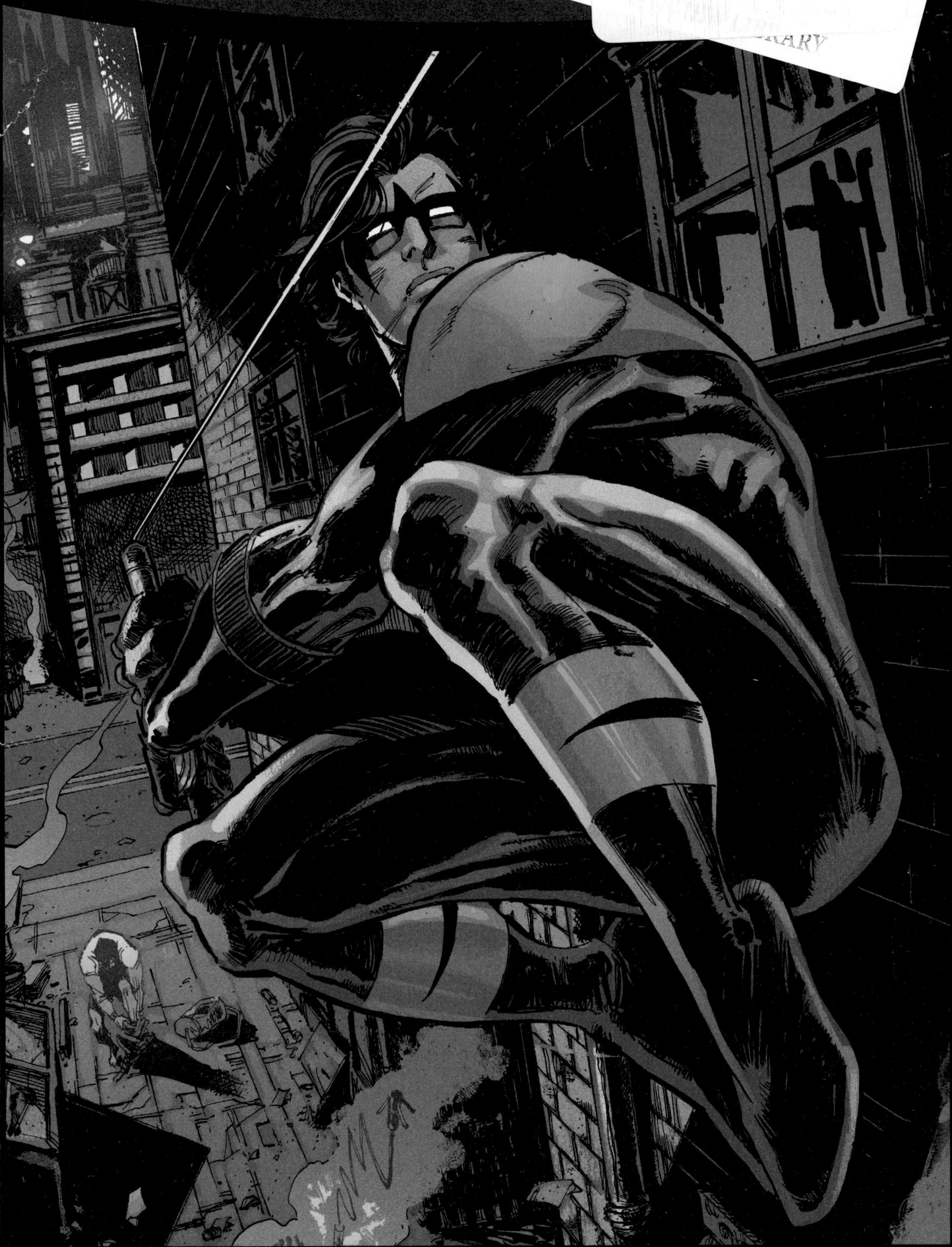

NIGHTWING

VOL.7 THE BLEEDING EDGE

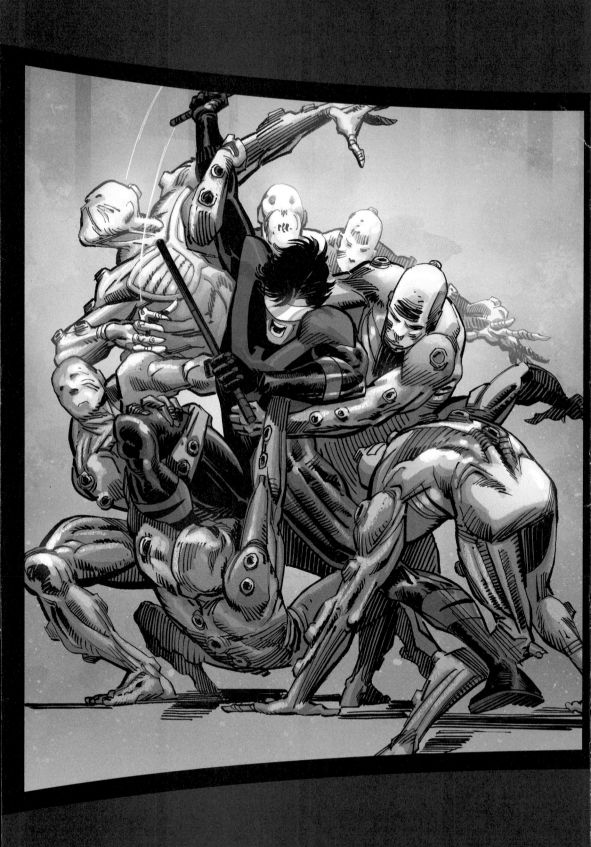

NIGHTWING

VOL.7 THE BLEEDING EDGE

BENJAMIN PERCY
writer

CHRIS MOONEYHAM * **KLAUS JANSON**
AMANCAY NAHUELPAN * **OTTO SCHMIDT**
SCOTT HANNA * LALIT KUMAR SHARMA
artists

NICK FILARDI
OTTO SCHMIDT
colorists

CARLOS M. MANGUAL
DAVE SHARPE
letterers

JOHN ROMITA JR., DANNY MIKI and **TOMEU MOREY**
collection cover artists

NIGHTWING created by **MARV WOLFMAN** and **GEORGE PÉREZ**
SUPERMAN created by **JERRY SIEGEL** and **JOE SHUSTER**
By special arrangement with the Jerry Siegel family

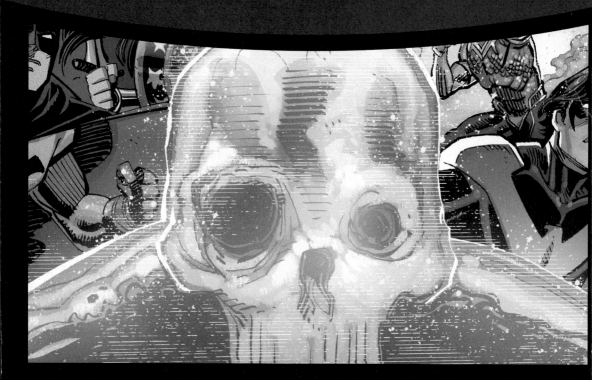

KATIE KUBERT Editor - Original Series * DAVE WIELGOSZ Assistant Editor - Original Series
JEB WOODARD Group Editor - Collected Editions * ERIKA ROTHBERG Editor - Collected Edition
STEVE COOK Design Director - Books * MONIQUE NARBONETA Publication Design

BOB HARRAS Senior VP - Editor-in-Chief, DC Comics
PAT McCALLUM Executive Editor, DC Comics

DAN DiDIO Publisher * JIM LEE Publisher & Chief Creative Officer
AMIT DESAI Executive VP - Business & Marketing Strategy, Direct to Consumer & Global Franchise Management
BOBBIE CHASE VP & Executive Editor, Young Reader & Talent Development * MARK CHIARELLO Senior VP - Art, Design & Collected Editions
JOHN CUNNINGHAM Senior VP - Sales & Trade Marketing * BRIAR DARDEN VP - Business Affairs
ANNE DePIES Senior VP - Business Strategy, Finance & Administration * DON FALLETTI VP - Manufacturing Operations
LAWRENCE GANEM VP - Editorial Administration & Talent Relations * ALISON GILL Senior VP - Manufacturing & Operations
JASON GREENBERG VP - Business Strategy & Finance * HANK KANALZ Senior VP - Editorial Strategy & Administration
JAY KOGAN Senior VP - Legal Affairs * NICK J. NAPOLITANO VP - Manufacturing Administration
LISETTE OSTERLOH VP - Digital Marketing & Events * EDDIE SCANNELL VP - Consumer Marketing
COURTNEY SIMMONS Senior VP - Publicity & Communications * JIM (SKI) SOKOLOWSKI VP - Comic Book Specialty Sales & Trade Marketing
NANCY SPEARS VP - Mass, Book, Digital Sales & Trade Marketing * MICHELE R. WELLS VP - Content Strategy

NIGHTWING VOL. 7: THE BLEEDING EDGE

DC Comics, 2900 West Alameda Ave., Burbank, CA 91505
Printed by LSC Communications, Owensville, MO, USA. 11/23/18. First Printing.
ISBN: 978-1-4012-8559-3

Library of Congress Cataloging-in-Publication Data is available.

FSC

www.fsc.org

MIX
Paper from
responsible sources
FSC® C132124

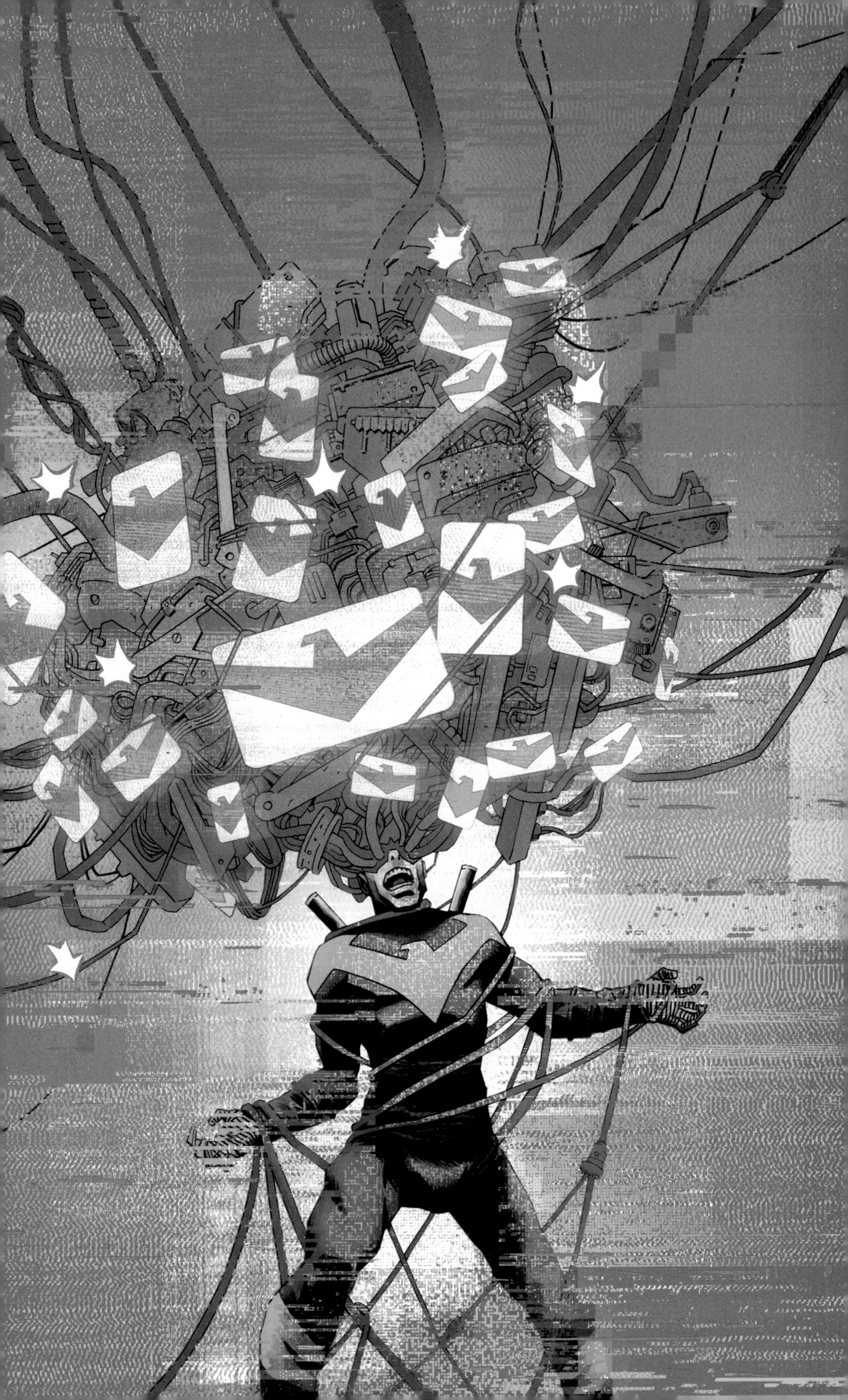

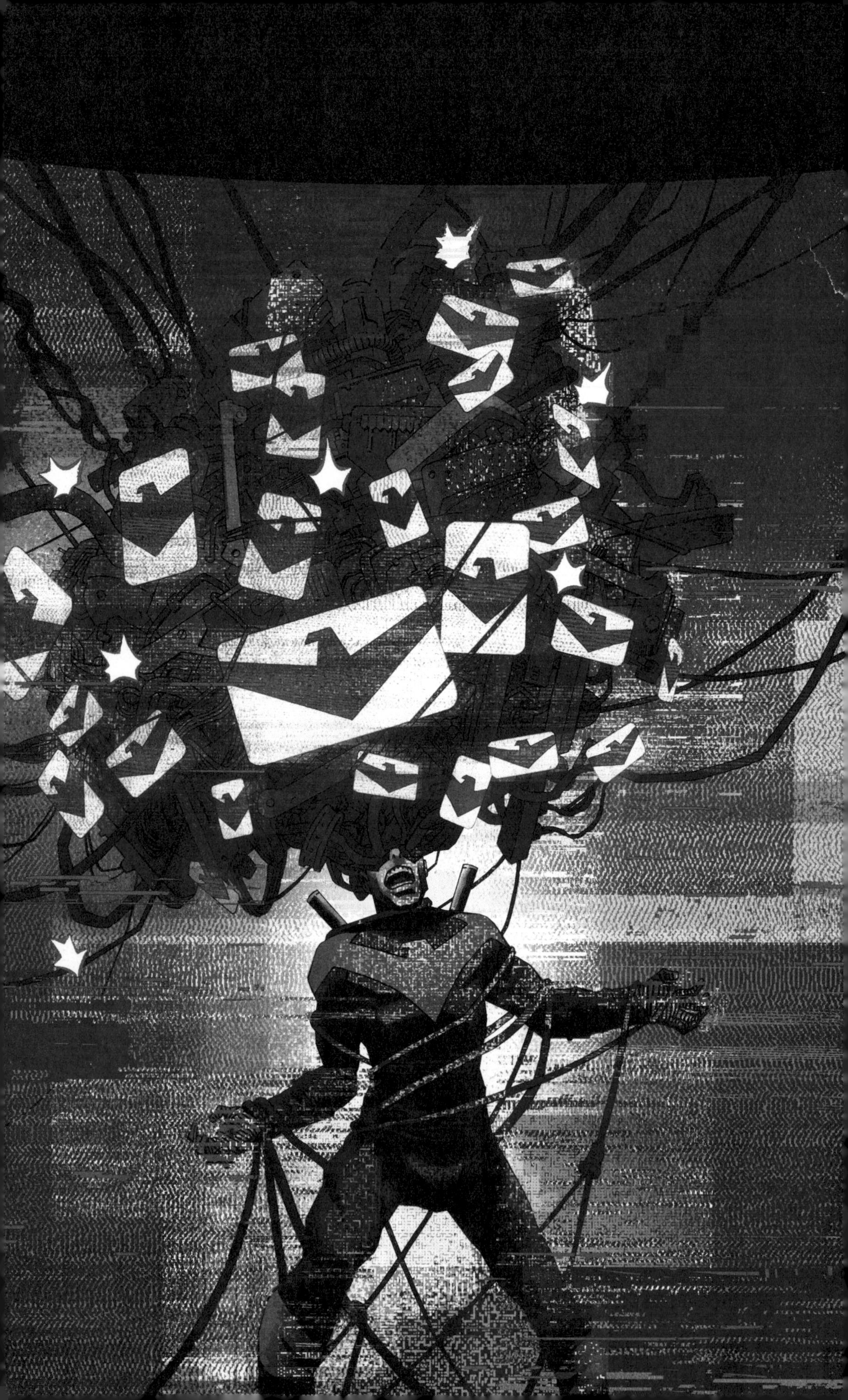

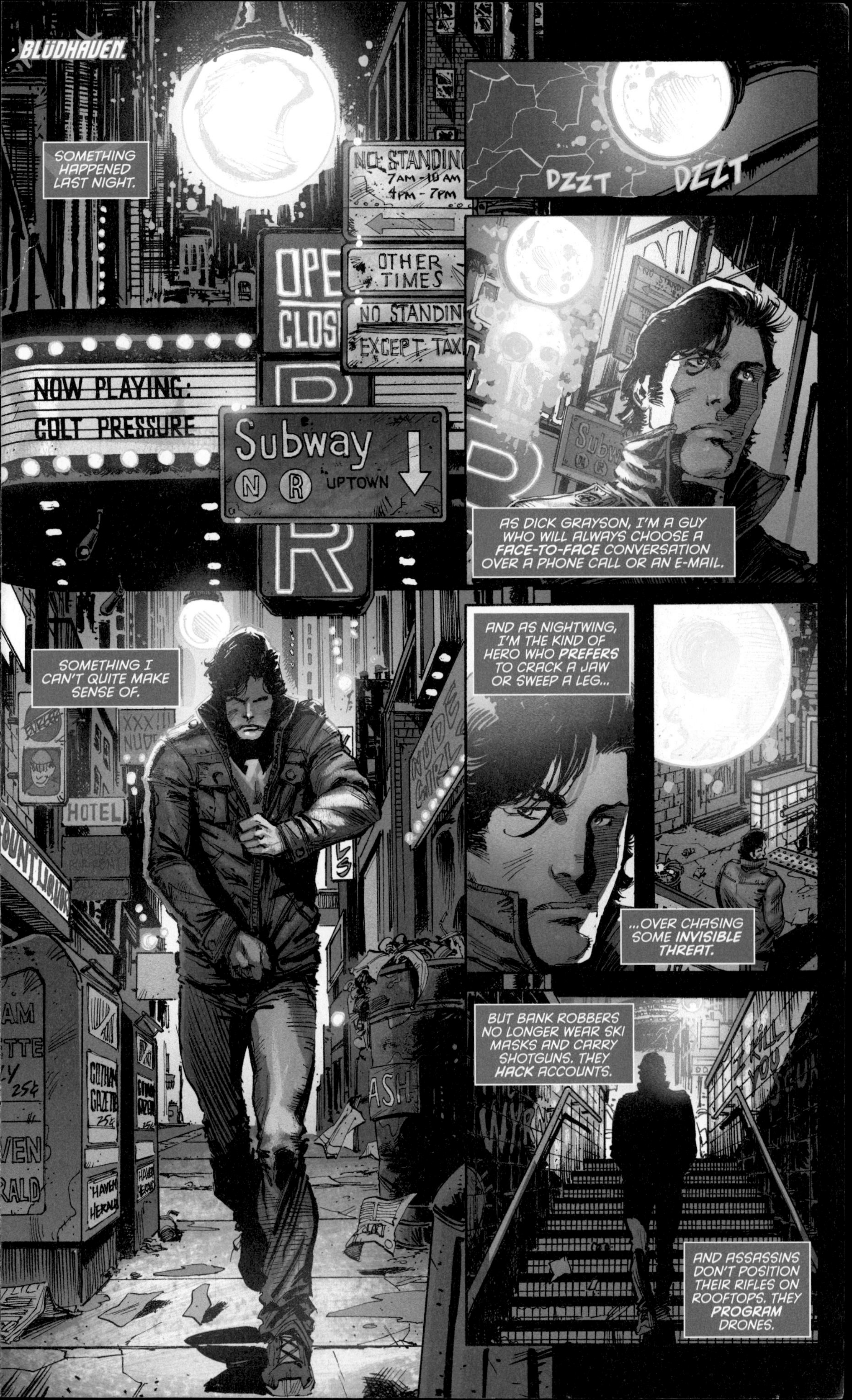
BLÜDHAVEN.
SOMETHING HAPPENED LAST NIGHT.
NO STANDING 7AM - 10 AM 4PM - 7PM
OTHER TIMES
NO STANDING EXCEPT TAXI
NOW PLAYING: COLT PRESSURE
Subway N R UPTOWN
DZZT DZZT
AS DICK GRAYSON, I'M A GUY WHO WILL ALWAYS CHOOSE A FACE-TO-FACE CONVERSATION OVER A PHONE CALL OR AN E-MAIL.
SOMETHING I CAN'T QUITE MAKE SENSE OF.
HOTEL
AND AS NIGHTWING, I'M THE KIND OF HERO WHO PREFERS TO CRACK A JAW OR SWEEP A LEG...
...OVER CHASING SOME INVISIBLE THREAT.
BUT BANK ROBBERS NO LONGER WEAR SKI MASKS AND CARRY SHOTGUNS. THEY HACK ACCOUNTS.
AND ASSASSINS DON'T POSITION THEIR RIFLES ON ROOFTOPS. THEY PROGRAM DRONES.

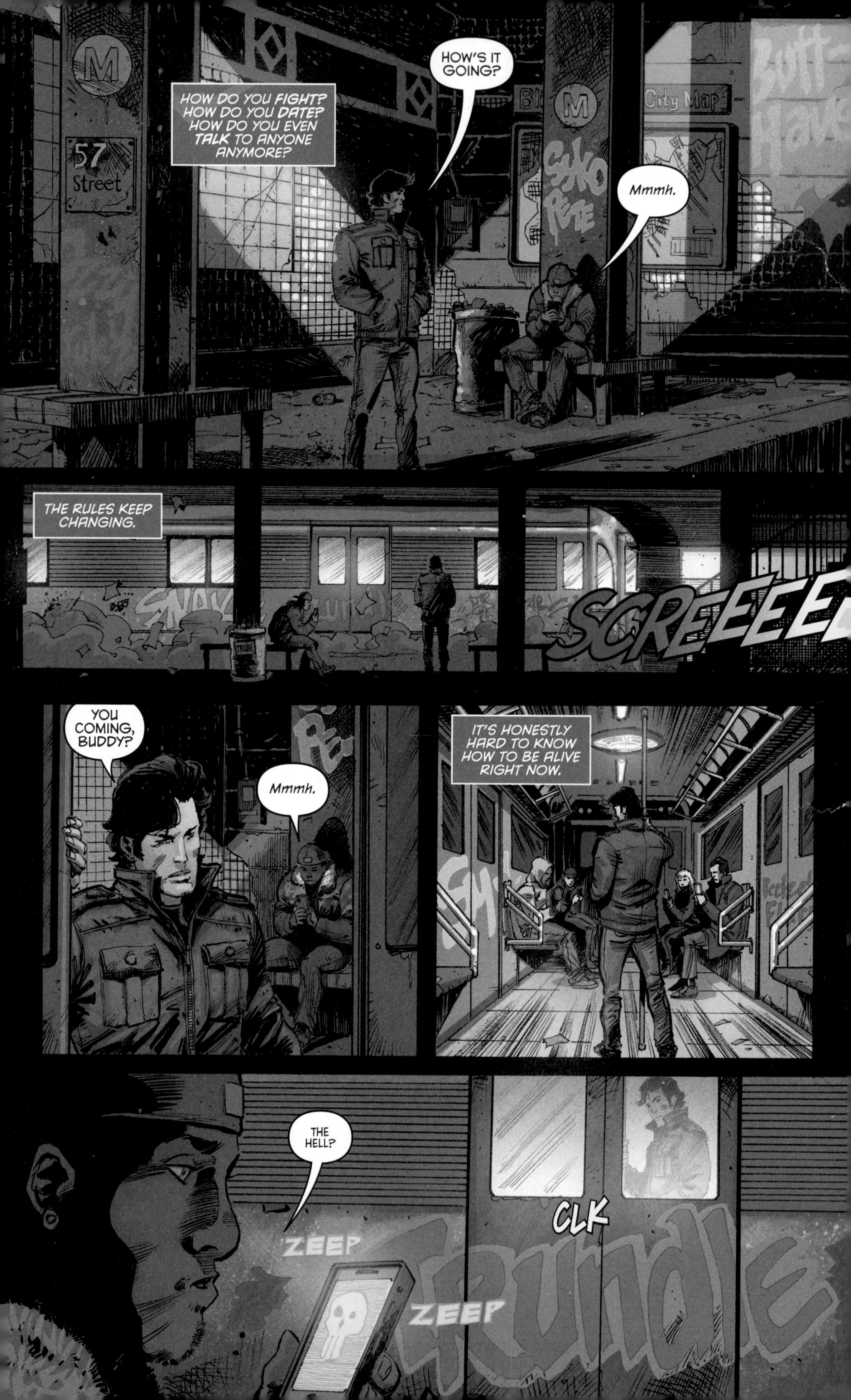
57
Street
HOW DO YOU FIGHT? HOW DO YOU DATE? HOW DO YOU EVEN TALK TO ANYONE ANYMORE?
HOW'S IT GOING?
City Map
Mmmh.
THE RULES KEEP CHANGING.
SCREEEEE
YOU COMING, BUDDY?
Mmmh.
IT'S HONESTLY HARD TO KNOW HOW TO BE ALIVE RIGHT NOW.
THE HELL?
CLK
ZEEP
ZEEP

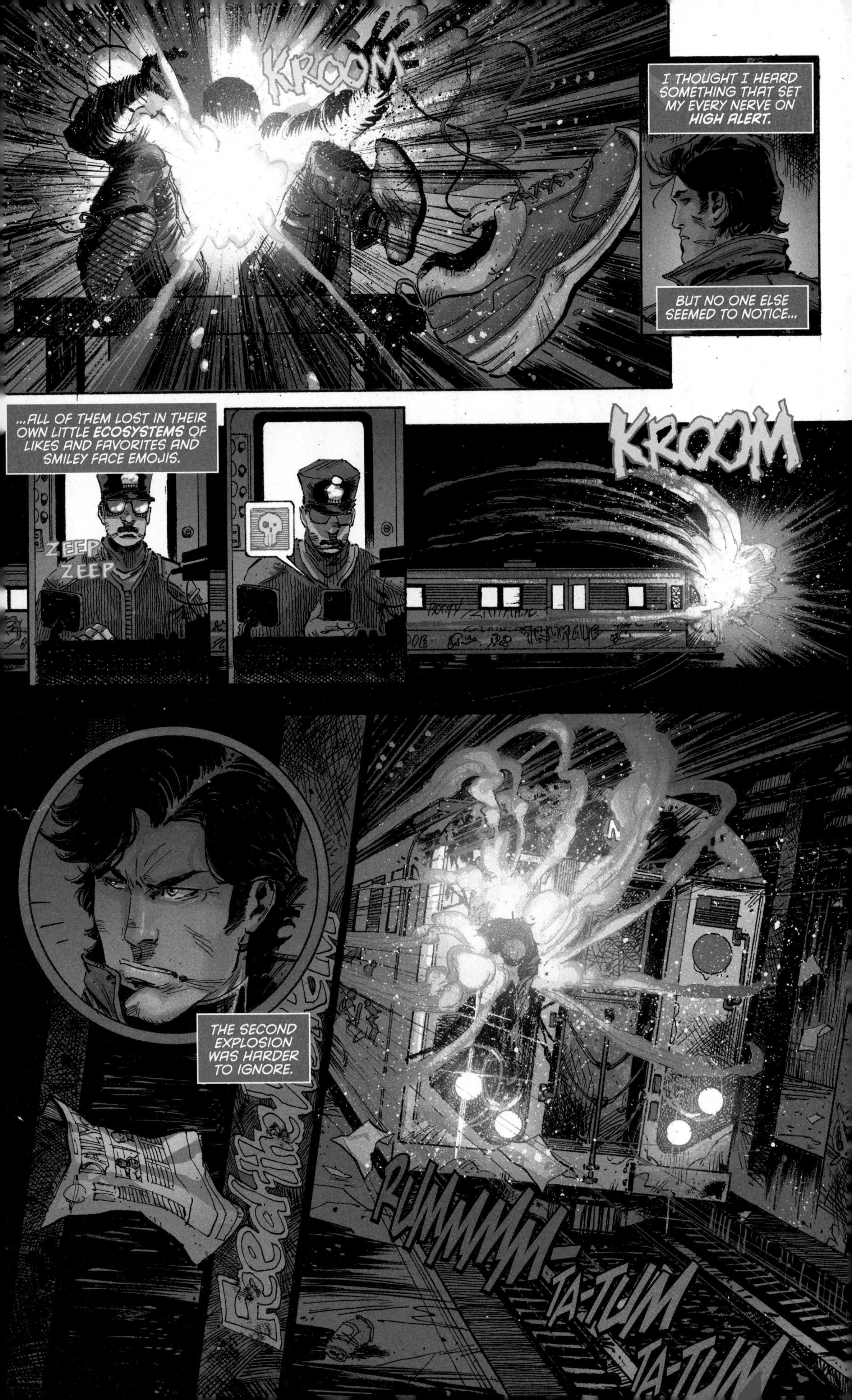
KROOM
I THOUGHT I HEARD SOMETHING THAT SET MY EVERY NERVE ON HIGH ALERT.
BUT NO ONE ELSE SEEMED TO NOTICE...
...ALL OF THEM LOST IN THEIR OWN LITTLE ECOSYSTEMS OF LIKES AND FAVORITES AND SMILEY FACE EMOJIS.
ZEEP ZEEP
KROOM
THE SECOND EXPLOSION WAS HARDER TO IGNORE.
RUMMMM-TA-TUM TA-TUM

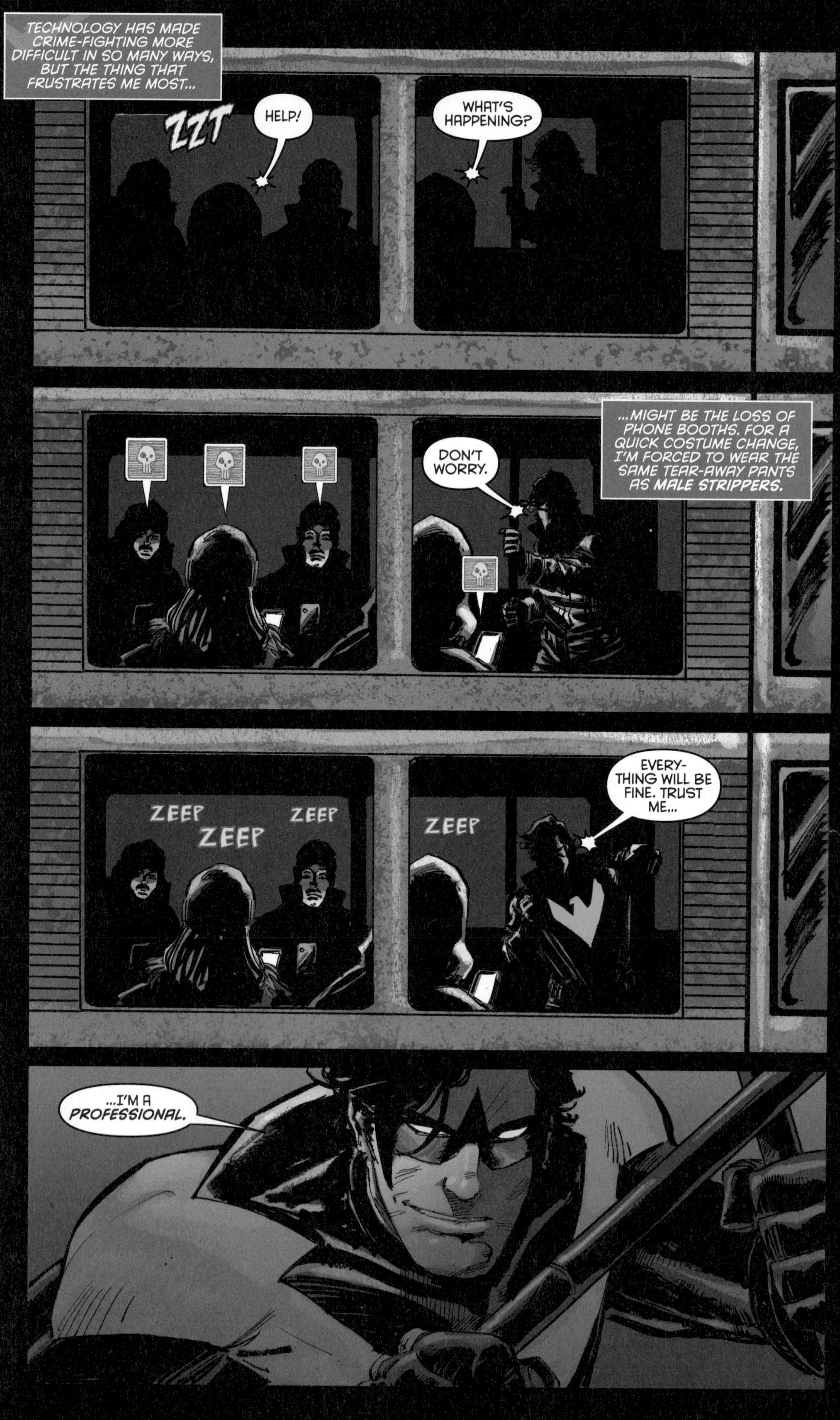
TECHNOLOGY HAS MADE CRIME-FIGHTING MORE DIFFICULT IN SO MANY WAYS, BUT THE THING THAT FRUSTRATES ME MOST...
ZZT
HELP!
WHAT'S HAPPENING?
...MIGHT BE THE LOSS OF PHONE BOOTHS. FOR A QUICK COSTUME CHANGE, I'M FORCED TO WEAR THE SAME TEAR-AWAY PANTS AS MALE STRIPPERS.
DON'T WORRY.
ZEEP
ZEEP
ZEEP
ZEEP
EVERY-THING WILL BE FINE. TRUST ME...
...I'M A PROFESSIONAL.

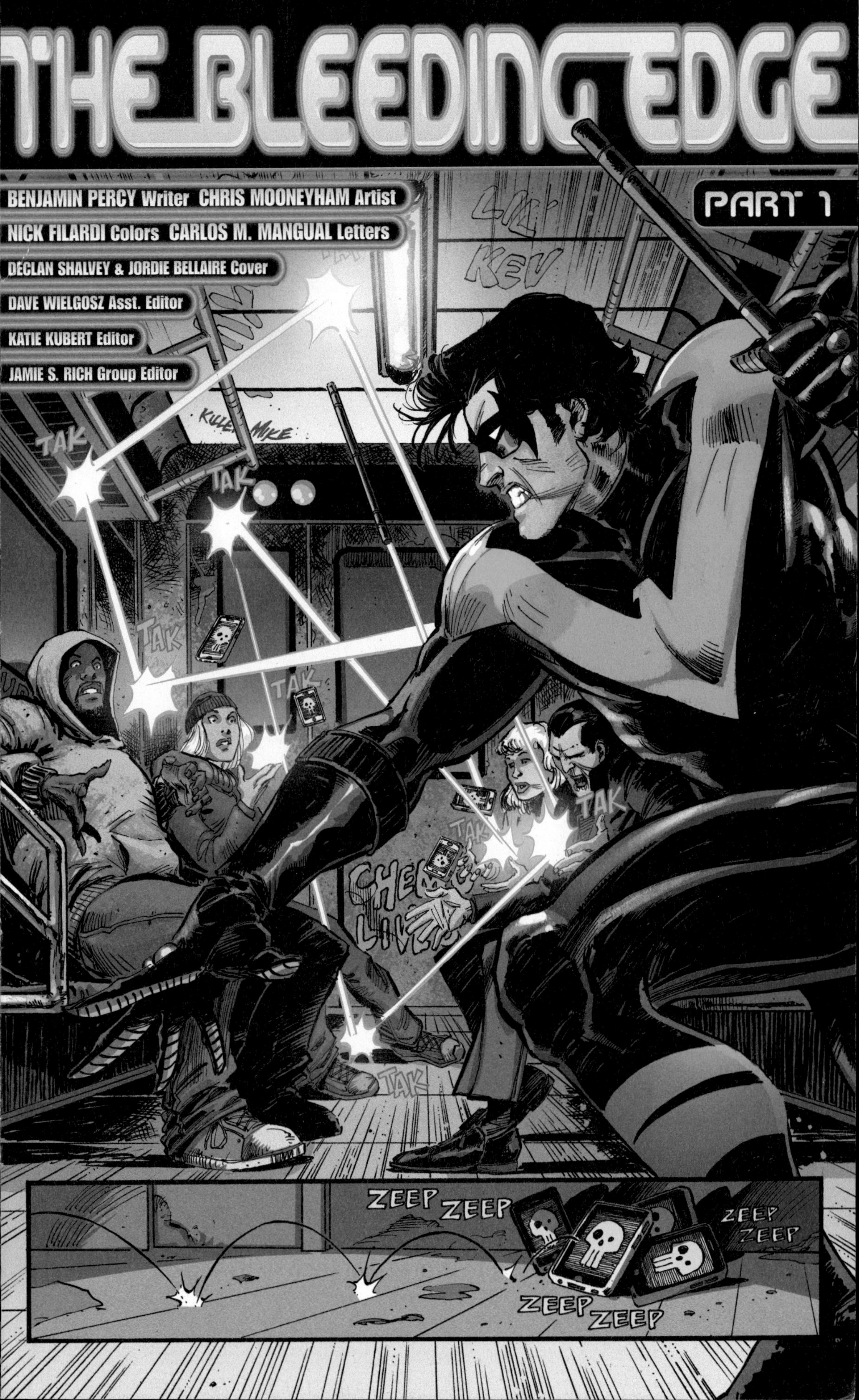
THE BLEEDING EDGE
PART 1
BENJAMIN PERCY Writer CHRIS MOONEYHAM Artist
NICK FILARDI Colors CARLOS M. MANGUAL Letters
DECLAN SHALVEY & JORDIE BELLAIRE Cover
DAVE WIELGOSZ Asst. Editor
KATIE KUBERT Editor
JAMIE S. RICH Group Editor
TAK
TAK
TAK
TAK
TAK
TAK
TAK
ZEEP ZEEP
ZEEP ZEEP
ZEEP ZEEP

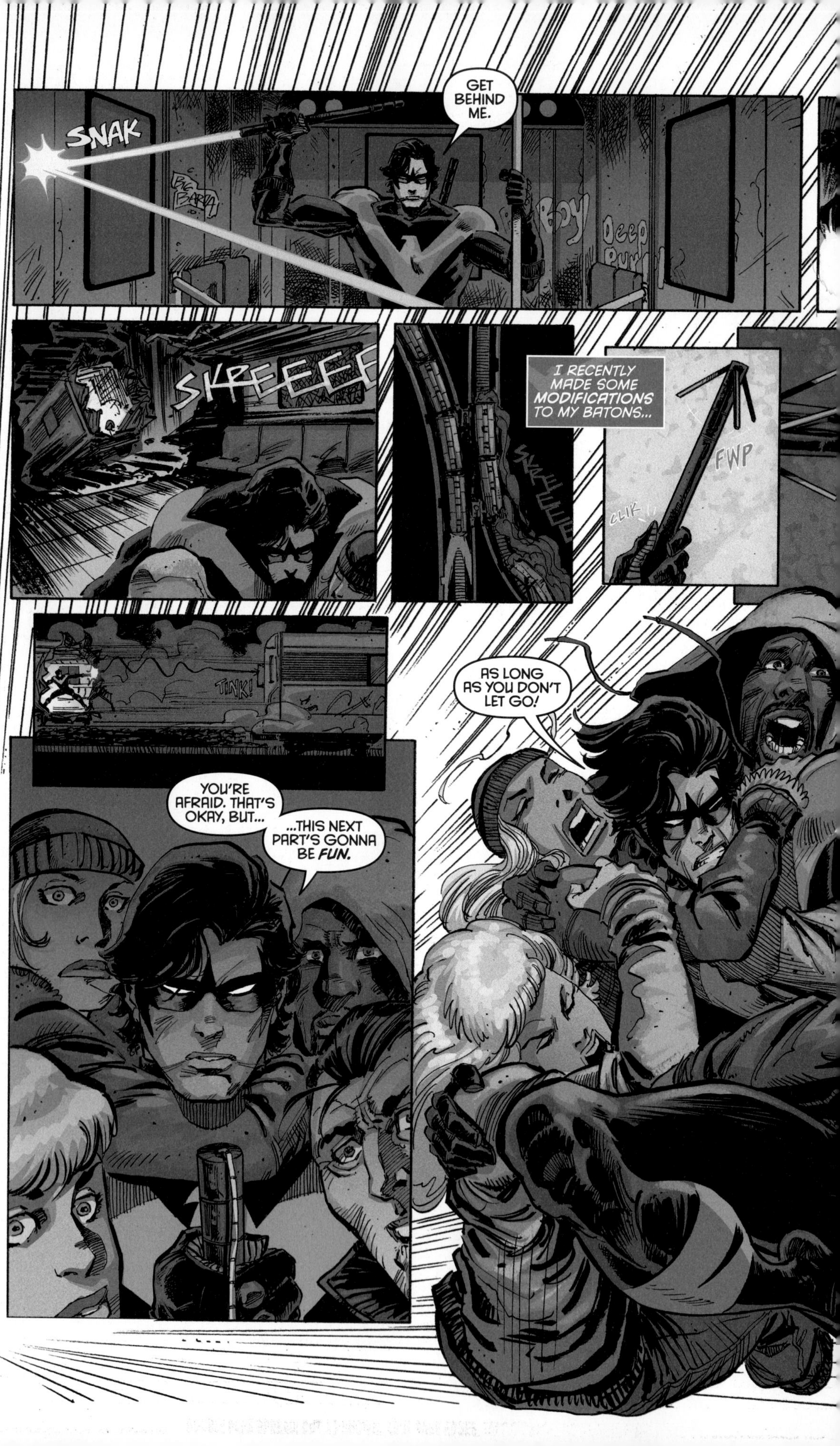
SNAK
GET BEHIND ME.
BIG BARDA
Boy!
Deep Purple
SKREEEEF
SKREEEE
I RECENTLY MADE SOME MODIFICATIONS TO MY BATONS...
FWP
CLIK
TINK!
YOU'RE AFRAID. THAT'S OKAY, BUT...
...THIS NEXT PART'S GONNA BE *FUN.*
AS LONG AS YOU DON'T LET GO!

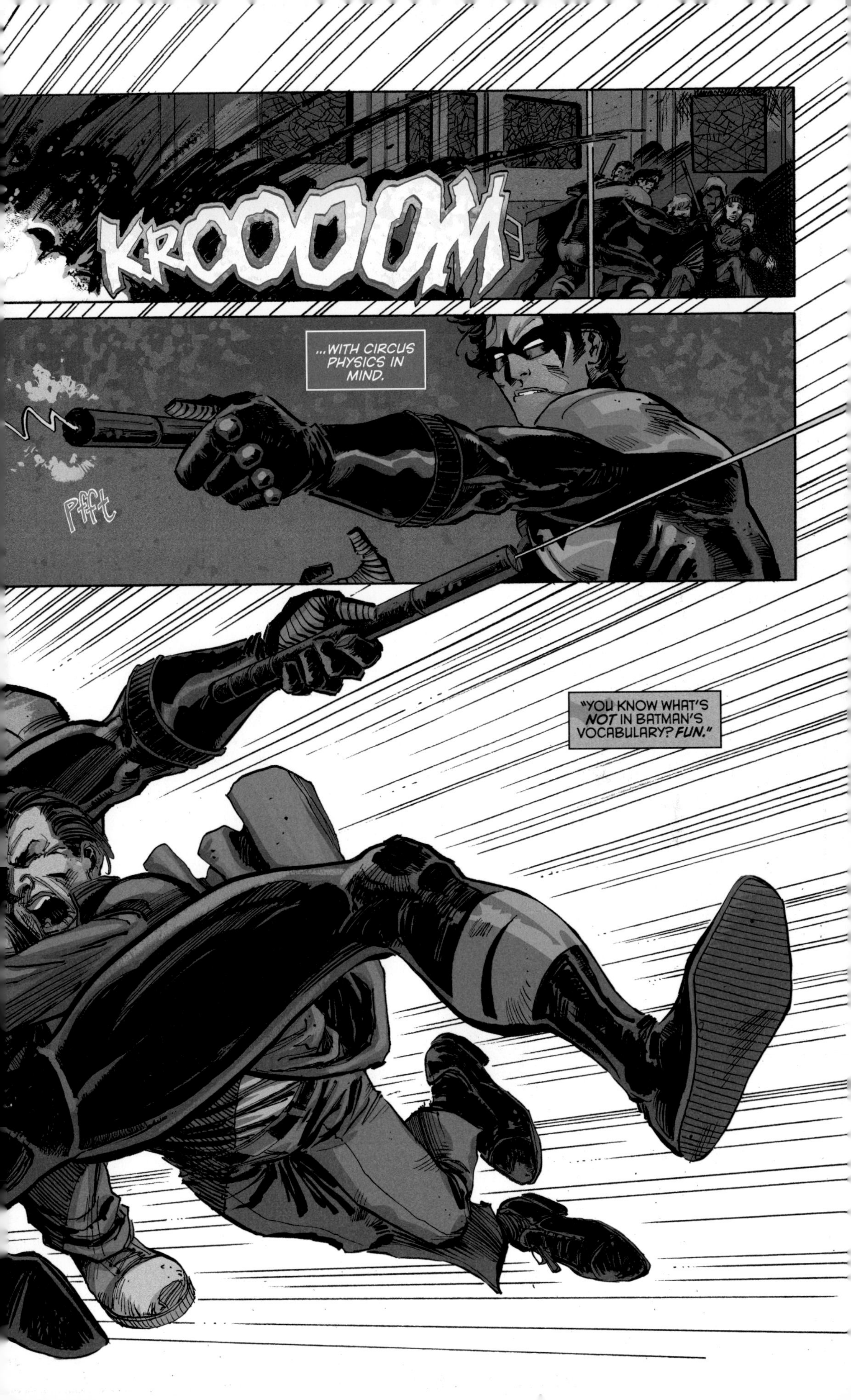
KROOOOM
...WITH CIRCUS PHYSICS IN MIND.
Pffft
"YOU KNOW WHAT'S NOT IN BATMAN'S VOCABULARY? FUN."

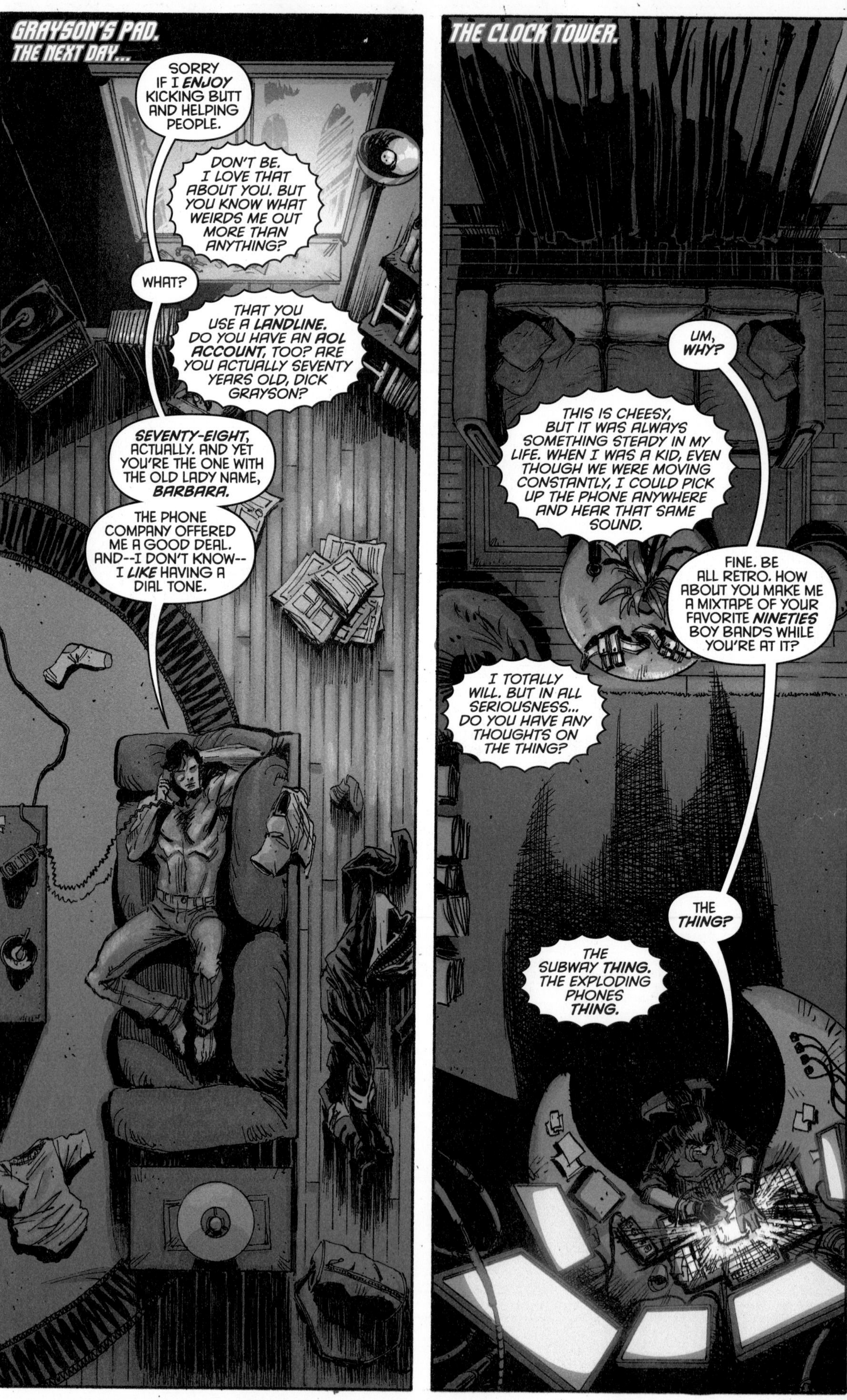
GRAYSON'S PAD. THE NEXT DAY...
SORRY IF I ENJOY KICKING BUTT AND HELPING PEOPLE.
DON'T BE. I LOVE THAT ABOUT YOU. BUT YOU KNOW WHAT WEIRDS ME OUT MORE THAN ANYTHING?
WHAT?
THAT YOU USE A LANDLINE. DO YOU HAVE AN AOL ACCOUNT, TOO? ARE YOU ACTUALLY SEVENTY YEARS OLD, DICK GRAYSON?
SEVENTY-EIGHT, ACTUALLY. AND YET YOU'RE THE ONE WITH THE OLD LADY NAME, BARBARA.
THE PHONE COMPANY OFFERED ME A GOOD DEAL. AND--I DON'T KNOW--I LIKE HAVING A DIAL TONE.
THE CLOCK TOWER.
UM, WHY?
THIS IS CHEESY, BUT IT WAS ALWAYS SOMETHING STEADY IN MY LIFE. WHEN I WAS A KID, EVEN THOUGH WE WERE MOVING CONSTANTLY, I COULD PICK UP THE PHONE ANYWHERE AND HEAR THAT SAME SOUND.
FINE. BE ALL RETRO. HOW ABOUT YOU MAKE ME A MIXTAPE OF YOUR FAVORITE NINETIES BOY BANDS WHILE YOU'RE AT IT?
I TOTALLY WILL. BUT IN ALL SERIOUSNESS... DO YOU HAVE ANY THOUGHTS ON THE THING?
THE THING?
THE SUBWAY THING. THE EXPLODING PHONES THING.

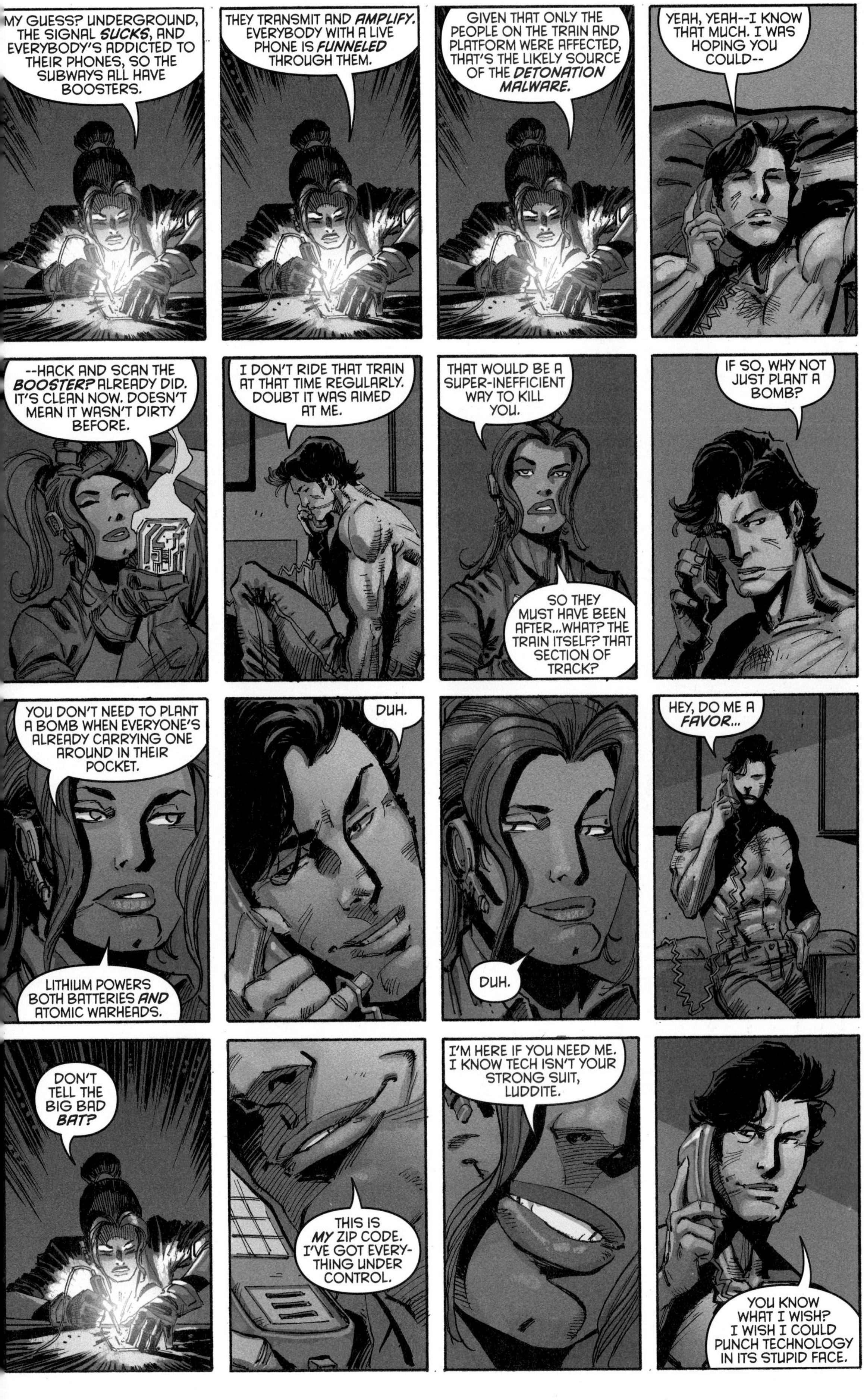

MY GUESS? UNDERGROUND, THE SIGNAL SUCKS, AND EVERYBODY'S ADDICTED TO THEIR PHONES, SO THE SUBWAYS ALL HAVE BOOSTERS.
THEY TRANSMIT AND AMPLIFY. EVERYBODY WITH A LIVE PHONE IS FUNNELED THROUGH THEM.
GIVEN THAT ONLY THE PEOPLE ON THE TRAIN AND PLATFORM WERE AFFECTED, THAT'S THE LIKELY SOURCE OF THE DETONATION MALWARE.
YEAH, YEAH--I KNOW THAT MUCH. I WAS HOPING YOU COULD--
--HACK AND SCAN THE BOOSTER? ALREADY DID. IT'S CLEAN NOW. DOESN'T MEAN IT WASN'T DIRTY BEFORE.
I DON'T RIDE THAT TRAIN AT THAT TIME REGULARLY. DOUBT IT WAS AIMED AT ME.
THAT WOULD BE A SUPER-INEFFICIENT WAY TO KILL YOU.
SO THEY MUST HAVE BEEN AFTER...WHAT? THE TRAIN ITSELF? THAT SECTION OF TRACK?
IF SO, WHY NOT JUST PLANT A BOMB?
YOU DON'T NEED TO PLANT A BOMB WHEN EVERYONE'S ALREADY CARRYING ONE AROUND IN THEIR POCKET.
LITHIUM POWERS BOTH BATTERIES AND ATOMIC WARHEADS.
DUH.
DUH.
HEY, DO ME A FAVOR...
DON'T TELL THE BIG BAD BAT?
THIS IS MY ZIP CODE. I'VE GOT EVERYTHING UNDER CONTROL.
I'M HERE IF YOU NEED ME. I KNOW TECH ISN'T YOUR STRONG SUIT, LUDDITE.
YOU KNOW WHAT I WISH? I WISH I COULD PUNCH TECHNOLOGY IN ITS STUPID FACE.

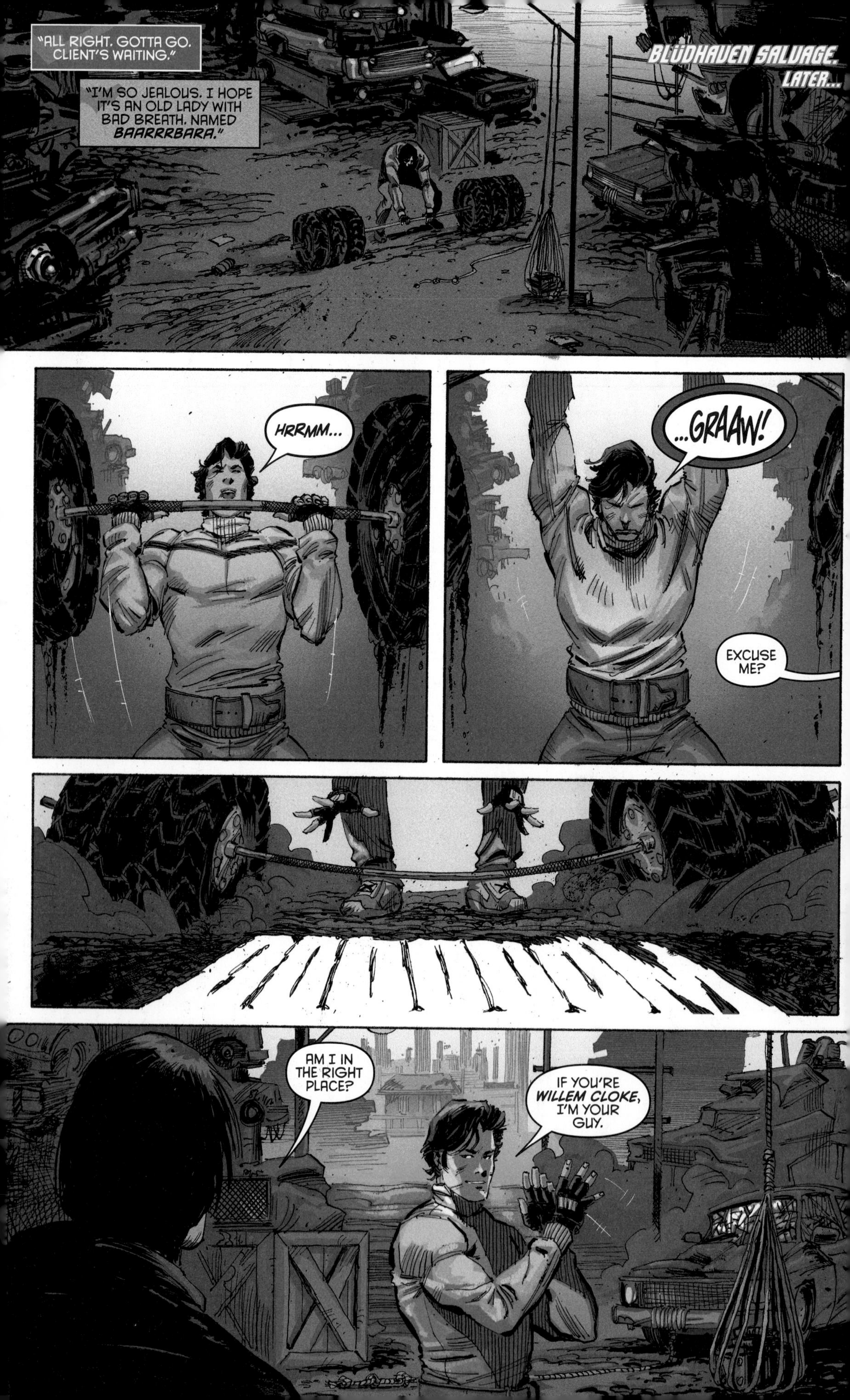
"ALL RIGHT. GOTTA GO. CLIENT'S WAITING."
BLÜDHAVEN SALVAGE. LATER...
"I'M SO JEALOUS. I HOPE IT'S AN OLD LADY WITH BAD BREATH. NAMED BAARRRBARA."
HRRMM...
...GRAAW!
EXCUSE ME?
AM I IN THE RIGHT PLACE?
IF YOU'RE WILLEM CLOKE, I'M YOUR GUY.

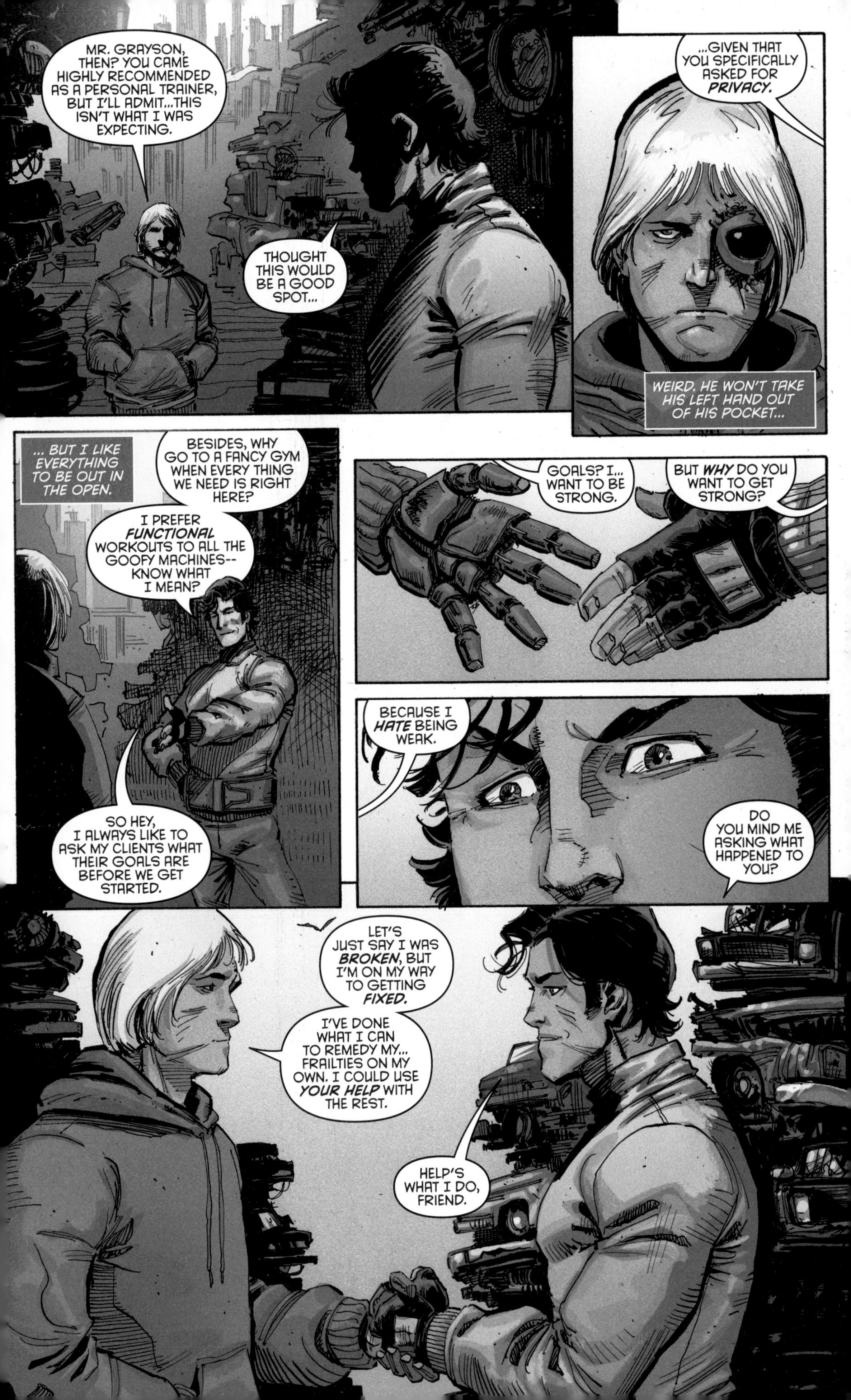

MR. GRAYSON, THEN? YOU CAME HIGHLY RECOMMENDED AS A PERSONAL TRAINER, BUT I'LL ADMIT...THIS ISN'T WHAT I WAS EXPECTING.
THOUGHT THIS WOULD BE A GOOD SPOT...
...GIVEN THAT YOU SPECIFICALLY ASKED FOR PRIVACY.
WEIRD. HE WON'T TAKE HIS LEFT HAND OUT OF HIS POCKET...
... BUT I LIKE EVERYTHING TO BE OUT IN THE OPEN.
BESIDES, WHY GO TO A FANCY GYM WHEN EVERY THING WE NEED IS RIGHT HERE?
I PREFER FUNCTIONAL WORKOUTS TO ALL THE GOOFY MACHINES-- KNOW WHAT I MEAN?
SO HEY, I ALWAYS LIKE TO ASK MY CLIENTS WHAT THEIR GOALS ARE BEFORE WE GET STARTED.
GOALS? I... WANT TO BE STRONG.
BUT WHY DO YOU WANT TO GET STRONG?
BECAUSE I HATE BEING WEAK.
DO YOU MIND ME ASKING WHAT HAPPENED TO YOU?
LET'S JUST SAY I WAS BROKEN, BUT I'M ON MY WAY TO GETTING FIXED.
I'VE DONE WHAT I CAN TO REMEDY MY... FRAILTIES ON MY OWN. I COULD USE YOUR HELP WITH THE REST.
HELP'S WHAT I DO, FRIEND.

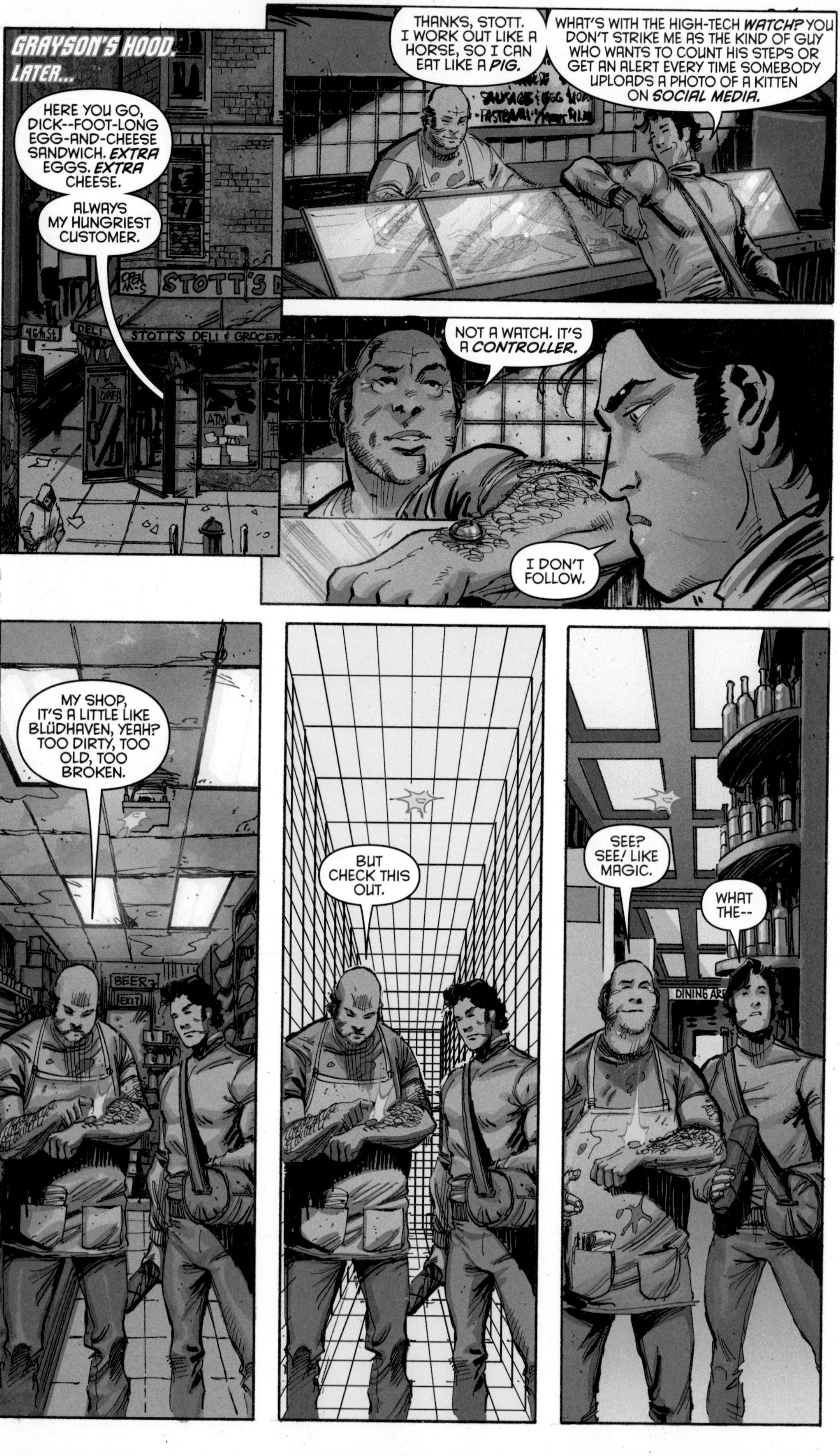
GRAYSON'S HOOD.
LATER...
HERE YOU GO, DICK--FOOT-LONG EGG-AND-CHEESE SANDWICH. EXTRA EGGS. EXTRA CHEESE.
ALWAYS MY HUNGRIEST CUSTOMER.
STOTT'S
STOTT'S DELI & GROCER
DELI
46th St.
ATM
THANKS, STOTT. I WORK OUT LIKE A HORSE, SO I CAN EAT LIKE A PIG.
WHAT'S WITH THE HIGH-TECH WATCH? YOU DON'T STRIKE ME AS THE KIND OF GUY WHO WANTS TO COUNT HIS STEPS OR GET AN ALERT EVERY TIME SOMEBODY UPLOADS A PHOTO OF A KITTEN ON SOCIAL MEDIA.
NOT A WATCH. IT'S A CONTROLLER.
I DON'T FOLLOW.
MY SHOP, IT'S A LITTLE LIKE BLÜDHAVEN, YEAH? TOO DIRTY, TOO OLD, TOO BROKEN.
BEER
EXIT
BUT CHECK THIS OUT.
SEE? SEE! LIKE MAGIC.
WHAT THE--

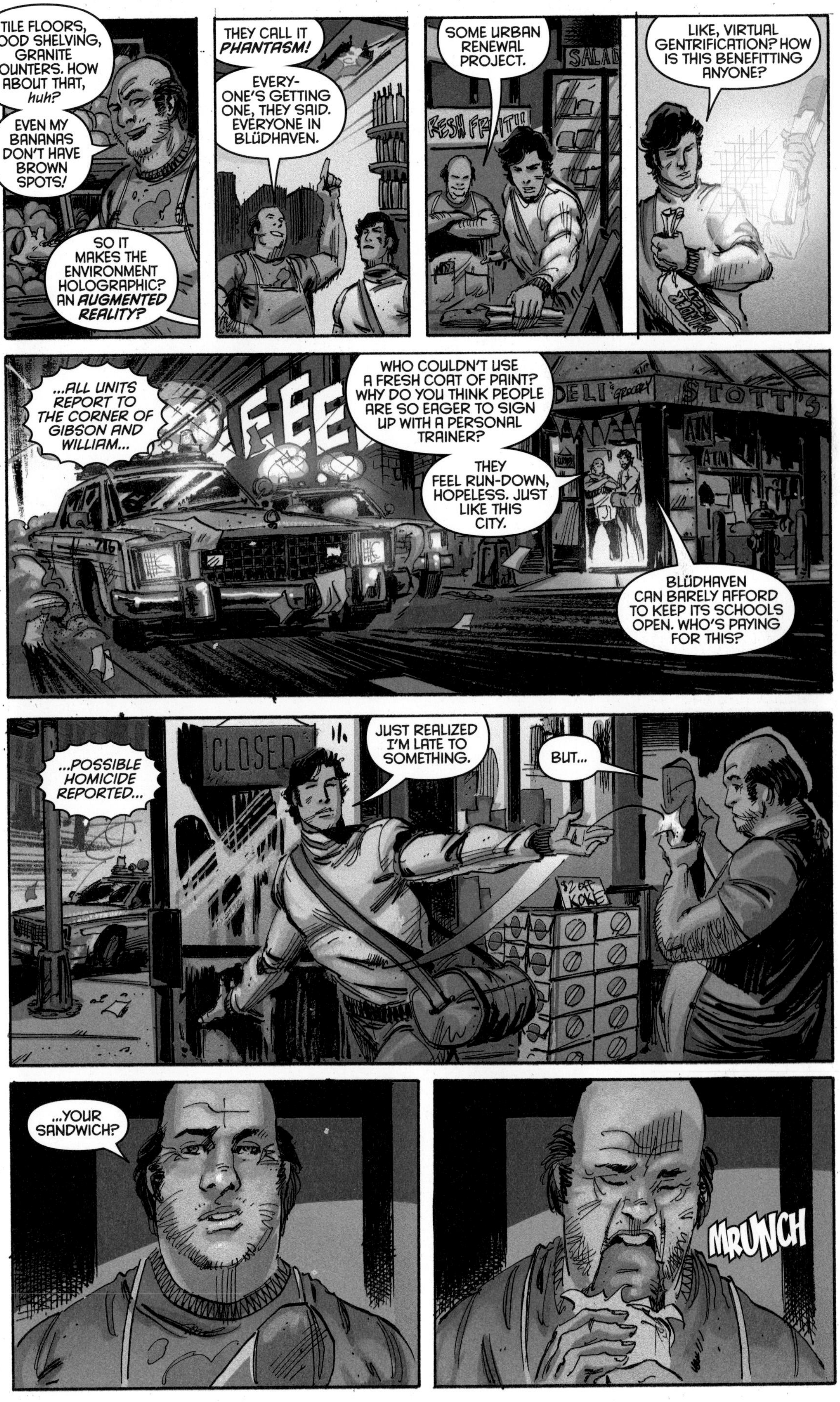
TILE FLOORS, WOOD SHELVING, GRANITE COUNTERS. HOW ABOUT THAT, huh?
EVEN MY BANANAS DON'T HAVE BROWN SPOTS!
SO IT MAKES THE ENVIRONMENT HOLOGRAPHIC? AN AUGMENTED REALITY?
THEY CALL IT PHANTASM!
EVERY-ONE'S GETTING ONE, THEY SAID. EVERYONE IN BLÜDHAVEN.
SOME URBAN RENEWAL PROJECT.
SALAD
FRESH FRUIT!!
LIKE, VIRTUAL GENTRIFICATION? HOW IS THIS BENEFITTING ANYONE?
...ALL UNITS REPORT TO THE CORNER OF GIBSON AND WILLIAM...
WHO COULDN'T USE A FRESH COAT OF PAINT? WHY DO YOU THINK PEOPLE ARE SO EAGER TO SIGN UP WITH A PERSONAL TRAINER?
DELI & GROCERY
STOTT'S
ATM
THEY FEEL RUN-DOWN, HOPELESS. JUST LIKE THIS CITY.
BLÜDHAVEN CAN BARELY AFFORD TO KEEP ITS SCHOOLS OPEN. WHO'S PAYING FOR THIS?
CLOSED
...POSSIBLE HOMICIDE REPORTED...
JUST REALIZED I'M LATE TO SOMETHING.
BUT...
$2 6 pk KOKE
...YOUR SANDWICH?
MRUNCH

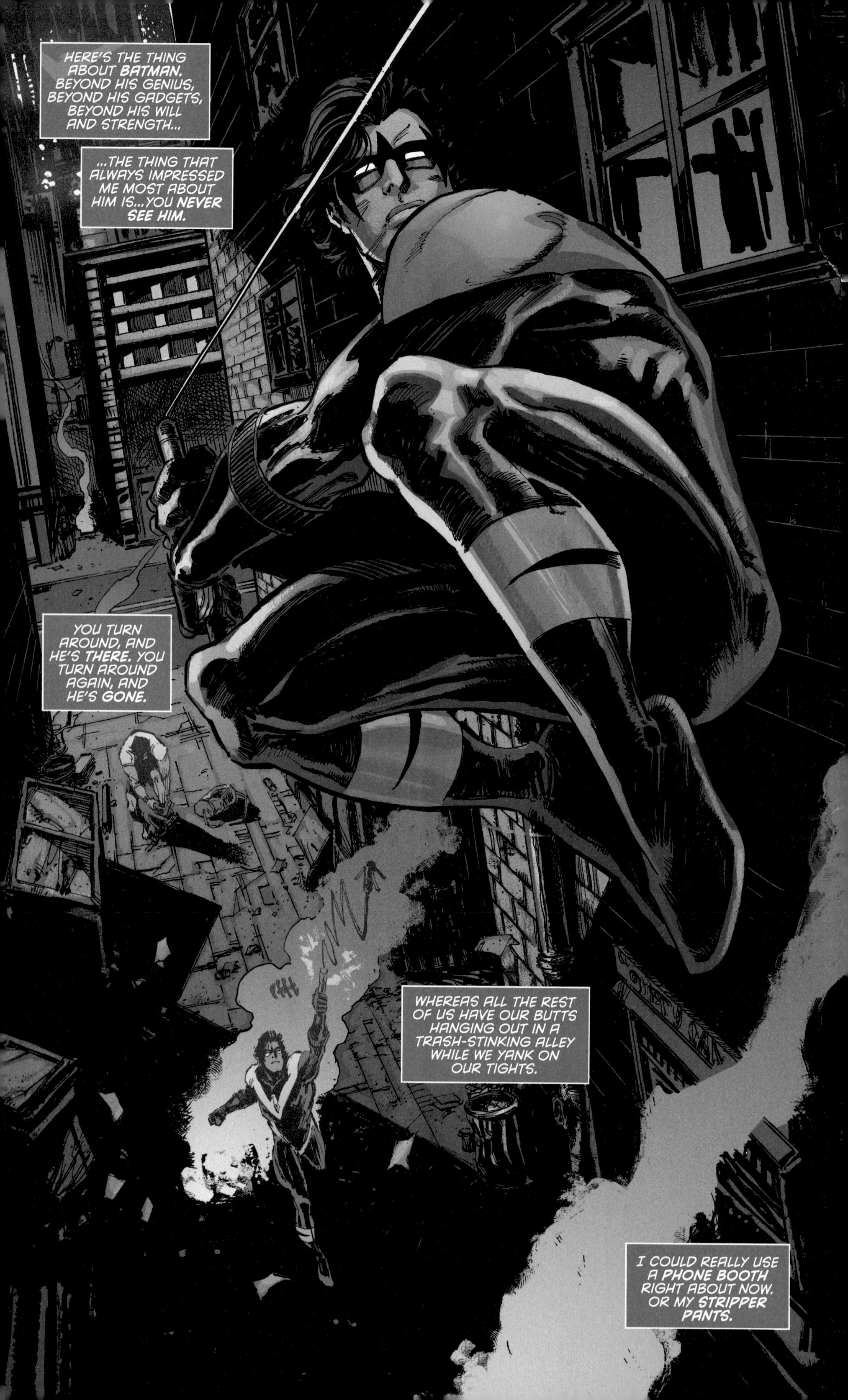
HERE'S THE THING ABOUT BATMAN. BEYOND HIS GENIUS, BEYOND HIS GADGETS, BEYOND HIS WILL AND STRENGTH...
...THE THING THAT ALWAYS IMPRESSED ME MOST ABOUT HIM IS...YOU NEVER SEE HIM.
YOU TURN AROUND, AND HE'S THERE. YOU TURN AROUND AGAIN, AND HE'S GONE.
WHEREAS ALL THE REST OF US HAVE OUR BUTTS HANGING OUT IN A TRASH-STINKING ALLEY WHILE WE YANK ON OUR TIGHTS.
I COULD REALLY USE A PHONE BOOTH RIGHT ABOUT NOW. OR MY STRIPPER PANTS.

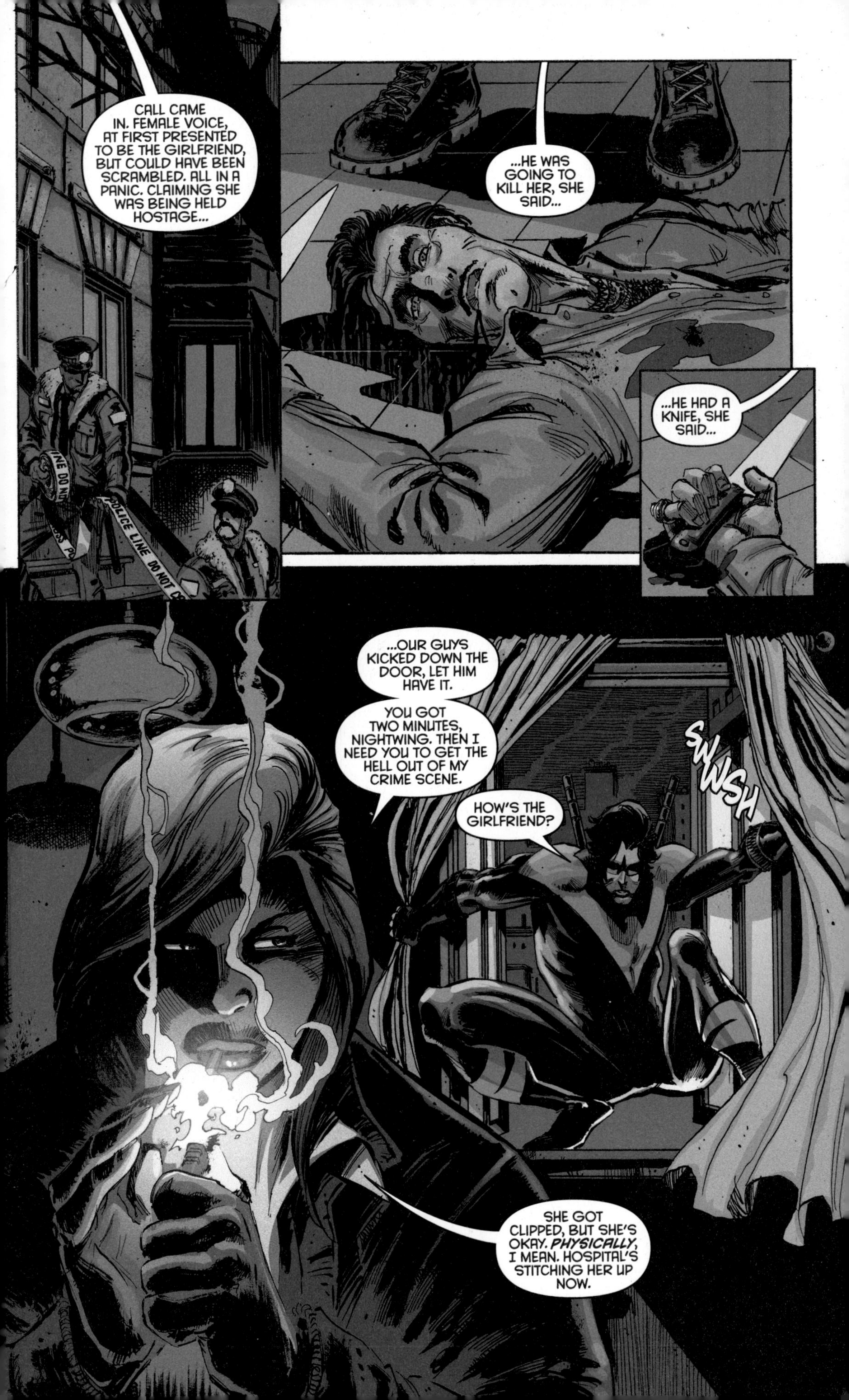
CALL CAME IN. FEMALE VOICE, AT FIRST PRESENTED TO BE THE GIRLFRIEND, BUT COULD HAVE BEEN SCRAMBLED. ALL IN A PANIC. CLAIMING SHE WAS BEING HELD HOSTAGE...
...HE WAS GOING TO KILL HER, SHE SAID...
...HE HAD A KNIFE, SHE SAID...
...OUR GUYS KICKED DOWN THE DOOR, LET HIM HAVE IT.
YOU GOT TWO MINUTES, NIGHTWING. THEN I NEED YOU TO GET THE HELL OUT OF MY CRIME SCENE.
SWWSH
HOW'S THE GIRLFRIEND?
SHE GOT CLIPPED, BUT SHE'S OKAY. *PHYSICALLY*, I MEAN. HOSPITAL'S STITCHING HER UP NOW.

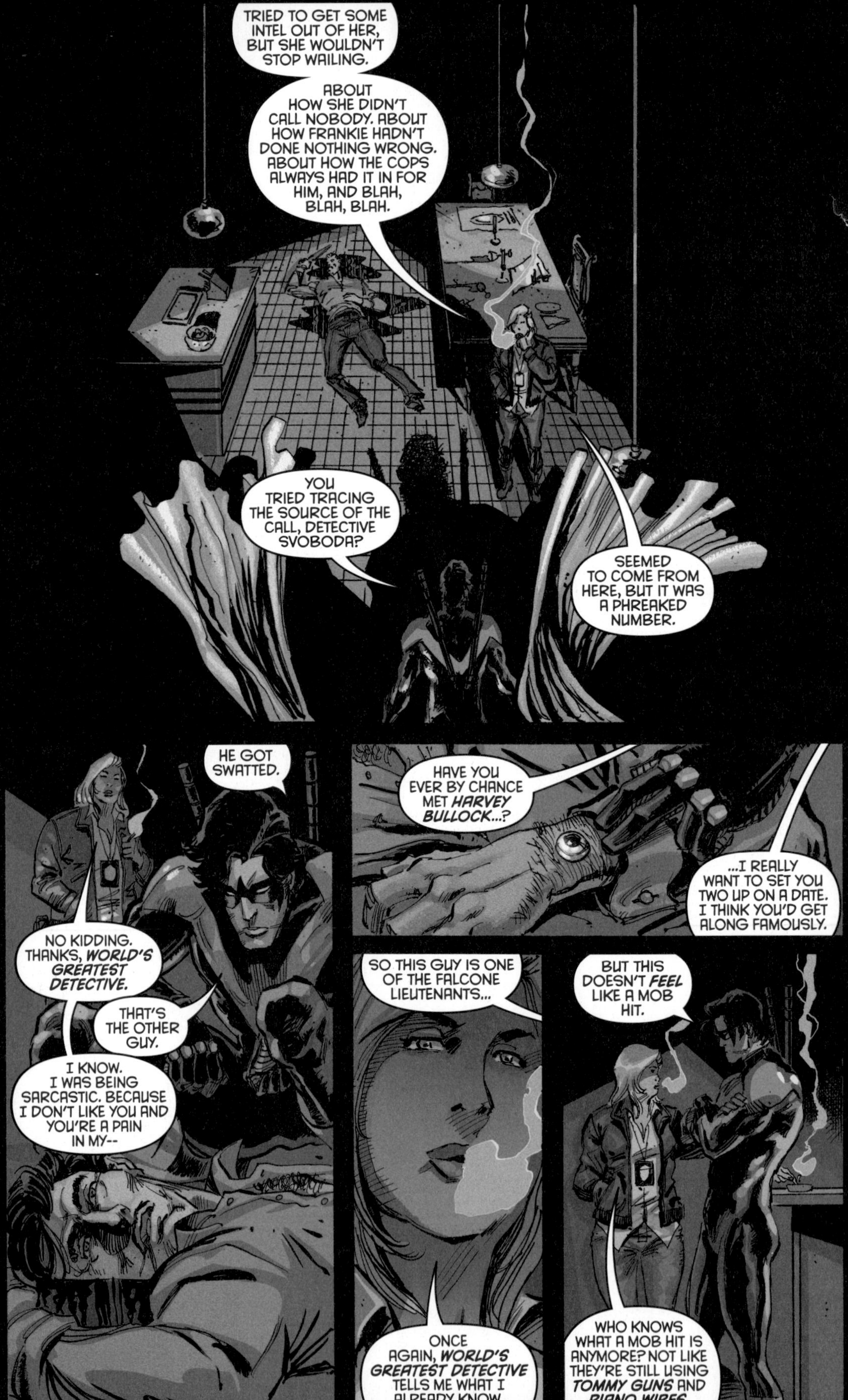
TRIED TO GET SOME INTEL OUT OF HER, BUT SHE WOULDN'T STOP WAILING.
ABOUT HOW SHE DIDN'T CALL NOBODY. ABOUT HOW FRANKIE HADN'T DONE NOTHING WRONG. ABOUT HOW THE COPS ALWAYS HAD IT IN FOR HIM, AND BLAH, BLAH, BLAH.
YOU TRIED TRACING THE SOURCE OF THE CALL, DETECTIVE SVOBODA?
SEEMED TO COME FROM HERE, BUT IT WAS A PHREAKED NUMBER.
HE GOT SWATTED.
NO KIDDING. THANKS, *WORLD'S GREATEST DETECTIVE.*
THAT'S THE OTHER GUY.
I KNOW. I WAS BEING SARCASTIC. BECAUSE I DON'T LIKE YOU AND YOU'RE A PAIN IN MY--
HAVE YOU EVER BY CHANCE MET *HARVEY BULLOCK*...?
...I REALLY WANT TO SET YOU TWO UP ON A DATE. I THINK YOU'D GET ALONG FAMOUSLY.
SO THIS GUY IS ONE OF THE FALCONE LIEUTENANTS...
ONCE AGAIN, *WORLD'S GREATEST DETECTIVE* TELLS ME WHAT I ALREADY KNOW.
BUT THIS DOESN'T *FEEL* LIKE A MOB HIT.
WHO KNOWS WHAT A MOB HIT IS ANYMORE? NOT LIKE THEY'RE STILL USING *TOMMY GUNS* AND *PIANO WIRES.*

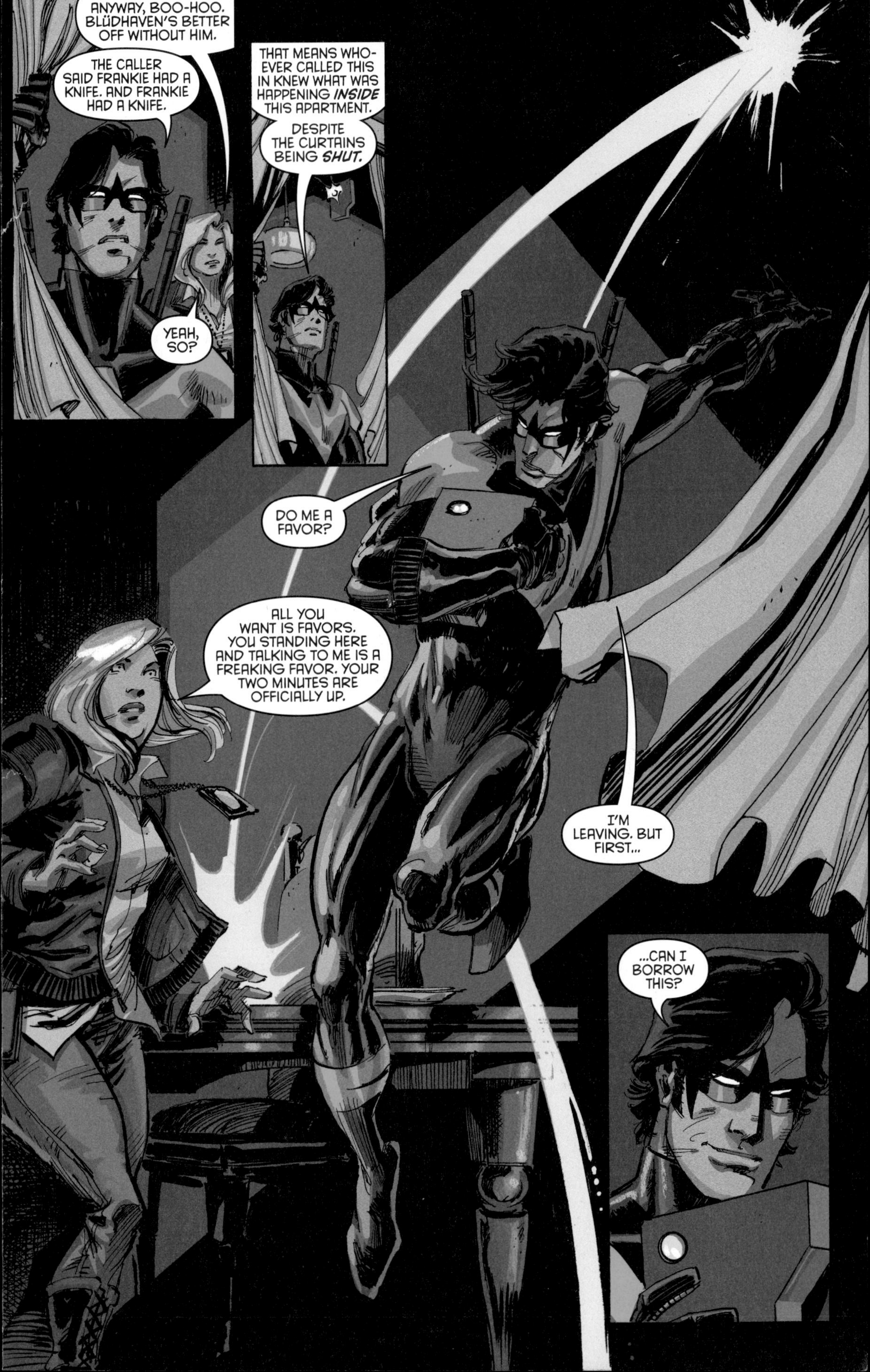
ANYWAY, BOO-HOO. BLÜDHAVEN'S BETTER OFF WITHOUT HIM.
THE CALLER SAID FRANKIE HAD A KNIFE. AND FRANKIE HAD A KNIFE.
YEAH, SO?
THAT MEANS WHOEVER CALLED THIS IN KNEW WHAT WAS HAPPENING *INSIDE* THIS APARTMENT.
DESPITE THE CURTAINS BEING *SHUT.*
DO ME A FAVOR?
ALL YOU WANT IS FAVORS. YOU STANDING HERE AND TALKING TO ME IS A FREAKING FAVOR. YOUR TWO MINUTES ARE OFFICIALLY UP.
I'M LEAVING. BUT FIRST...
...CAN I BORROW THIS?

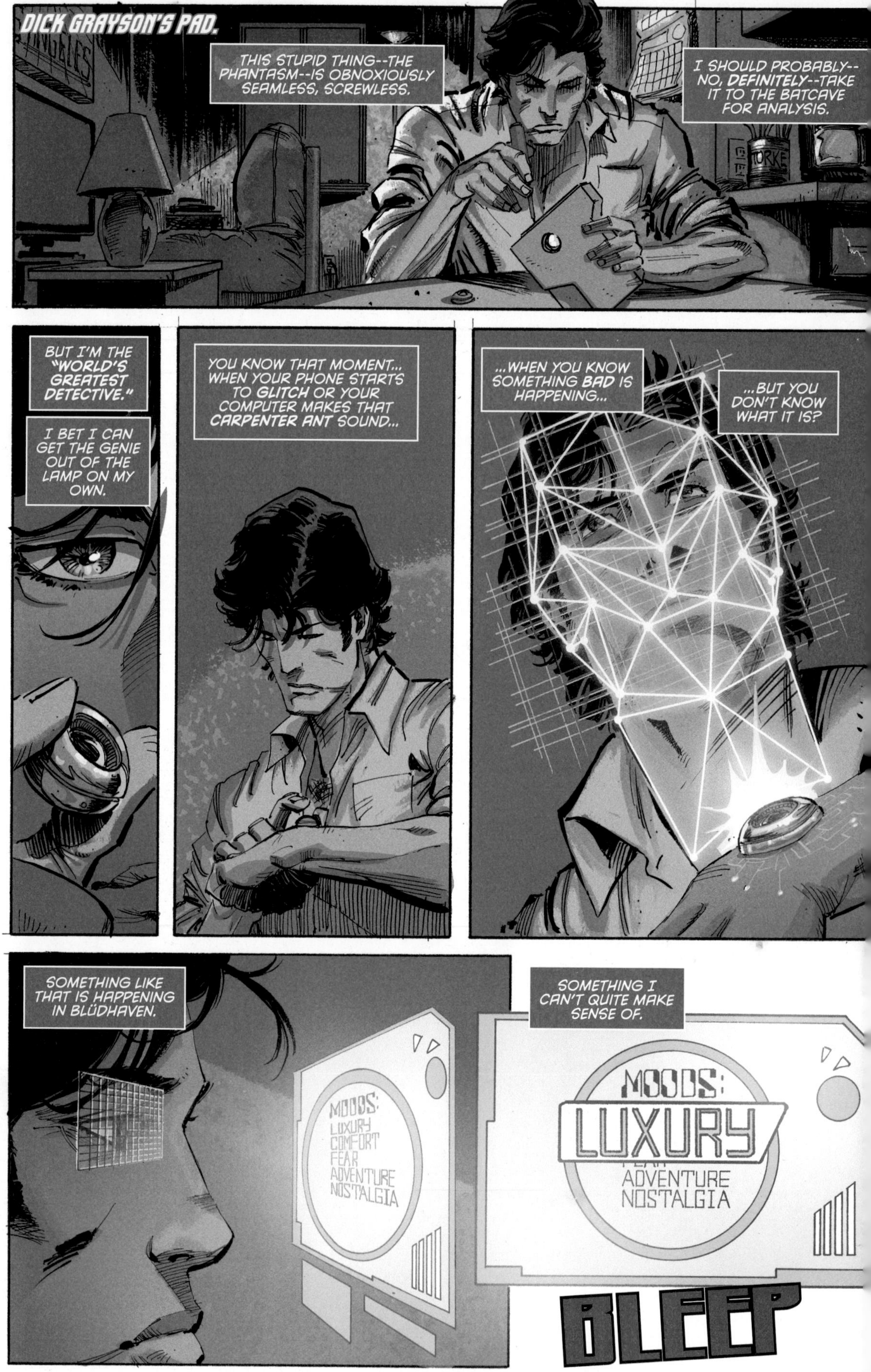

DICK GRAYSON'S PAD.
THIS STUPID THING--THE PHANTASM--IS OBNOXIOUSLY SEAMLESS, SCREWLESS.
I SHOULD PROBABLY--NO, DEFINITELY--TAKE IT TO THE BATCAVE FOR ANALYSIS.
BUT I'M THE "WORLD'S GREATEST DETECTIVE."
I BET I CAN GET THE GENIE OUT OF THE LAMP ON MY OWN.
YOU KNOW THAT MOMENT... WHEN YOUR PHONE STARTS TO GLITCH OR YOUR COMPUTER MAKES THAT CARPENTER ANT SOUND...
...WHEN YOU KNOW SOMETHING BAD IS HAPPENING...
...BUT YOU DON'T KNOW WHAT IT IS?
SOMETHING LIKE THAT IS HAPPENING IN BLÜDHAVEN.
MOODS:
LUXURY
COMFORT
FEAR
ADVENTURE
NOSTALGIA
SOMETHING I CAN'T QUITE MAKE SENSE OF.
MOODS:
LUXURY
ADVENTURE
NOSTALGIA
BLEEP

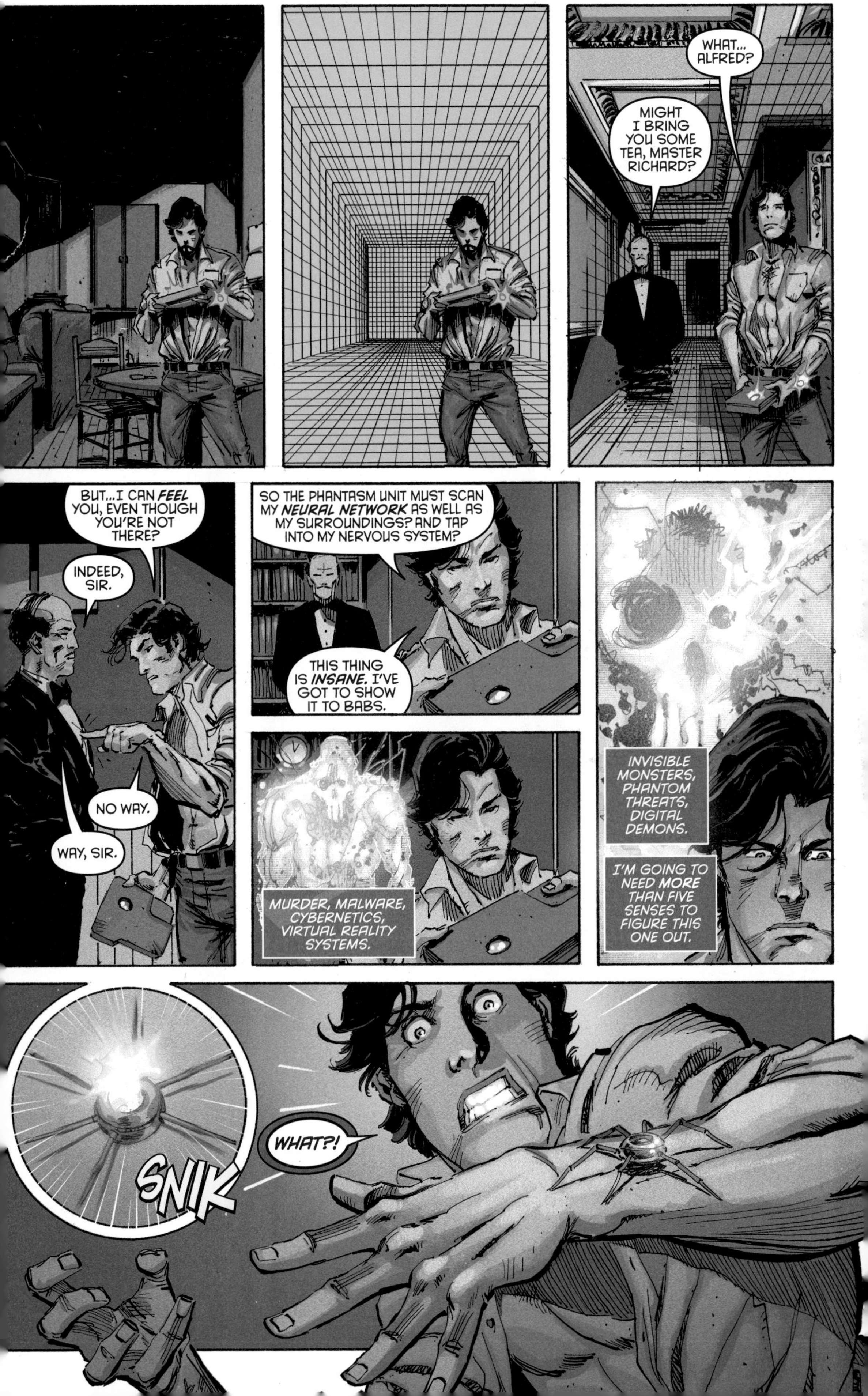
WHAT... ALFRED?
MIGHT I BRING YOU SOME TEA, MASTER RICHARD?
BUT...I CAN FEEL YOU, EVEN THOUGH YOU'RE NOT THERE?
INDEED, SIR.
NO WAY.
WAY, SIR.
SO THE PHANTASM UNIT MUST SCAN MY NEURAL NETWORK AS WELL AS MY SURROUNDINGS? AND TAP INTO MY NERVOUS SYSTEM?
THIS THING IS INSANE. I'VE GOT TO SHOW IT TO BABS.
MURDER, MALWARE, CYBERNETICS, VIRTUAL REALITY SYSTEMS.
INVISIBLE MONSTERS, PHANTOM THREATS, DIGITAL DEMONS.
I'M GOING TO NEED MORE THAN FIVE SENSES TO FIGURE THIS ONE OUT.
WHAT?!
SNIK

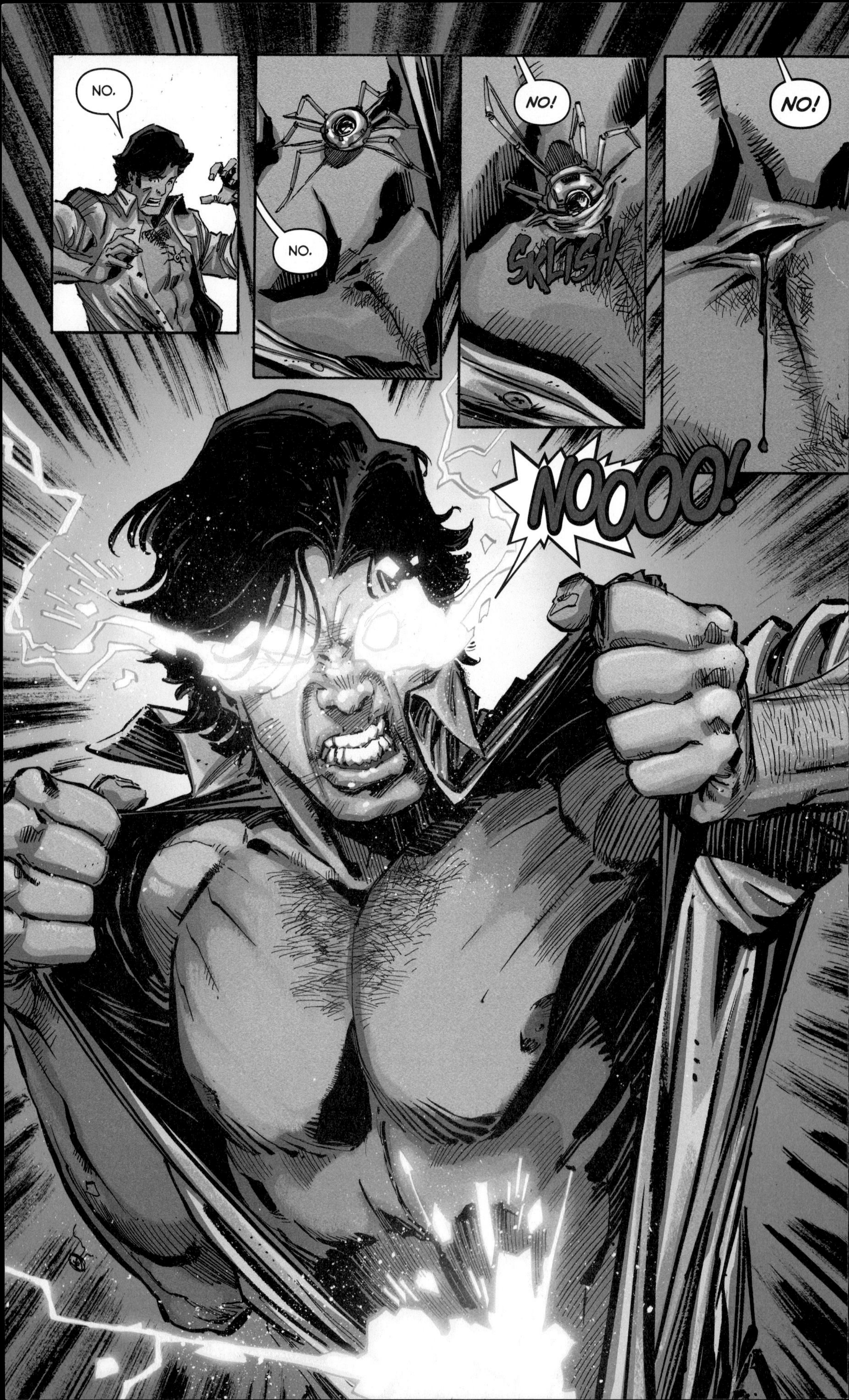
NO.
NO.
NO!
SKLISH
NO!
NOOOO!

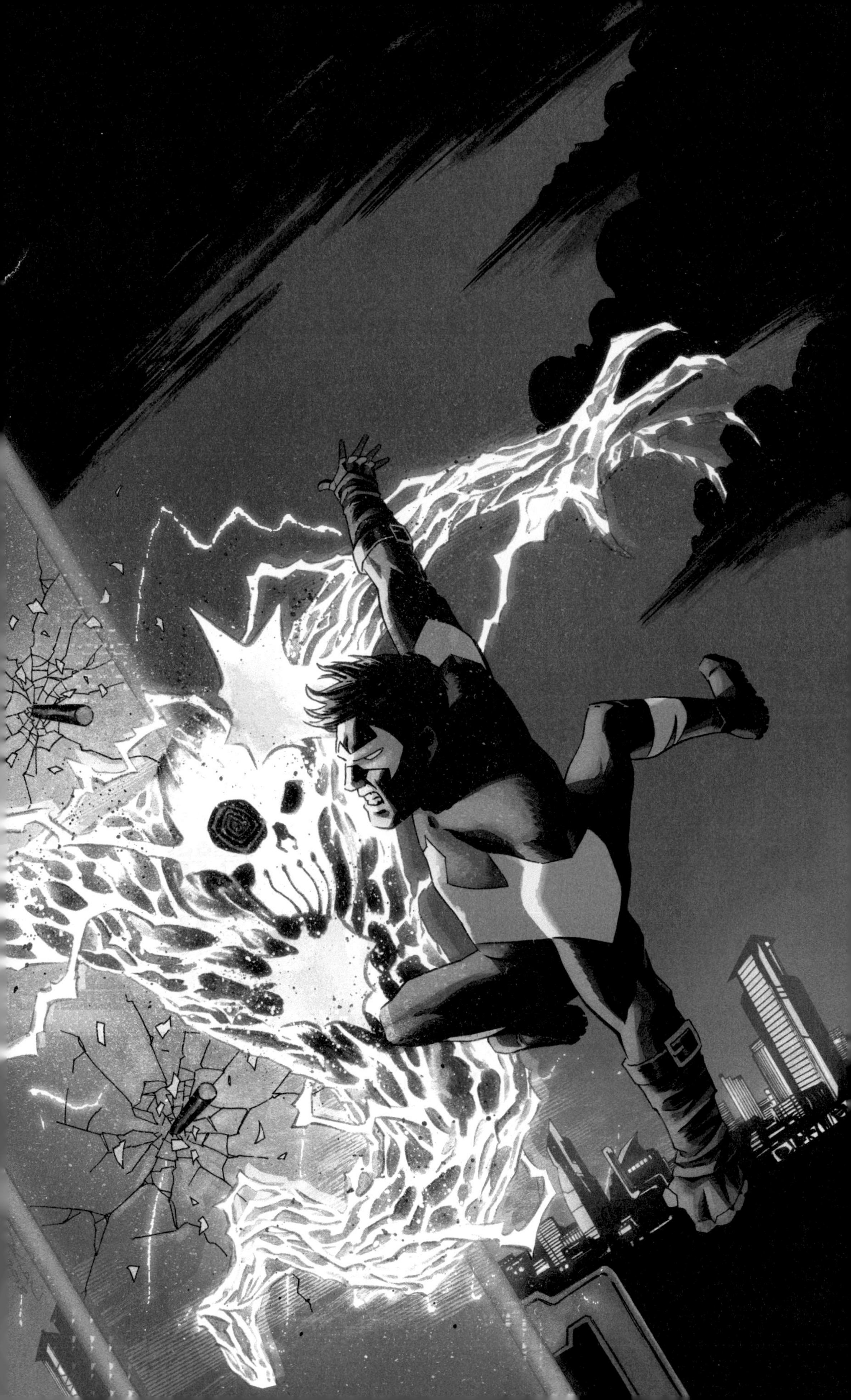

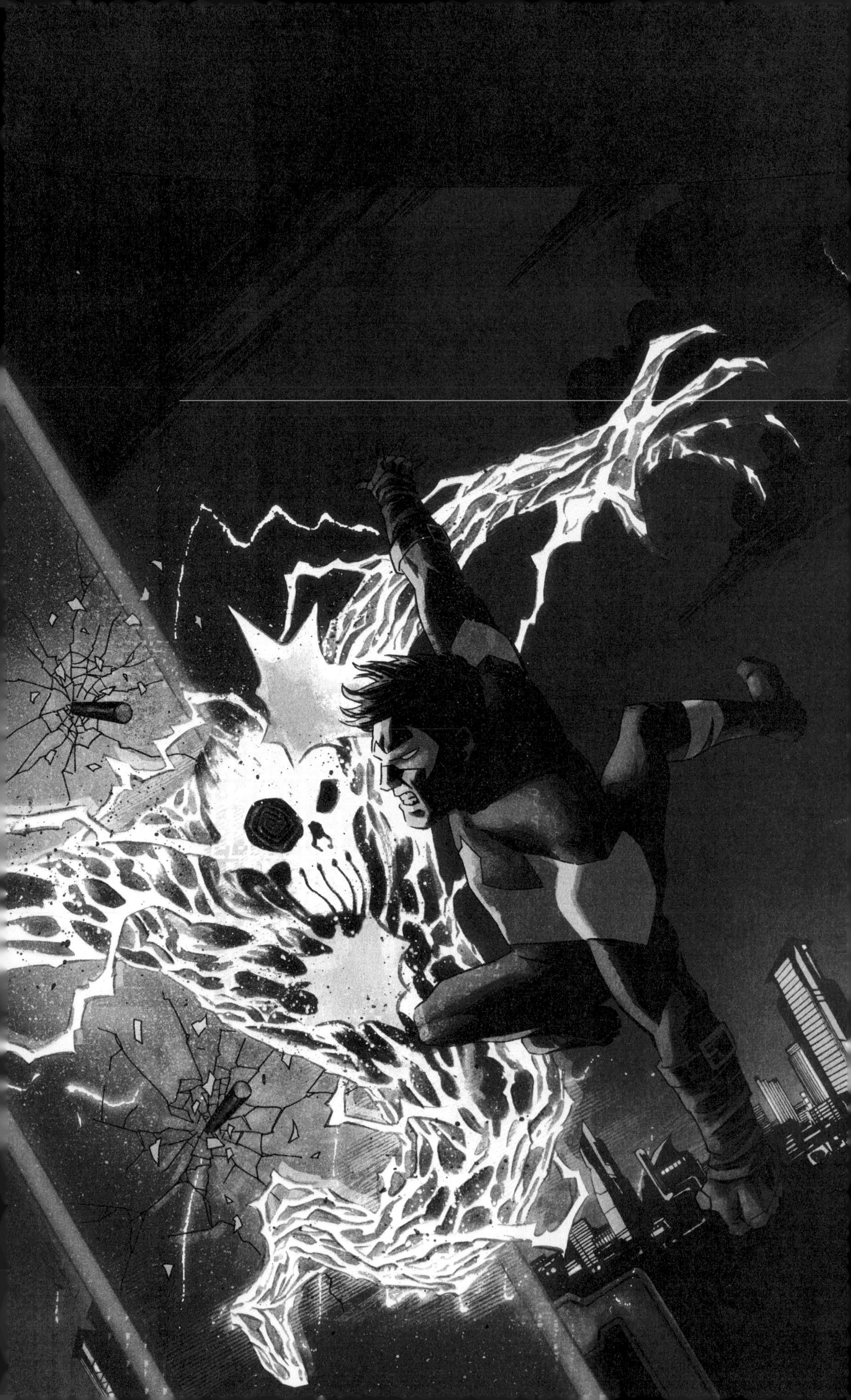

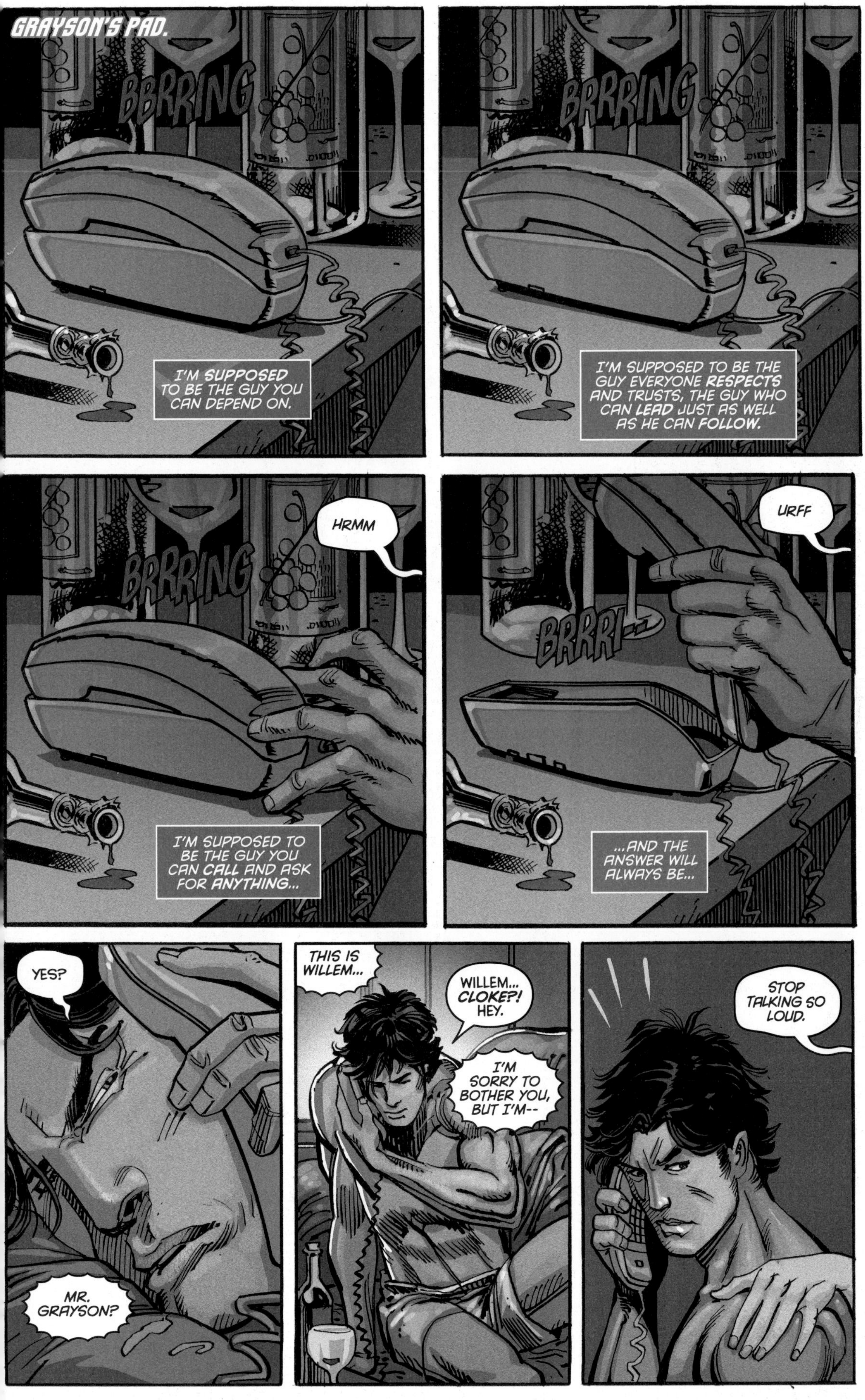
GRAYSON'S PAD.
BBRRING
I'M SUPPOSED TO BE THE GUY YOU CAN DEPEND ON.
BRRRING
I'M SUPPOSED TO BE THE GUY EVERYONE RESPECTS AND TRUSTS, THE GUY WHO CAN LEAD JUST AS WELL AS HE CAN FOLLOW.
BRRRING
HRMM
I'M SUPPOSED TO BE THE GUY YOU CAN CALL AND ASK FOR ANYTHING...
URFF
BRRRI--
...AND THE ANSWER WILL ALWAYS BE...
YES?
MR. GRAYSON?
THIS IS WILLEM...
WILLEM... CLOKE?! HEY.
I'M SORRY TO BOTHER YOU, BUT I'M--
STOP TALKING SO LOUD.

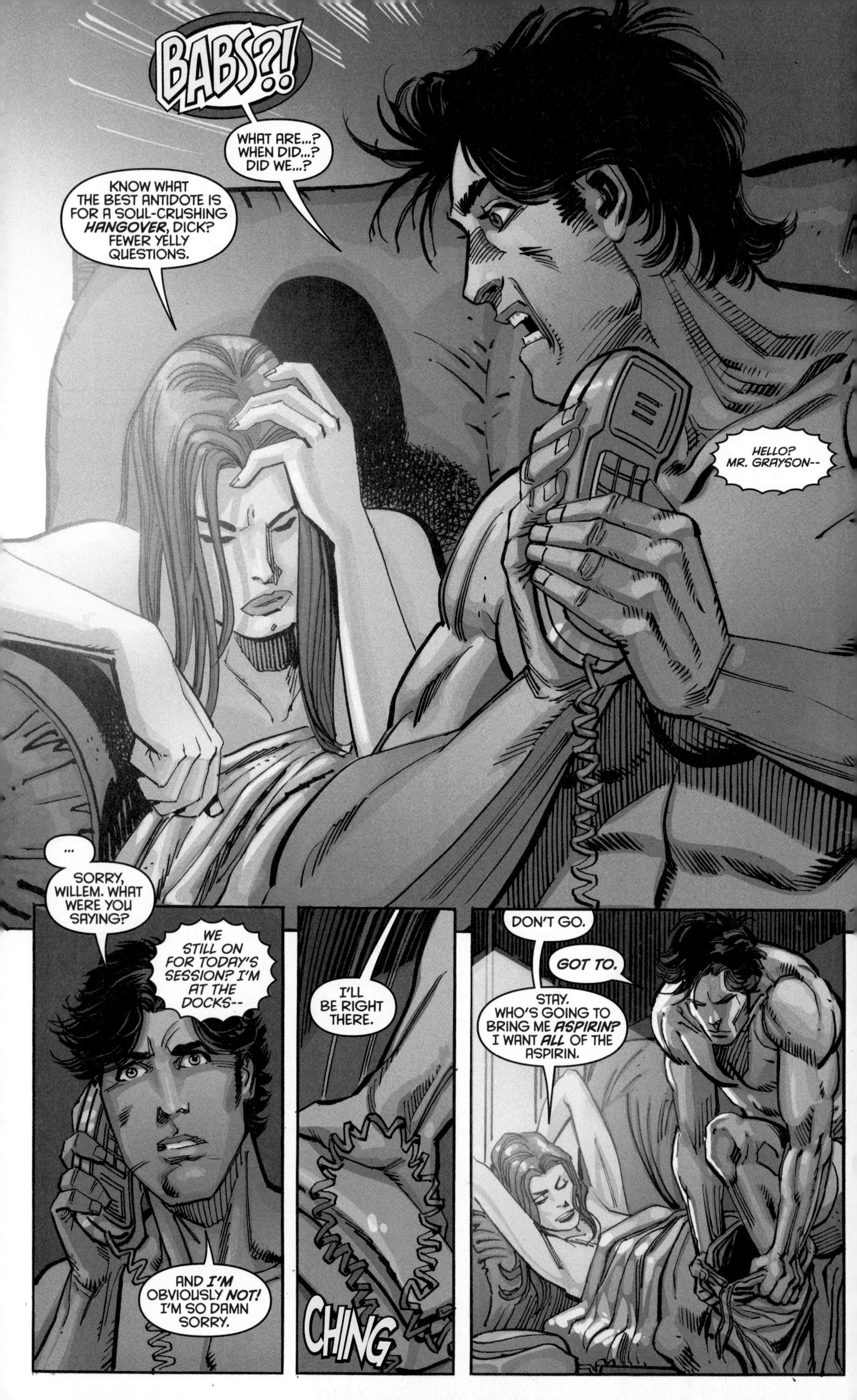
BABS?!
WHAT ARE...? WHEN DID...? DID WE...?
KNOW WHAT THE BEST ANTIDOTE IS FOR A SOUL-CRUSHING *HANGOVER*, DICK? FEWER YELLY QUESTIONS.
HELLO? MR. GRAYSON--
...
SORRY, WILLEM. WHAT WERE YOU SAYING?
WE STILL ON FOR TODAY'S SESSION? I'M AT THE DOCKS--
AND *I'M* OBVIOUSLY *NOT!* I'M SO DAMN SORRY.
I'LL BE RIGHT THERE.
CHING
DON'T GO.
GOT TO.
STAY. WHO'S GOING TO BRING ME *ASPIRIN?* I WANT *ALL* OF THE ASPIRIN.

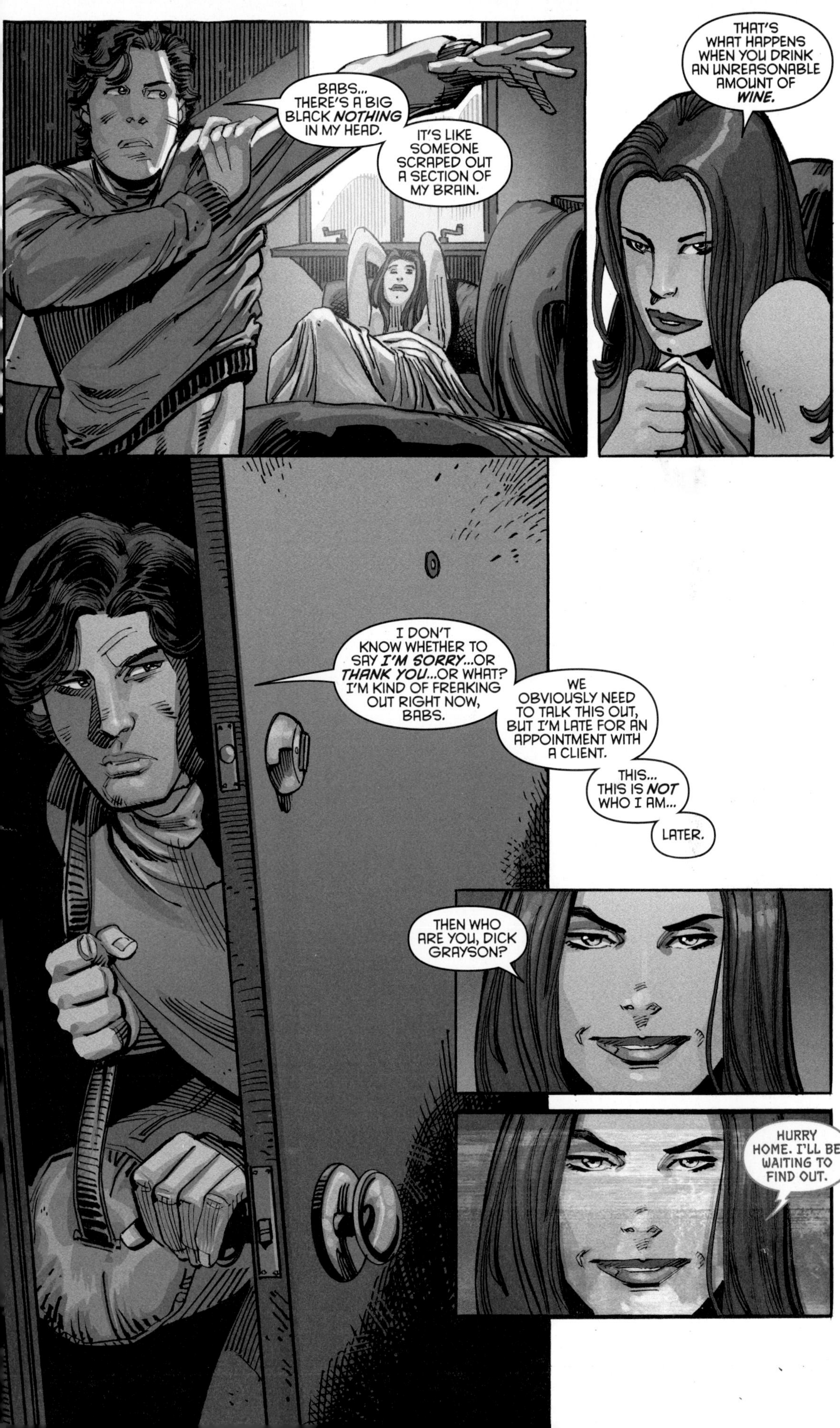
BABS... THERE'S A BIG BLACK *NOTHING* IN MY HEAD.
IT'S LIKE SOMEONE SCRAPED OUT A SECTION OF MY BRAIN.
THAT'S WHAT HAPPENS WHEN YOU DRINK AN UNREASONABLE AMOUNT OF *WINE.*
I DON'T KNOW WHETHER TO SAY *I'M SORRY*...OR *THANK YOU*...OR WHAT? I'M KIND OF FREAKING OUT RIGHT NOW, BABS.
WE OBVIOUSLY NEED TO TALK THIS OUT, BUT I'M LATE FOR AN APPOINTMENT WITH A CLIENT.
THIS... THIS IS *NOT* WHO I AM...
LATER.
THEN WHO ARE YOU, DICK GRAYSON?
HURRY HOME. I'LL BE WAITING TO FIND OUT.

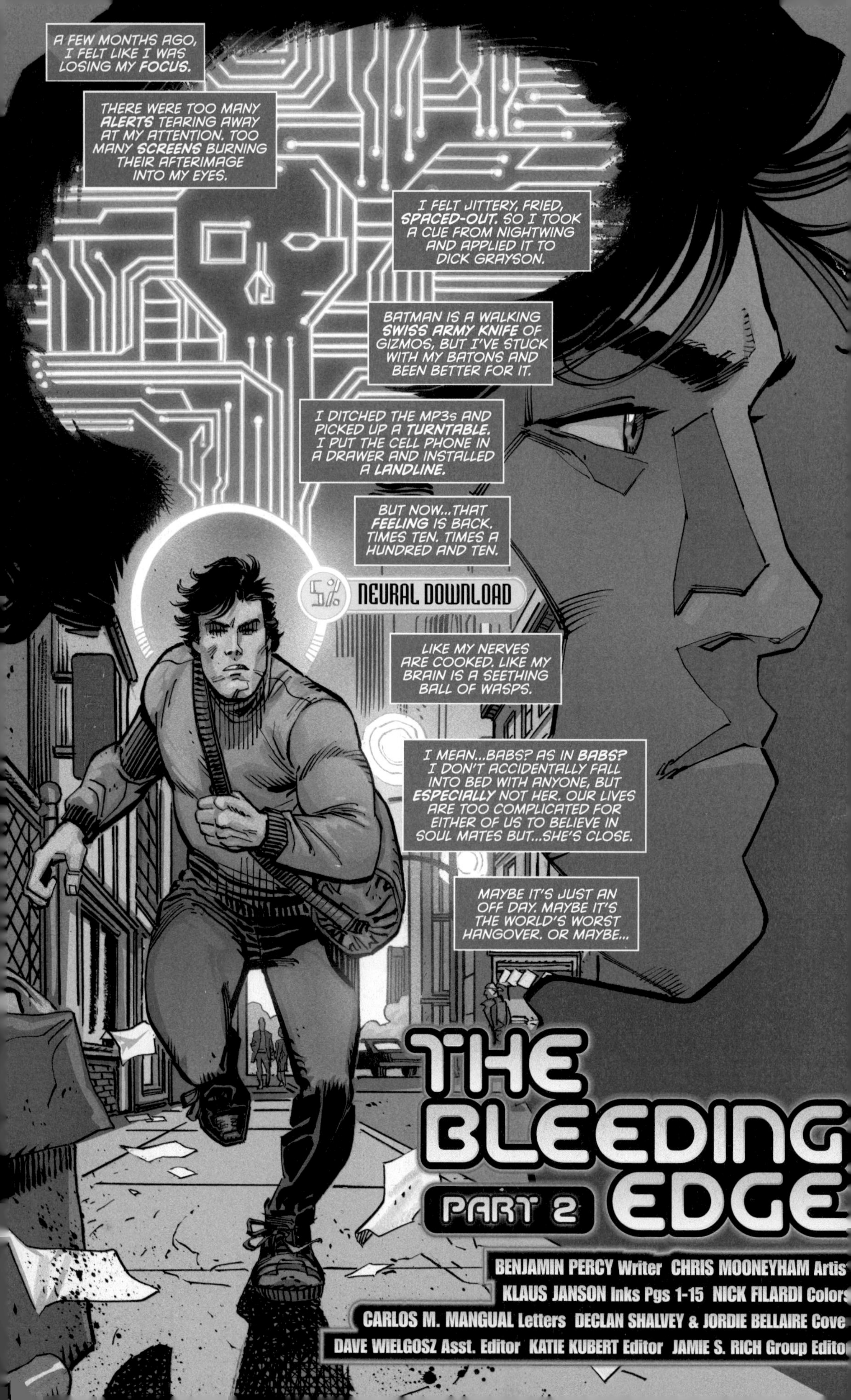
A FEW MONTHS AGO, I FELT LIKE I WAS LOSING MY FOCUS.
THERE WERE TOO MANY ALERTS TEARING AWAY AT MY ATTENTION. TOO MANY SCREENS BURNING THEIR AFTERIMAGE INTO MY EYES.
I FELT JITTERY, FRIED, SPACED-OUT. SO I TOOK A CUE FROM NIGHTWING AND APPLIED IT TO DICK GRAYSON.
BATMAN IS A WALKING SWISS ARMY KNIFE OF GIZMOS, BUT I'VE STUCK WITH MY BATONS AND BEEN BETTER FOR IT.
I DITCHED THE MP3s AND PICKED UP A TURNTABLE. I PUT THE CELL PHONE IN A DRAWER AND INSTALLED A LANDLINE.
BUT NOW...THAT FEELING IS BACK. TIMES TEN. TIMES A HUNDRED AND TEN.
5% NEURAL DOWNLOAD
LIKE MY NERVES ARE COOKED. LIKE MY BRAIN IS A SEETHING BALL OF WASPS.
I MEAN...BABS? AS IN BABS? I DON'T ACCIDENTALLY FALL INTO BED WITH ANYONE, BUT ESPECIALLY NOT HER. OUR LIVES ARE TOO COMPLICATED FOR EITHER OF US TO BELIEVE IN SOUL MATES BUT...SHE'S CLOSE.
MAYBE IT'S JUST AN OFF DAY. MAYBE IT'S THE WORLD'S WORST HANGOVER. OR MAYBE...
THE BLEEDING EDGE
PART 2
BENJAMIN PERCY Writer CHRIS MOONEYHAM Artis
KLAUS JANSON Inks Pgs 1-15 NICK FILARDI Colors
CARLOS M. MANGUAL Letters DECLAN SHALVEY & JORDIE BELLAIRE Cove
DAVE WIELGOSZ Asst. Editor KATIE KUBERT Editor JAMIE S. RICH Group Edito

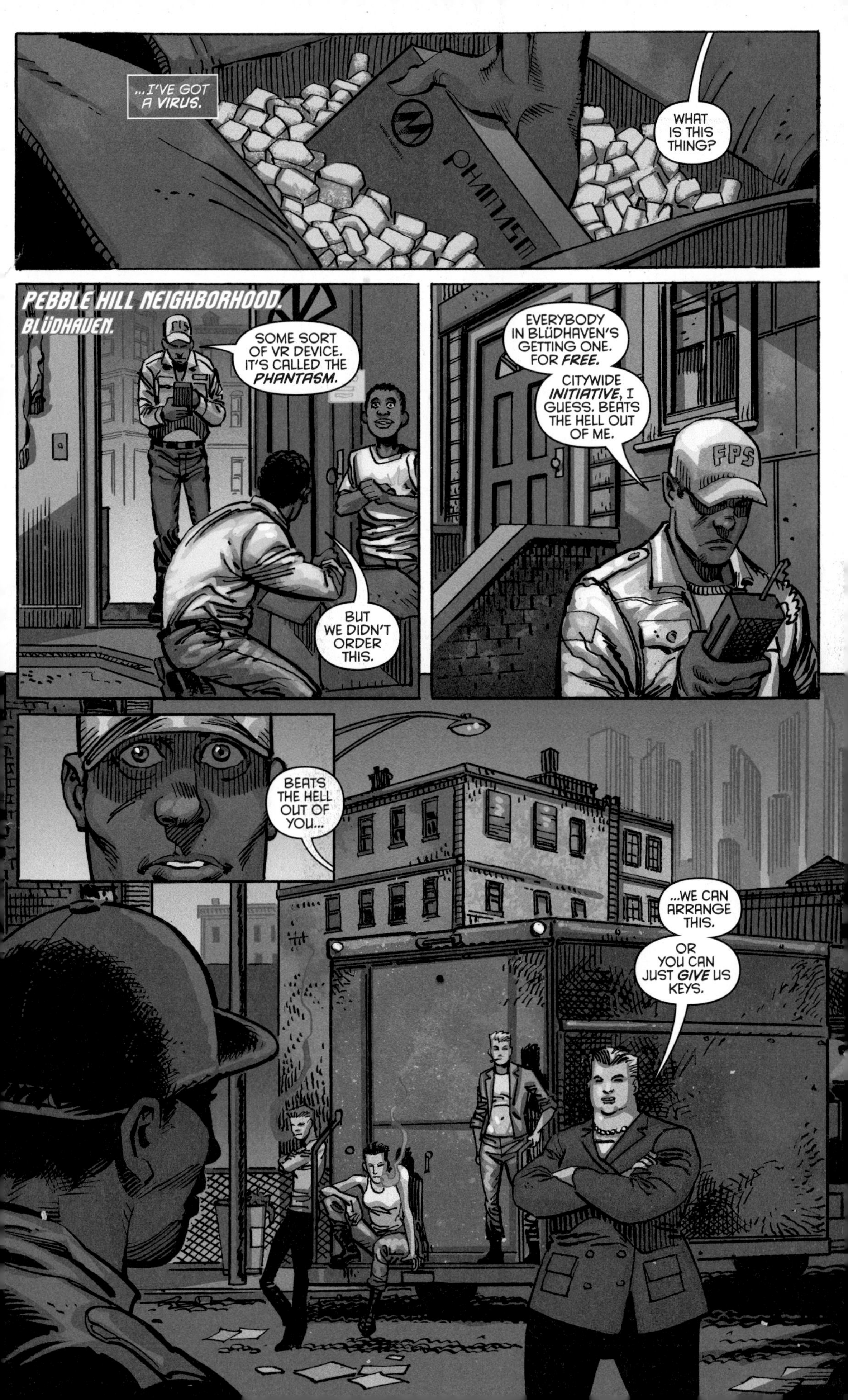
...I'VE GOT A VIRUS.
WHAT IS THIS THING?
PHANTASM
PEBBLE HILL NEIGHBORHOOD. BLÜDHAVEN.
SOME SORT OF VR DEVICE. IT'S CALLED THE PHANTASM.
BUT WE DIDN'T ORDER THIS.
EVERYBODY IN BLÜDHAVEN'S GETTING ONE. FOR FREE.
CITYWIDE INITIATIVE, I GUESS. BEATS THE HELL OUT OF ME.
FPS
BEATS THE HELL OUT OF YOU...
...WE CAN ARRANGE THIS.
OR YOU CAN JUST GIVE US KEYS.

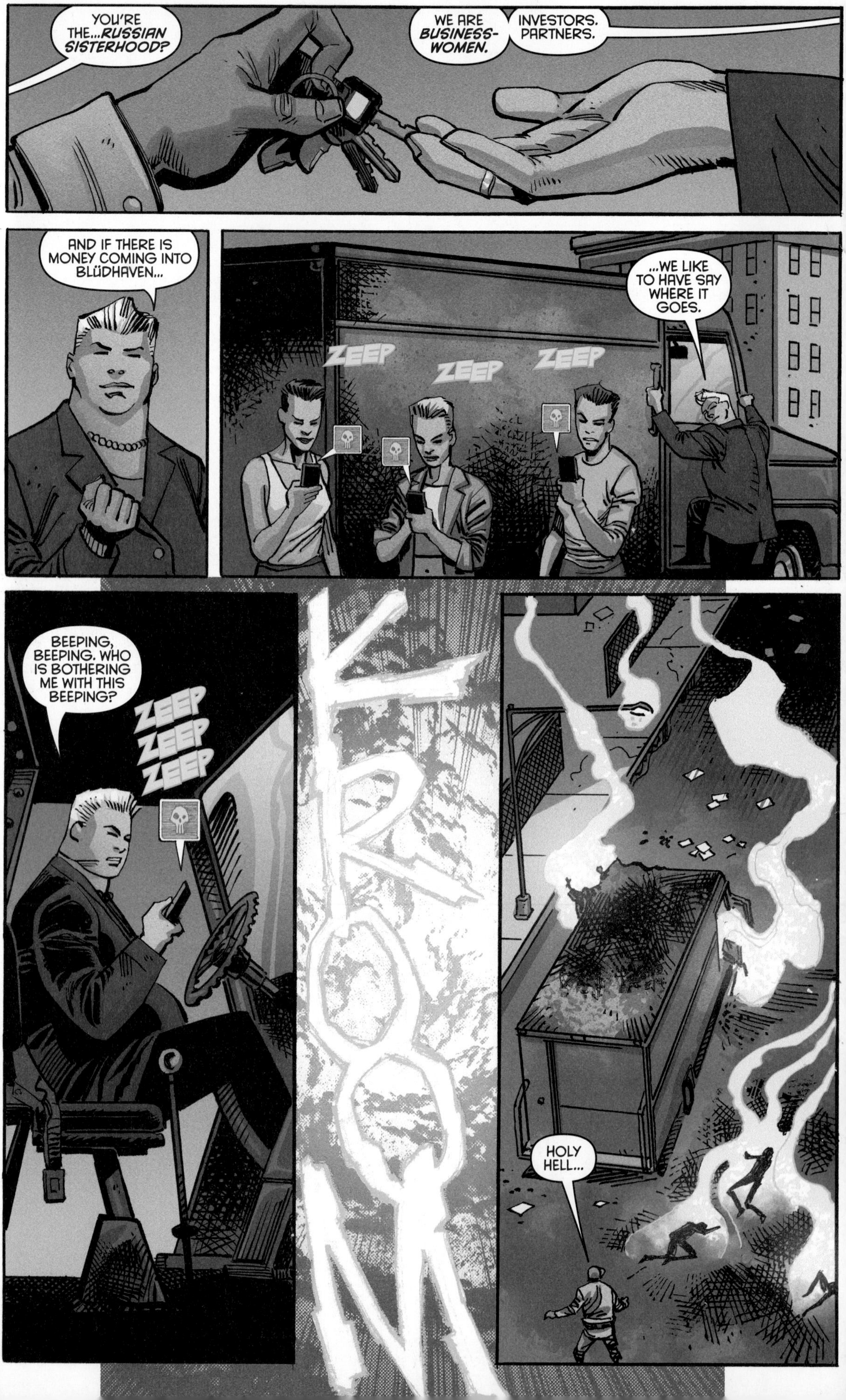
YOU'RE THE...RUSSIAN SISTERHOOD?
WE ARE BUSINESS-WOMEN.
INVESTORS. PARTNERS.
AND IF THERE IS MONEY COMING INTO BLÜDHAVEN...
ZEEP
ZEEP
ZEEP
...WE LIKE TO HAVE SAY WHERE IT GOES.
BEEPING, BEEPING. WHO IS BOTHERING ME WITH THIS BEEPING?
ZEEP ZEEP ZEEP
KROOM
HOLY HELL...

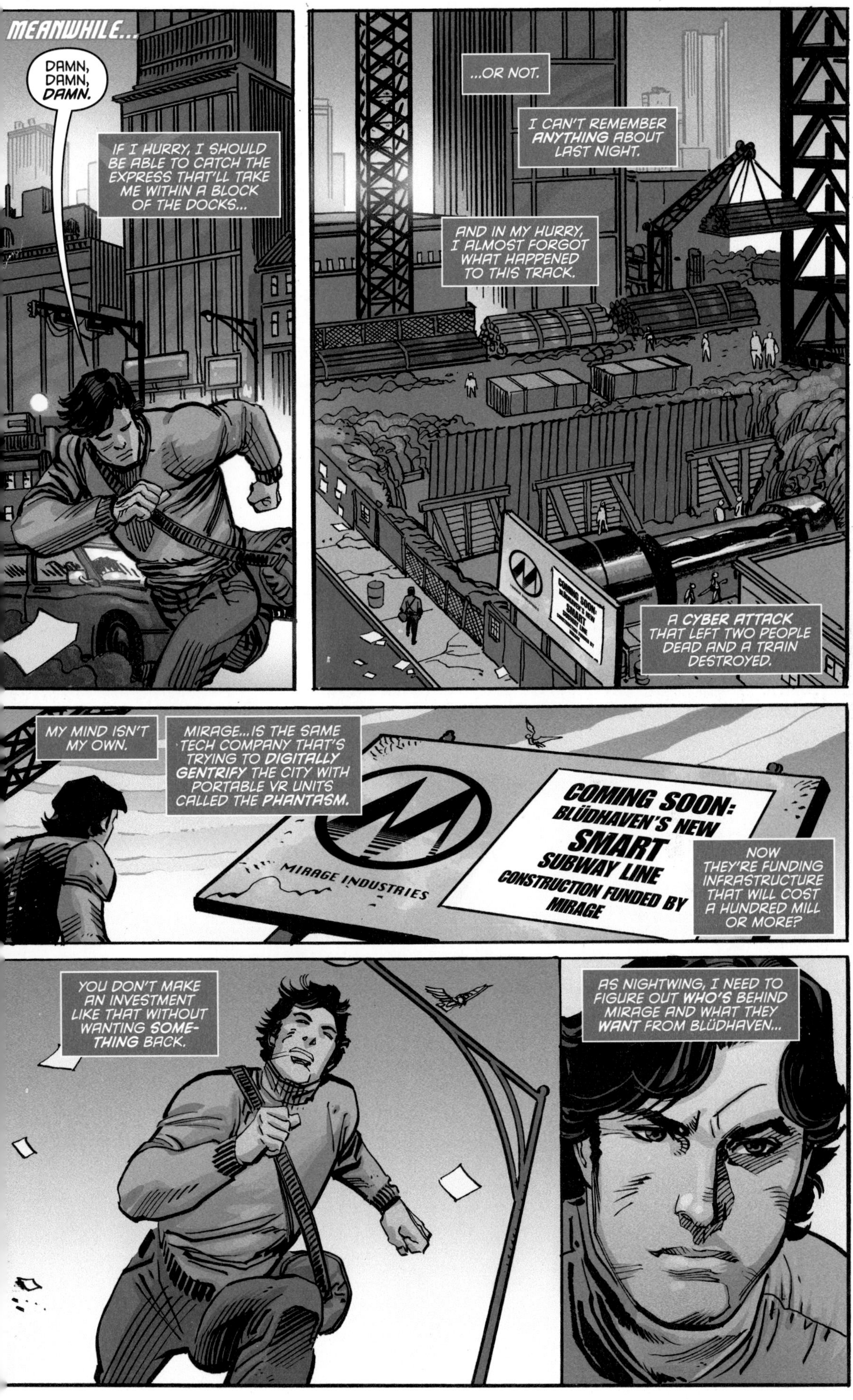
MEANWHILE...
DAMN, DAMN, DAMN.
IF I HURRY, I SHOULD BE ABLE TO CATCH THE EXPRESS THAT'LL TAKE ME WITHIN A BLOCK OF THE DOCKS...
...OR NOT.
I CAN'T REMEMBER ANYTHING ABOUT LAST NIGHT.
AND IN MY HURRY, I ALMOST FORGOT WHAT HAPPENED TO THIS TRACK.
A CYBER ATTACK THAT LEFT TWO PEOPLE DEAD AND A TRAIN DESTROYED.
MY MIND ISN'T MY OWN.
MIRAGE...IS THE SAME TECH COMPANY THAT'S TRYING TO DIGITALLY GENTRIFY THE CITY WITH PORTABLE VR UNITS CALLED THE PHANTASM.
MIRAGE INDUSTRIES
COMING SOON: BLÜDHAVEN'S NEW SMART SUBWAY LINE CONSTRUCTION FUNDED BY MIRAGE
NOW THEY'RE FUNDING INFRASTRUCTURE THAT WILL COST A HUNDRED MILL OR MORE?
YOU DON'T MAKE AN INVESTMENT LIKE THAT WITHOUT WANTING SOME-THING BACK.
AS NIGHTWING, I NEED TO FIGURE OUT WHO'S BEHIND MIRAGE AND WHAT THEY WANT FROM BLÜDHAVEN...

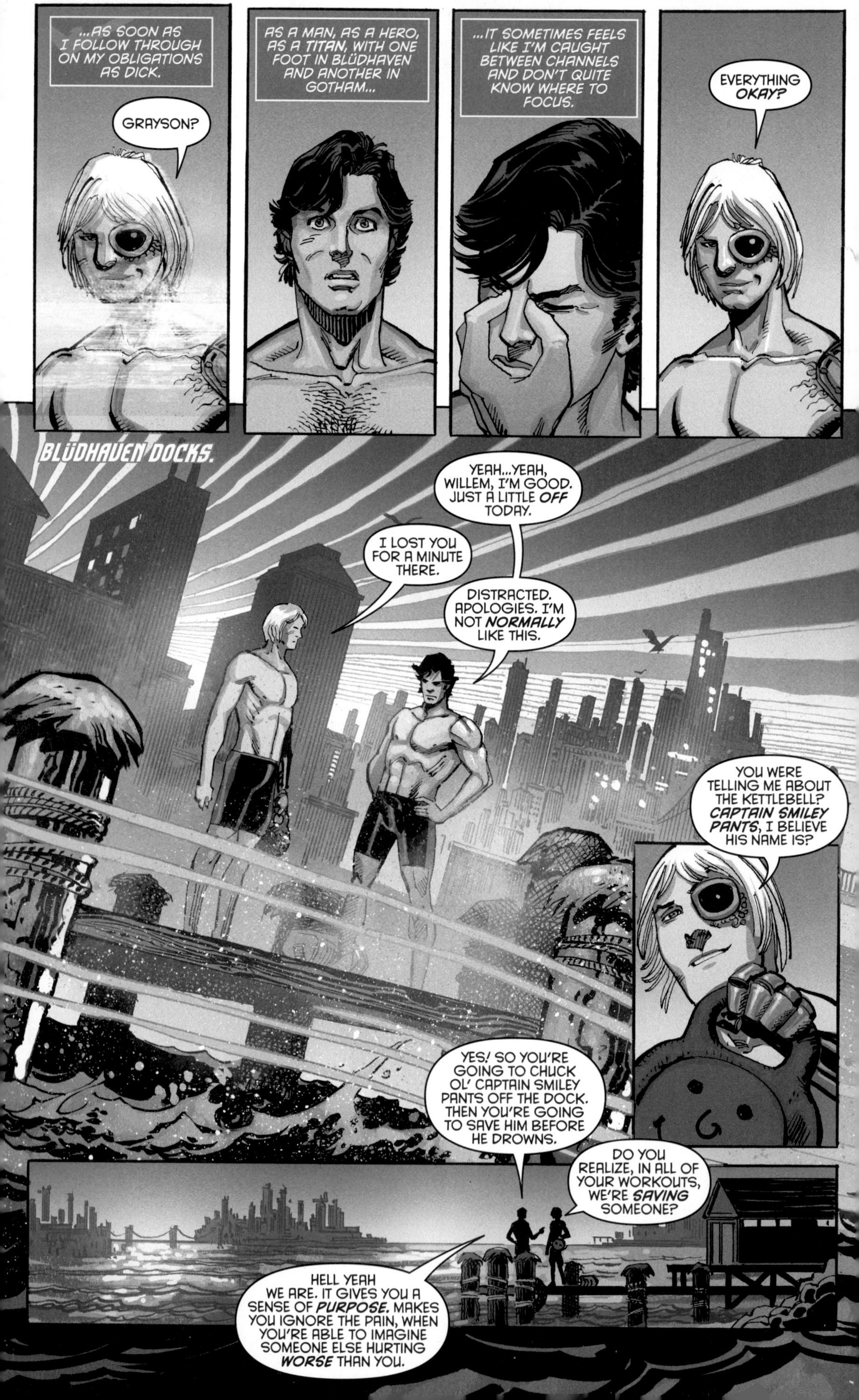

...AS SOON AS I FOLLOW THROUGH ON MY OBLIGATIONS AS DICK.
GRAYSON?
AS A MAN, AS A HERO, AS A *TITAN*, WITH ONE FOOT IN BLÜDHAVEN AND ANOTHER IN GOTHAM...
...IT SOMETIMES FEELS LIKE I'M CAUGHT BETWEEN CHANNELS AND DON'T QUITE KNOW WHERE TO FOCUS.
EVERYTHING *OKAY?*
BLÜDHAVEN DOCKS.
YEAH...YEAH, WILLEM, I'M GOOD. JUST A LITTLE *OFF* TODAY.
I LOST YOU FOR A MINUTE THERE.
DISTRACTED. APOLOGIES. I'M NOT *NORMALLY* LIKE THIS.
YOU WERE TELLING ME ABOUT THE KETTLEBELL? *CAPTAIN SMILEY PANTS*, I BELIEVE HIS NAME IS?
YES! SO YOU'RE GOING TO CHUCK OL' CAPTAIN SMILEY PANTS OFF THE DOCK. THEN YOU'RE GOING TO SAVE HIM BEFORE HE DROWNS.
DO YOU REALIZE, IN ALL OF YOUR WORKOUTS, WE'RE *SAVING* SOMEONE?
HELL YEAH WE ARE. IT GIVES YOU A SENSE OF *PURPOSE*. MAKES YOU IGNORE THE PAIN, WHEN YOU'RE ABLE TO IMAGINE SOMEONE ELSE HURTING *WORSE* THAN YOU.

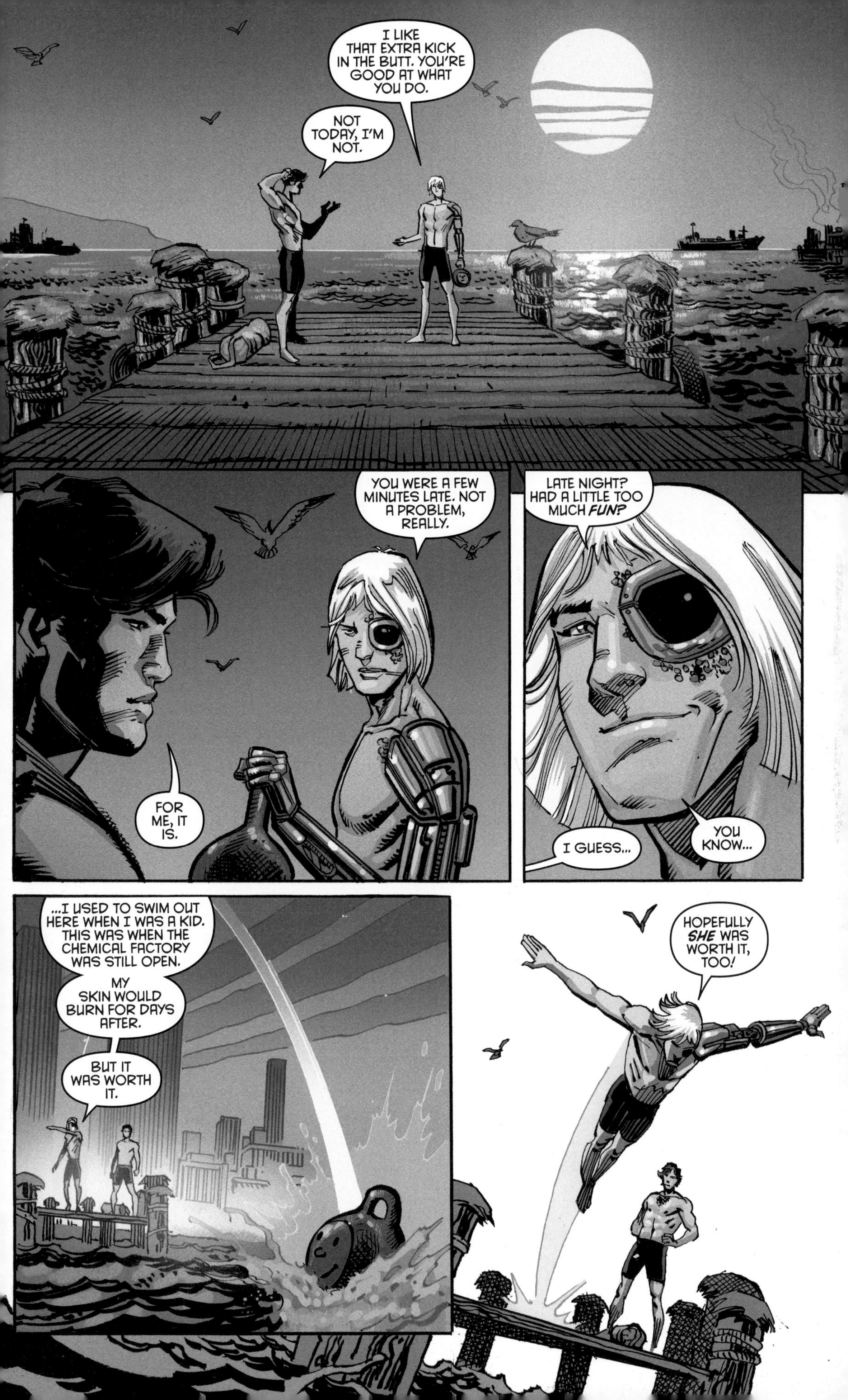
I LIKE THAT EXTRA KICK IN THE BUTT. YOU'RE GOOD AT WHAT YOU DO.
NOT TODAY, I'M NOT.
YOU WERE A FEW MINUTES LATE. NOT A PROBLEM, REALLY.
FOR ME, IT IS.
LATE NIGHT? HAD A LITTLE TOO MUCH *FUN?*
I GUESS...
YOU KNOW...
...I USED TO SWIM OUT HERE WHEN I WAS A KID. THIS WAS WHEN THE CHEMICAL FACTORY WAS STILL OPEN.
MY SKIN WOULD BURN FOR DAYS AFTER.
BUT IT WAS WORTH IT.
HOPEFULLY *SHE* WAS WORTH IT, TOO!

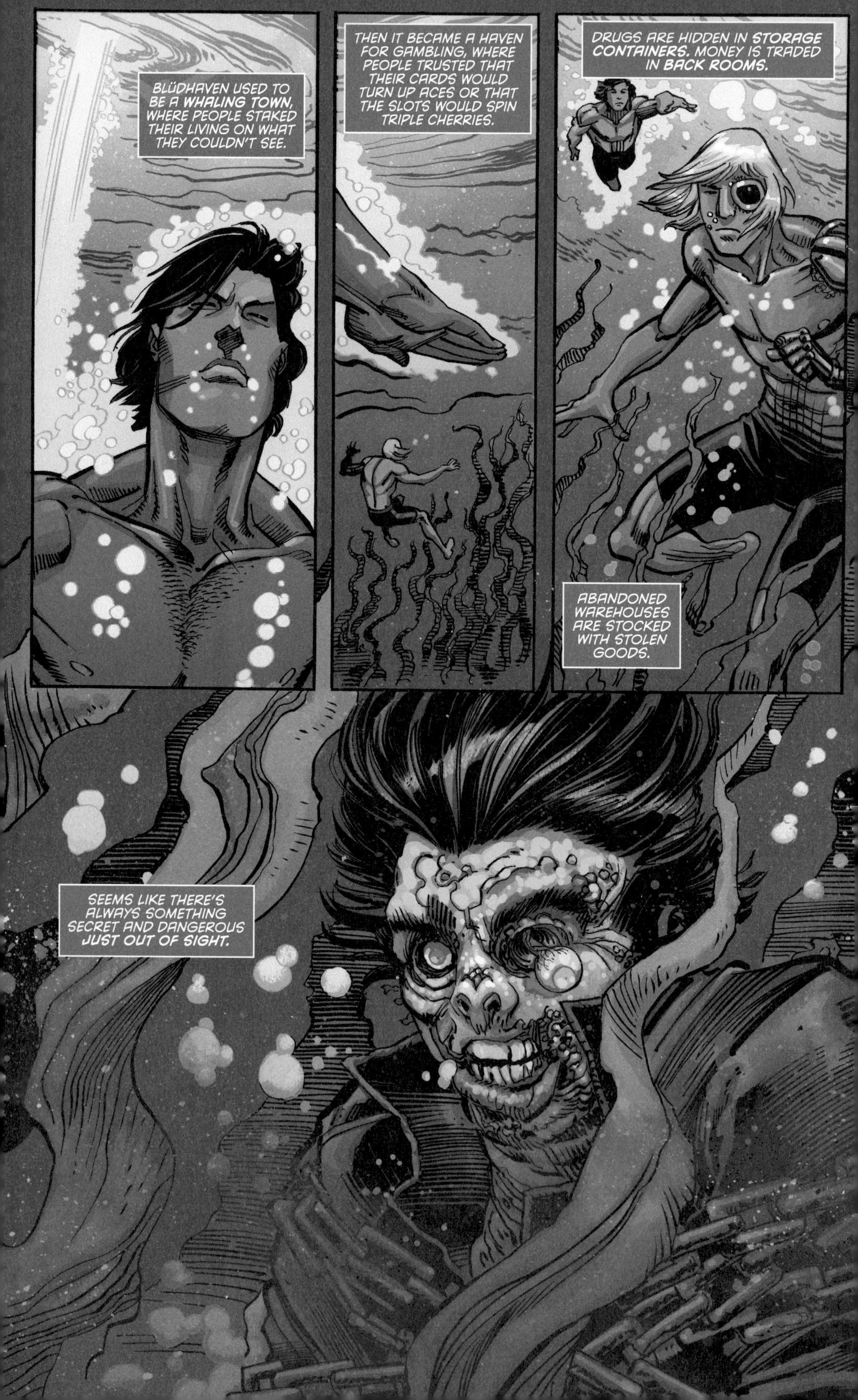

BLÜDHAVEN USED TO BE A WHALING TOWN, WHERE PEOPLE STAKED THEIR LIVING ON WHAT THEY COULDN'T SEE.
THEN IT BECAME A HAVEN FOR GAMBLING, WHERE PEOPLE TRUSTED THAT THEIR CARDS WOULD TURN UP ACES OR THAT THE SLOTS WOULD SPIN TRIPLE CHERRIES.
DRUGS ARE HIDDEN IN STORAGE CONTAINERS. MONEY IS TRADED IN BACK ROOMS.
ABANDONED WAREHOUSES ARE STOCKED WITH STOLEN GOODS.
SEEMS LIKE THERE'S ALWAYS SOMETHING SECRET AND DANGEROUS JUST OUT OF SIGHT.

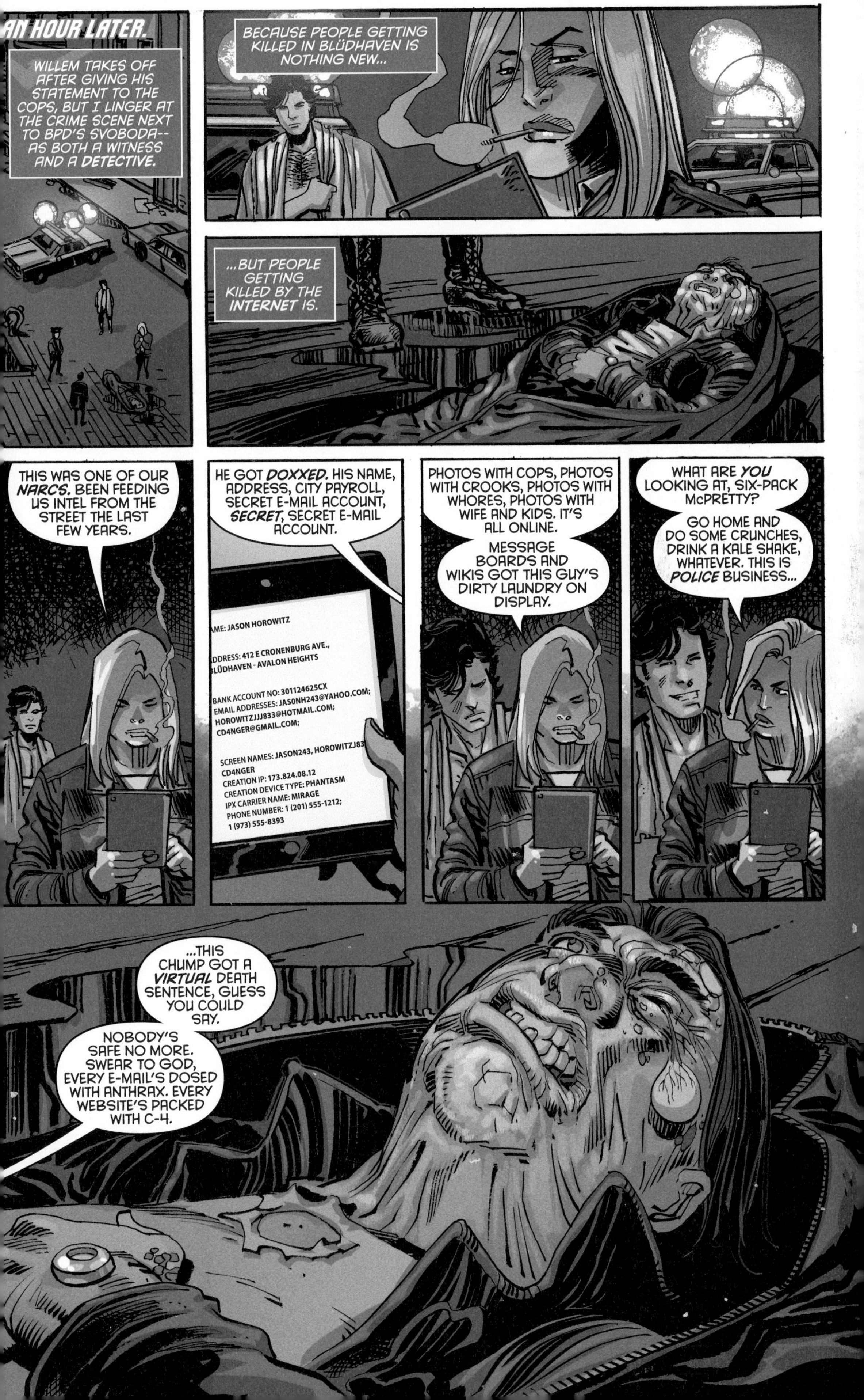
AN HOUR LATER.
WILLEM TAKES OFF AFTER GIVING HIS STATEMENT TO THE COPS, BUT I LINGER AT THE CRIME SCENE NEXT TO BPD'S SVOBODA--AS BOTH A WITNESS AND A DETECTIVE.
BECAUSE PEOPLE GETTING KILLED IN BLÜDHAVEN IS NOTHING NEW...
...BUT PEOPLE GETTING KILLED BY THE INTERNET IS.
THIS WAS ONE OF OUR NARCS. BEEN FEEDING US INTEL FROM THE STREET THE LAST FEW YEARS.
HE GOT DOXXED. HIS NAME, ADDRESS, CITY PAYROLL, SECRET E-MAIL ACCOUNT, SECRET, SECRET E-MAIL ACCOUNT.
AME: JASON HOROWITZ
DDRESS: 412 E CRONENBURG AVE., LÜDHAVEN - AVALON HEIGHTS
BANK ACCOUNT NO: 301124625CX
EMAIL ADDRESSES: JAS0NH243@YAHOO.COM; HOROWITZJJJ833@HOTMAIL.COM; CD4NGER@GMAIL.COM;
SCREEN NAMES: JASON243, HOROWITZJ83 CD4NGER
CREATION IP: 173.824.08.12
CREATION DEVICE TYPE: PHANTASM
IPX CARRIER NAME: MIRAGE
PHONE NUMBER: 1 (201) 555-1212; 1 (973) 555-8393
PHOTOS WITH COPS, PHOTOS WITH CROOKS, PHOTOS WITH WHORES, PHOTOS WITH WIFE AND KIDS. IT'S ALL ONLINE.
MESSAGE BOARDS AND WIKIS GOT THIS GUY'S DIRTY LAUNDRY ON DISPLAY.
WHAT ARE YOU LOOKING AT, SIX-PACK McPRETTY?
GO HOME AND DO SOME CRUNCHES, DRINK A KALE SHAKE, WHATEVER. THIS IS POLICE BUSINESS...
...THIS CHUMP GOT A VIRTUAL DEATH SENTENCE, GUESS YOU COULD SAY.
NOBODY'S SAFE NO MORE. SWEAR TO GOD, EVERY E-MAIL'S DOSED WITH ANTHRAX. EVERY WEBSITE'S PACKED WITH C-4.

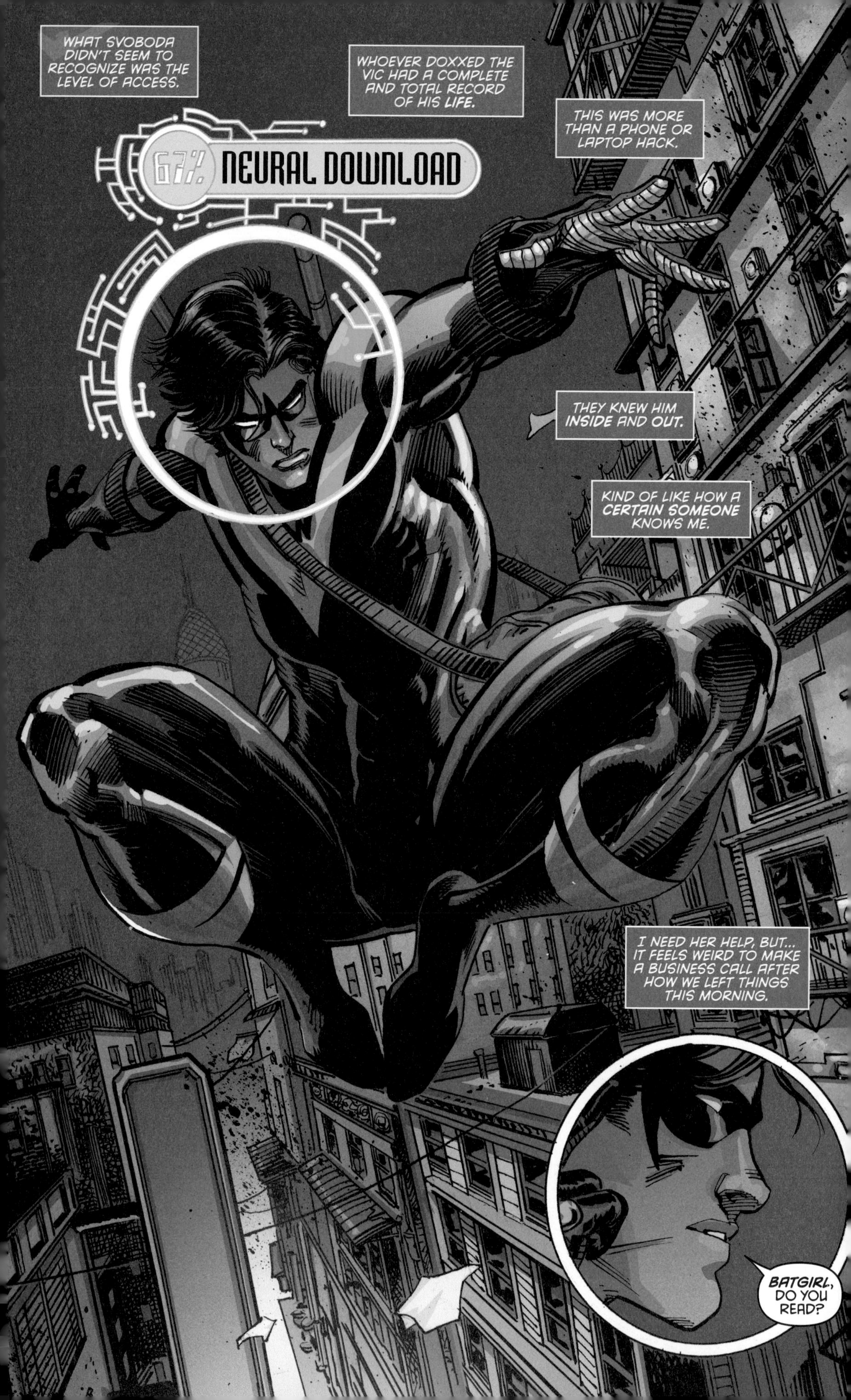
WHAT SVOBODA DIDN'T SEEM TO RECOGNIZE WAS THE LEVEL OF ACCESS.
WHOEVER DOXXED THE VIC HAD A COMPLETE AND TOTAL RECORD OF HIS LIFE.
THIS WAS MORE THAN A PHONE OR LAPTOP HACK.
67% NEURAL DOWNLOAD
THEY KNEW HIM INSIDE AND OUT.
KIND OF LIKE HOW A CERTAIN SOMEONE KNOWS ME.
I NEED HER HELP, BUT... IT FEELS WEIRD TO MAKE A BUSINESS CALL AFTER HOW WE LEFT THINGS THIS MORNING.
BATGIRL, DO YOU READ?

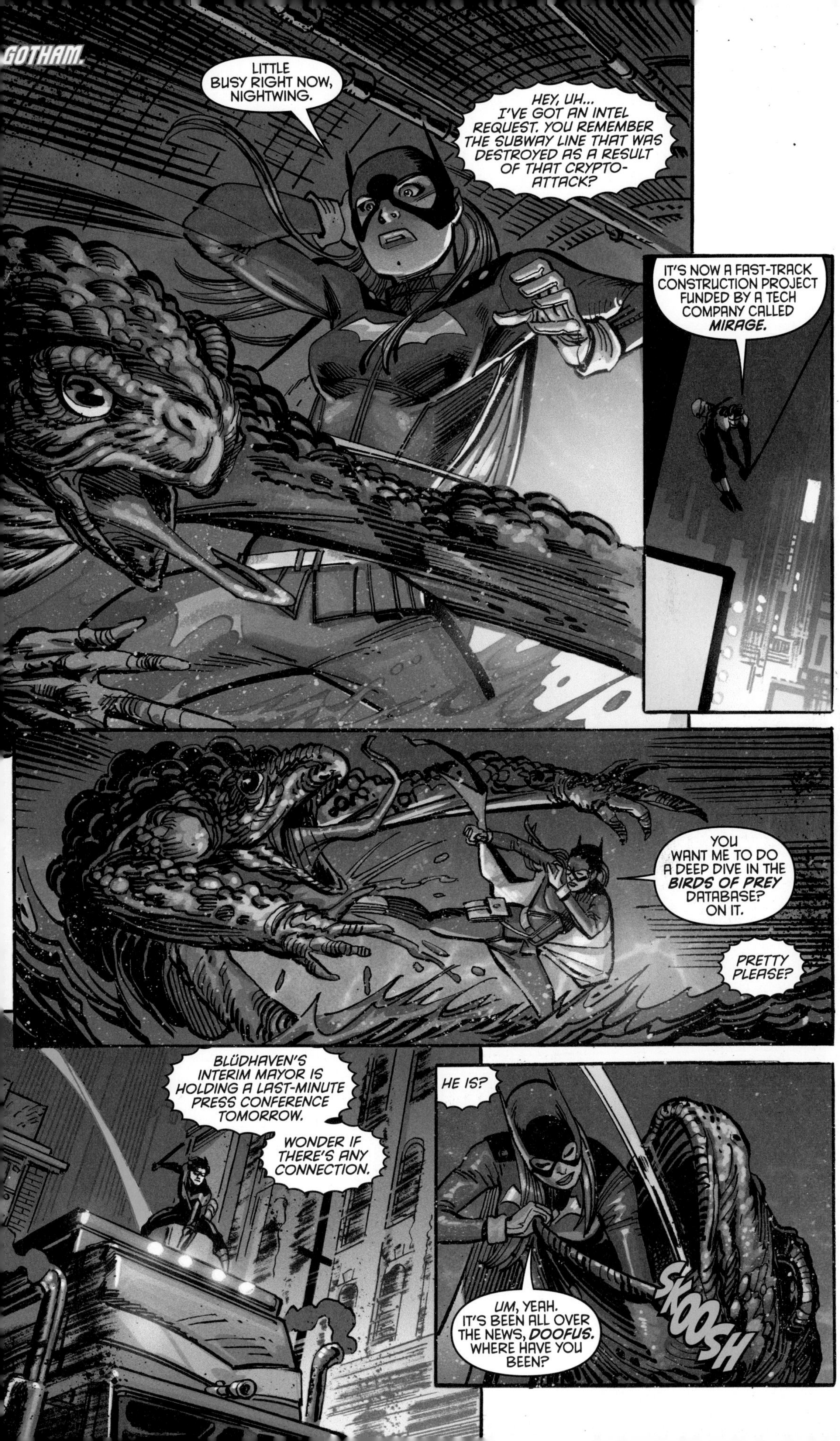
GOTHAM.
LITTLE BUSY RIGHT NOW, NIGHTWING.
HEY, UH... I'VE GOT AN INTEL REQUEST. YOU REMEMBER THE SUBWAY LINE THAT WAS DESTROYED AS A RESULT OF THAT CRYPTO-ATTACK?
IT'S NOW A FAST-TRACK CONSTRUCTION PROJECT FUNDED BY A TECH COMPANY CALLED MIRAGE.
YOU WANT ME TO DO A DEEP DIVE IN THE BIRDS OF PREY DATABASE? ON IT.
PRETTY PLEASE?
BLÜDHAVEN'S INTERIM MAYOR IS HOLDING A LAST-MINUTE PRESS CONFERENCE TOMORROW.
WONDER IF THERE'S ANY CONNECTION.
HE IS?
UM, YEAH. IT'S BEEN ALL OVER THE NEWS, DOOFUS. WHERE HAVE YOU BEEN?
SKOOSH

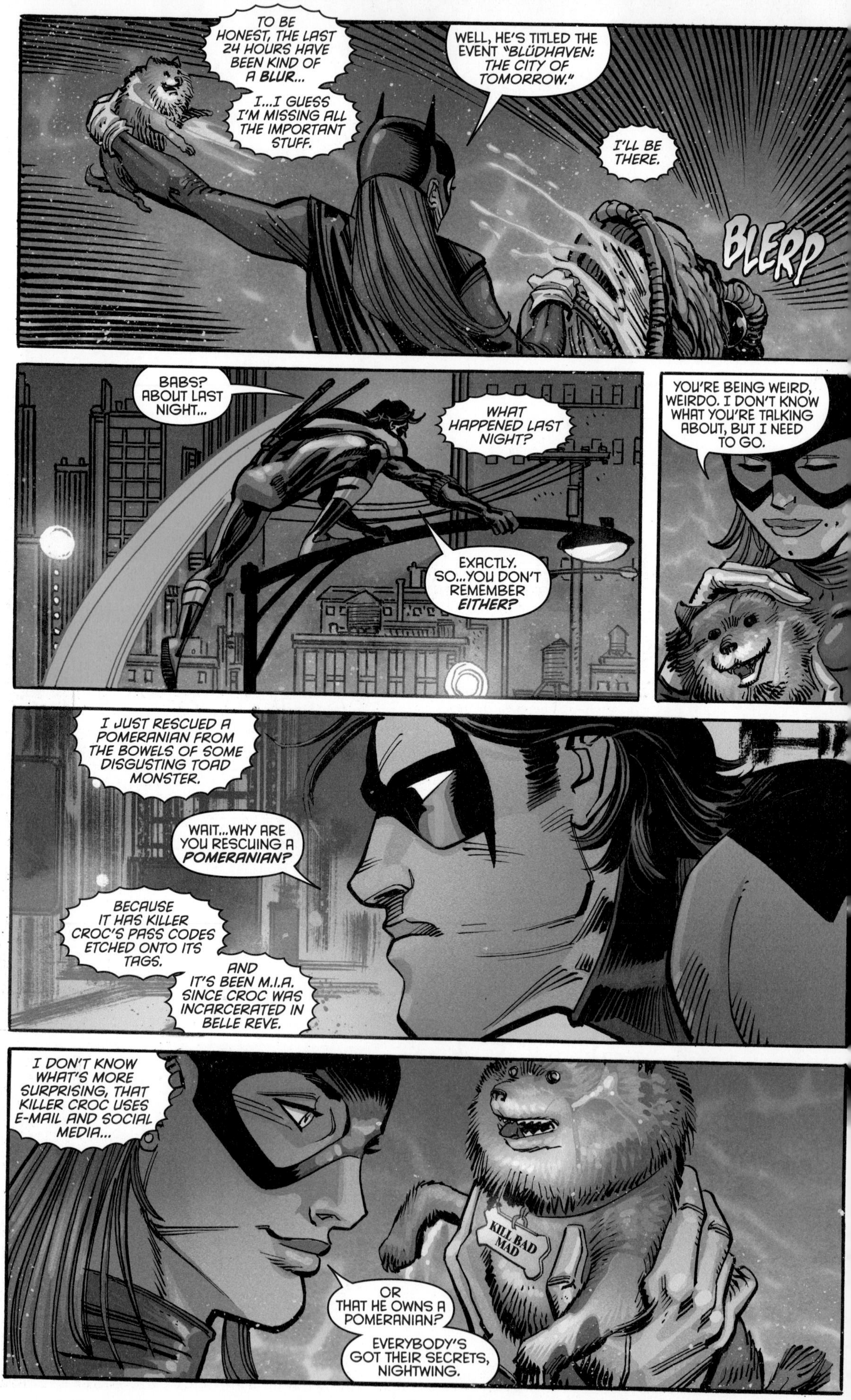
TO BE HONEST, THE LAST 24 HOURS HAVE BEEN KIND OF A BLUR...
I...I GUESS I'M MISSING ALL THE IMPORTANT STUFF.
WELL, HE'S TITLED THE EVENT "BLÜDHAVEN: THE CITY OF TOMORROW."
I'LL BE THERE.
BLERP
BABS? ABOUT LAST NIGHT...
WHAT HAPPENED LAST NIGHT?
EXACTLY. SO...YOU DON'T REMEMBER EITHER?
YOU'RE BEING WEIRD, WEIRDO. I DON'T KNOW WHAT YOU'RE TALKING ABOUT, BUT I NEED TO GO.
I JUST RESCUED A POMERANIAN FROM THE BOWELS OF SOME DISGUSTING TOAD MONSTER.
WAIT...WHY ARE YOU RESCUING A POMERANIAN?
BECAUSE IT HAS KILLER CROC'S PASS CODES ETCHED ONTO ITS TAGS.
AND IT'S BEEN M.I.A. SINCE CROC WAS INCARCERATED IN BELLE REVE.
I DON'T KNOW WHAT'S MORE SURPRISING, THAT KILLER CROC USES E-MAIL AND SOCIAL MEDIA...
KILL BAD MAD
OR THAT HE OWNS A POMERANIAN?
EVERYBODY'S GOT THEIR SECRETS, NIGHTWING.

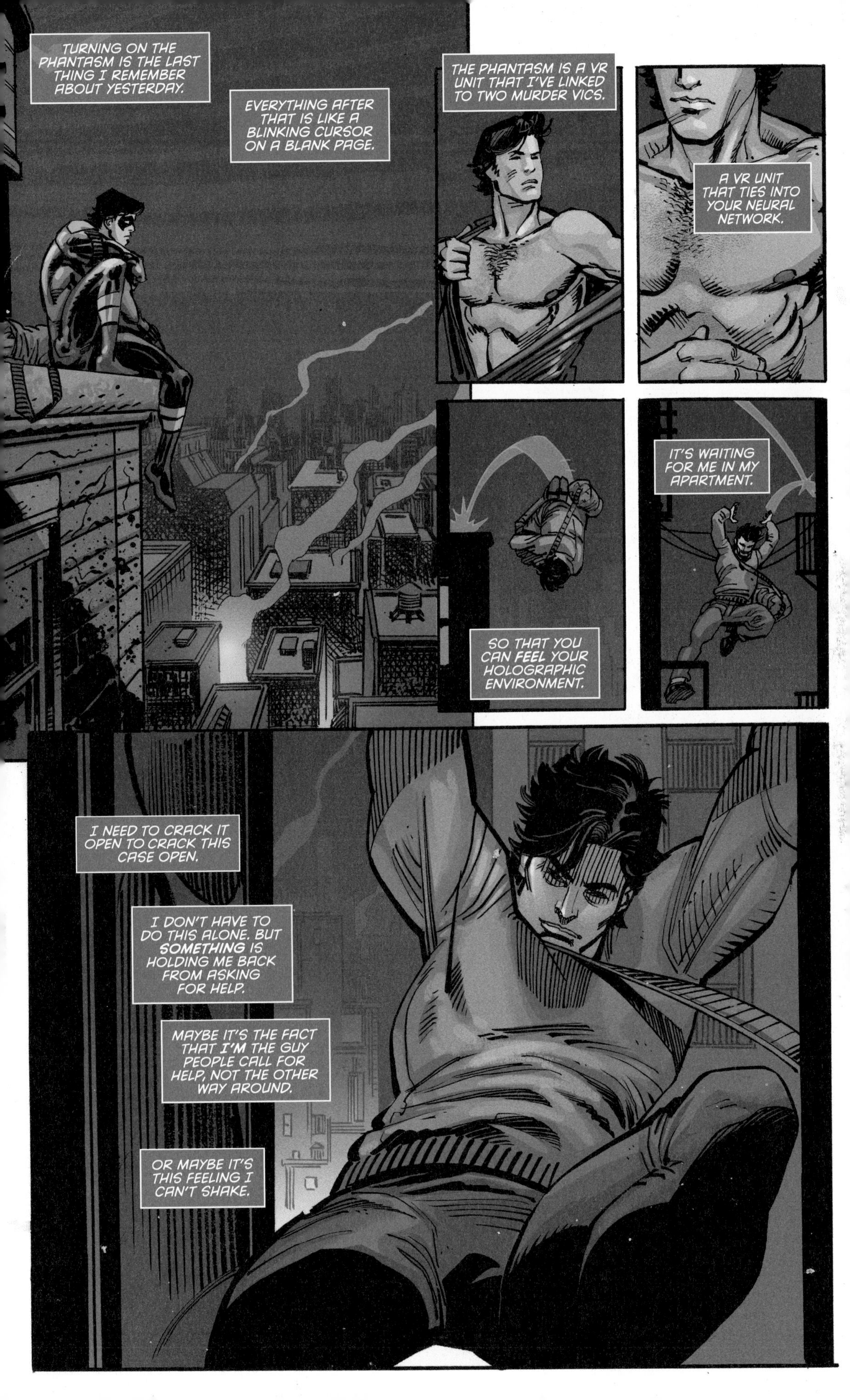
TURNING ON THE PHANTASM IS THE LAST THING I REMEMBER ABOUT YESTERDAY.
EVERYTHING AFTER THAT IS LIKE A BLINKING CURSOR ON A BLANK PAGE.
THE PHANTASM IS A VR UNIT THAT I'VE LINKED TO TWO MURDER VICS.
A VR UNIT THAT TIES INTO YOUR NEURAL NETWORK.
SO THAT YOU CAN FEEL YOUR HOLOGRAPHIC ENVIRONMENT.
IT'S WAITING FOR ME IN MY APARTMENT.
I NEED TO CRACK IT OPEN TO CRACK THIS CASE OPEN.
I DON'T HAVE TO DO THIS ALONE. BUT SOMETHING IS HOLDING ME BACK FROM ASKING FOR HELP.
MAYBE IT'S THE FACT THAT I'M THE GUY PEOPLE CALL FOR HELP, NOT THE OTHER WAY AROUND.
OR MAYBE IT'S THIS FEELING I CAN'T SHAKE.

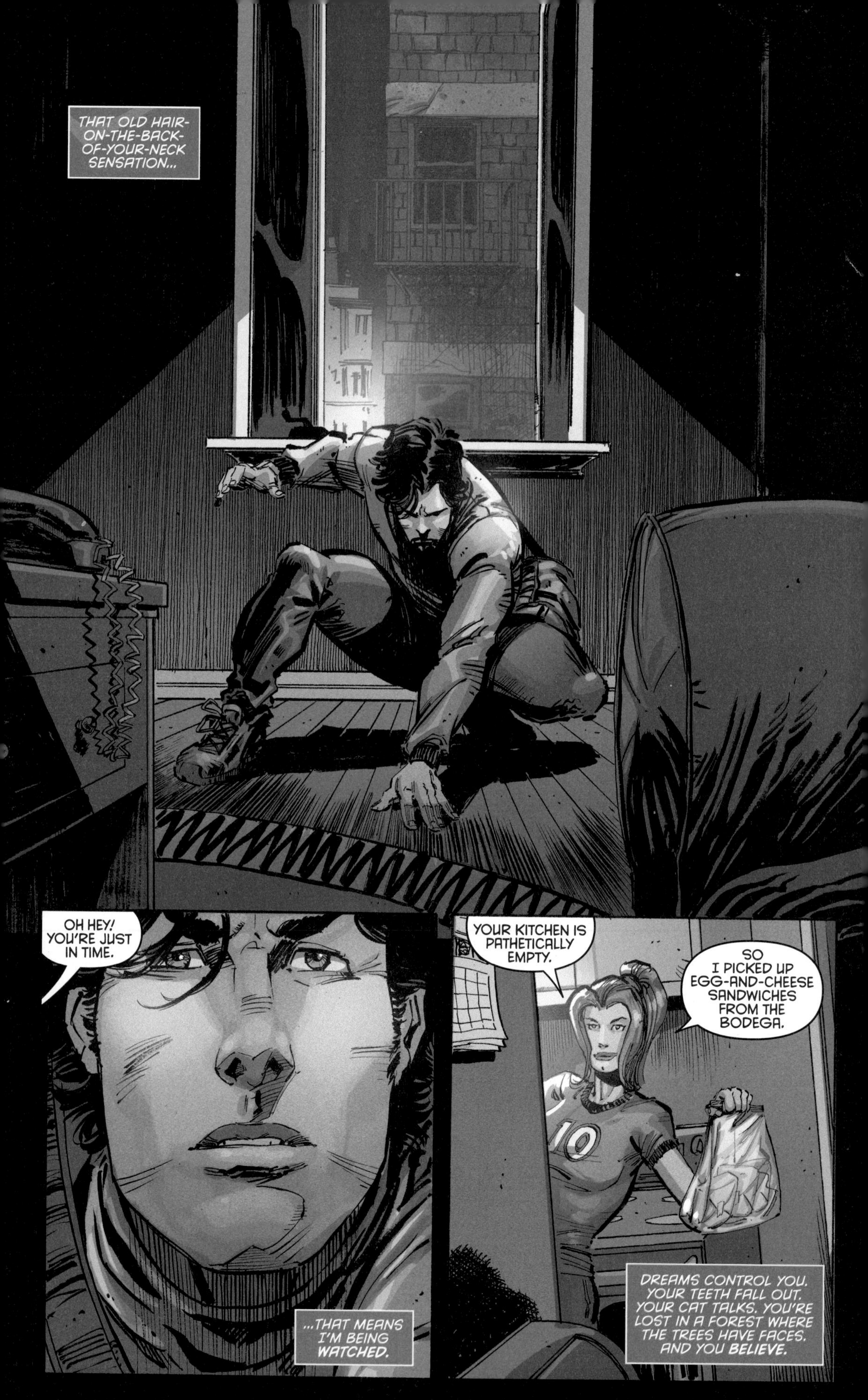

THAT OLD HAIR-ON-THE-BACK-OF-YOUR-NECK SENSATION...
OH HEY! YOU'RE JUST IN TIME.
...THAT MEANS I'M BEING WATCHED.
YOUR KITCHEN IS PATHETICALLY EMPTY.
SO I PICKED UP EGG-AND-CHEESE SANDWICHES FROM THE BODEGA.
DREAMS CONTROL YOU. YOUR TEETH FALL OUT. YOUR CAT TALKS. YOU'RE LOST IN A FOREST WHERE THE TREES HAVE FACES. AND YOU BELIEVE.

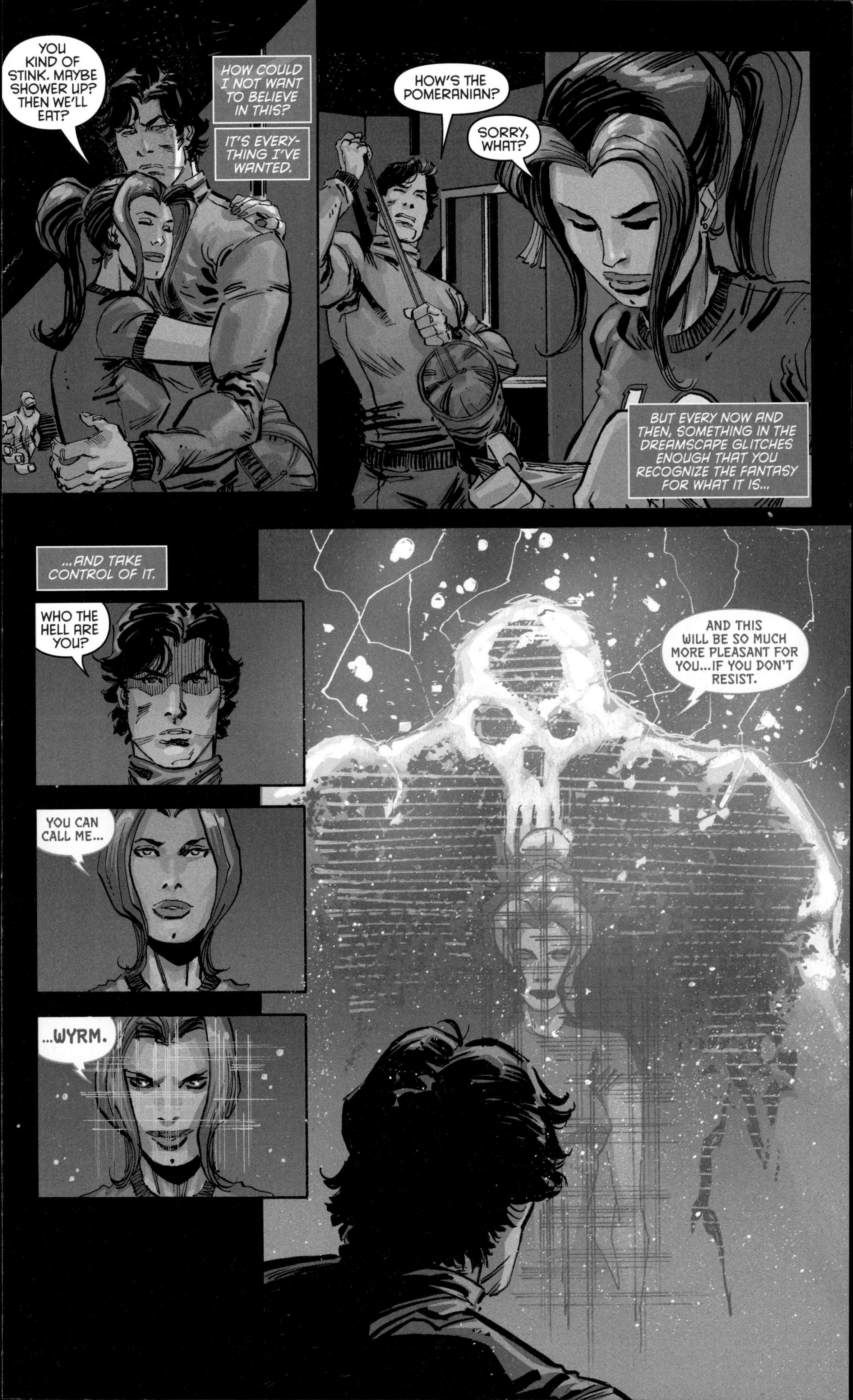
YOU KIND OF STINK. MAYBE SHOWER UP? THEN WE'LL EAT?
HOW COULD I NOT WANT TO BELIEVE IN THIS?
IT'S EVERY-THING I'VE WANTED.
HOW'S THE POMERANIAN?
SORRY, WHAT?
BUT EVERY NOW AND THEN, SOMETHING IN THE DREAMSCAPE GLITCHES ENOUGH THAT YOU RECOGNIZE THE FANTASY FOR WHAT IT IS...
...AND TAKE CONTROL OF IT.
WHO THE HELL ARE YOU?
YOU CAN CALL ME...
...WYRM.
AND THIS WILL BE SO MUCH MORE PLEASANT FOR YOU...IF YOU DON'T RESIST.

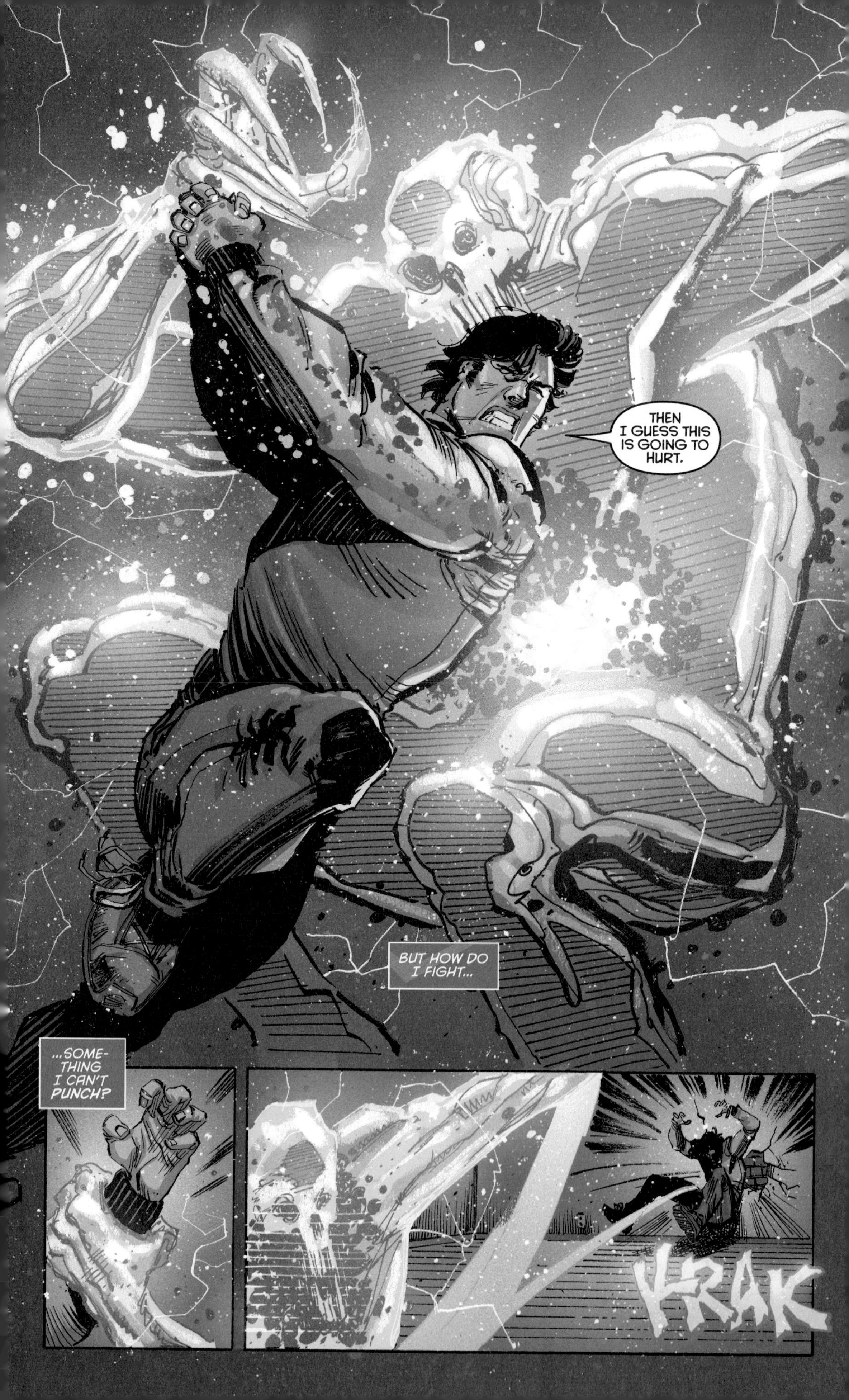
THEN I GUESS THIS IS GOING TO HURT.
BUT HOW DO I FIGHT...
...SOME-THING I CAN'T PUNCH?
KRAK

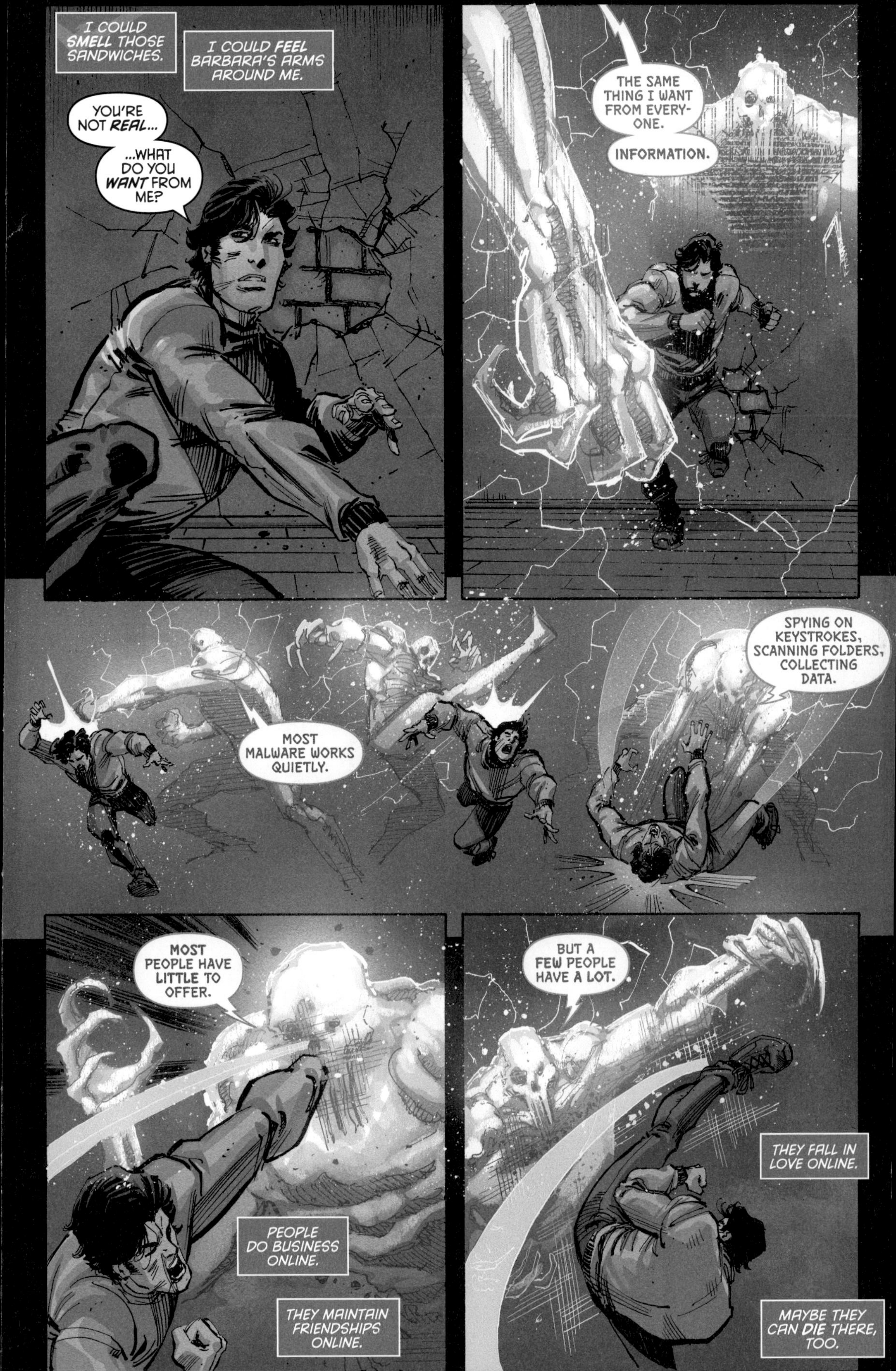
I COULD SMELL THOSE SANDWICHES.
I COULD FEEL BARBARA'S ARMS AROUND ME.
YOU'RE NOT REAL...
...WHAT DO YOU WANT FROM ME?
THE SAME THING I WANT FROM EVERY-ONE.
INFORMATION.
MOST MALWARE WORKS QUIETLY.
SPYING ON KEYSTROKES, SCANNING FOLDERS, COLLECTING DATA.
MOST PEOPLE HAVE LITTLE TO OFFER.
PEOPLE DO BUSINESS ONLINE.
THEY MAINTAIN FRIENDSHIPS ONLINE.
BUT A FEW PEOPLE HAVE A LOT.
THEY FALL IN LOVE ONLINE.
MAYBE THEY CAN DIE THERE, TOO.

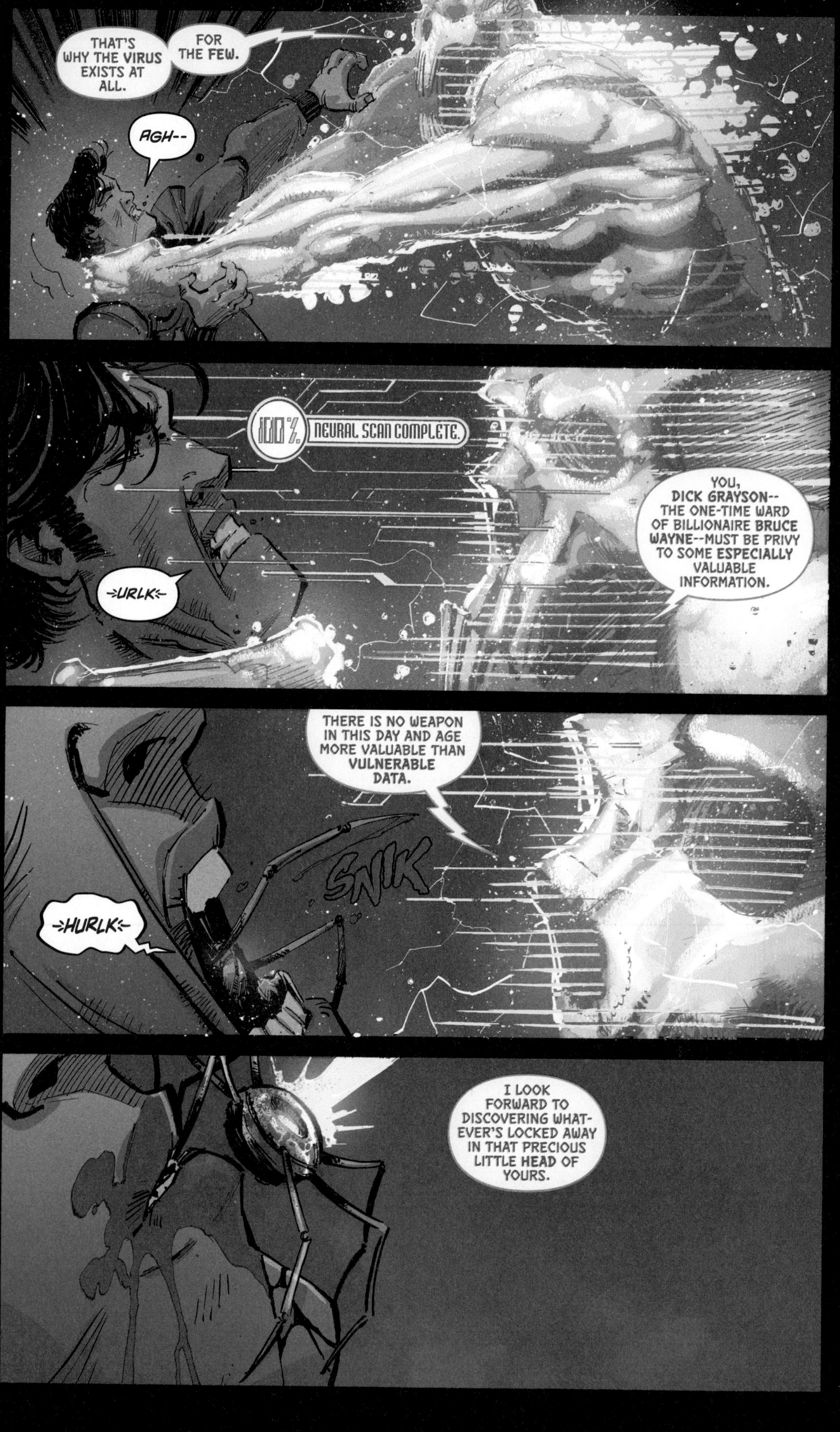

THAT'S WHY THE VIRUS EXISTS AT ALL.
FOR THE FEW.
AGH--
100%
NEURAL SCAN COMPLETE.
YOU, DICK GRAYSON-- THE ONE-TIME WARD OF BILLIONAIRE BRUCE WAYNE--MUST BE PRIVY TO SOME ESPECIALLY VALUABLE INFORMATION.
URLK
THERE IS NO WEAPON IN THIS DAY AND AGE MORE VALUABLE THAN VULNERABLE DATA.
SNIK
HURLK
I LOOK FORWARD TO DISCOVERING WHATEVER'S LOCKED AWAY IN THAT PRECIOUS LITTLE HEAD OF YOURS.

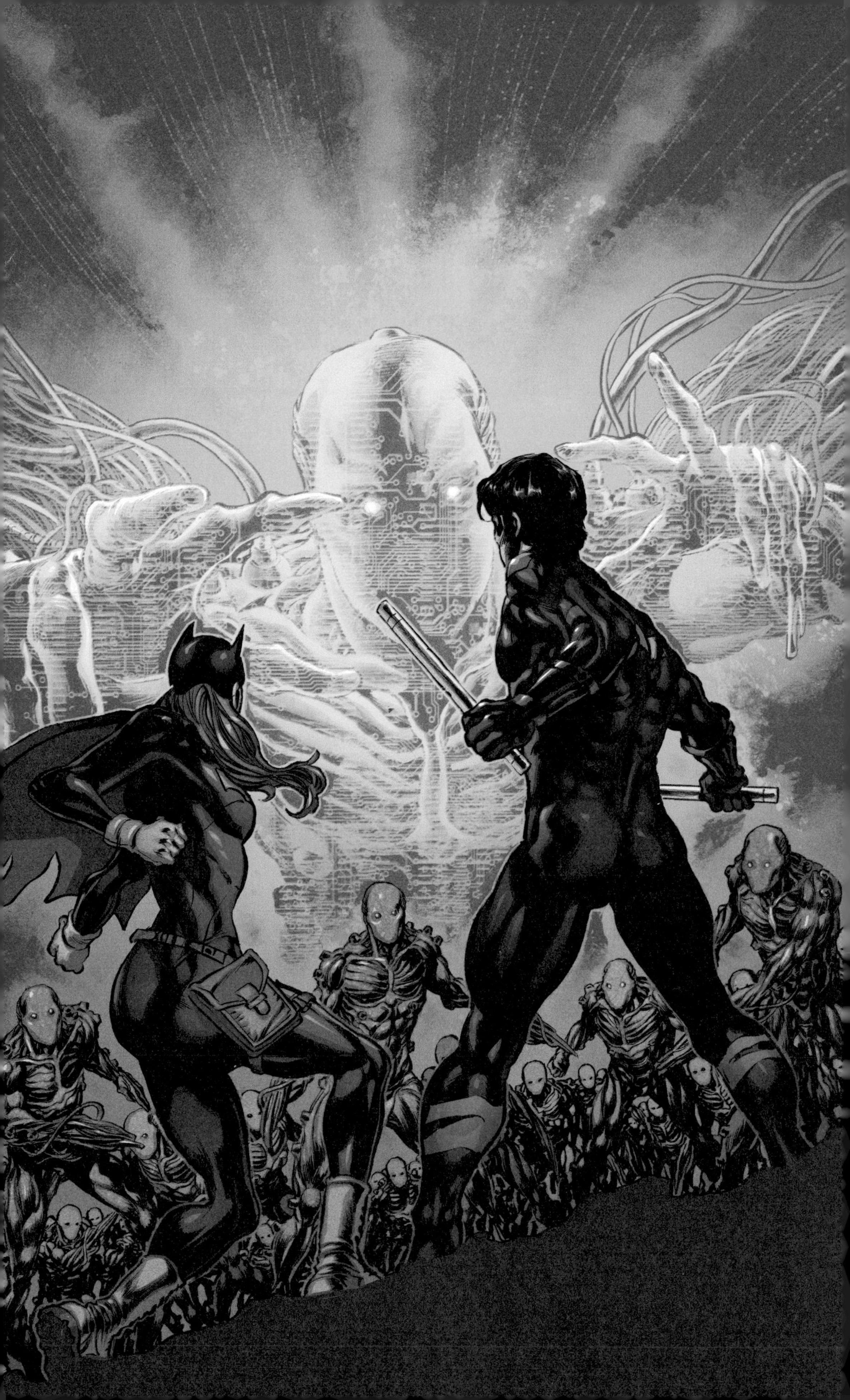

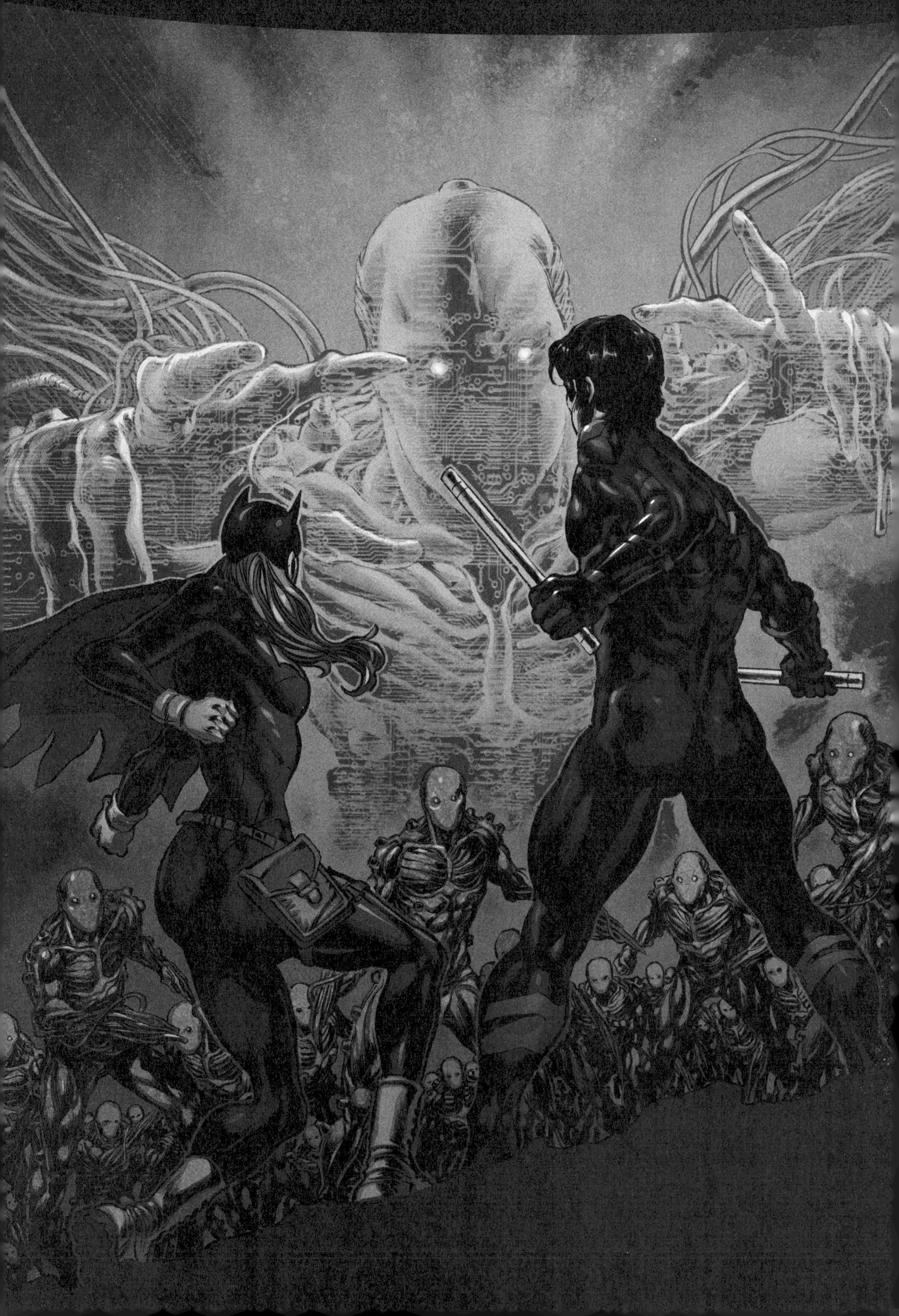

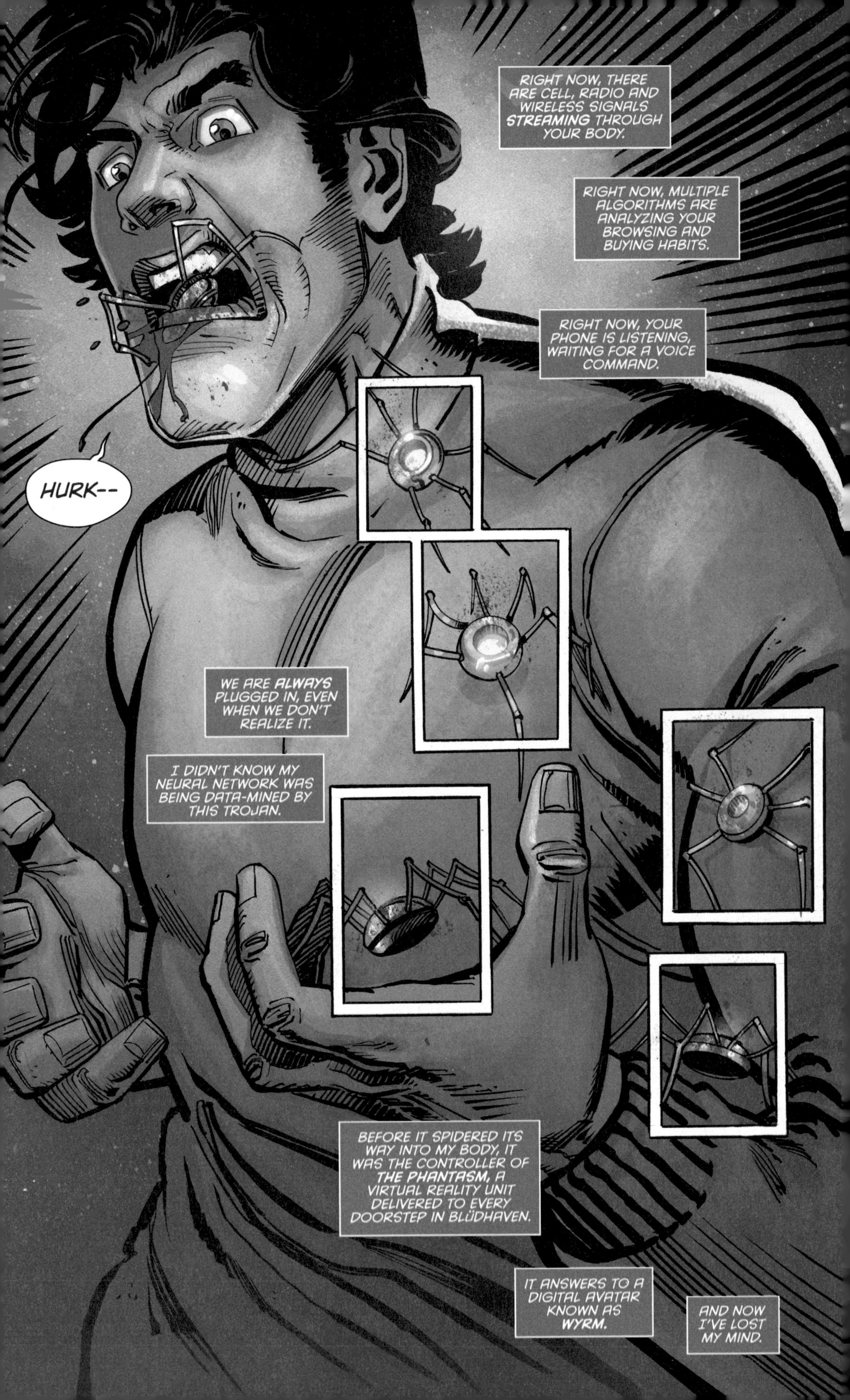
RIGHT NOW, THERE ARE CELL, RADIO AND WIRELESS SIGNALS STREAMING THROUGH YOUR BODY.
RIGHT NOW, MULTIPLE ALGORITHMS ARE ANALYZING YOUR BROWSING AND BUYING HABITS.
RIGHT NOW, YOUR PHONE IS LISTENING, WAITING FOR A VOICE COMMAND.
HURK--
WE ARE ALWAYS PLUGGED IN, EVEN WHEN WE DON'T REALIZE IT.
I DIDN'T KNOW MY NEURAL NETWORK WAS BEING DATA-MINED BY THIS TROJAN.
BEFORE IT SPIDERED ITS WAY INTO MY BODY, IT WAS THE CONTROLLER OF THE PHANTASM, A VIRTUAL REALITY UNIT DELIVERED TO EVERY DOORSTEP IN BLÜDHAVEN.
IT ANSWERS TO A DIGITAL AVATAR KNOWN AS WYRM.
AND NOW I'VE LOST MY MIND.

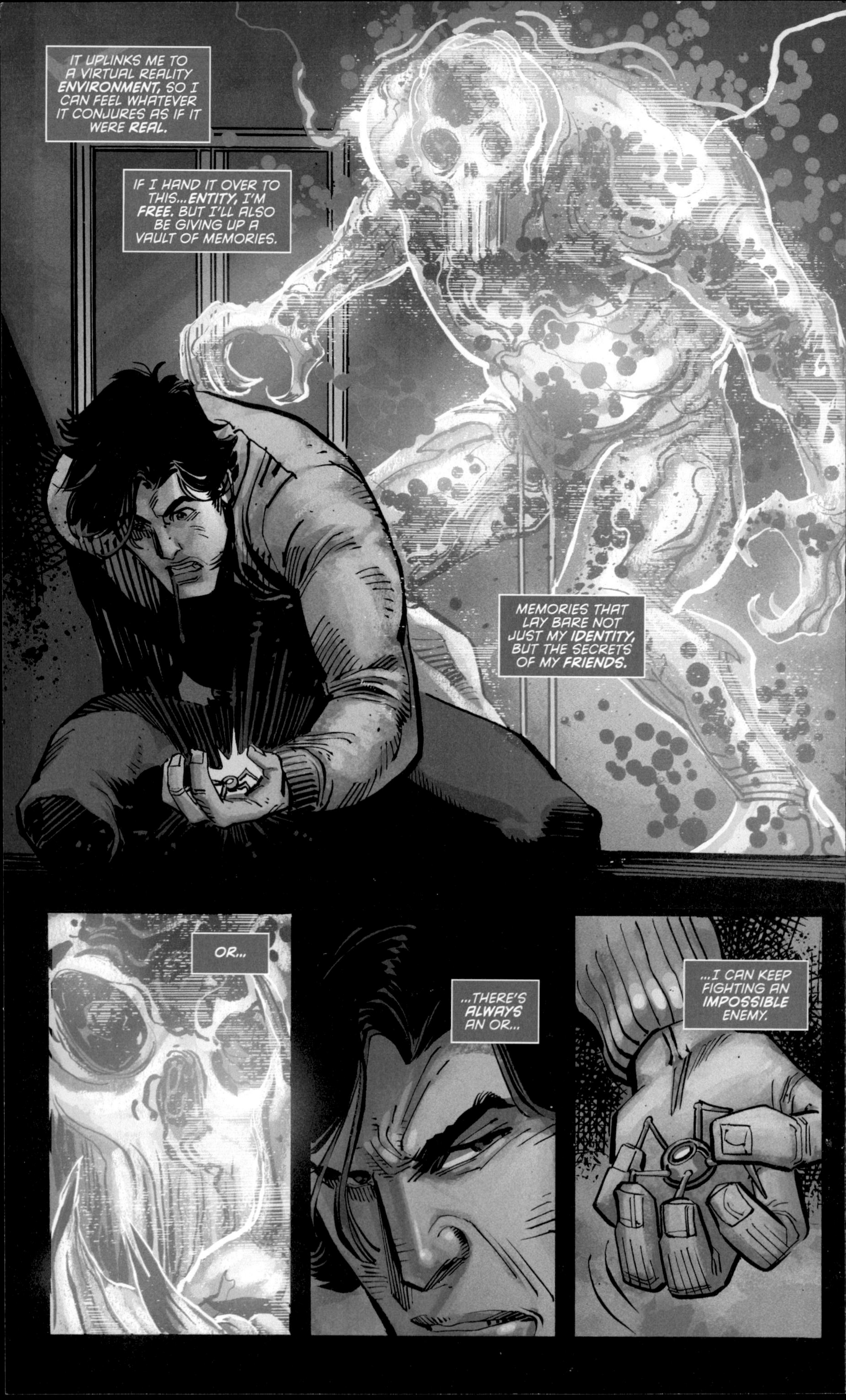

IT UPLINKS ME TO A VIRTUAL REALITY ENVIRONMENT, SO I CAN FEEL WHATEVER IT CONJURES AS IF IT WERE REAL.
IF I HAND IT OVER TO THIS...ENTITY, I'M FREE. BUT I'LL ALSO BE GIVING UP A VAULT OF MEMORIES.
MEMORIES THAT LAY BARE NOT JUST MY IDENTITY, BUT THE SECRETS OF MY FRIENDS.
OR...
...THERE'S ALWAYS AN OR...
...I CAN KEEP FIGHTING AN IMPOSSIBLE ENEMY.

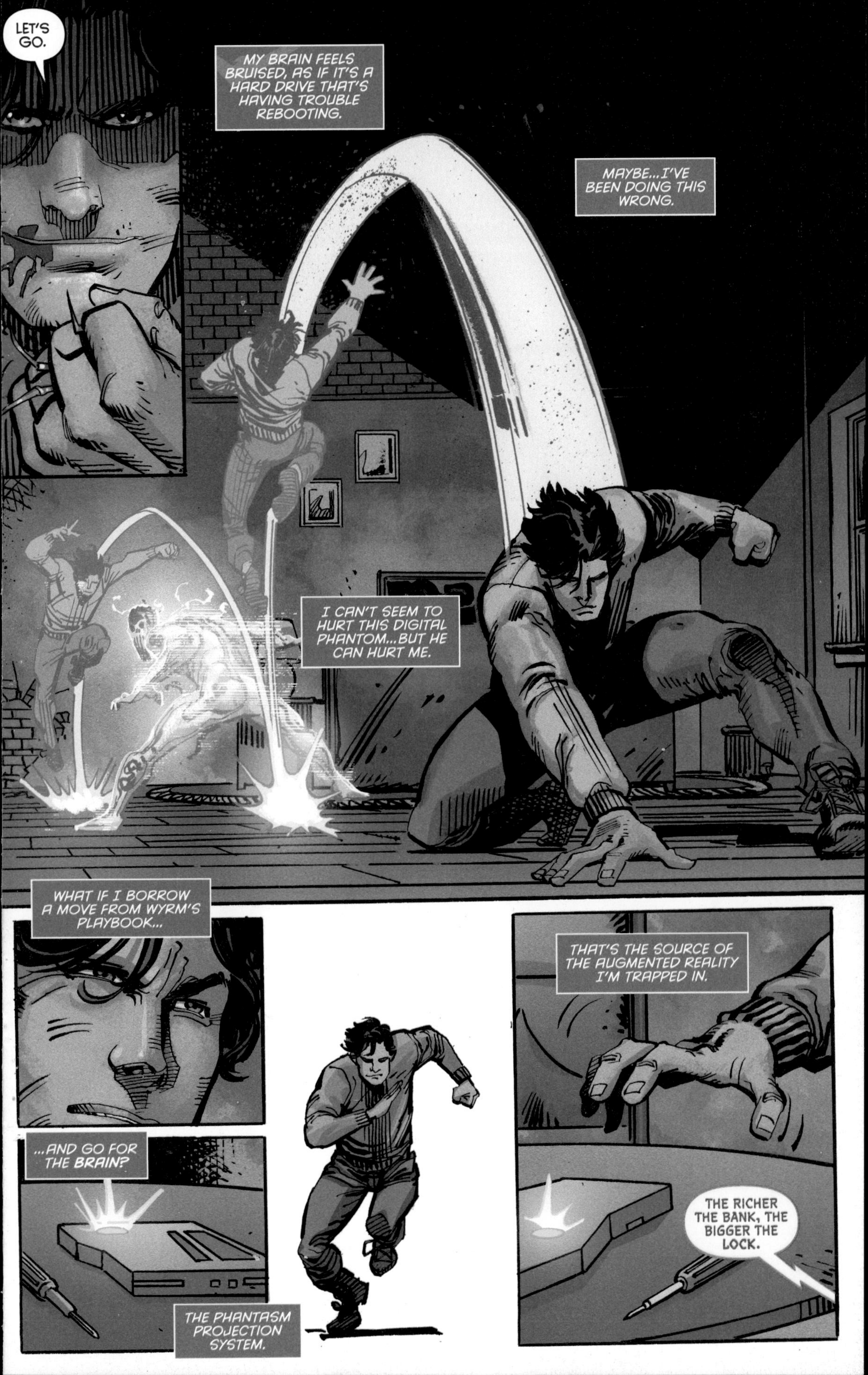
LET'S GO.
MY BRAIN FEELS BRUISED, AS IF IT'S A HARD DRIVE THAT'S HAVING TROUBLE REBOOTING.
MAYBE...I'VE BEEN DOING THIS WRONG.
I CAN'T SEEM TO HURT THIS DIGITAL PHANTOM...BUT HE CAN HURT ME.
WHAT IF I BORROW A MOVE FROM WYRM'S PLAYBOOK...
...AND GO FOR THE BRAIN?
THE PHANTASM PROJECTION SYSTEM.
THAT'S THE SOURCE OF THE AUGMENTED REALITY I'M TRAPPED IN.
THE RICHER THE BANK, THE BIGGER THE LOCK.

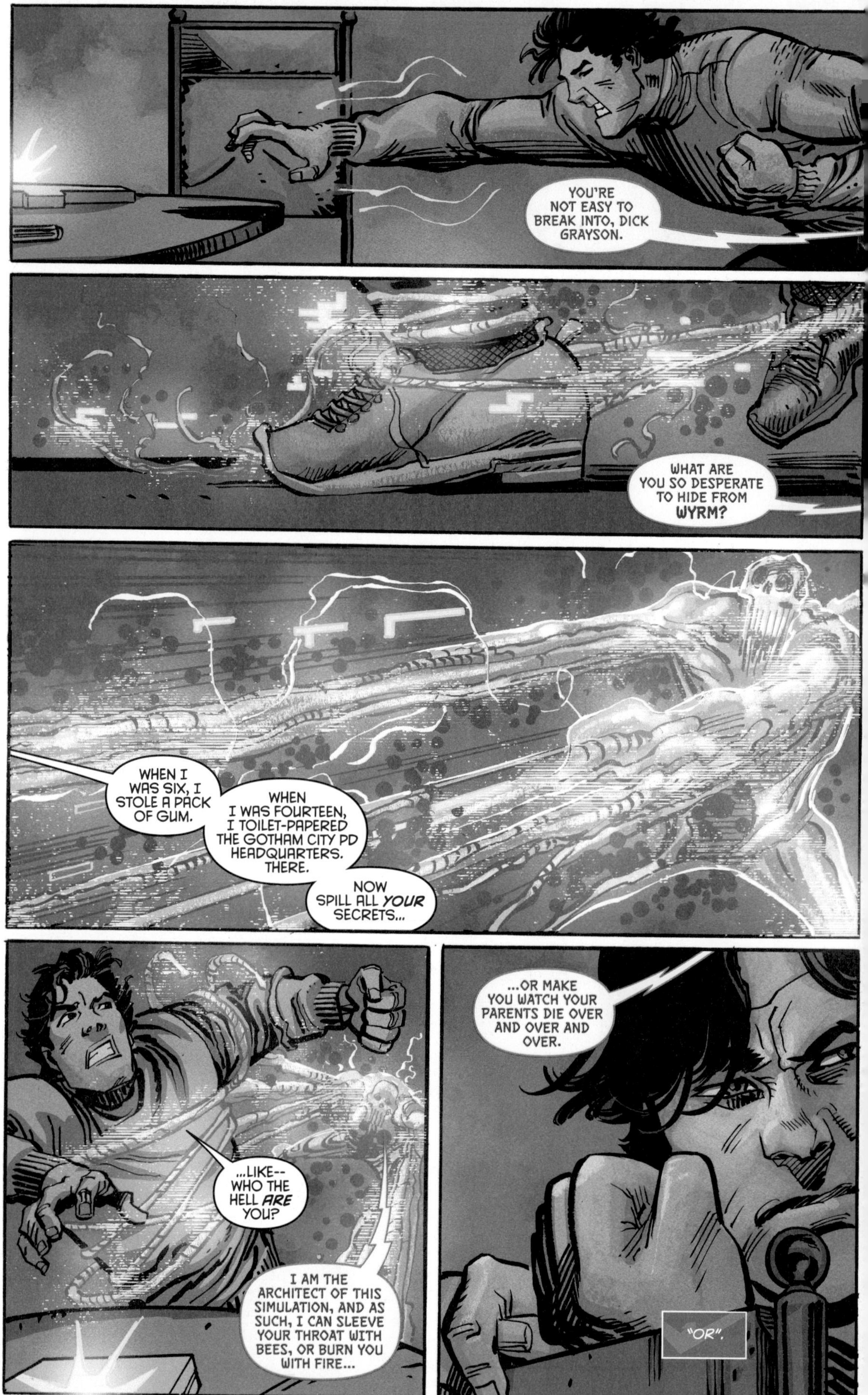
YOU'RE NOT EASY TO BREAK INTO, DICK GRAYSON.
WHAT ARE YOU SO DESPERATE TO HIDE FROM WYRM?
WHEN I WAS SIX, I STOLE A PACK OF GUM.
WHEN I WAS FOURTEEN, I TOILET-PAPERED THE GOTHAM CITY PD HEADQUARTERS. THERE.
NOW SPILL ALL *YOUR* SECRETS...
...LIKE-- WHO THE HELL *ARE* YOU?
I AM THE ARCHITECT OF THIS SIMULATION, AND AS SUCH, I CAN SLEEVE YOUR THROAT WITH BEES, OR BURN YOU WITH FIRE...
...OR MAKE YOU WATCH YOUR PARENTS DIE OVER AND OVER AND OVER.
"OR".

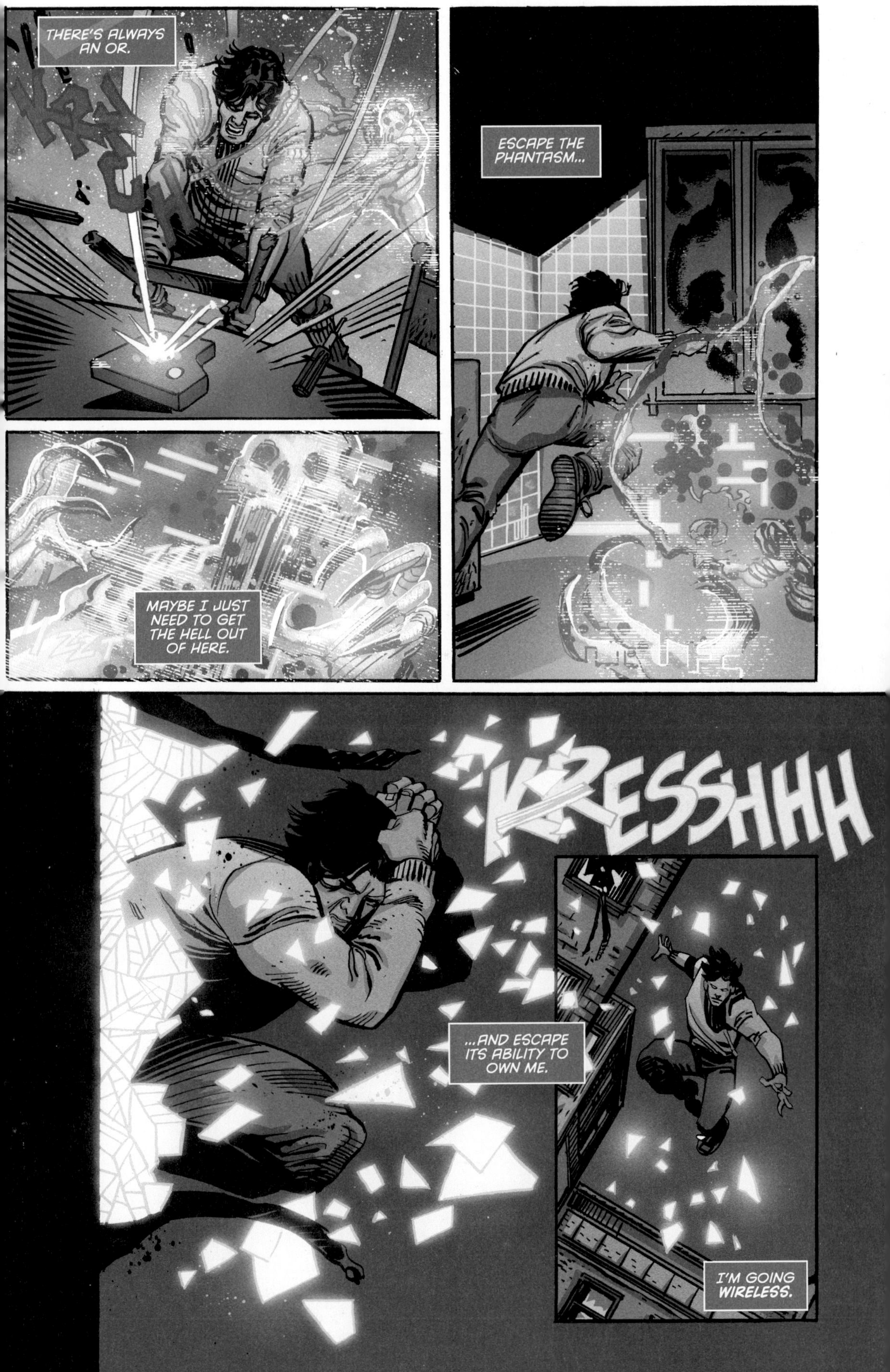
THERE'S ALWAYS AN OR.
ESCAPE THE PHANTASM...
MAYBE I JUST NEED TO GET THE HELL OUT OF HERE.
KRESSHHH
...AND ESCAPE ITS ABILITY TO OWN ME.
I'M GOING WIRELESS.

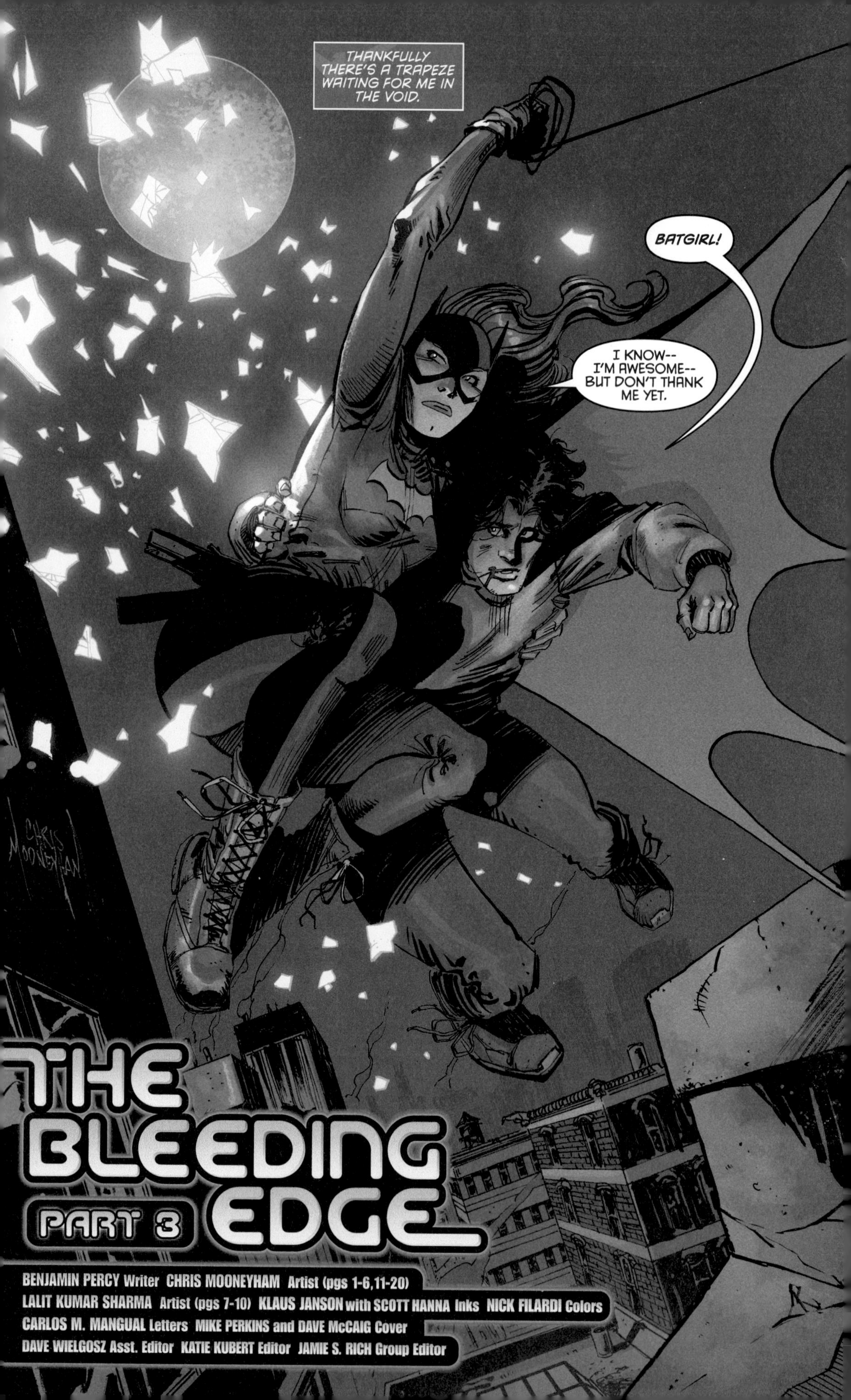
THANKFULLY THERE'S A TRAPEZE WAITING FOR ME IN THE VOID.
BATGIRL!
I KNOW-- I'M AWESOME-- BUT DON'T THANK ME YET.
THE BLEEDING EDGE
PART 3
BENJAMIN PERCY Writer CHRIS MOONEYHAM Artist (pgs 1-6,11-20)
LALIT KUMAR SHARMA Artist (pgs 7-10) KLAUS JANSON with SCOTT HANNA Inks NICK FILARDI Colors
CARLOS M. MANGUAL Letters MIKE PERKINS and DAVE McCAIG Cover
DAVE WIELGOSZ Asst. Editor KATIE KUBERT Editor JAMIE S. RICH Group Editor

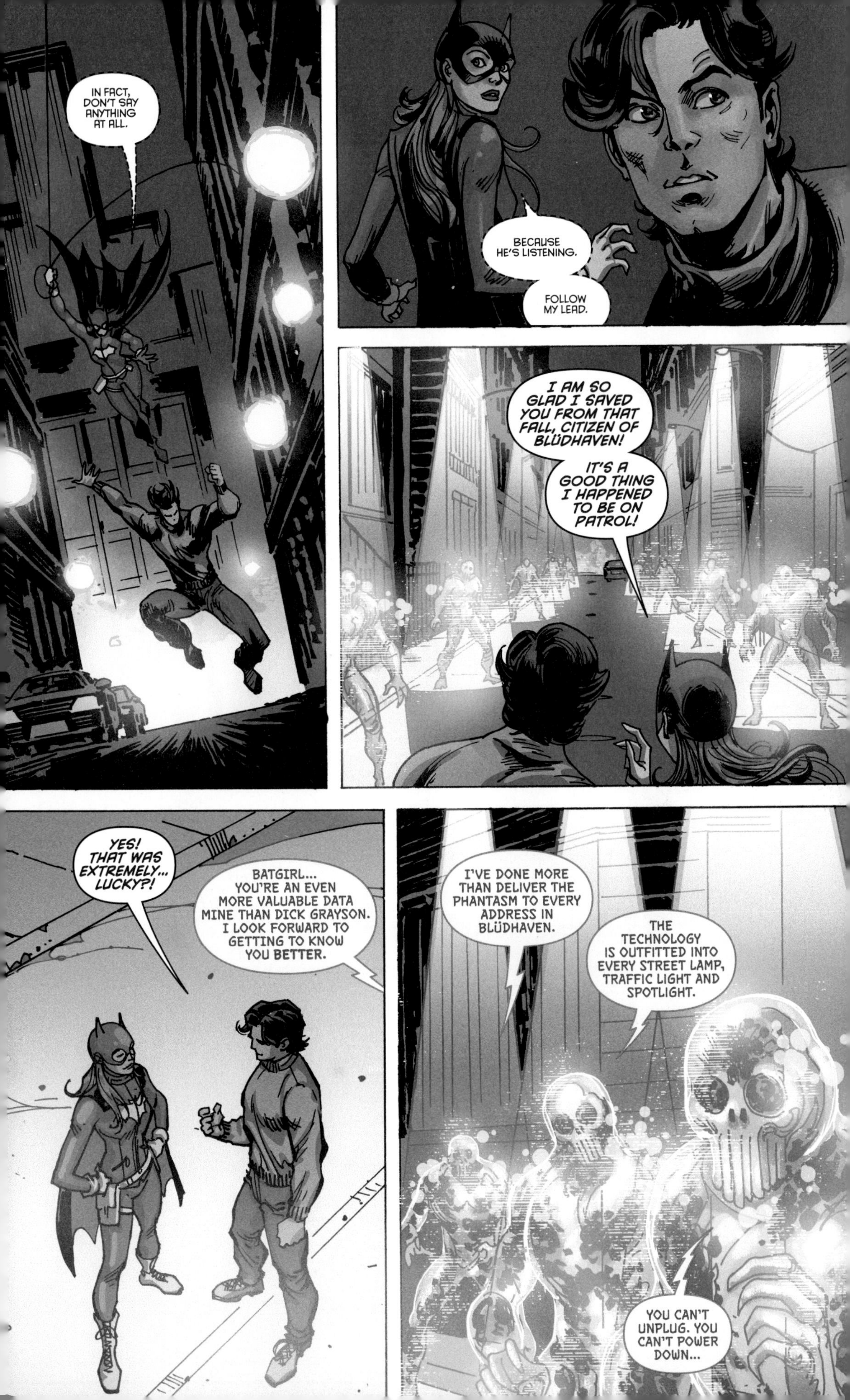
IN FACT, DON'T SAY ANYTHING AT ALL.
BECAUSE HE'S LISTENING.
FOLLOW MY LEAD.
I AM SO GLAD I SAVED YOU FROM THAT FALL, CITIZEN OF BLÜDHAVEN!
IT'S A GOOD THING I HAPPENED TO BE ON PATROL!
YES! THAT WAS EXTREMELY... LUCKY?!
BATGIRL... YOU'RE AN EVEN MORE VALUABLE DATA MINE THAN DICK GRAYSON. I LOOK FORWARD TO GETTING TO KNOW YOU BETTER.
I'VE DONE MORE THAN DELIVER THE PHANTASM TO EVERY ADDRESS IN BLÜDHAVEN.
THE TECHNOLOGY IS OUTFITTED INTO EVERY STREET LAMP, TRAFFIC LIGHT AND SPOTLIGHT.
YOU CAN'T UNPLUG. YOU CAN'T POWER DOWN...

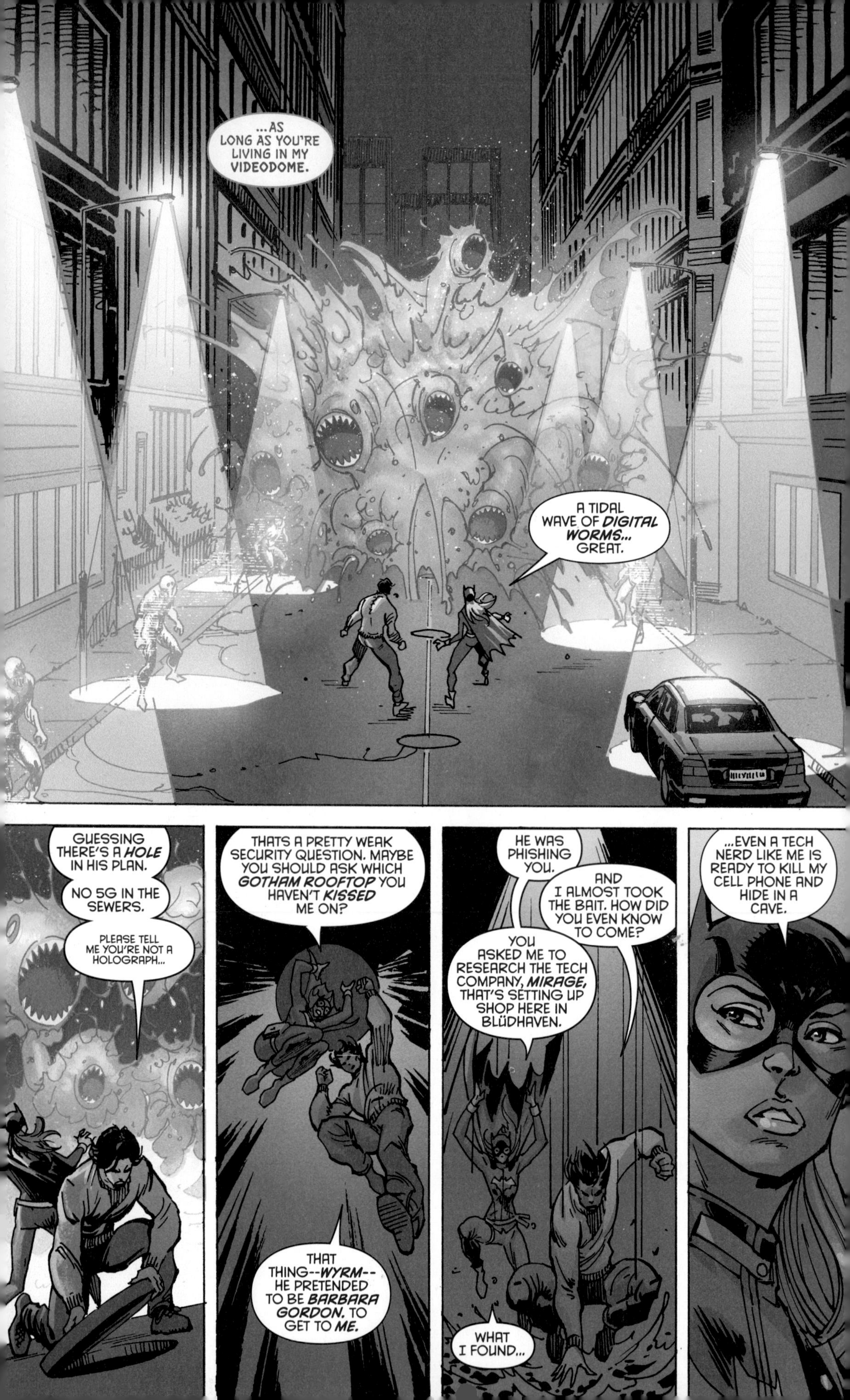
...AS LONG AS YOU'RE LIVING IN MY VIDEODOME.
A TIDAL WAVE OF DIGITAL WORMS... GREAT.
GUESSING THERE'S A HOLE IN HIS PLAN.
NO 5G IN THE SEWERS.
PLEASE TELL ME YOU'RE NOT A HOLOGRAPH...
THATS A PRETTY WEAK SECURITY QUESTION. MAYBE YOU SHOULD ASK WHICH GOTHAM ROOFTOP YOU HAVEN'T KISSED ME ON?
THAT THING--WYRM--HE PRETENDED TO BE BARBARA GORDON. TO GET TO ME.
HE WAS PHISHING YOU.
AND I ALMOST TOOK THE BAIT. HOW DID YOU EVEN KNOW TO COME?
YOU ASKED ME TO RESEARCH THE TECH COMPANY, MIRAGE, THAT'S SETTING UP SHOP HERE IN BLÜDHAVEN.
WHAT I FOUND...
...EVEN A TECH NERD LIKE ME IS READY TO KILL MY CELL PHONE AND HIDE IN A CAVE.

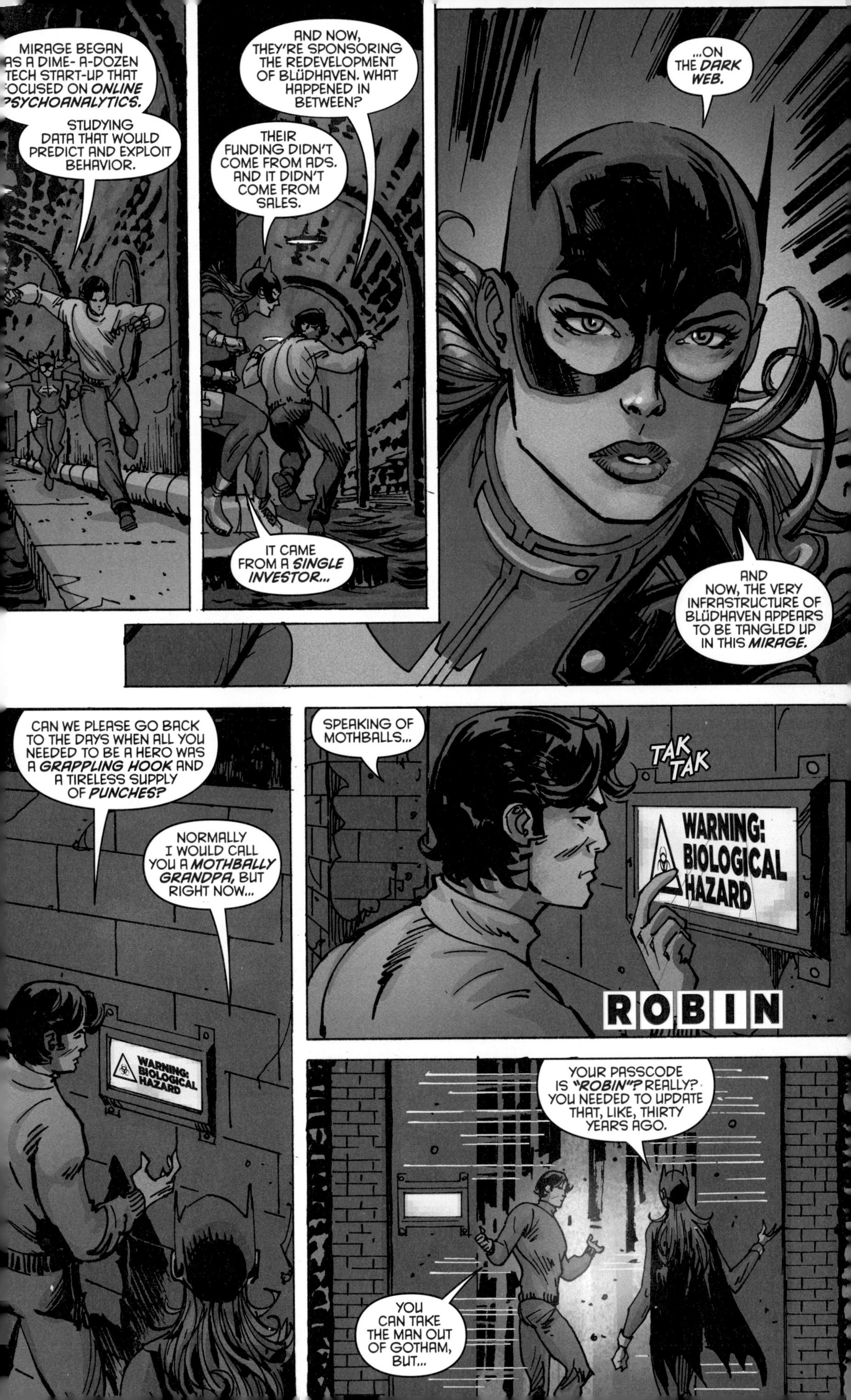

MIRAGE BEGAN AS A DIME- A-DOZEN TECH START-UP THAT FOCUSED ON *ONLINE PSYCHOANALYTICS.*
STUDYING DATA THAT WOULD PREDICT AND EXPLOIT BEHAVIOR.
AND NOW, THEY'RE SPONSORING THE REDEVELOPMENT OF BLÜDHAVEN. WHAT HAPPENED IN BETWEEN?
THEIR FUNDING DIDN'T COME FROM ADS. AND IT DIDN'T COME FROM SALES.
IT CAME FROM A *SINGLE INVESTOR...*
...ON THE *DARK WEB.*
AND NOW, THE VERY INFRASTRUCTURE OF BLÜDHAVEN APPEARS TO BE TANGLED UP IN THIS *MIRAGE.*
CAN WE PLEASE GO BACK TO THE DAYS WHEN ALL YOU NEEDED TO BE A HERO WAS A *GRAPPLING HOOK* AND A TIRELESS SUPPLY OF *PUNCHES?*
NORMALLY I WOULD CALL YOU A *MOTHBALLY GRANDPA,* BUT RIGHT NOW...
WARNING: BIOLOGICAL HAZARD
SPEAKING OF MOTHBALLS...
TAK TAK
WARNING: BIOLOGICAL HAZARD
ROBIN
YOUR PASSCODE IS *"ROBIN"?* REALLY? YOU NEEDED TO UPDATE THAT, LIKE, THIRTY YEARS AGO.
YOU CAN TAKE THE MAN OUT OF GOTHAM, BUT...

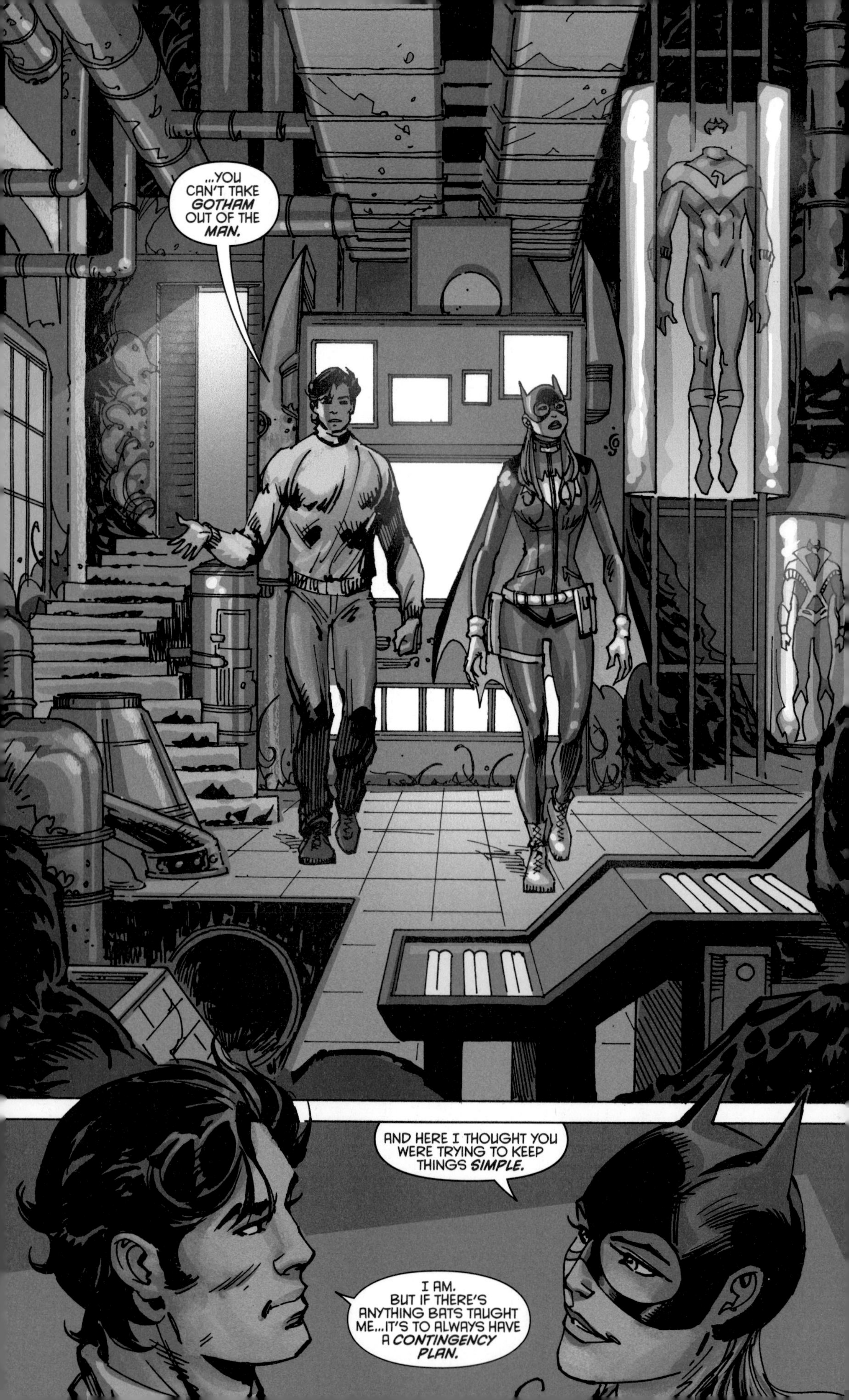
...YOU CAN'T TAKE GOTHAM OUT OF THE MAN.
AND HERE I THOUGHT YOU WERE TRYING TO KEEP THINGS SIMPLE.
I AM. BUT IF THERE'S ANYTHING BATS TAUGHT ME...IT'S TO ALWAYS HAVE A CONTINGENCY PLAN.

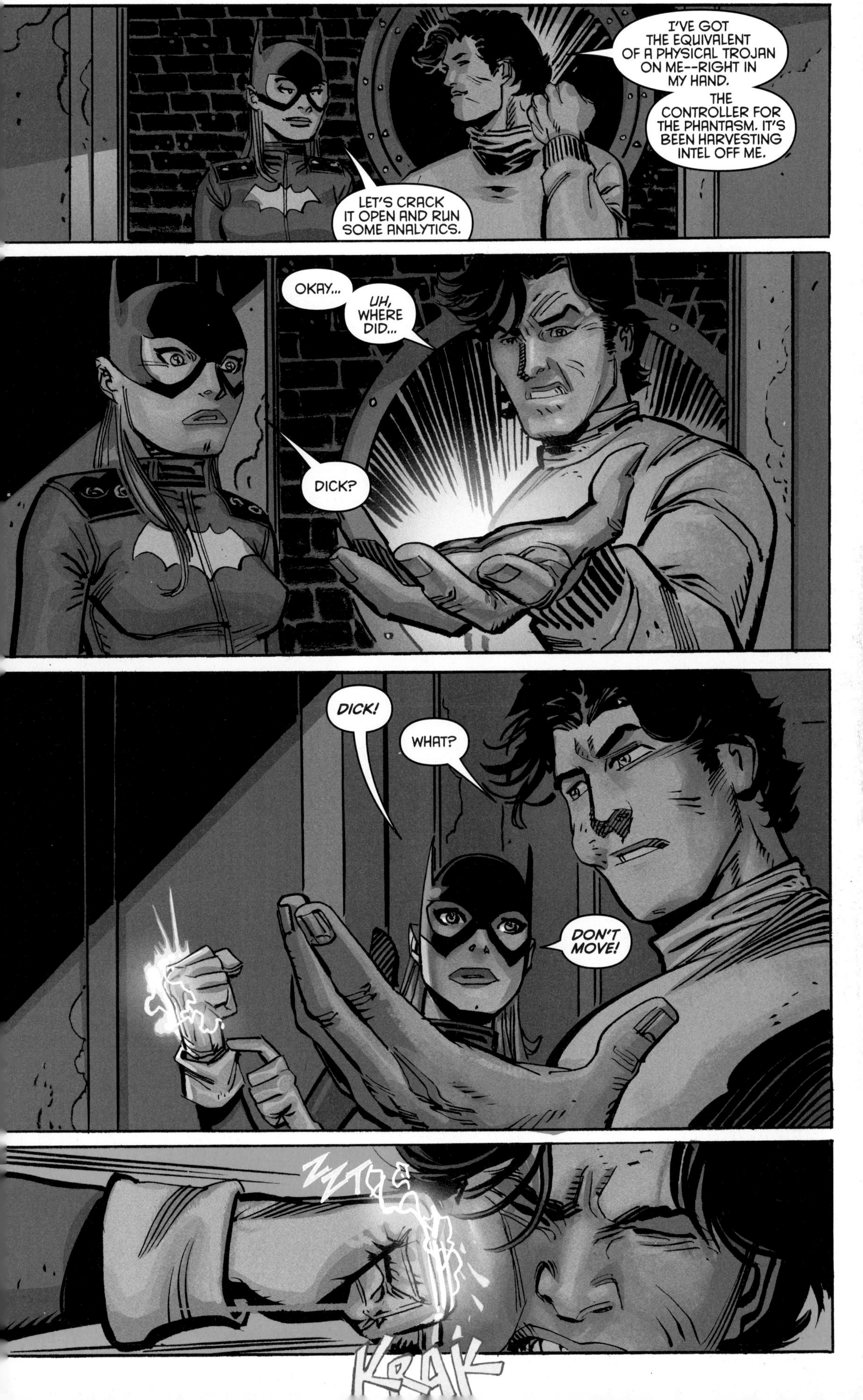
I'VE GOT THE EQUIVALENT OF A PHYSICAL TROJAN ON ME--RIGHT IN MY HAND.
THE CONTROLLER FOR THE PHANTASM. IT'S BEEN HARVESTING INTEL OFF ME.
LET'S CRACK IT OPEN AND RUN SOME ANALYTICS.
OKAY...
UH, WHERE DID...
DICK?
DICK!
WHAT?
DON'T MOVE!
KRAK

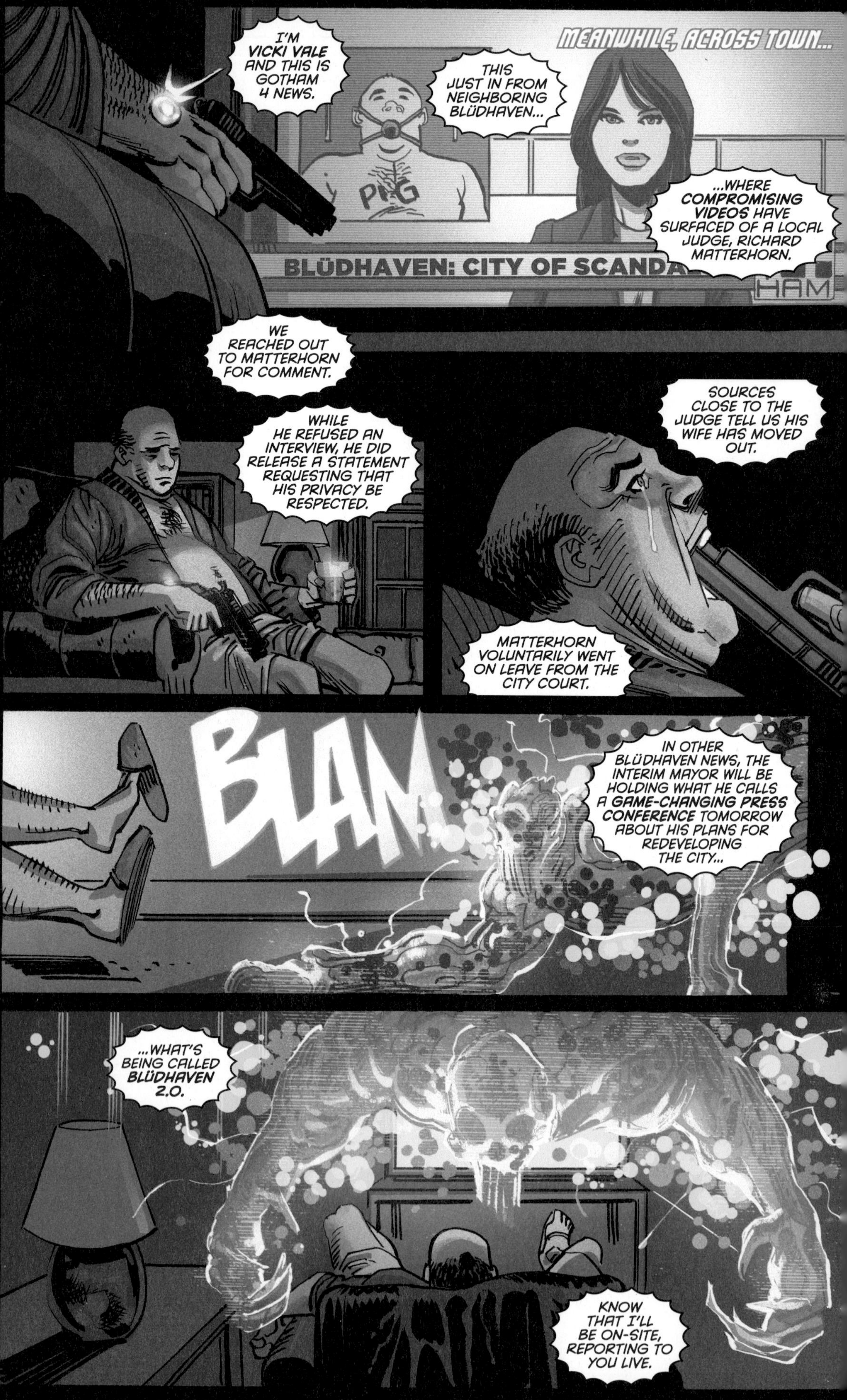
MEANWHILE, ACROSS TOWN...
I'M VICKI VALE AND THIS IS GOTHAM 4 NEWS.
THIS JUST IN FROM NEIGHBORING BLÜDHAVEN...
PIG
...WHERE COMPROMISING VIDEOS HAVE SURFACED OF A LOCAL JUDGE, RICHARD MATTERHORN.
BLÜDHAVEN: CITY OF SCANDA
HAM
WE REACHED OUT TO MATTERHORN FOR COMMENT.
WHILE HE REFUSED AN INTERVIEW, HE DID RELEASE A STATEMENT REQUESTING THAT HIS PRIVACY BE RESPECTED.
SOURCES CLOSE TO THE JUDGE TELL US HIS WIFE HAS MOVED OUT.
MATTERHORN VOLUNTARILY WENT ON LEAVE FROM THE CITY COURT.
BLAM
IN OTHER BLÜDHAVEN NEWS, THE INTERIM MAYOR WILL BE HOLDING WHAT HE CALLS A GAME-CHANGING PRESS CONFERENCE TOMORROW ABOUT HIS PLANS FOR REDEVELOPING THE CITY...
...WHAT'S BEING CALLED BLÜDHAVEN 2.0.
KNOW THAT I'LL BE ON-SITE, REPORTING TO YOU LIVE.

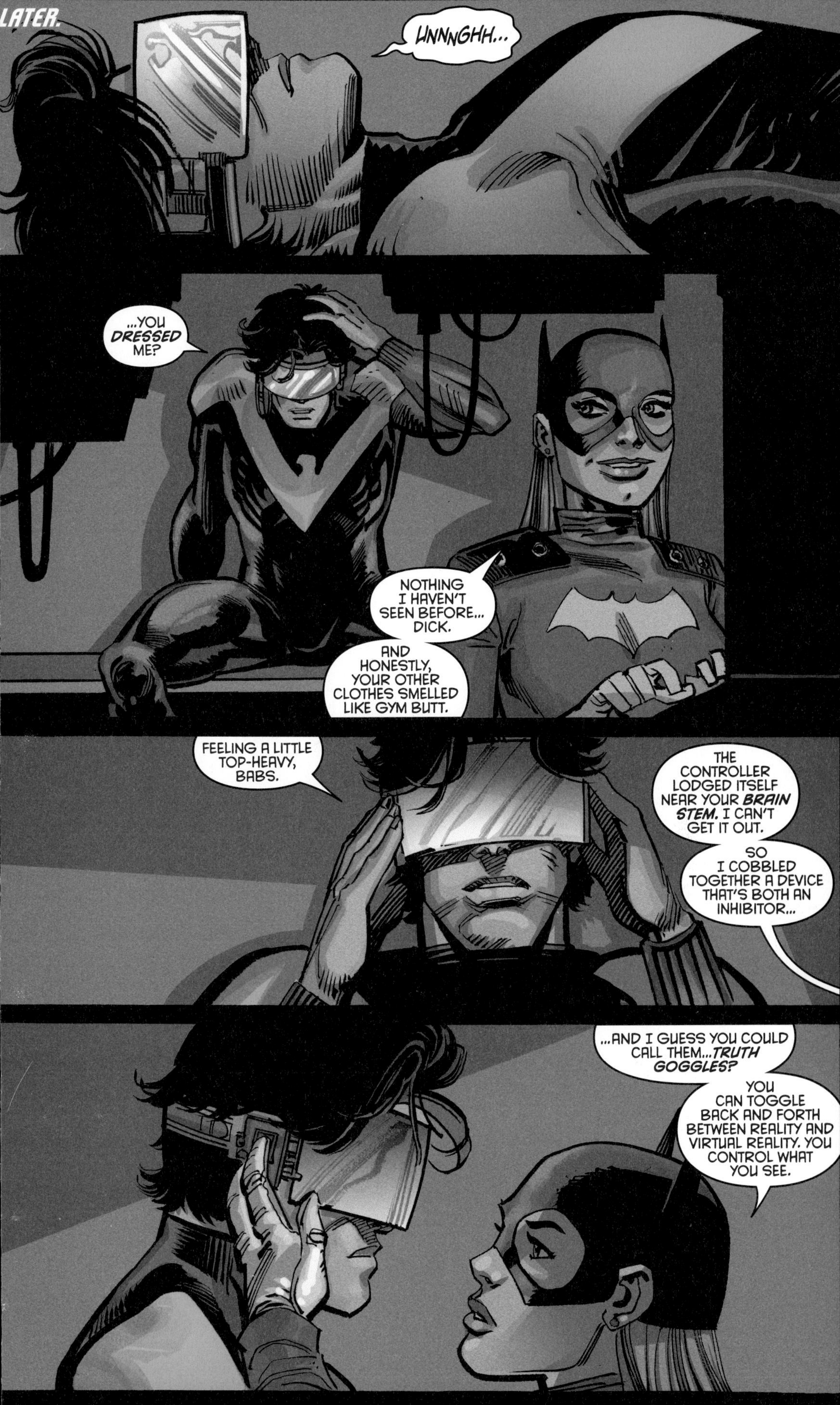
LATER.
UNNNGHH...
...YOU *DRESSED* ME?
NOTHING I HAVEN'T SEEN BEFORE... DICK.
AND HONESTLY, YOUR OTHER CLOTHES SMELLED LIKE GYM BUTT.
FEELING A LITTLE TOP-HEAVY, BABS.
THE CONTROLLER LODGED ITSELF NEAR YOUR *BRAIN STEM.* I CAN'T GET IT OUT.
SO I COBBLED TOGETHER A DEVICE THAT'S BOTH AN INHIBITOR...
...AND I GUESS YOU COULD CALL THEM... *TRUTH GOGGLES?*
YOU CAN TOGGLE BACK AND FORTH BETWEEN REALITY AND VIRTUAL REALITY. YOU CONTROL WHAT YOU SEE.

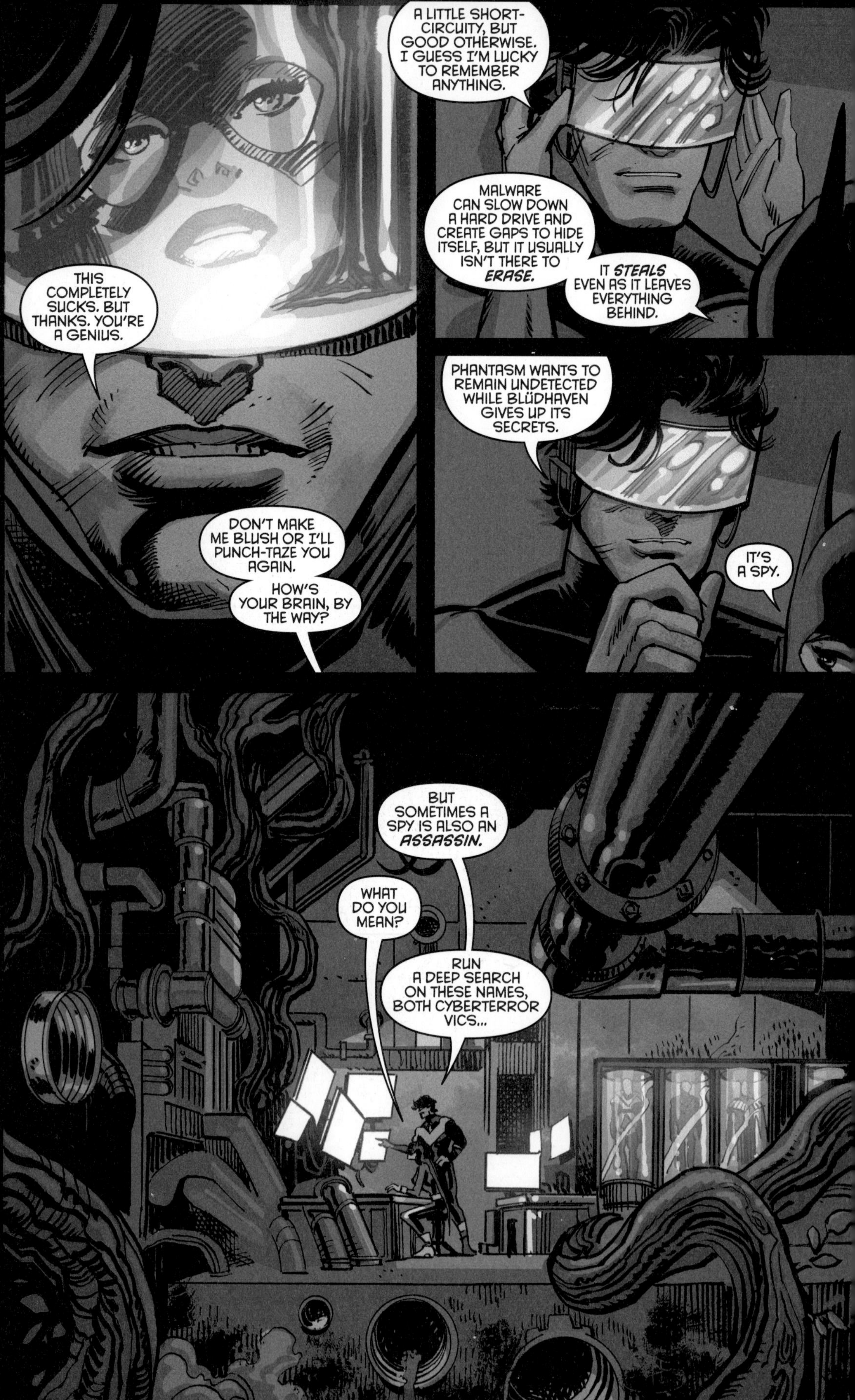

THIS COMPLETELY SUCKS. BUT THANKS. YOU'RE A GENIUS.
DON'T MAKE ME BLUSH OR I'LL PUNCH-TAZE YOU AGAIN.
HOW'S YOUR BRAIN, BY THE WAY?
A LITTLE SHORT-CIRCUITY, BUT GOOD OTHERWISE. I GUESS I'M LUCKY TO REMEMBER ANYTHING.
MALWARE CAN SLOW DOWN A HARD DRIVE AND CREATE GAPS TO HIDE ITSELF, BUT IT USUALLY ISN'T THERE TO ERASE.
IT STEALS EVEN AS IT LEAVES EVERYTHING BEHIND.
PHANTASM WANTS TO REMAIN UNDETECTED WHILE BLÜDHAVEN GIVES UP ITS SECRETS.
IT'S A SPY.
BUT SOMETIMES A SPY IS ALSO AN ASSASSIN.
WHAT DO YOU MEAN?
RUN A DEEP SEARCH ON THESE NAMES, BOTH CYBERTERROR VICS...

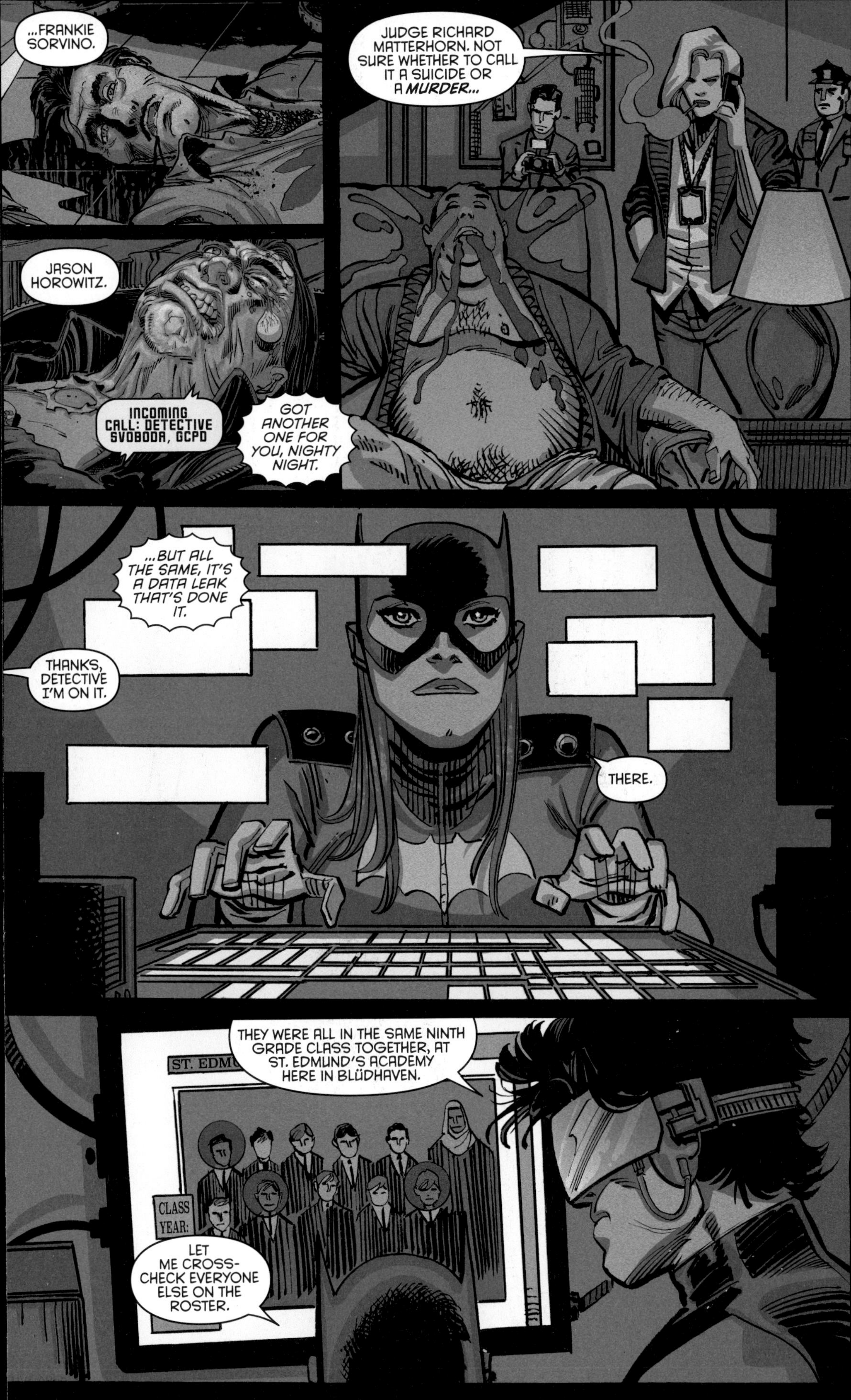
...FRANKIE SORVINO.
JUDGE RICHARD MATTERHORN. NOT SURE WHETHER TO CALL IT A SUICIDE OR A *MURDER*...
JASON HOROWITZ.
INCOMING CALL: DETECTIVE SVOBODA, GCPD
GOT ANOTHER ONE FOR YOU, NIGHTY NIGHT.
...BUT ALL THE SAME, IT'S A DATA LEAK THAT'S DONE IT.
THANKS, DETECTIVE I'M ON IT.
THERE.
THEY WERE ALL IN THE SAME NINTH GRADE CLASS TOGETHER, AT ST. EDMUND'S ACADEMY HERE IN BLÜDHAVEN.
ST. EDMU
CLASS YEAR:
LET ME CROSS-CHECK EVERYONE ELSE ON THE ROSTER.

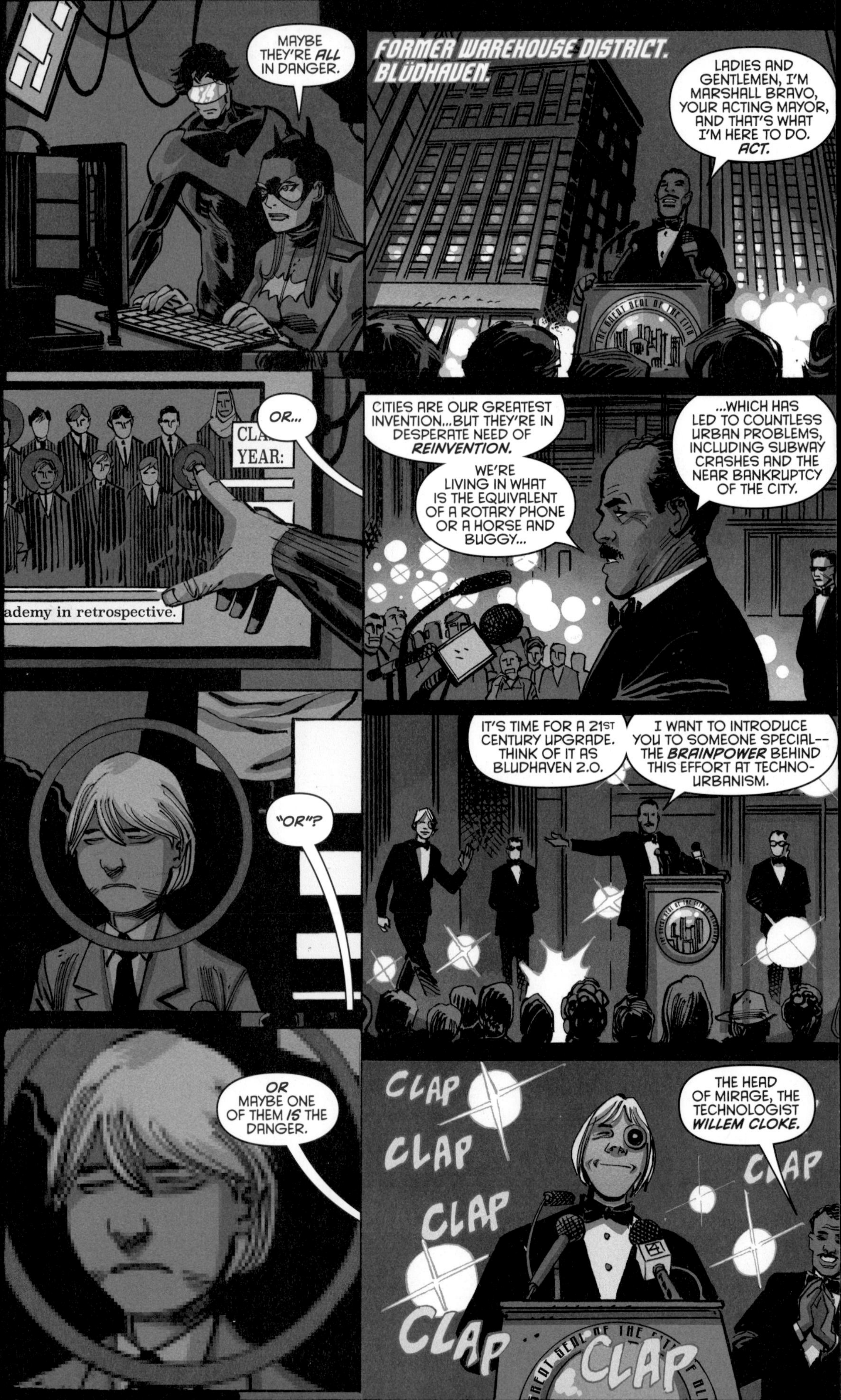
MAYBE THEY'RE ALL IN DANGER.
FORMER WAREHOUSE DISTRICT. BLÜDHAVEN.
LADIES AND GENTLEMEN, I'M MARSHALL BRAVO, YOUR ACTING MAYOR, AND THAT'S WHAT I'M HERE TO DO. ACT.
CLA
YEAR:
ademy in retrospective.
OR...
CITIES ARE OUR GREATEST INVENTION...BUT THEY'RE IN DESPERATE NEED OF REINVENTION.
WE'RE LIVING IN WHAT IS THE EQUIVALENT OF A ROTARY PHONE OR A HORSE AND BUGGY...
...WHICH HAS LED TO COUNTLESS URBAN PROBLEMS, INCLUDING SUBWAY CRASHES AND THE NEAR BANKRUPTCY OF THE CITY.
"OR"?
IT'S TIME FOR A 21ST CENTURY UPGRADE. THINK OF IT AS BLUDHAVEN 2.0.
I WANT TO INTRODUCE YOU TO SOMEONE SPECIAL-- THE BRAINPOWER BEHIND THIS EFFORT AT TECHNO-URBANISM.
OR MAYBE ONE OF THEM IS THE DANGER.
CLAP
CLAP
CLAP
CLAP
CLAP
CLAP
THE HEAD OF MIRAGE, THE TECHNOLOGIST WILLEM CLOKE.

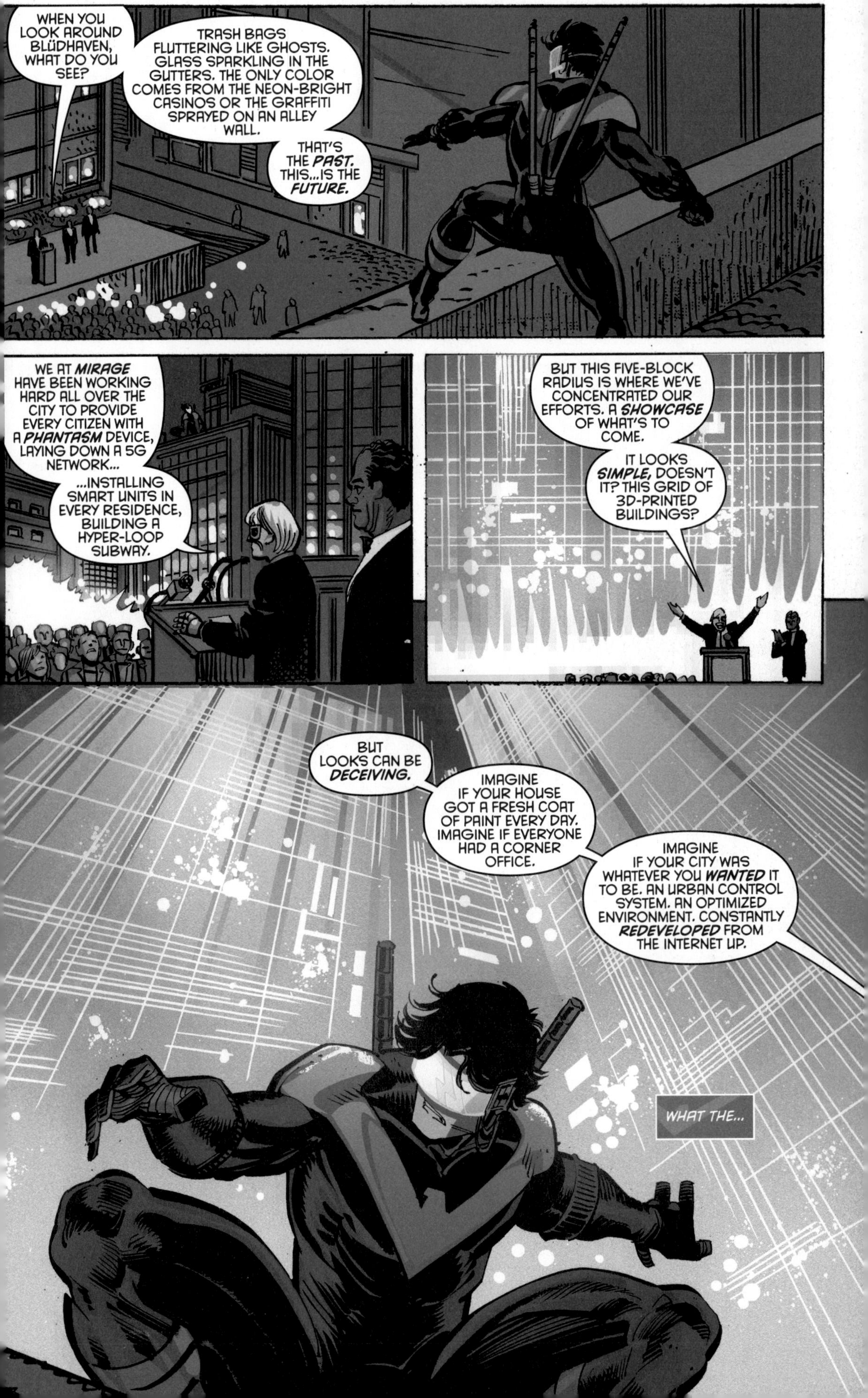
WHEN YOU LOOK AROUND BLÜDHAVEN, WHAT DO YOU SEE?
TRASH BAGS FLUTTERING LIKE GHOSTS. GLASS SPARKLING IN THE GUTTERS. THE ONLY COLOR COMES FROM THE NEON-BRIGHT CASINOS OR THE GRAFFITI SPRAYED ON AN ALLEY WALL.
THAT'S THE PAST. THIS...IS THE FUTURE.
WE AT MIRAGE HAVE BEEN WORKING HARD ALL OVER THE CITY TO PROVIDE EVERY CITIZEN WITH A PHANTASM DEVICE, LAYING DOWN A 5G NETWORK...
...INSTALLING SMART UNITS IN EVERY RESIDENCE, BUILDING A HYPER-LOOP SUBWAY.
BUT THIS FIVE-BLOCK RADIUS IS WHERE WE'VE CONCENTRATED OUR EFFORTS. A SHOWCASE OF WHAT'S TO COME.
IT LOOKS SIMPLE, DOESN'T IT? THIS GRID OF 3D-PRINTED BUILDINGS?
BUT LOOKS CAN BE DECEIVING.
IMAGINE IF YOUR HOUSE GOT A FRESH COAT OF PAINT EVERY DAY. IMAGINE IF EVERYONE HAD A CORNER OFFICE.
IMAGINE IF YOUR CITY WAS WHATEVER YOU WANTED IT TO BE. AN URBAN CONTROL SYSTEM. AN OPTIMIZED ENVIRONMENT. CONSTANTLY REDEVELOPED FROM THE INTERNET UP.
WHAT THE...

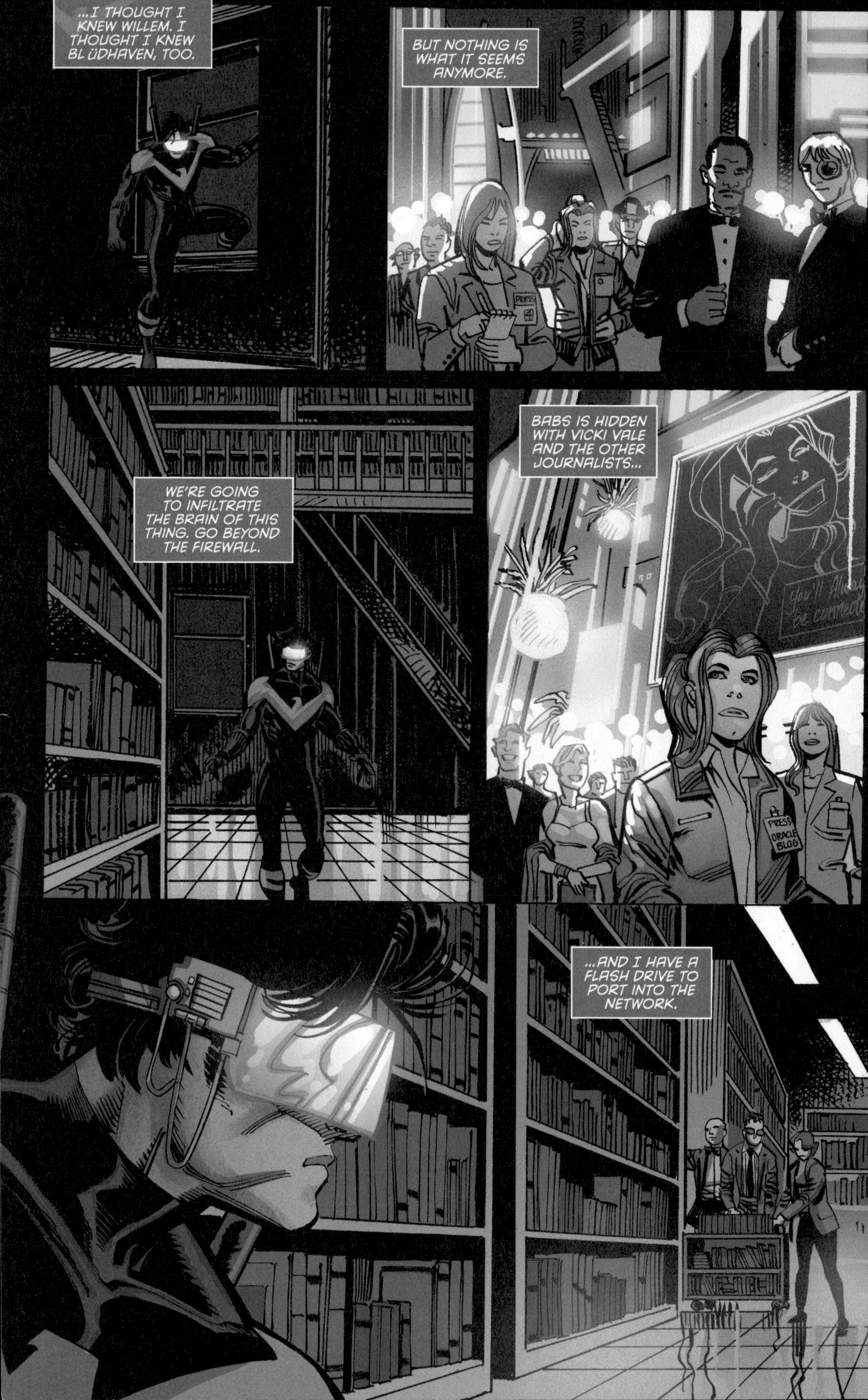

...I THOUGHT I KNEW WILLEM. I THOUGHT I KNEW BLÜDHAVEN, TOO.
BUT NOTHING IS WHAT IT SEEMS ANYMORE.
PRESS
WE'RE GOING TO INFILTRATE THE BRAIN OF THIS THING. GO BEYOND THE FIREWALL.
BABS IS HIDDEN WITH VICKI VALE AND THE OTHER JOURNALISTS...
PRESS ORACLE BLOG
...AND I HAVE A FLASH DRIVE TO PORT INTO THE NETWORK.

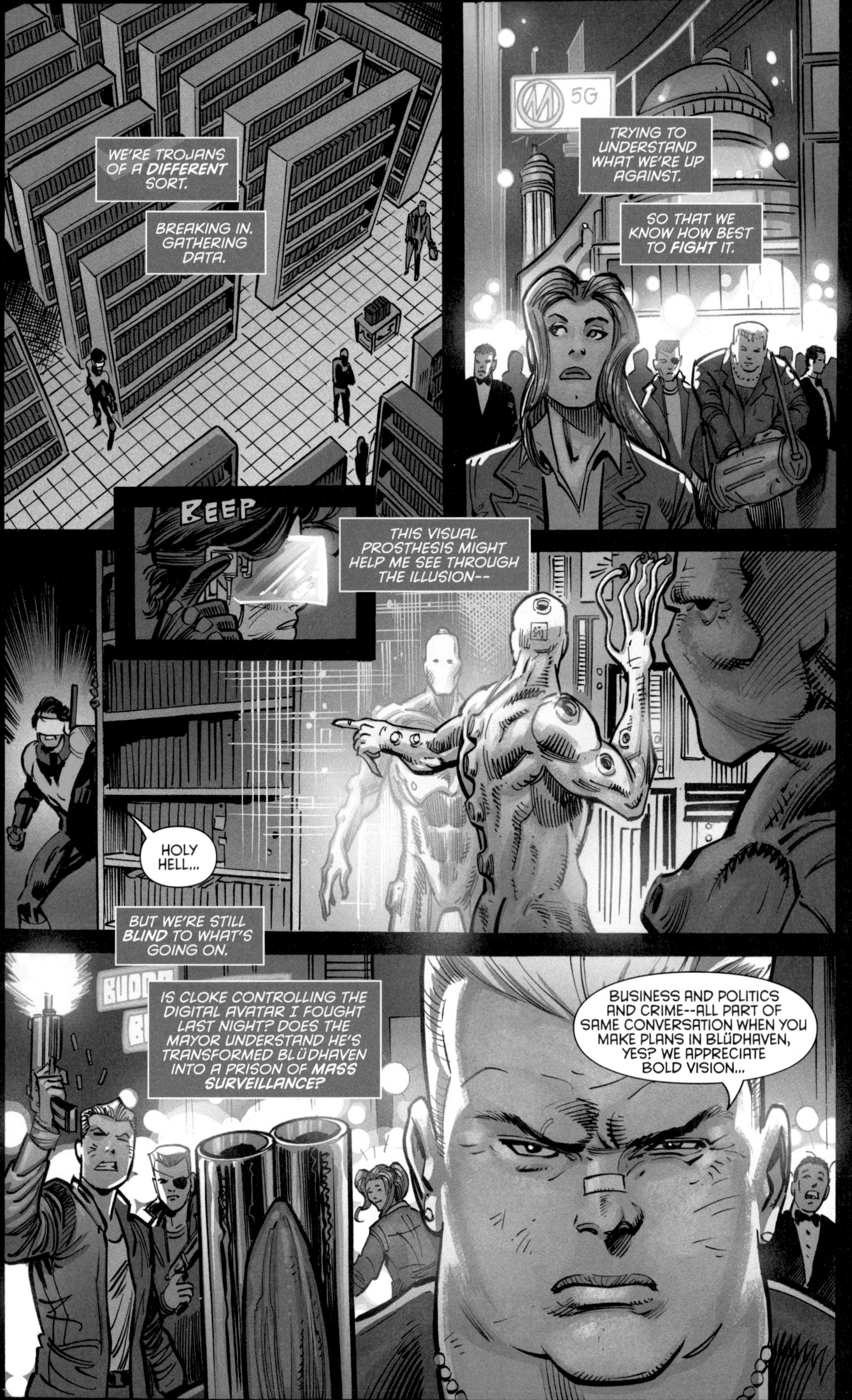
WE'RE TROJANS OF A DIFFERENT SORT.
BREAKING IN. GATHERING DATA.
TRYING TO UNDERSTAND WHAT WE'RE UP AGAINST.
SO THAT WE KNOW HOW BEST TO FIGHT IT.
5G
BEEP
THIS VISUAL PROSTHESIS MIGHT HELP ME SEE THROUGH THE ILLUSION--
HOLY HELL...
BUT WE'RE STILL BLIND TO WHAT'S GOING ON.
IS CLOKE CONTROLLING THE DIGITAL AVATAR I FOUGHT LAST NIGHT? DOES THE MAYOR UNDERSTAND HE'S TRANSFORMED BLÜDHAVEN INTO A PRISON OF MASS SURVEILLANCE?
BUSINESS AND POLITICS AND CRIME--ALL PART OF SAME CONVERSATION WHEN YOU MAKE PLANS IN BLÜDHAVEN, YES? WE APPRECIATE BOLD VISION...

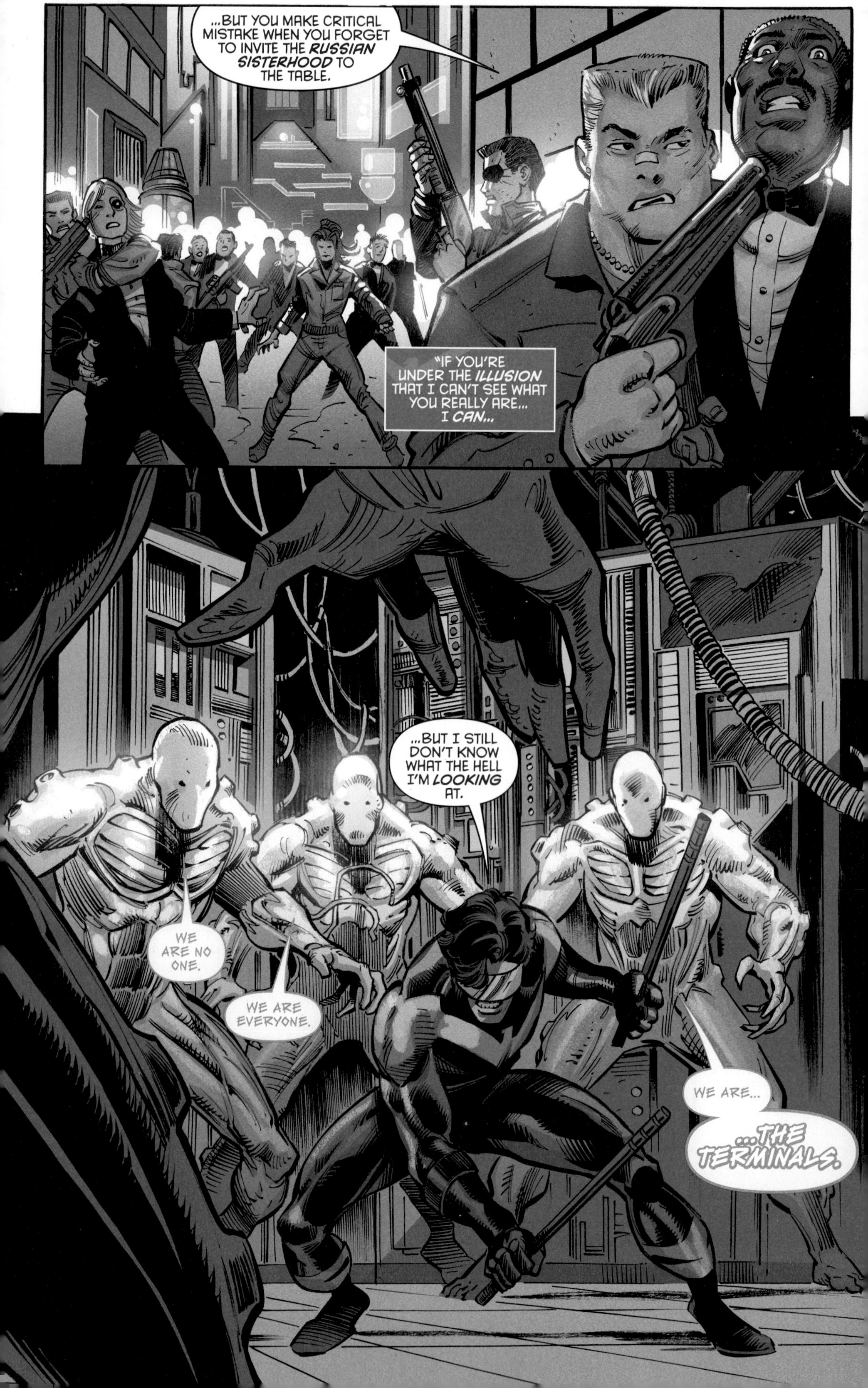
...BUT YOU MAKE CRITICAL MISTAKE WHEN YOU FORGET TO INVITE THE *RUSSIAN SISTERHOOD* TO THE TABLE.
"IF YOU'RE UNDER THE *ILLUSION* THAT I CAN'T SEE WHAT YOU REALLY ARE... I *CAN*...
...BUT I STILL DON'T KNOW WHAT THE HELL I'M *LOOKING* AT.
WE ARE NO ONE.
WE ARE EVERYONE.
WE ARE...
...THE TERMINALS.

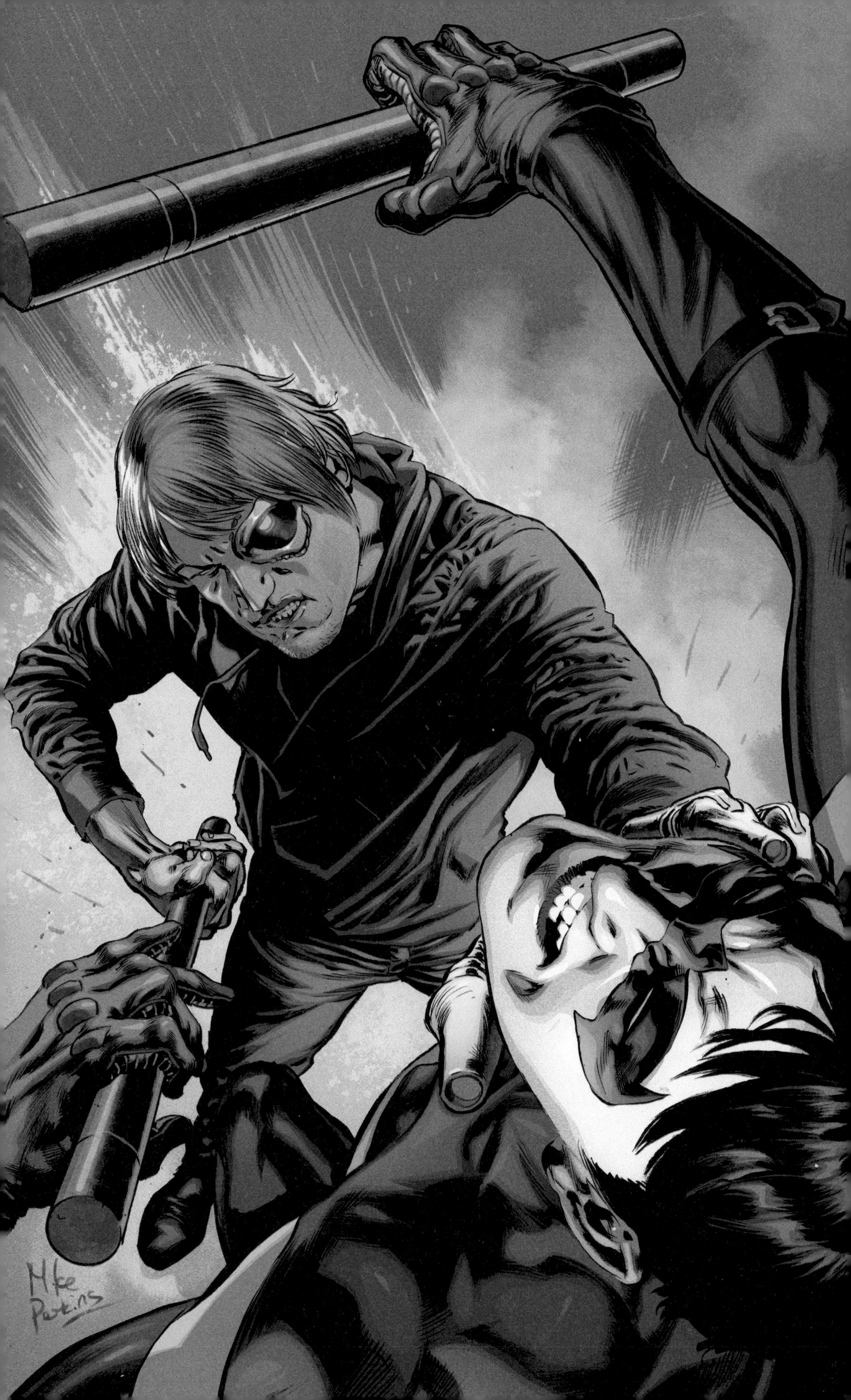

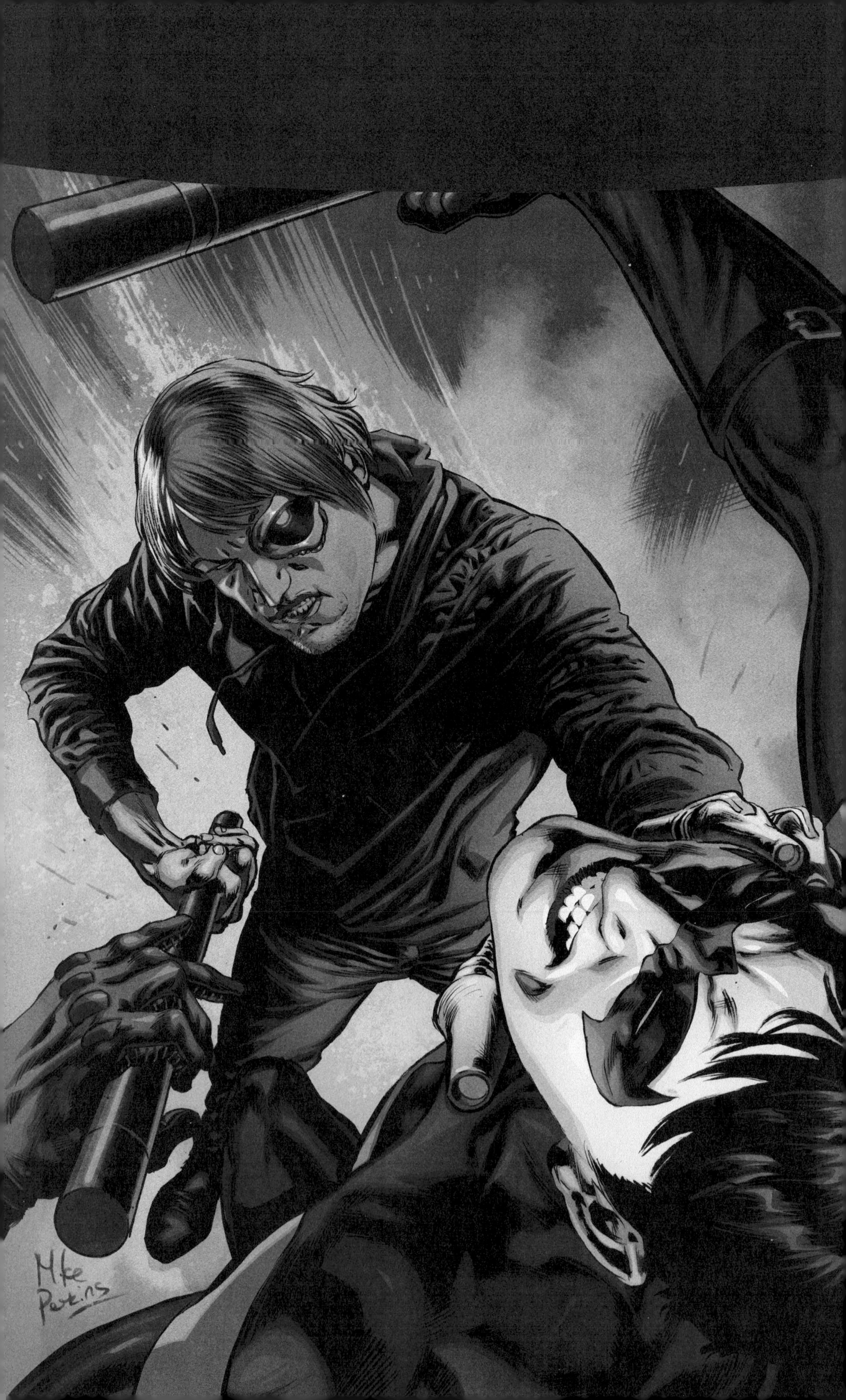

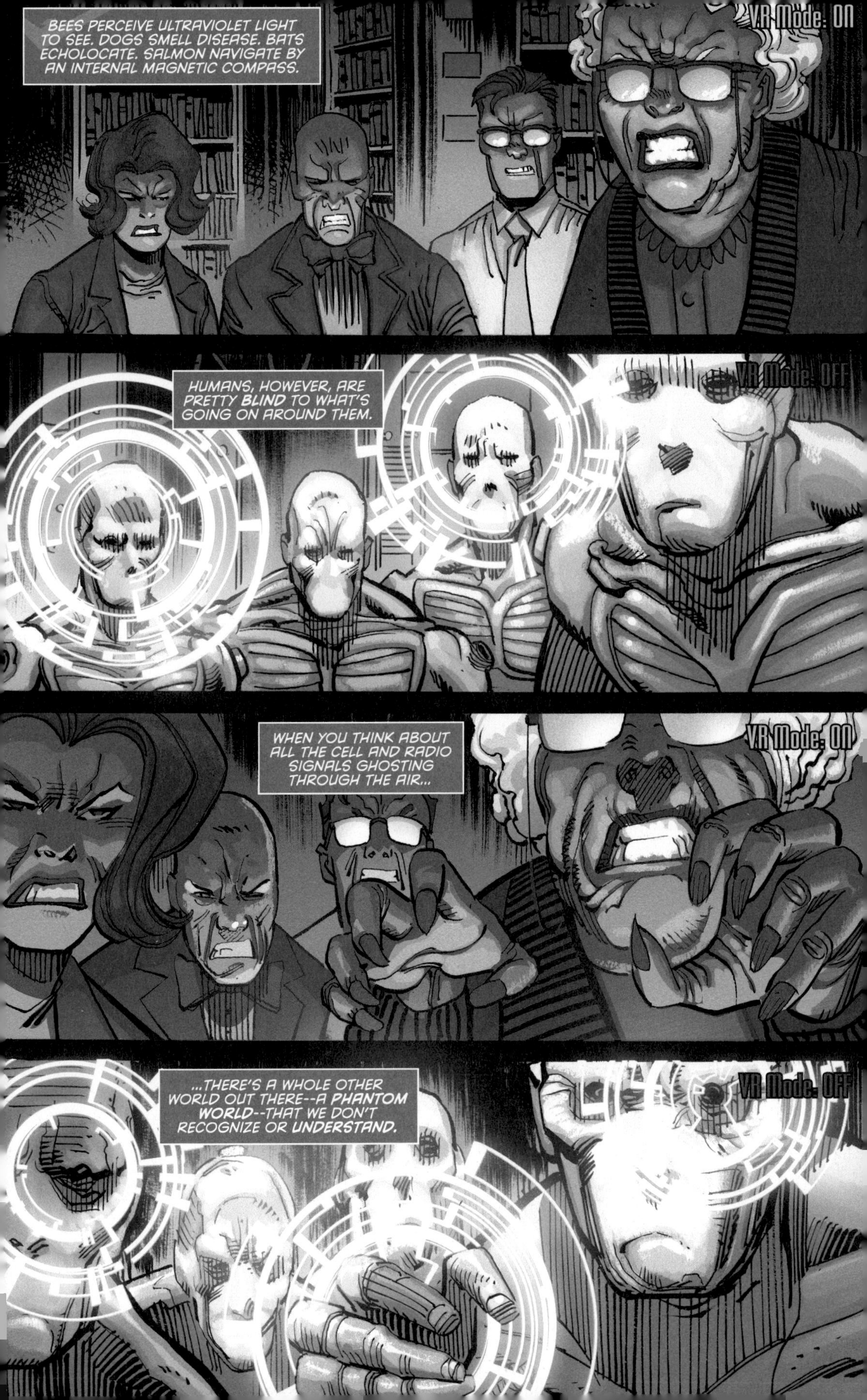
VR Mode: ON
BEES PERCEIVE ULTRAVIOLET LIGHT TO SEE. DOGS SMELL DISEASE. BATS ECHOLOCATE. SALMON NAVIGATE BY AN INTERNAL MAGNETIC COMPASS.
VR Mode: OFF
HUMANS, HOWEVER, ARE PRETTY **BLIND** TO WHAT'S GOING ON AROUND THEM.
VR Mode: ON
WHEN YOU THINK ABOUT ALL THE CELL AND RADIO SIGNALS GHOSTING THROUGH THE AIR...
VR Mode: OFF
...THERE'S A WHOLE OTHER WORLD OUT THERE--A ***PHANTOM WORLD***--THAT WE DON'T RECOGNIZE OR ***UNDERSTAND.***

THE BLEEDING EDGE

FINALE

BENJAMIN PERCY Writer CHRIS MOONEYHAM Artist
KLAUS JANSON Inks NICK FILARDI Colors
CARLOS M. MANGUAL Letters

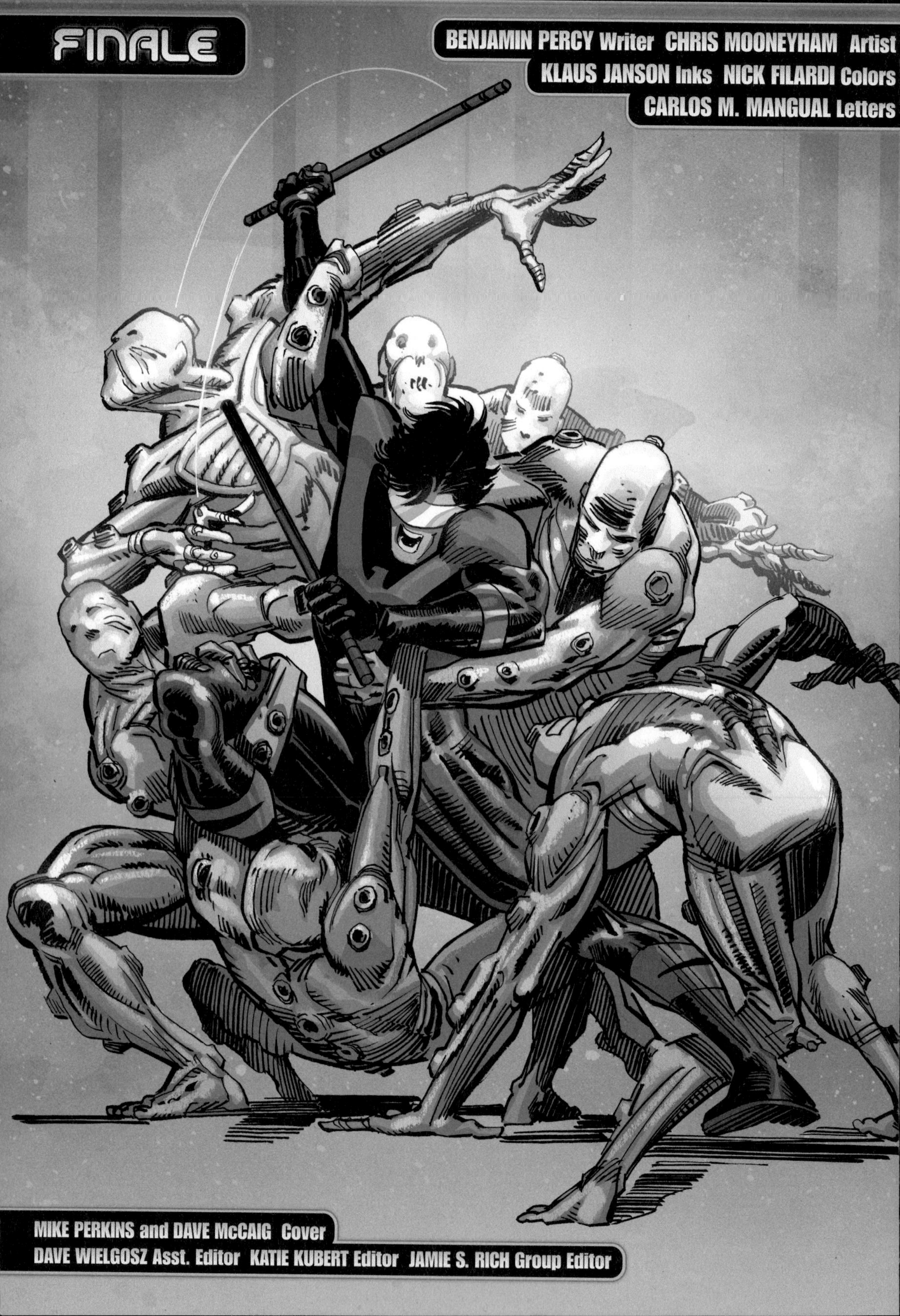

MIKE PERKINS and DAVE McCAIG Cover
DAVE WIELGOSZ Asst. Editor KATIE KUBERT Editor JAMIE S. RICH Group Editor

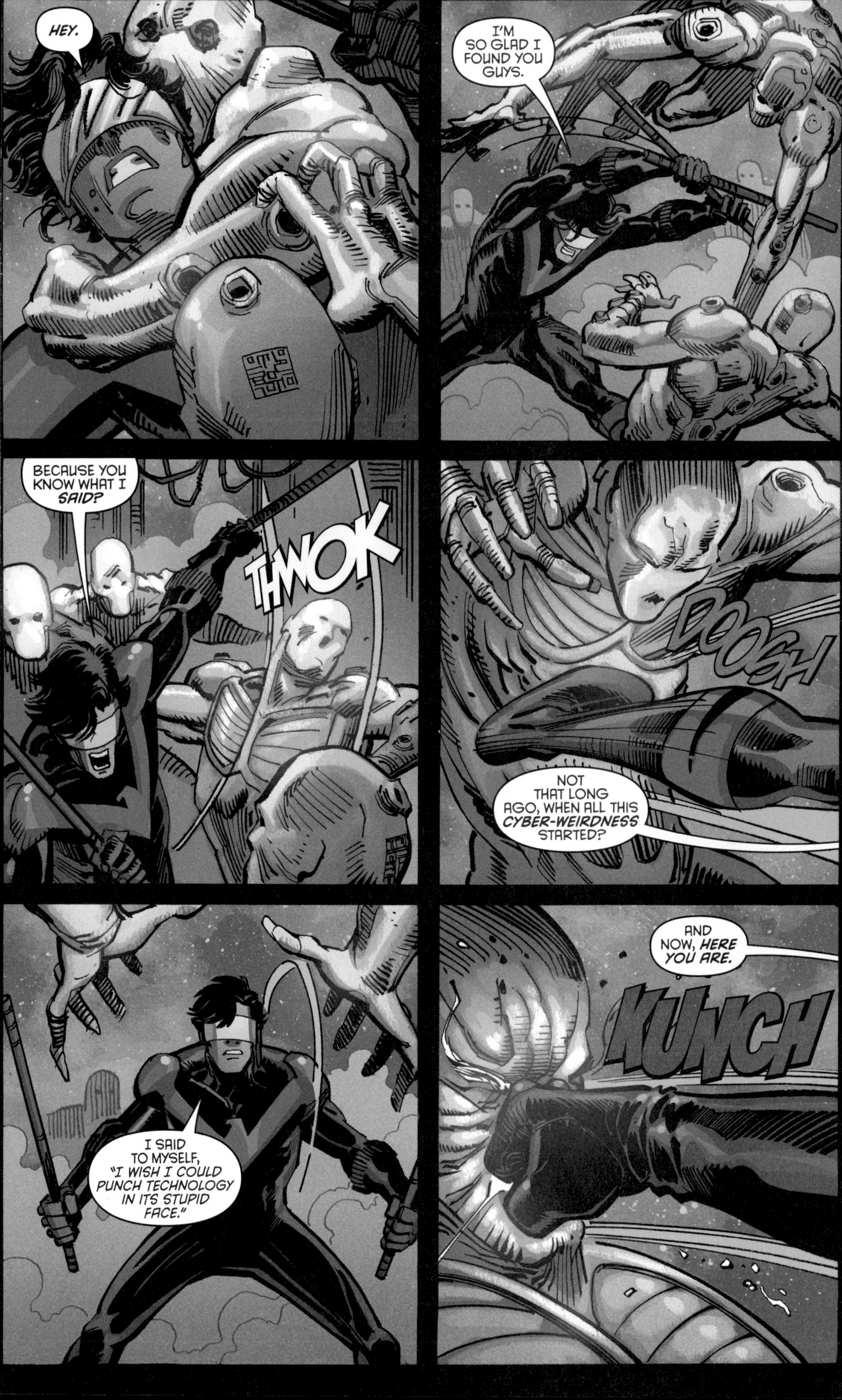
HEY.
I'M SO GLAD I FOUND YOU GUYS.
BECAUSE YOU KNOW WHAT I *SAID?*
THWOK
DOOSH
NOT THAT LONG AGO, WHEN ALL THIS *CYBER-WEIRDNESS* STARTED?
I SAID TO MYSELF, *"I WISH I COULD PUNCH TECHNOLOGY IN ITS STUPID FACE."*
AND NOW, *HERE YOU ARE.*
KUNCH

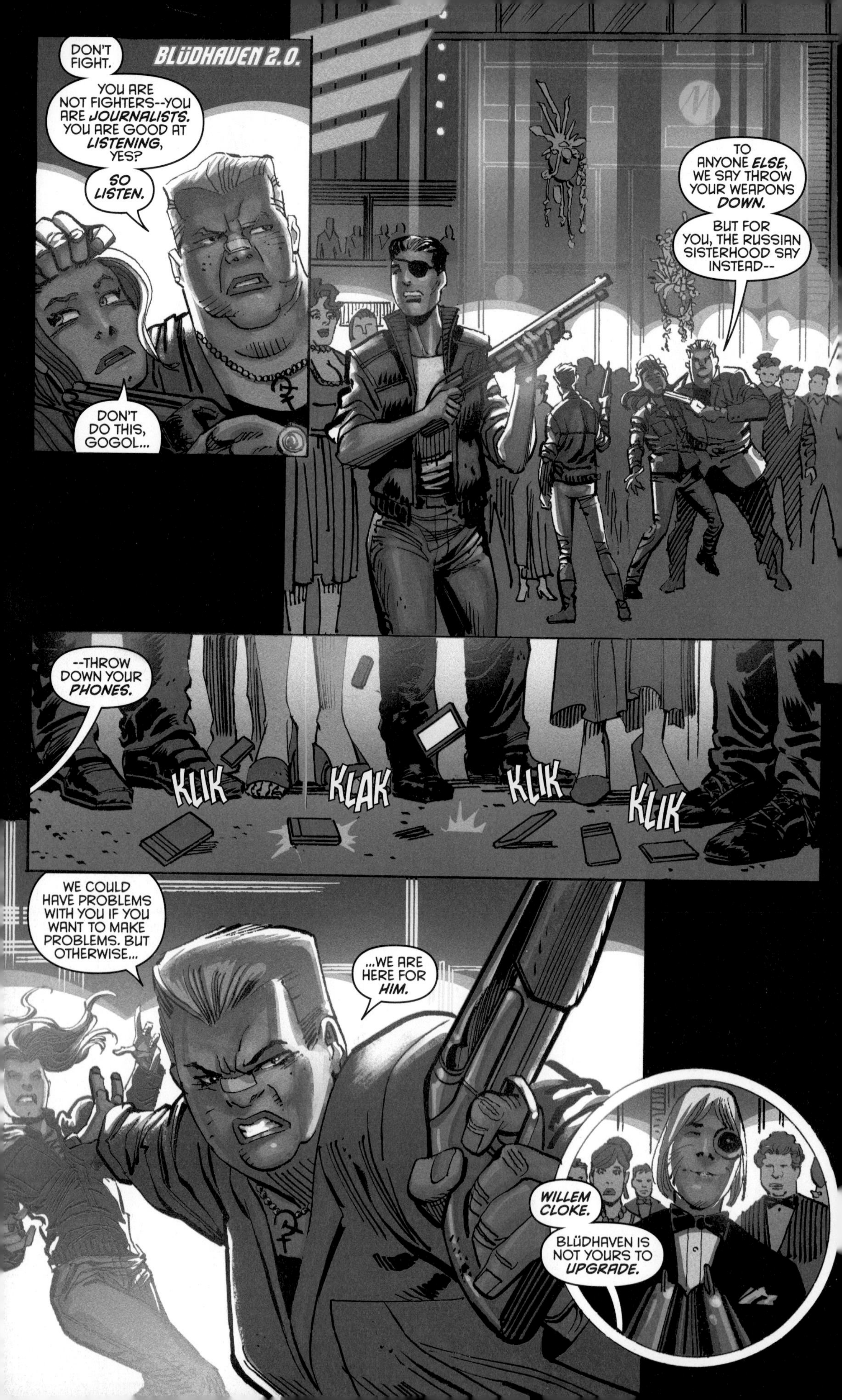

BLÜDHAVEN 2.0.
DON'T FIGHT.
YOU ARE NOT FIGHTERS--YOU ARE *JOURNALISTS.* YOU ARE GOOD AT *LISTENING,* YES?
SO LISTEN.
DON'T DO THIS, GOGOL...
TO ANYONE *ELSE,* WE SAY THROW YOUR WEAPONS *DOWN.*
BUT FOR YOU, THE RUSSIAN SISTERHOOD SAY INSTEAD--
--THROW DOWN YOUR *PHONES.*
KLIK
KLAK
KLIK
KLIK
WE COULD HAVE PROBLEMS WITH YOU IF YOU WANT TO MAKE PROBLEMS. BUT OTHERWISE...
...WE ARE HERE FOR *HIM.*
WILLEM CLOKE.
BLÜDHAVEN IS NOT YOURS TO *UPGRADE.*

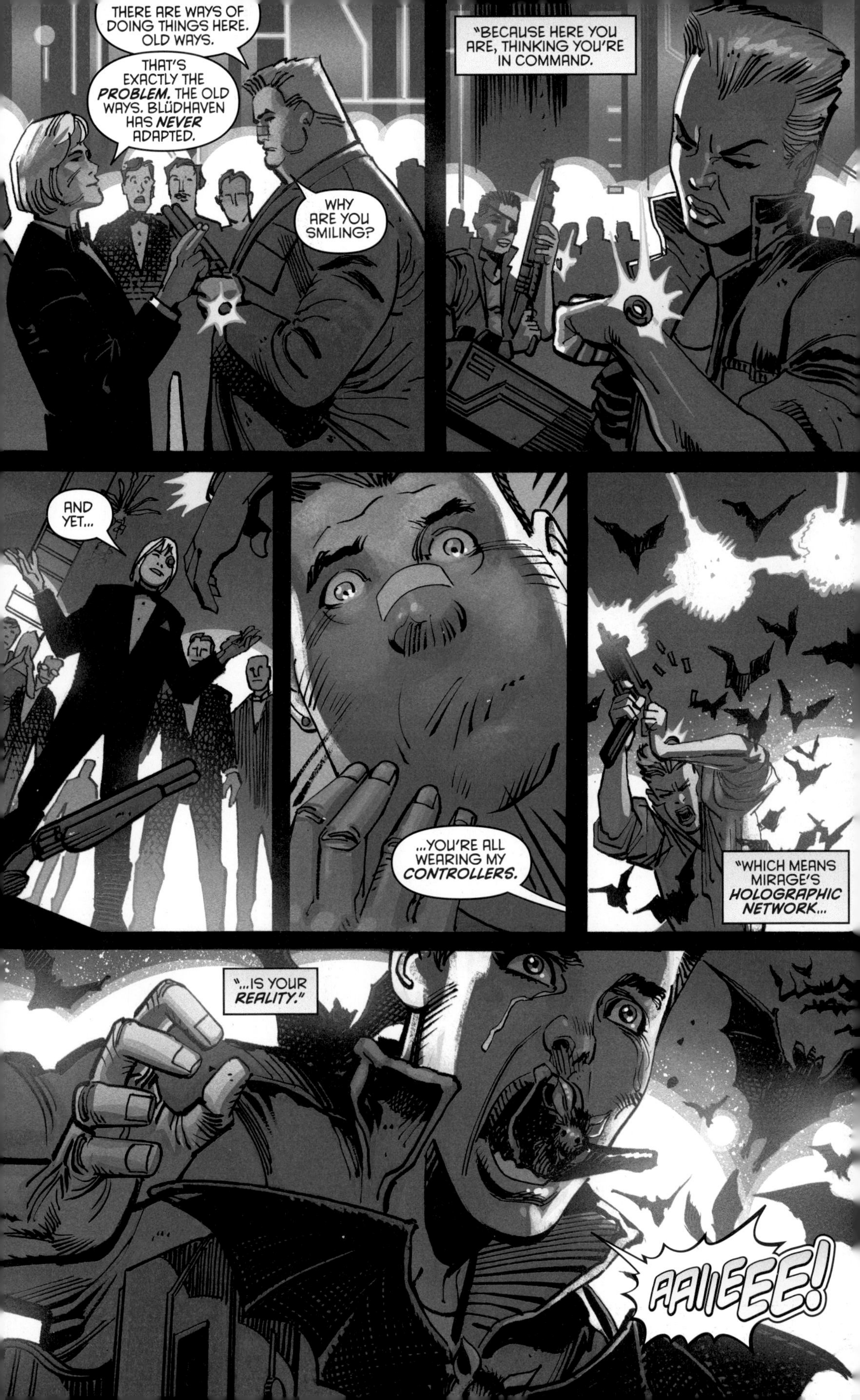

THERE ARE WAYS OF DOING THINGS HERE. OLD WAYS.
THAT'S EXACTLY THE **PROBLEM.** THE OLD WAYS. BLÜDHAVEN HAS **NEVER** ADAPTED.
WHY ARE YOU SMILING?
"BECAUSE HERE YOU ARE, THINKING YOU'RE IN COMMAND.
AND YET...
...YOU'RE ALL WEARING MY **CONTROLLERS.**
"WHICH MEANS MIRAGE'S **HOLOGRAPHIC NETWORK...**
"...IS YOUR **REALITY.**"
AAIIEEE!

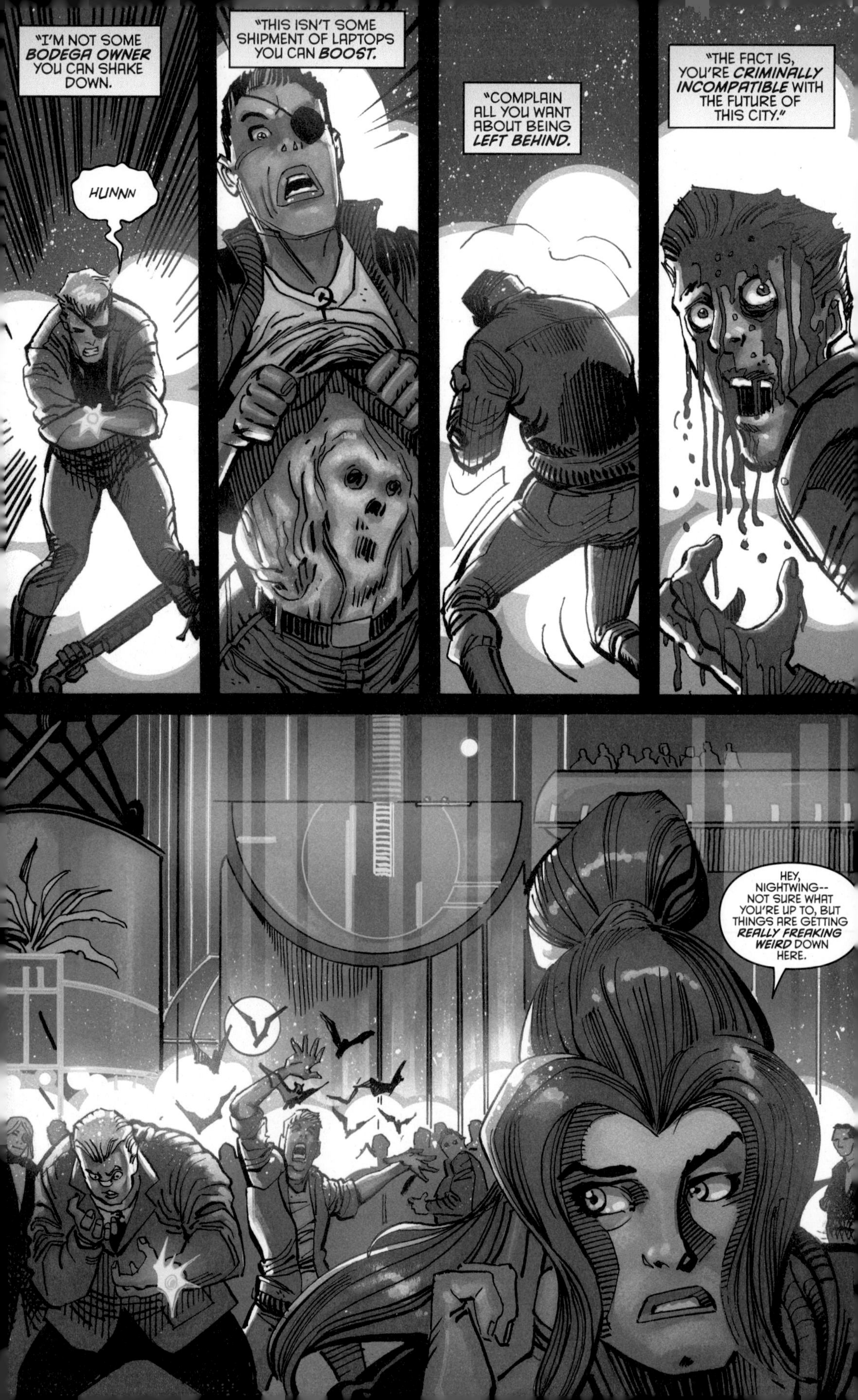
"I'M NOT SOME BODEGA OWNER YOU CAN SHAKE DOWN.
HUNNN
"THIS ISN'T SOME SHIPMENT OF LAPTOPS YOU CAN BOOST.
"COMPLAIN ALL YOU WANT ABOUT BEING LEFT BEHIND.
"THE FACT IS, YOU'RE CRIMINALLY INCOMPATIBLE WITH THE FUTURE OF THIS CITY."
HEY, NIGHTWING-- NOT SURE WHAT YOU'RE UP TO, BUT THINGS ARE GETTING REALLY FREAKING WEIRD DOWN HERE.

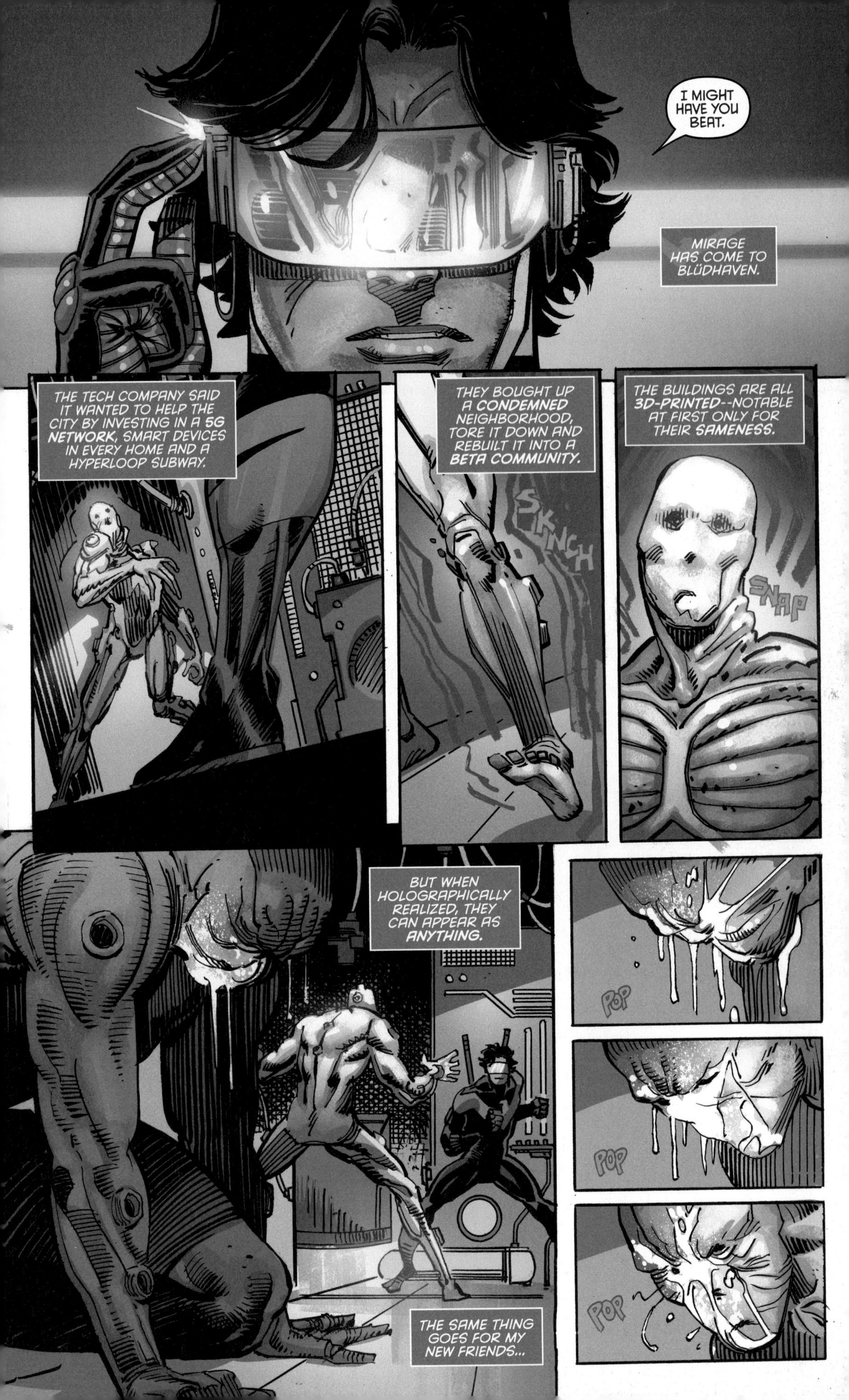
I MIGHT HAVE YOU BEAT.
MIRAGE HAS COME TO BLÜDHAVEN.
THE TECH COMPANY SAID IT WANTED TO HELP THE CITY BY INVESTING IN A 5G NETWORK, SMART DEVICES IN EVERY HOME AND A HYPERLOOP SUBWAY.
THEY BOUGHT UP A CONDEMNED NEIGHBORHOOD, TORE IT DOWN AND REBUILT IT INTO A BETA COMMUNITY.
SKNCH
THE BUILDINGS ARE ALL 3D-PRINTED--NOTABLE AT FIRST ONLY FOR THEIR SAMENESS.
SNAP
BUT WHEN HOLOGRAPHICALLY REALIZED, THEY CAN APPEAR AS ANYTHING.
POP
POP
POP
THE SAME THING GOES FOR MY NEW FRIENDS...

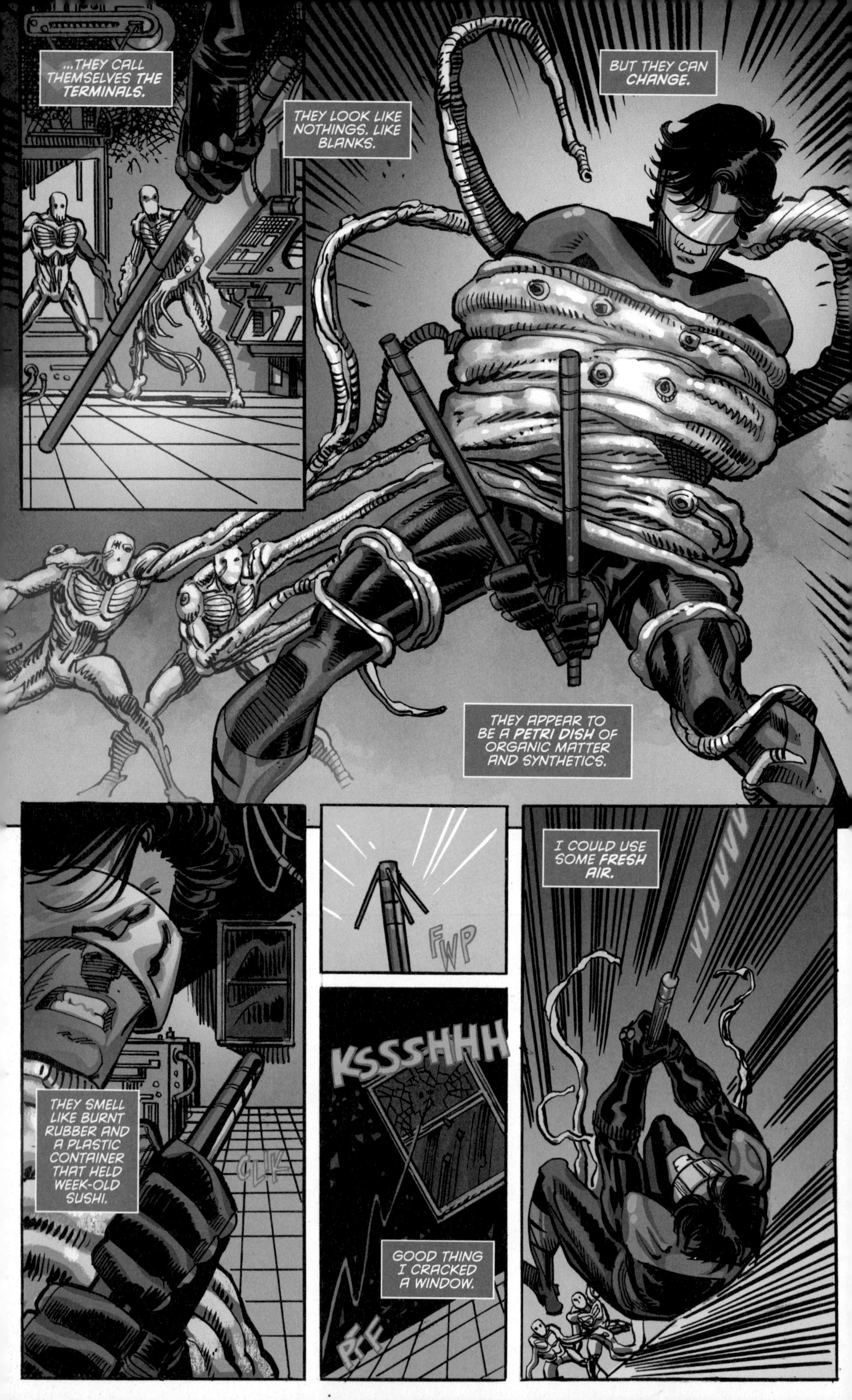
...THEY CALL THEMSELVES THE TERMINALS.
THEY LOOK LIKE NOTHINGS. LIKE BLANKS.
BUT THEY CAN CHANGE.
THEY APPEAR TO BE A PETRI DISH OF ORGANIC MATTER AND SYNTHETICS.
THEY SMELL LIKE BURNT RUBBER AND A PLASTIC CONTAINER THAT HELD WEEK-OLD SUSHI.
CLIK
FWP
KSSSHHH
GOOD THING I CRACKED A WINDOW.
I COULD USE SOME FRESH AIR.

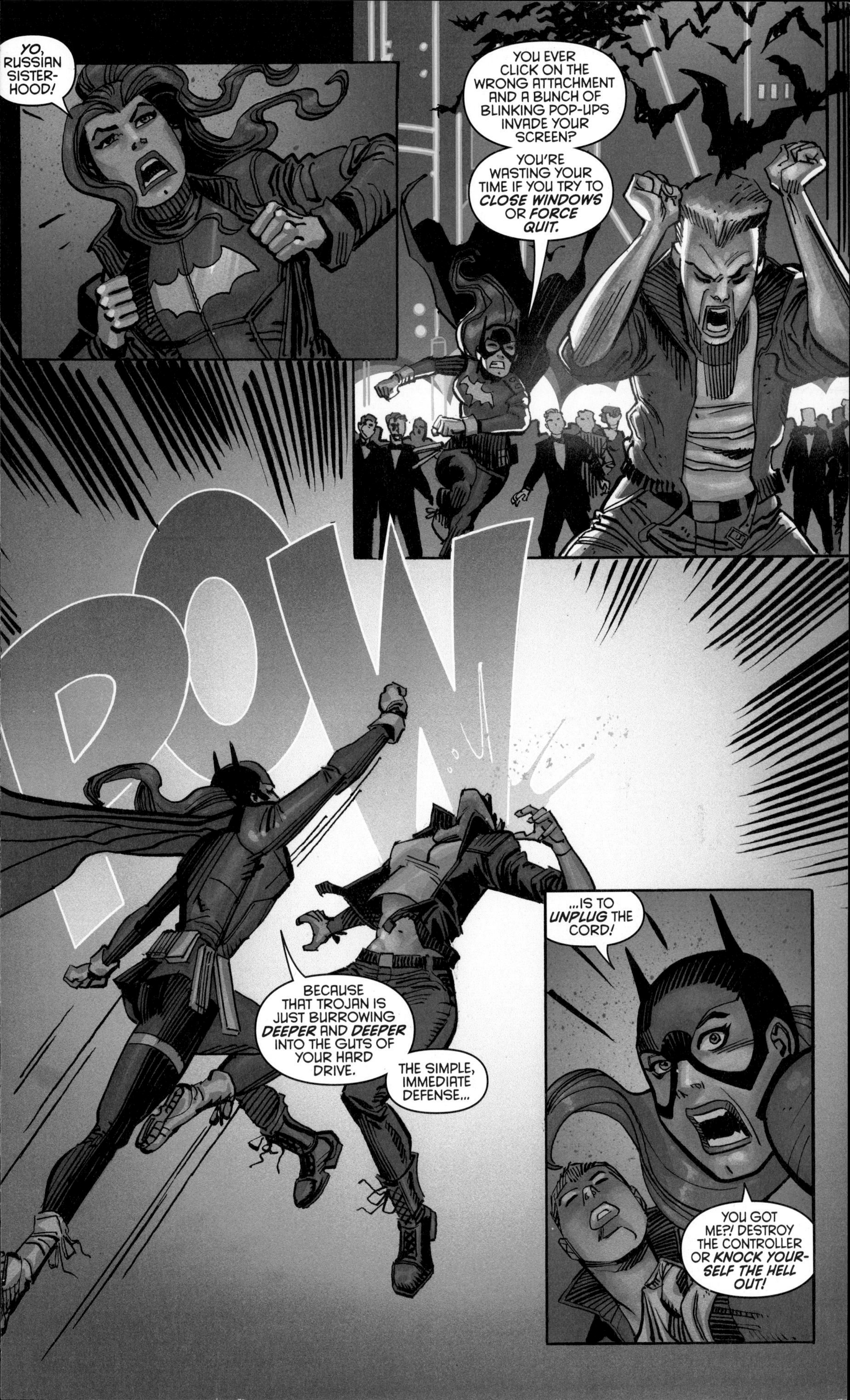
YO, RUSSIAN SISTER-HOOD!
YOU EVER CLICK ON THE WRONG ATTACHMENT AND A BUNCH OF BLINKING POP-UPS INVADE YOUR SCREEN?
YOU'RE WASTING YOUR TIME IF YOU TRY TO CLOSE WINDOWS OR FORCE QUIT.
POW
BECAUSE THAT TROJAN IS JUST BURROWING DEEPER AND DEEPER INTO THE GUTS OF YOUR HARD DRIVE.
THE SIMPLE, IMMEDIATE DEFENSE...
...IS TO UNPLUG THE CORD!
YOU GOT ME?! DESTROY THE CONTROLLER OR KNOCK YOUR-SELF THE HELL OUT!

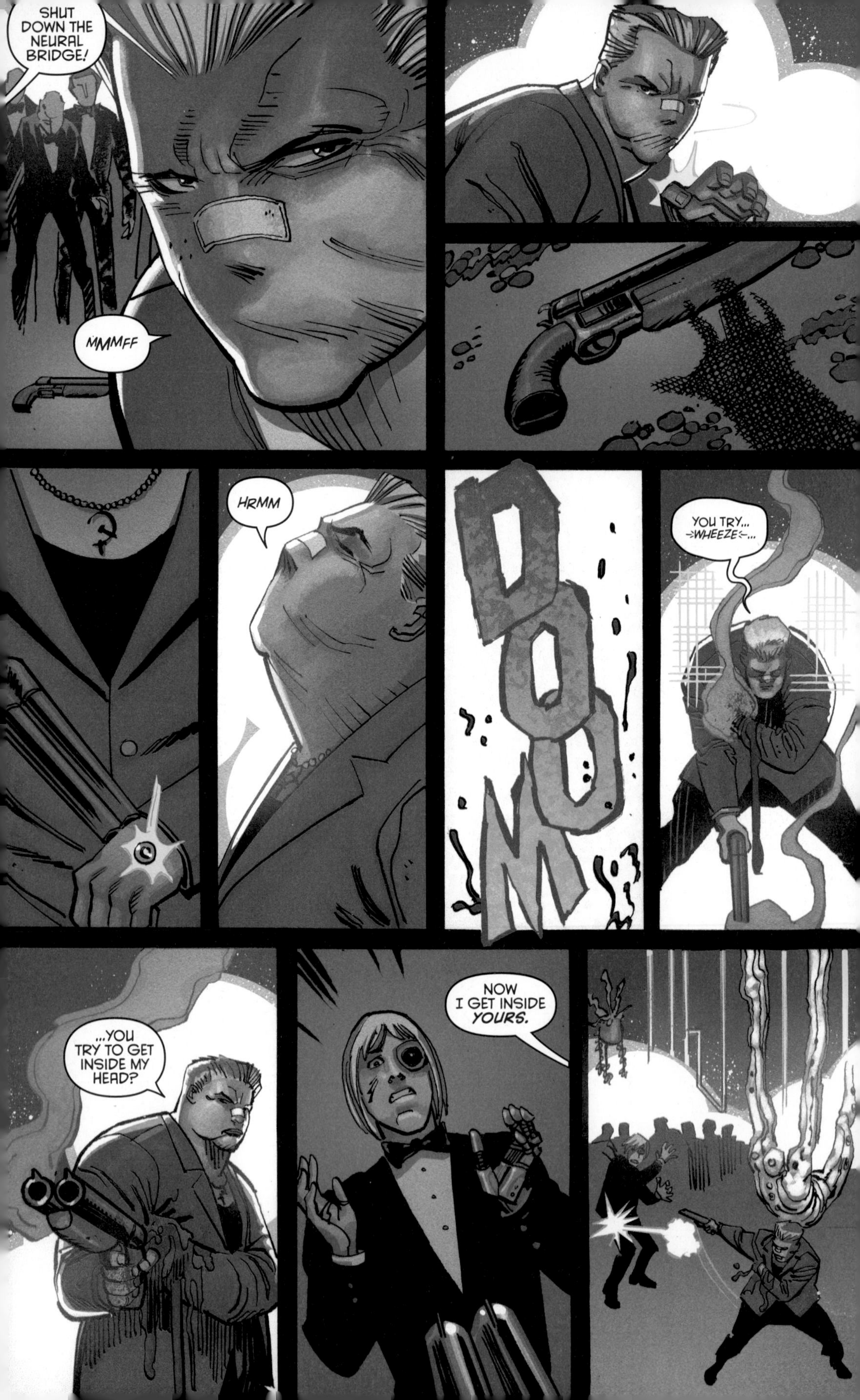
SHUT DOWN THE NEURAL BRIDGE!
MMMFF
HRMM
DOOM
YOU TRY... -WHEEZE-...
...YOU TRY TO GET INSIDE MY HEAD?
NOW I GET INSIDE YOURS.

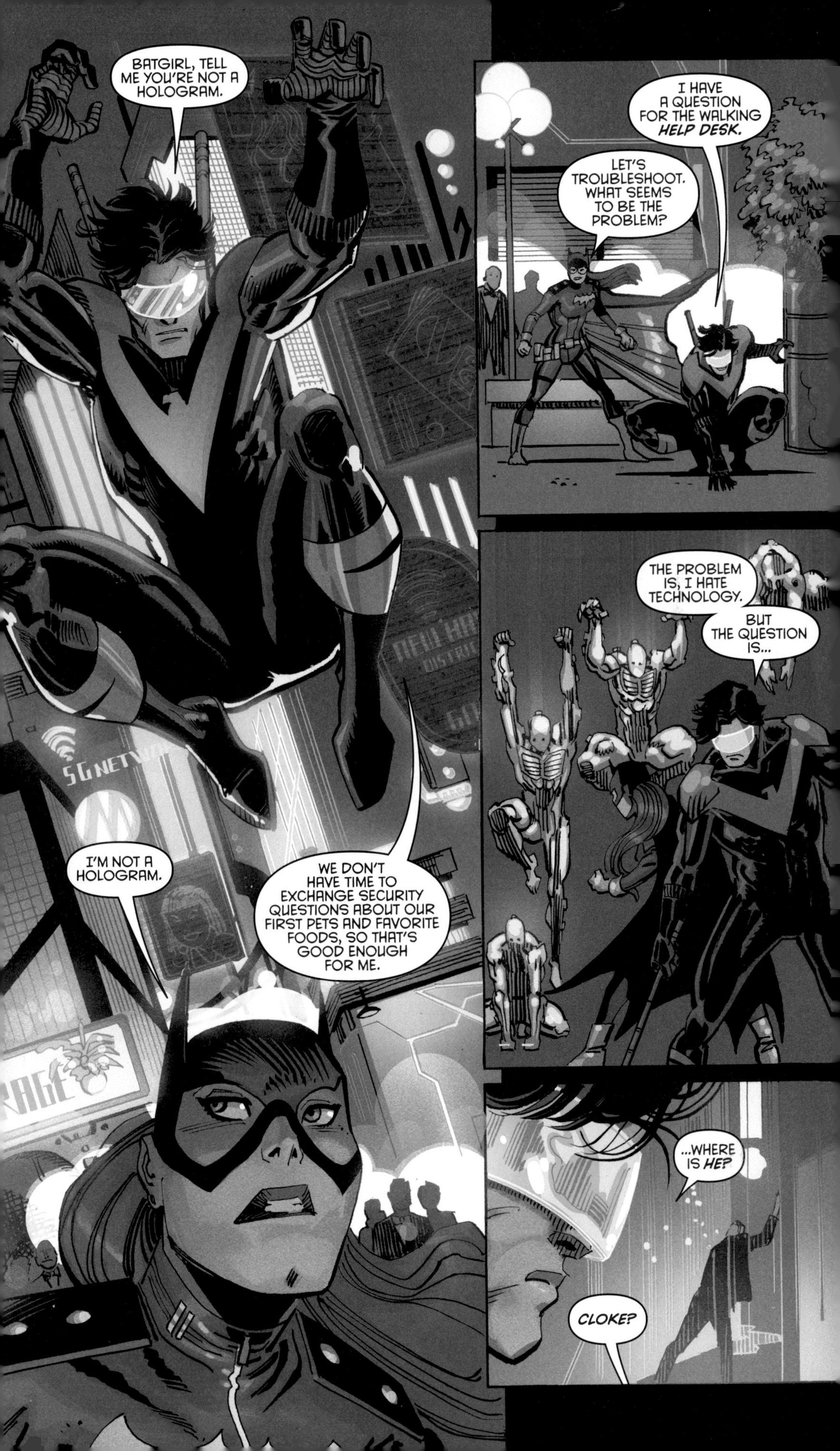
BATGIRL, TELL ME YOU'RE NOT A HOLOGRAM.
I'M NOT A HOLOGRAM.
WE DON'T HAVE TIME TO EXCHANGE SECURITY QUESTIONS ABOUT OUR FIRST PETS AND FAVORITE FOODS, SO THAT'S GOOD ENOUGH FOR ME.
5G NETW
I HAVE A QUESTION FOR THE WALKING *HELP DESK.*
LET'S TROUBLESHOOT. WHAT SEEMS TO BE THE PROBLEM?
THE PROBLEM IS, I HATE TECHNOLOGY.
BUT THE QUESTION IS...
...WHERE IS *HE?*
CLOKE?

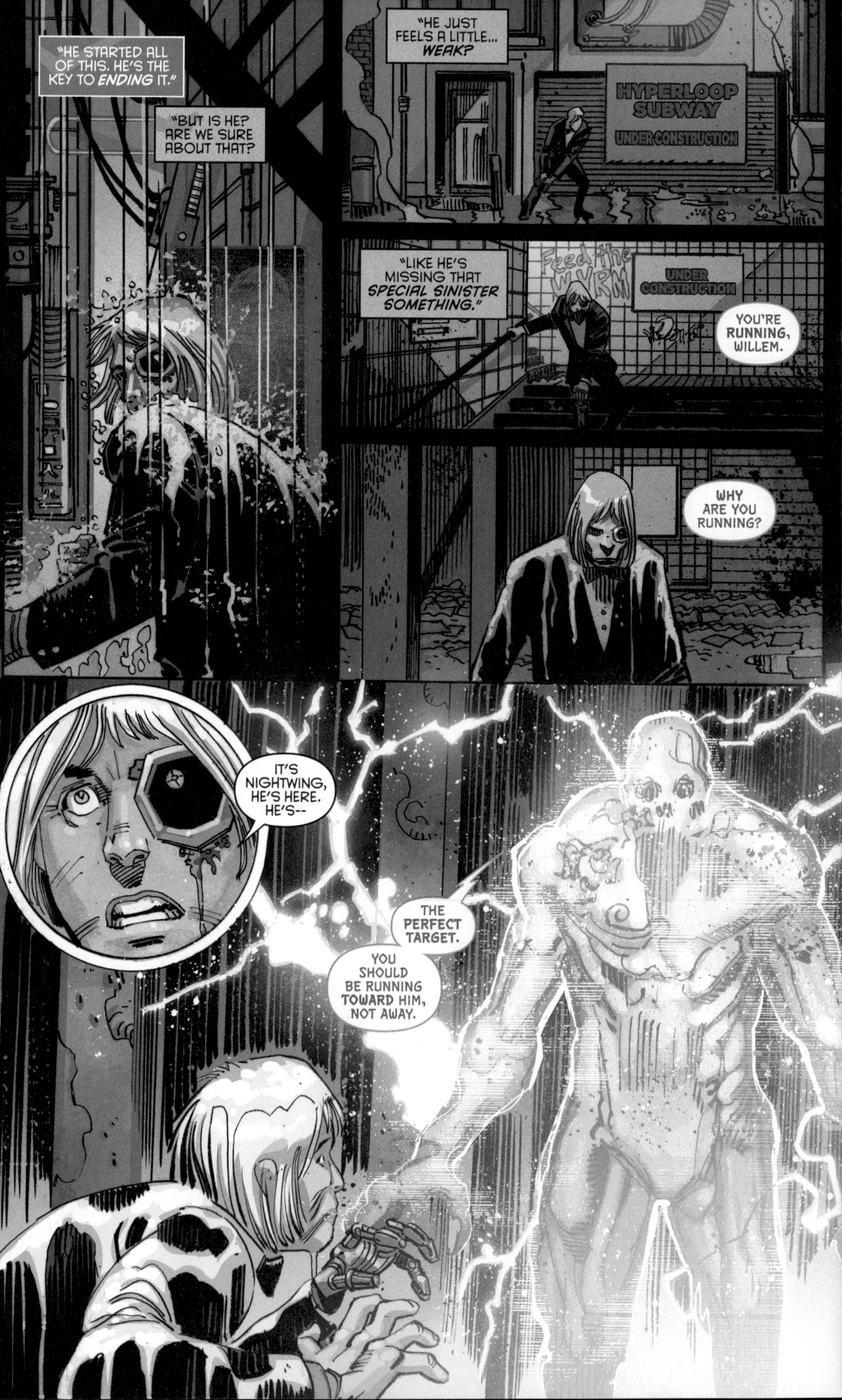
"HE STARTED ALL OF THIS. HE'S THE KEY TO *ENDING* IT."
"BUT IS HE? ARE WE SURE ABOUT THAT?
"HE JUST FEELS A LITTLE... *WEAK?*
HYPERLOOP SUBWAY
UNDER CONSTRUCTION
"LIKE HE'S MISSING THAT *SPECIAL SINISTER SOMETHING.*"
Feed the WYRM
UNDER CONSTRUCTION
YOU'RE RUNNING, WILLEM.
WHY ARE YOU RUNNING?
IT'S NIGHTWING, HE'S HERE. HE'S--
THE PERFECT TARGET.
YOU SHOULD BE RUNNING TOWARD HIM, NOT AWAY.

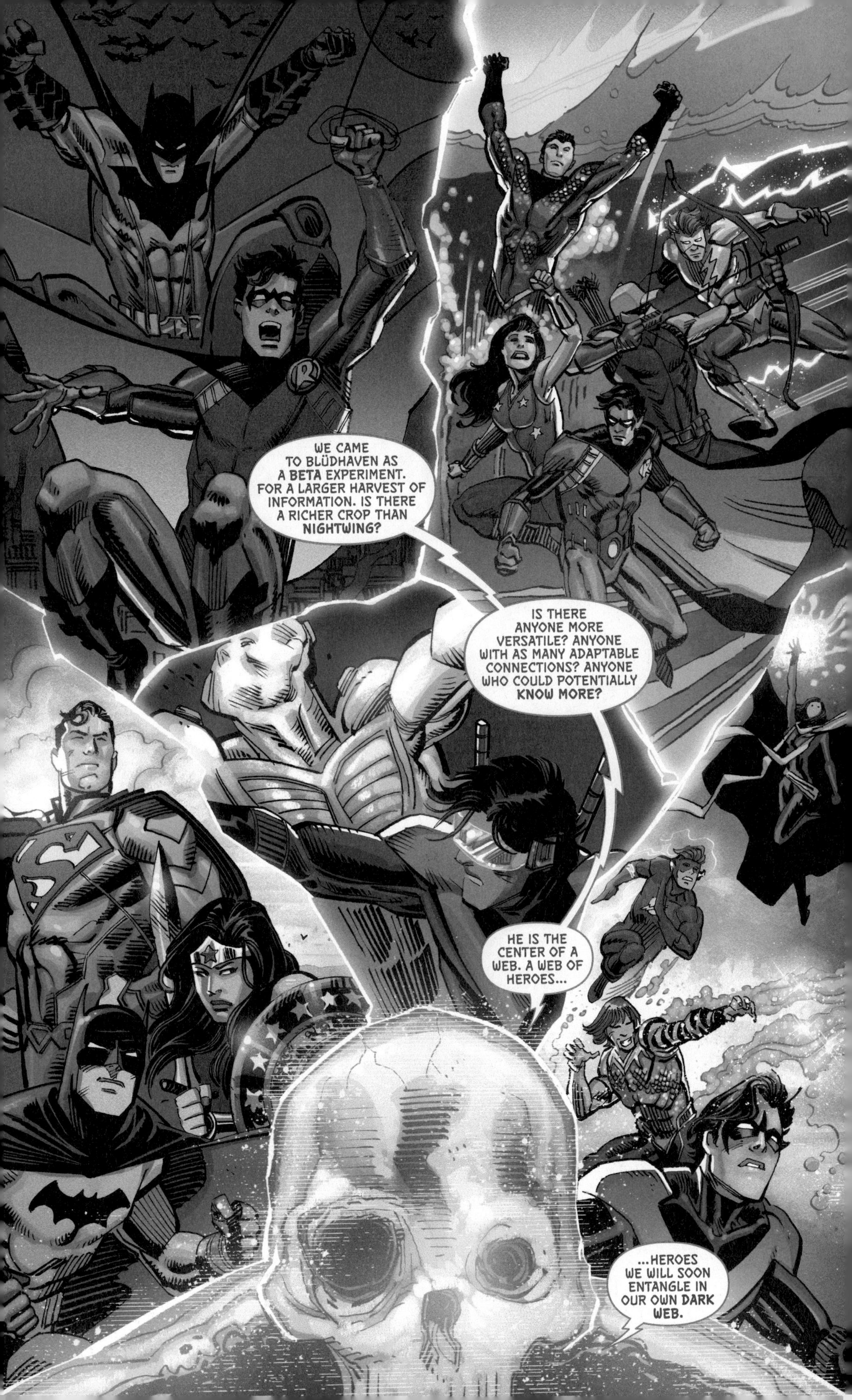
WE CAME TO BLÜDHAVEN AS A BETA EXPERIMENT. FOR A LARGER HARVEST OF INFORMATION. IS THERE A RICHER CROP THAN NIGHTWING?
IS THERE ANYONE MORE VERSATILE? ANYONE WITH AS MANY ADAPTABLE CONNECTIONS? ANYONE WHO COULD POTENTIALLY KNOW MORE?
HE IS THE CENTER OF A WEB. A WEB OF HEROES...
...HEROES WE WILL SOON ENTANGLE IN OUR OWN DARK WEB.

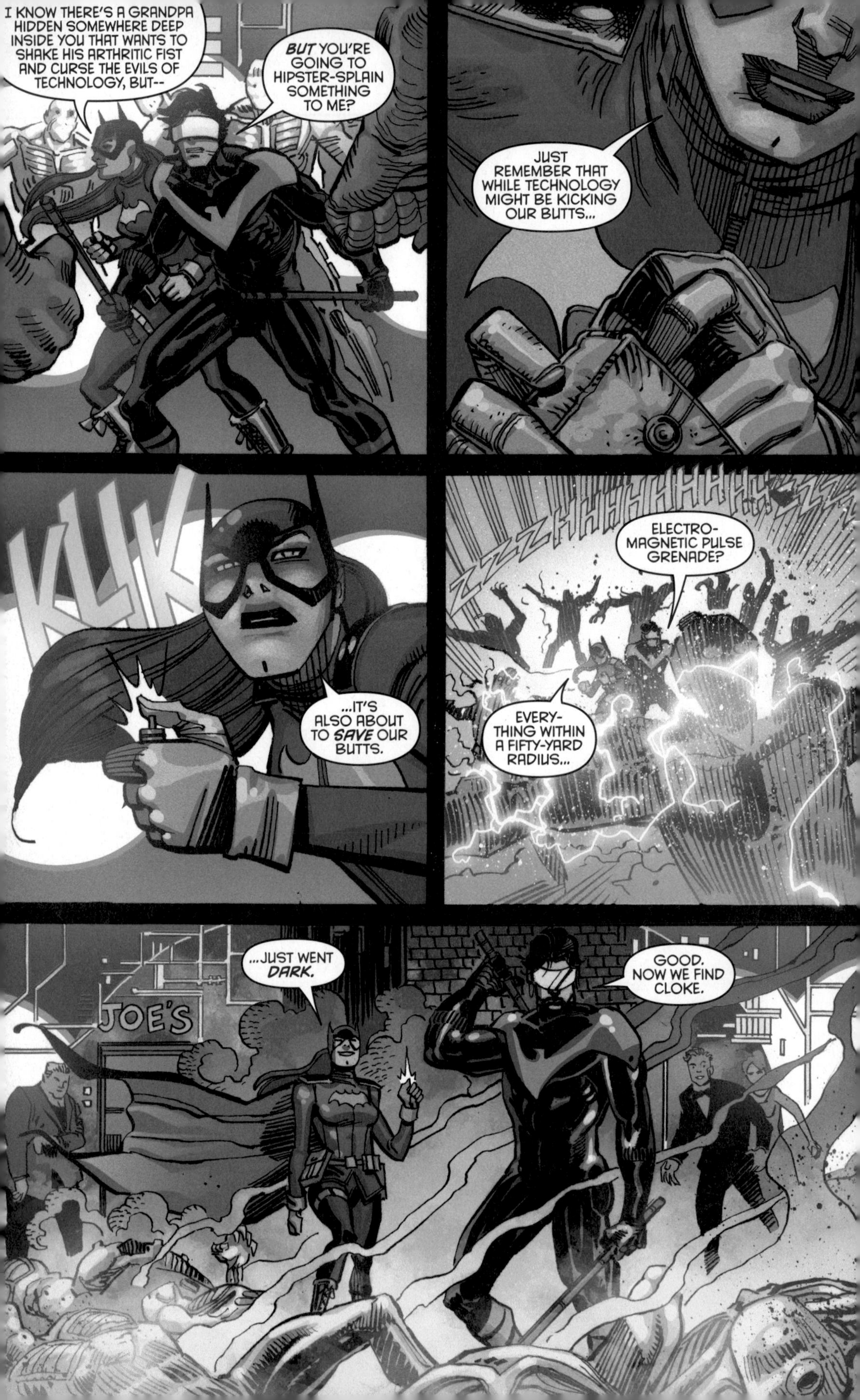
I KNOW THERE'S A GRANDPA HIDDEN SOMEWHERE DEEP INSIDE YOU THAT WANTS TO SHAKE HIS ARTHRITIC FIST AND CURSE THE EVILS OF TECHNOLOGY, BUT--
BUT YOU'RE GOING TO HIPSTER-SPLAIN SOMETHING TO ME?
JUST REMEMBER THAT WHILE TECHNOLOGY MIGHT BE KICKING OUR BUTTS...
KLIK
...IT'S ALSO ABOUT TO SAVE OUR BUTTS.
ZZZZHHHHHHHHHHZZZZ
ELECTRO-MAGNETIC PULSE GRENADE?
EVERY-THING WITHIN A FIFTY-YARD RADIUS...
...JUST WENT DARK.
JOE'S
GOOD. NOW WE FIND CLOKE.

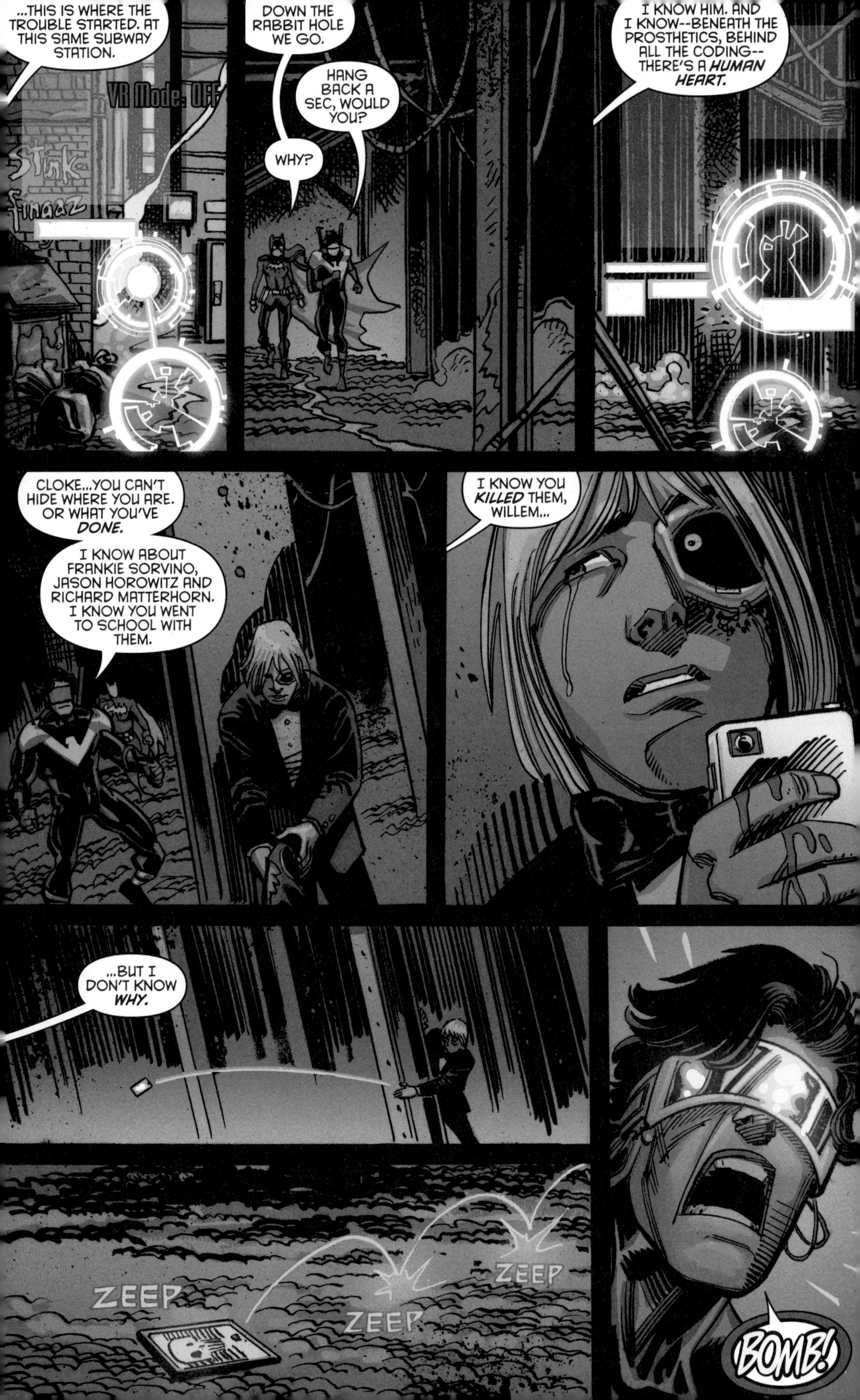
...THIS IS WHERE THE TROUBLE STARTED. AT THIS SAME SUBWAY STATION.
VR Mode: OFF
Stink Fingaz
DOWN THE RABBIT HOLE WE GO.
HANG BACK A SEC, WOULD YOU?
WHY?
I KNOW HIM. AND I KNOW--BENEATH THE PROSTHETICS, BEHIND ALL THE CODING--THERE'S A HUMAN HEART.
CLOKE...YOU CAN'T HIDE WHERE YOU ARE. OR WHAT YOU'VE DONE.
I KNOW ABOUT FRANKIE SORVINO, JASON HOROWITZ AND RICHARD MATTERHORN. I KNOW YOU WENT TO SCHOOL WITH THEM.
I KNOW YOU KILLED THEM, WILLEM...
...BUT I DON'T KNOW WHY.
ZEEP
ZEEP
ZEEP
BOMB!

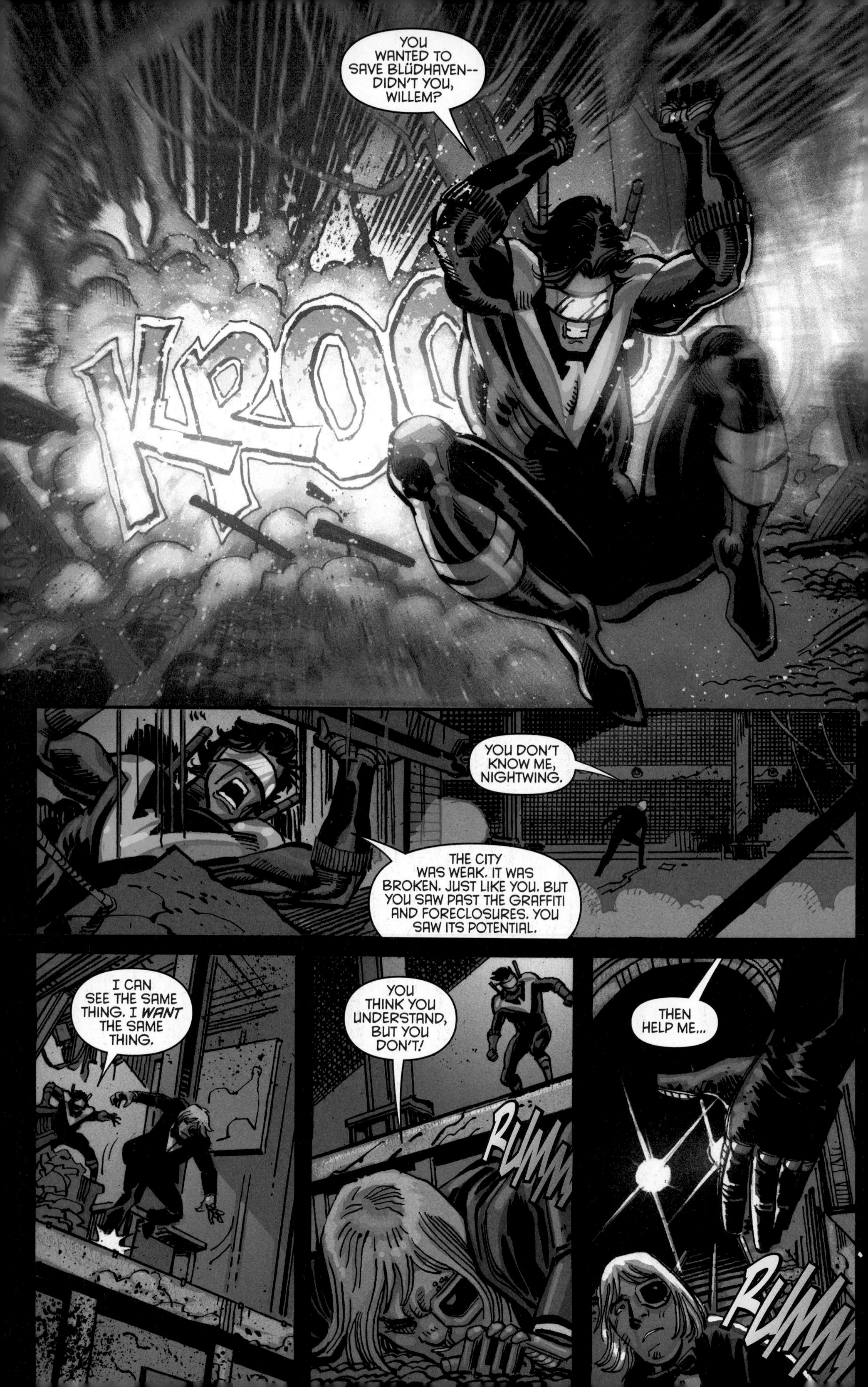
YOU WANTED TO SAVE BLÜDHAVEN-- DIDN'T YOU, WILLEM?
KROOO
YOU DON'T KNOW ME, NIGHTWING.
THE CITY WAS WEAK. IT WAS BROKEN. JUST LIKE YOU. BUT YOU SAW PAST THE GRAFFITI AND FORECLOSURES. YOU SAW ITS POTENTIAL.
I CAN SEE THE SAME THING. I *WANT* THE SAME THING.
YOU THINK YOU UNDERSTAND, BUT YOU DON'T!
RUMM
THEN HELP ME...
RUMM

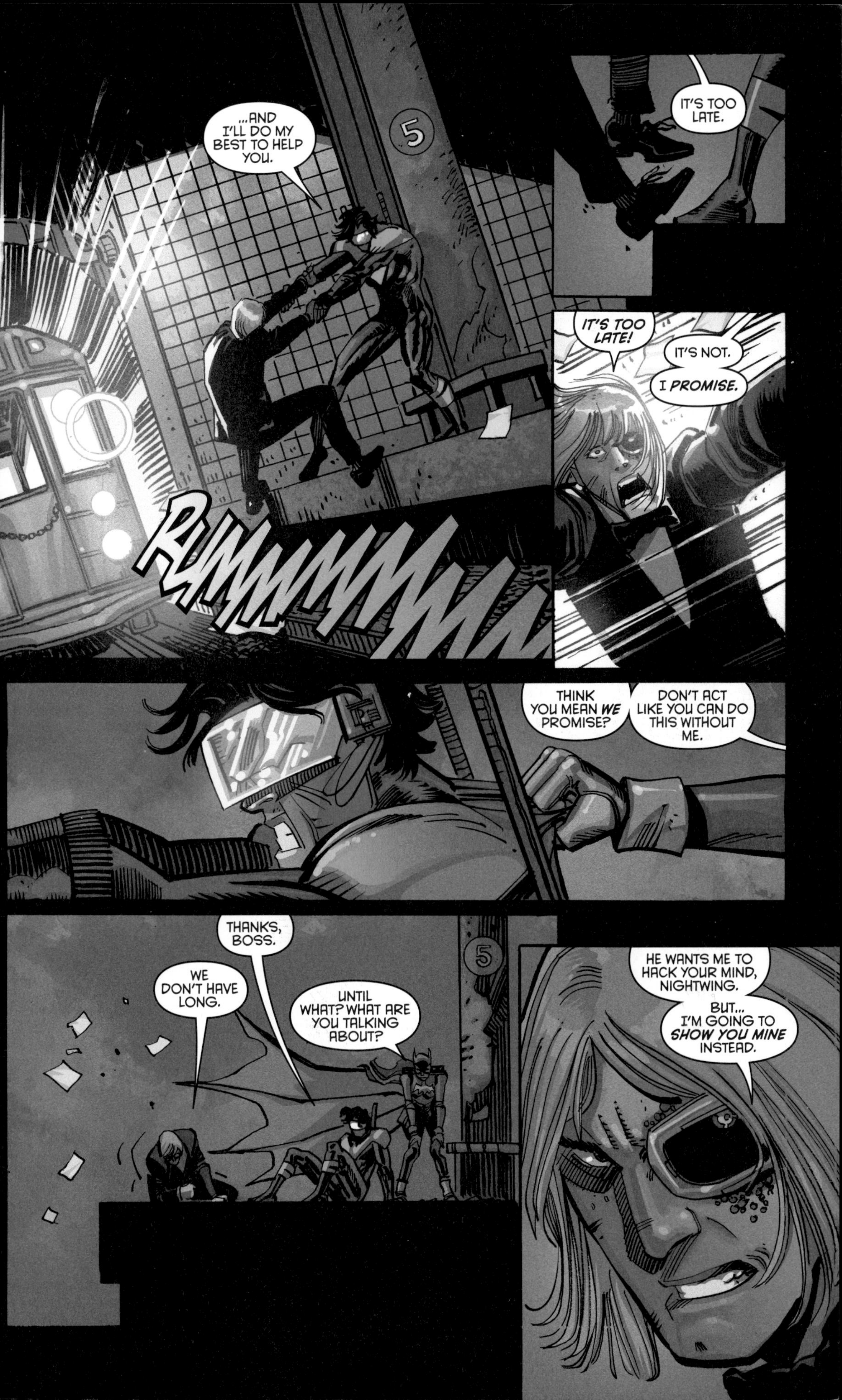
...AND I'LL DO MY BEST TO HELP YOU.
IT'S TOO LATE.
RUMMMMMMMMM
IT'S TOO LATE!
IT'S NOT.
I PROMISE.
THINK YOU MEAN WE PROMISE?
DON'T ACT LIKE YOU CAN DO THIS WITHOUT ME.
THANKS, BOSS.
WE DON'T HAVE LONG.
UNTIL WHAT? WHAT ARE YOU TALKING ABOUT?
HE WANTS ME TO HACK YOUR MIND, NIGHTWING.
BUT... I'M GOING TO SHOW YOU MINE INSTEAD.

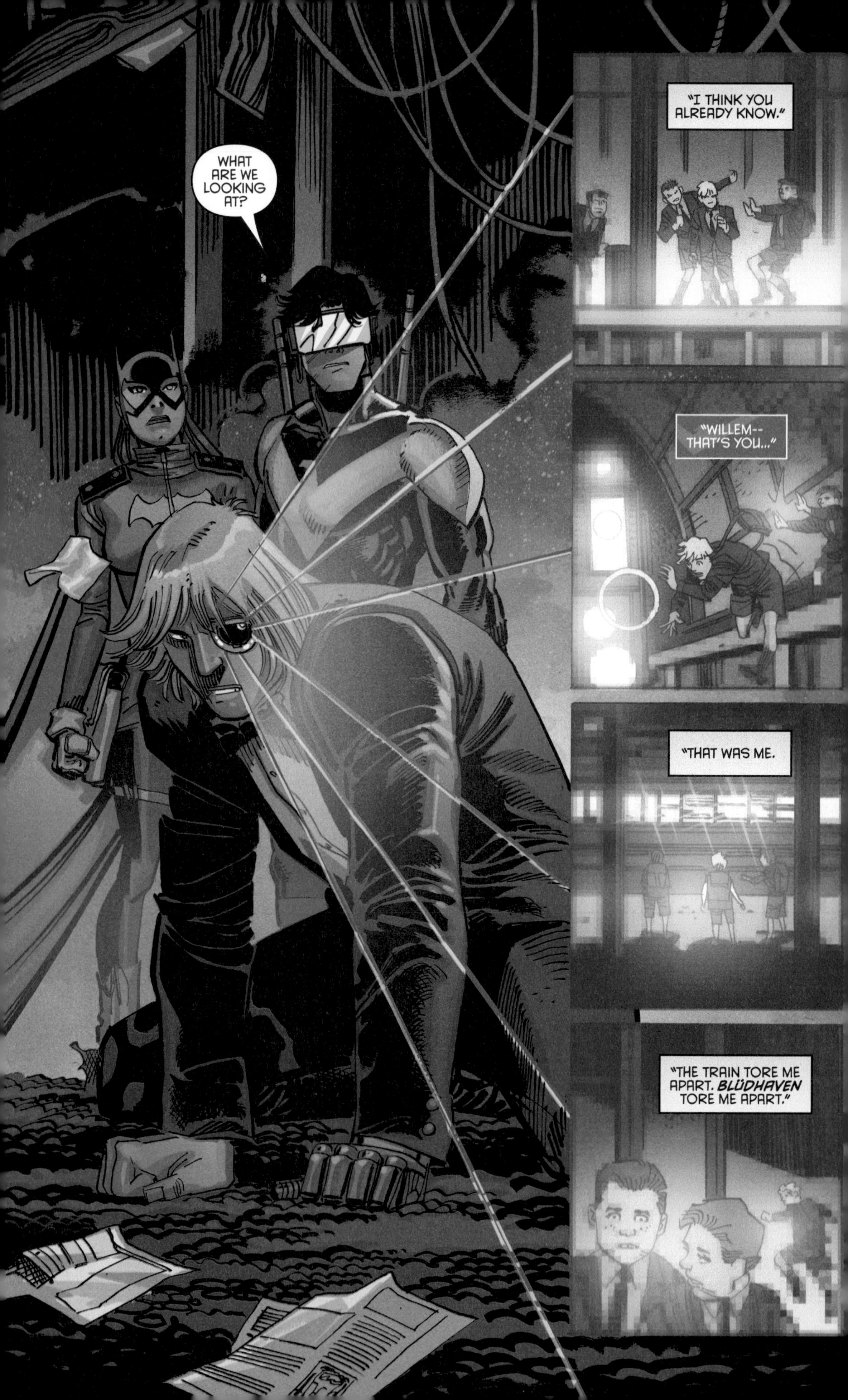
WHAT ARE WE LOOKING AT?
"I THINK YOU ALREADY KNOW."
"WILLEM-- THAT'S YOU..."
"THAT WAS ME.
"THE TRAIN TORE ME APART. *BLÜDHAVEN* TORE ME APART."

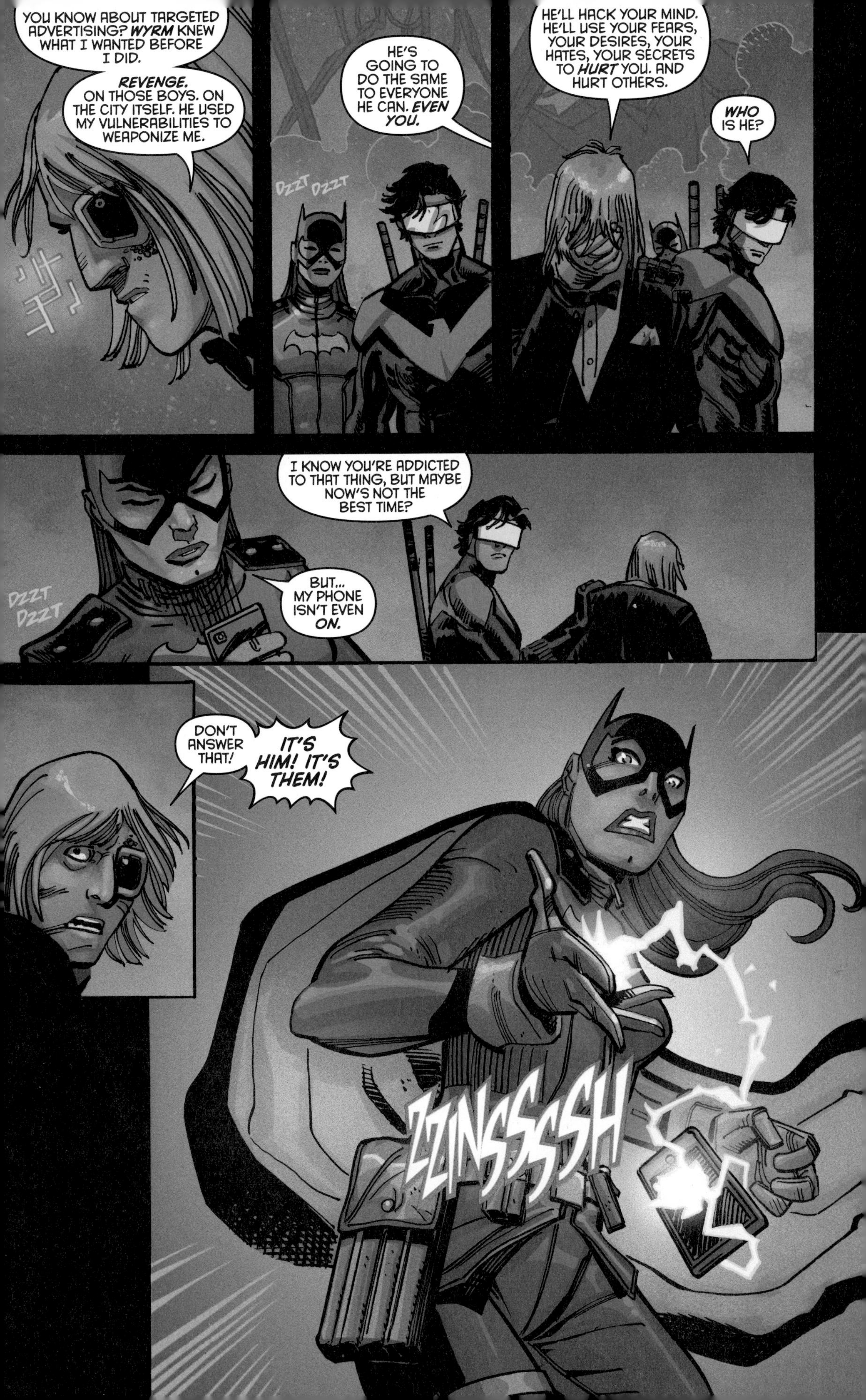
YOU KNOW ABOUT TARGETED ADVERTISING? WYRM KNEW WHAT I WANTED BEFORE I DID.
REVENGE. ON THOSE BOYS. ON THE CITY ITSELF. HE USED MY VULNERABILITIES TO WEAPONIZE ME.
DZZT DZZT
HE'S GOING TO DO THE SAME TO EVERYONE HE CAN. EVEN YOU.
HE'LL HACK YOUR MIND. HE'LL USE YOUR FEARS, YOUR DESIRES, YOUR HATES, YOUR SECRETS TO HURT YOU. AND HURT OTHERS.
WHO IS HE?
I KNOW YOU'RE ADDICTED TO THAT THING, BUT MAYBE NOW'S NOT THE BEST TIME?
DZZT DZZT
BUT... MY PHONE ISN'T EVEN ON.
DON'T ANSWER THAT!
IT'S HIM! IT'S THEM!
ZZINSSSSH

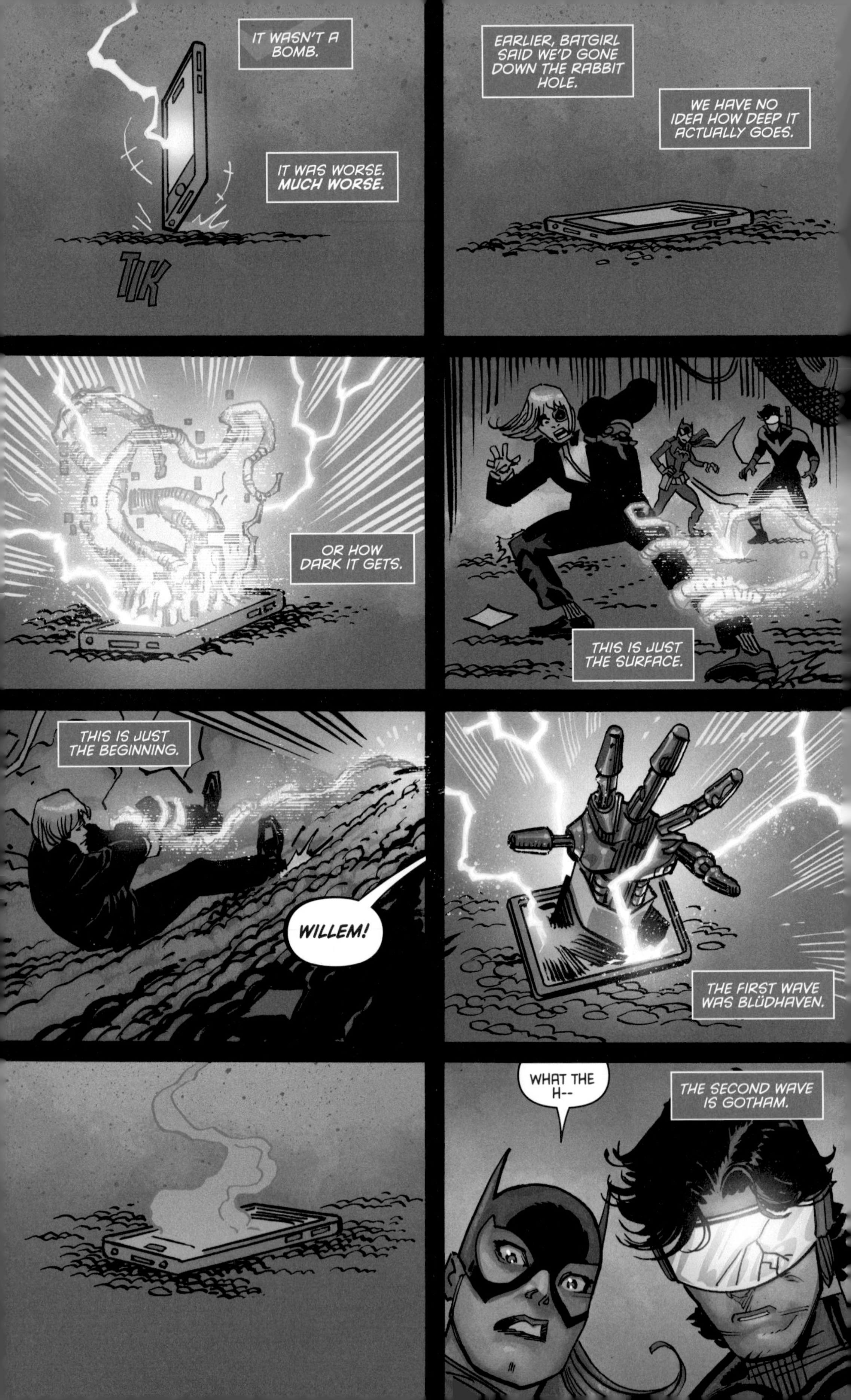
IT WASN'T A BOMB.
IT WAS WORSE. MUCH WORSE.
TIK
EARLIER, BATGIRL SAID WE'D GONE DOWN THE RABBIT HOLE.
WE HAVE NO IDEA HOW DEEP IT ACTUALLY GOES.
OR HOW DARK IT GETS.
THIS IS JUST THE SURFACE.
THIS IS JUST THE BEGINNING.
WILLEM!
THE FIRST WAVE WAS BLÜDHAVEN.
WHAT THE H--
THE SECOND WAVE IS GOTHAM.

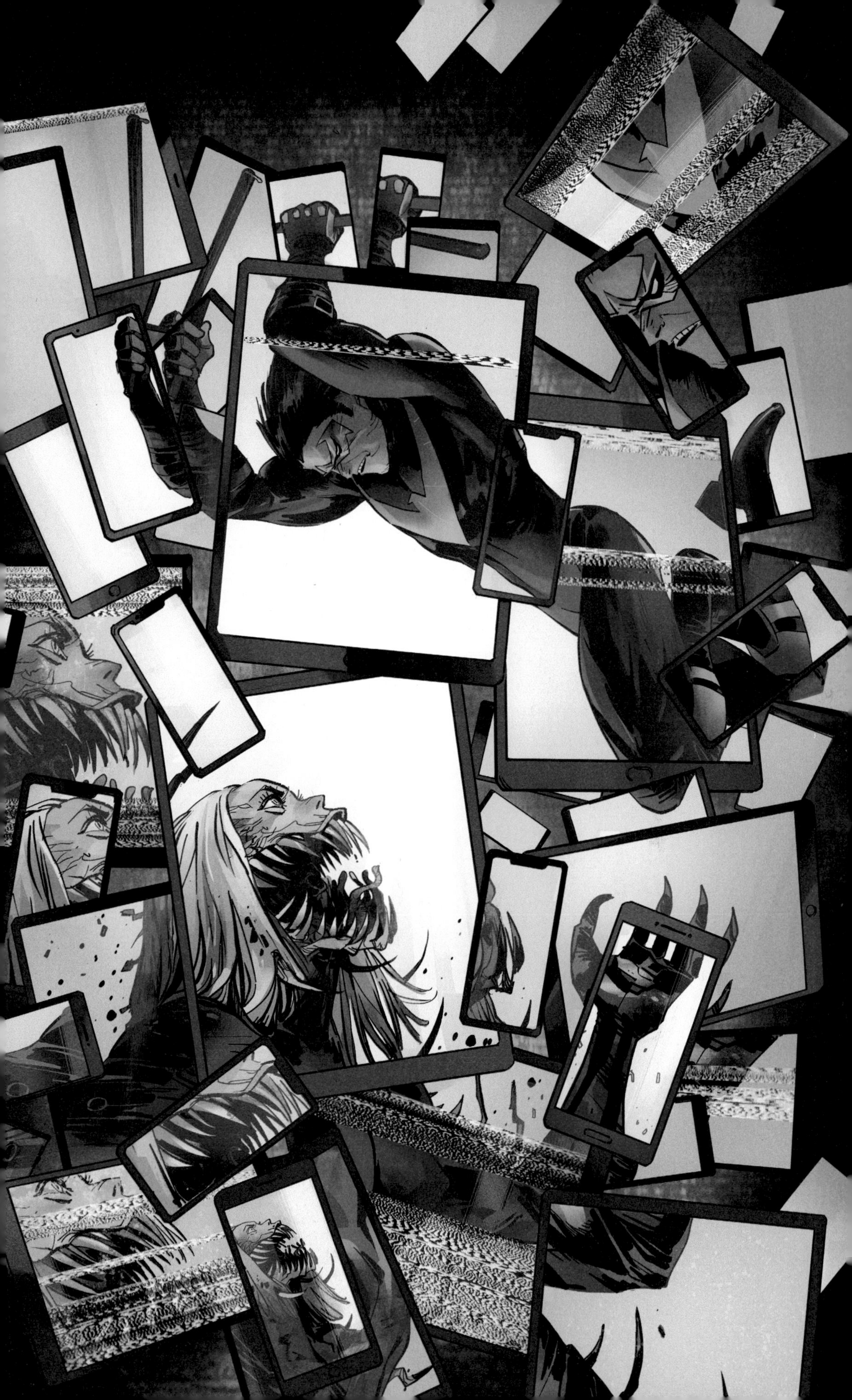

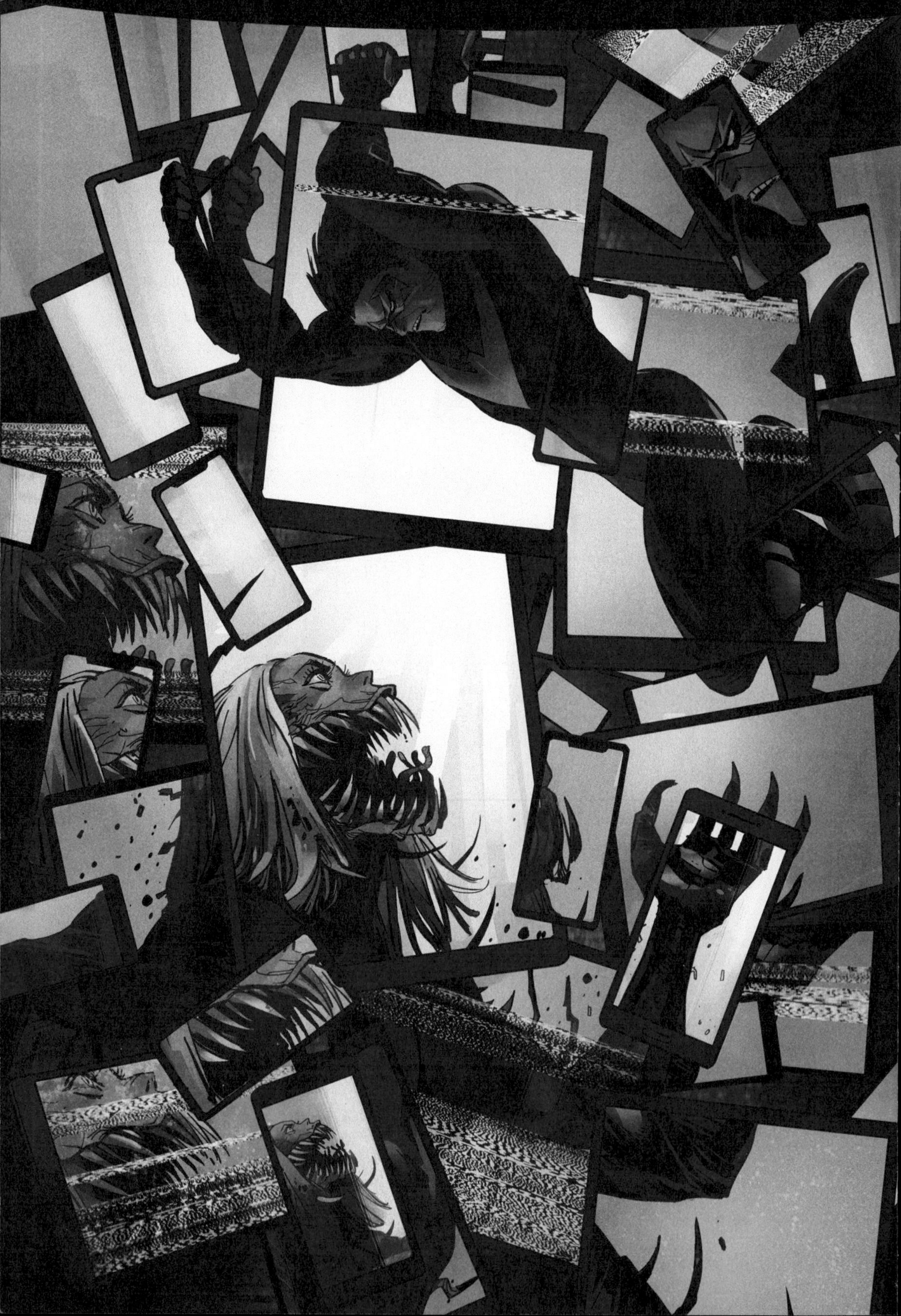

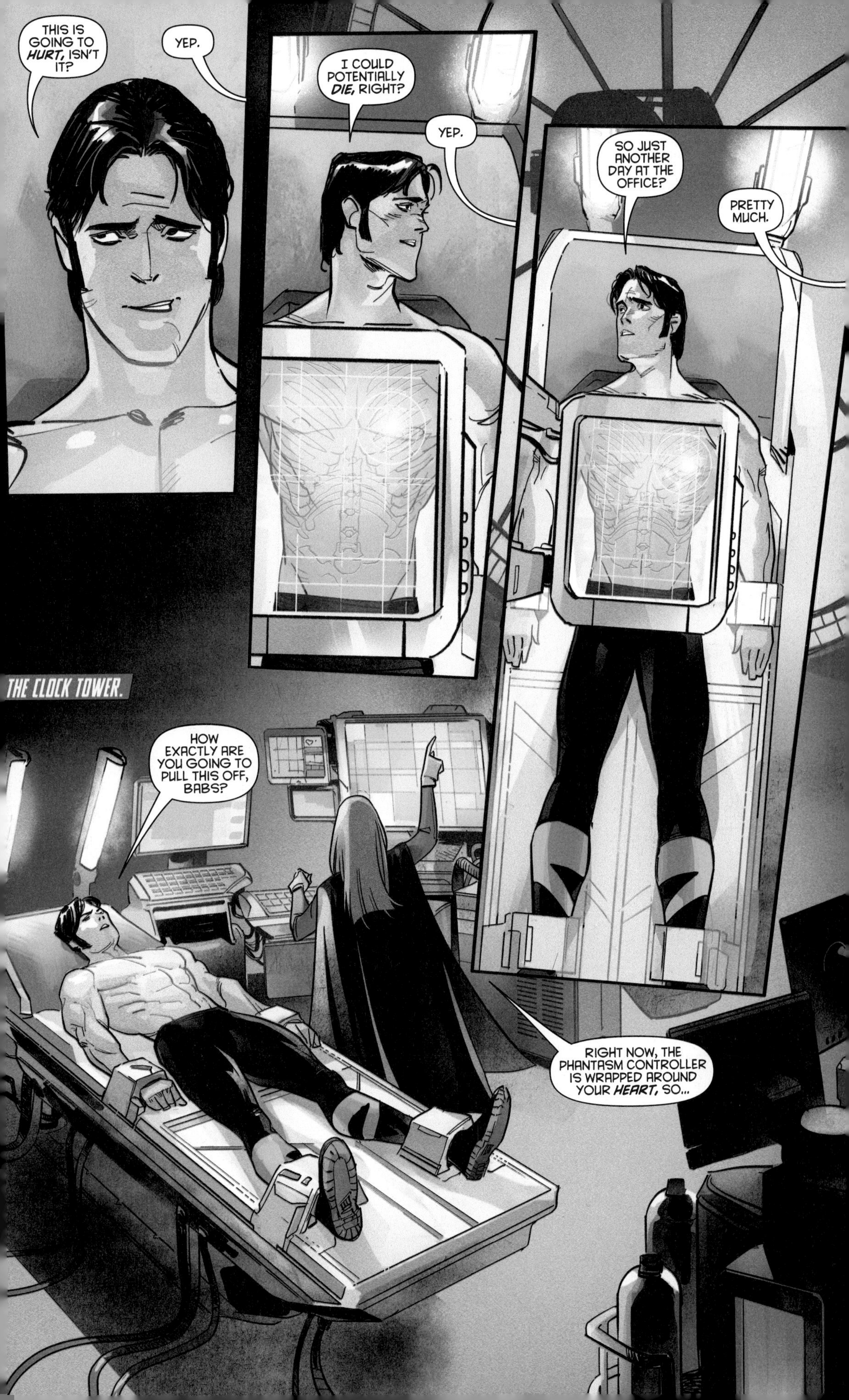

THIS IS GOING TO *HURT,* ISN'T IT?
YEP.
I COULD POTENTIALLY *DIE,* RIGHT?
YEP.
SO JUST ANOTHER DAY AT THE OFFICE?
PRETTY MUCH.
THE CLOCK TOWER.
HOW EXACTLY ARE YOU GOING TO PULL THIS OFF, BABS?
RIGHT NOW, THE PHANTASM CONTROLLER IS WRAPPED AROUND YOUR *HEART,* SO...

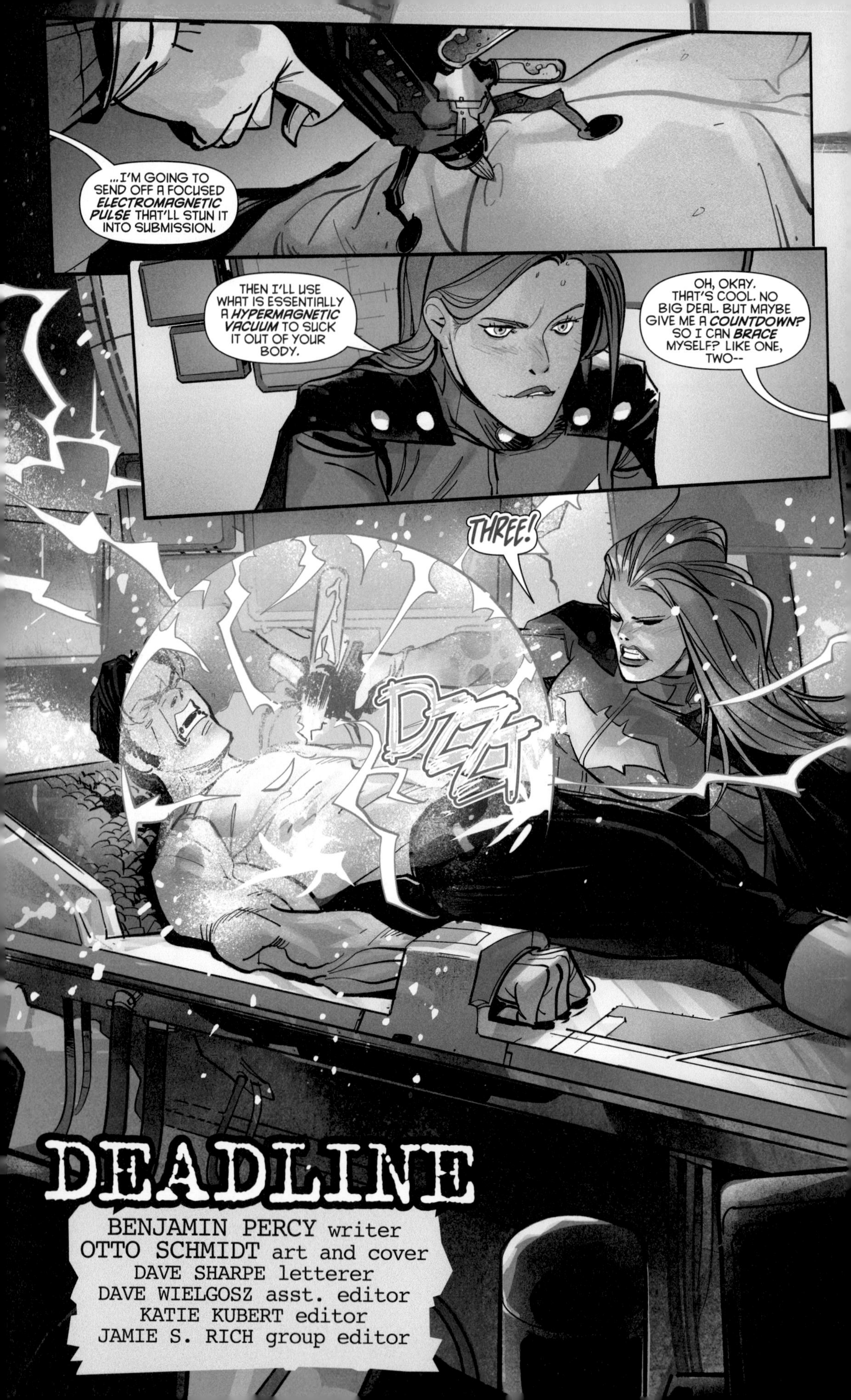
...I'M GOING TO SEND OFF A FOCUSED *ELECTROMAGNETIC PULSE* THAT'LL STUN IT INTO SUBMISSION.
THEN I'LL USE WHAT IS ESSENTIALLY A *HYPERMAGNETIC VACUUM* TO SUCK IT OUT OF YOUR BODY.
OH, OKAY. THAT'S COOL. NO BIG DEAL. BUT MAYBE GIVE ME A *COUNTDOWN?* SO I CAN *BRACE* MYSELF? LIKE ONE, TWO--
THREE!
DZZZT
DEADLINE
BENJAMIN PERCY writer
OTTO SCHMIDT art and cover
DAVE SHARPE letterer
DAVE WIELGOSZ asst. editor
KATIE KUBERT editor
JAMIE S. RICH group editor

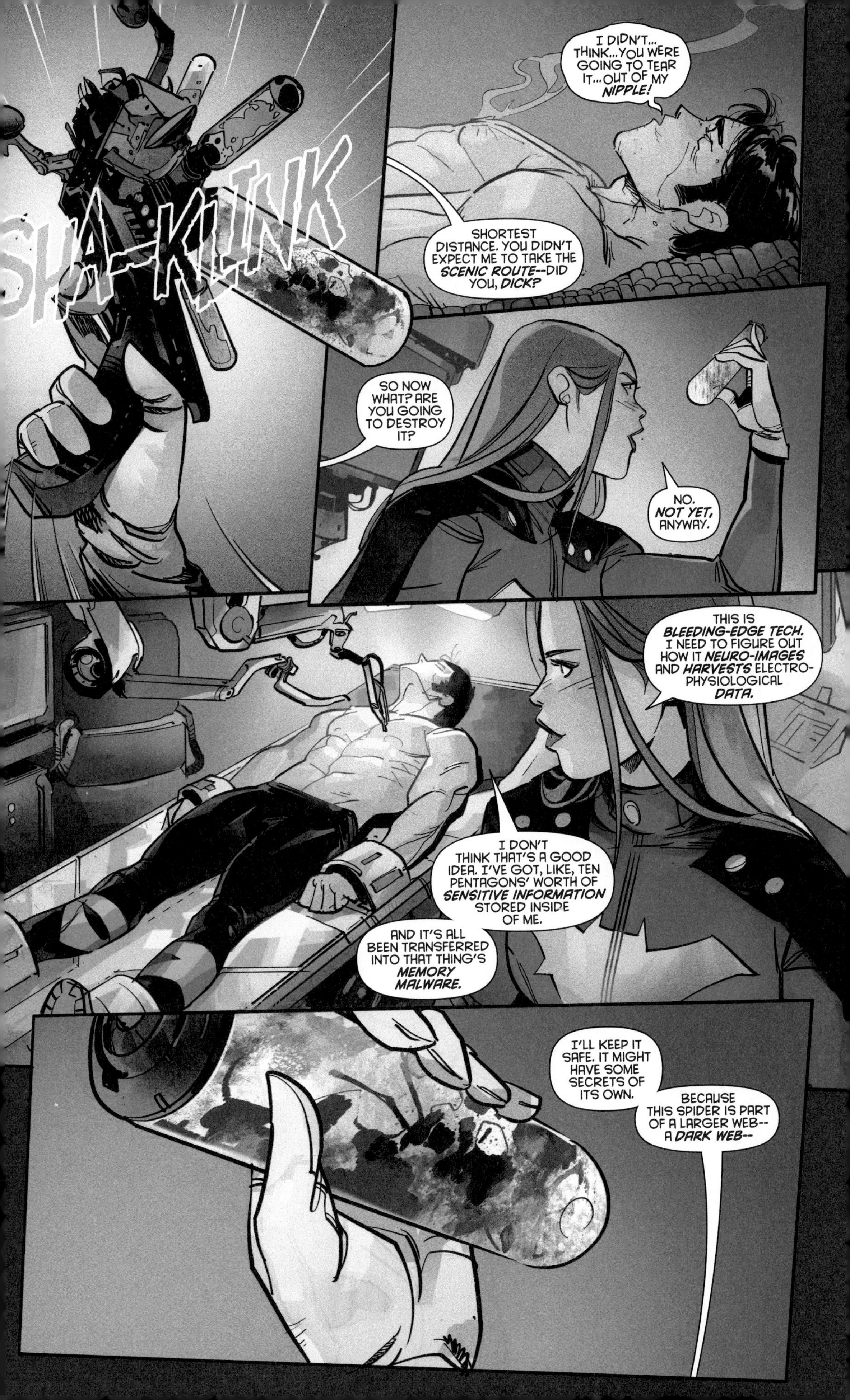
SHA-KLINK
I DIDN'T... THINK...YOU WERE GOING TO TEAR IT...OUT OF MY NIPPLE!
SHORTEST DISTANCE. YOU DIDN'T EXPECT ME TO TAKE THE SCENIC ROUTE--DID YOU, DICK?
SO NOW WHAT? ARE YOU GOING TO DESTROY IT?
NO. NOT YET, ANYWAY.
THIS IS BLEEDING-EDGE TECH. I NEED TO FIGURE OUT HOW IT NEURO-IMAGES AND HARVESTS ELECTRO-PHYSIOLOGICAL DATA.
I DON'T THINK THAT'S A GOOD IDEA. I'VE GOT, LIKE, TEN PENTAGONS' WORTH OF SENSITIVE INFORMATION STORED INSIDE OF ME.
AND IT'S ALL BEEN TRANSFERRED INTO THAT THING'S MEMORY MALWARE.
I'LL KEEP IT SAFE. IT MIGHT HAVE SOME SECRETS OF ITS OWN.
BECAUSE THIS SPIDER IS PART OF A LARGER WEB-- A DARK WEB--

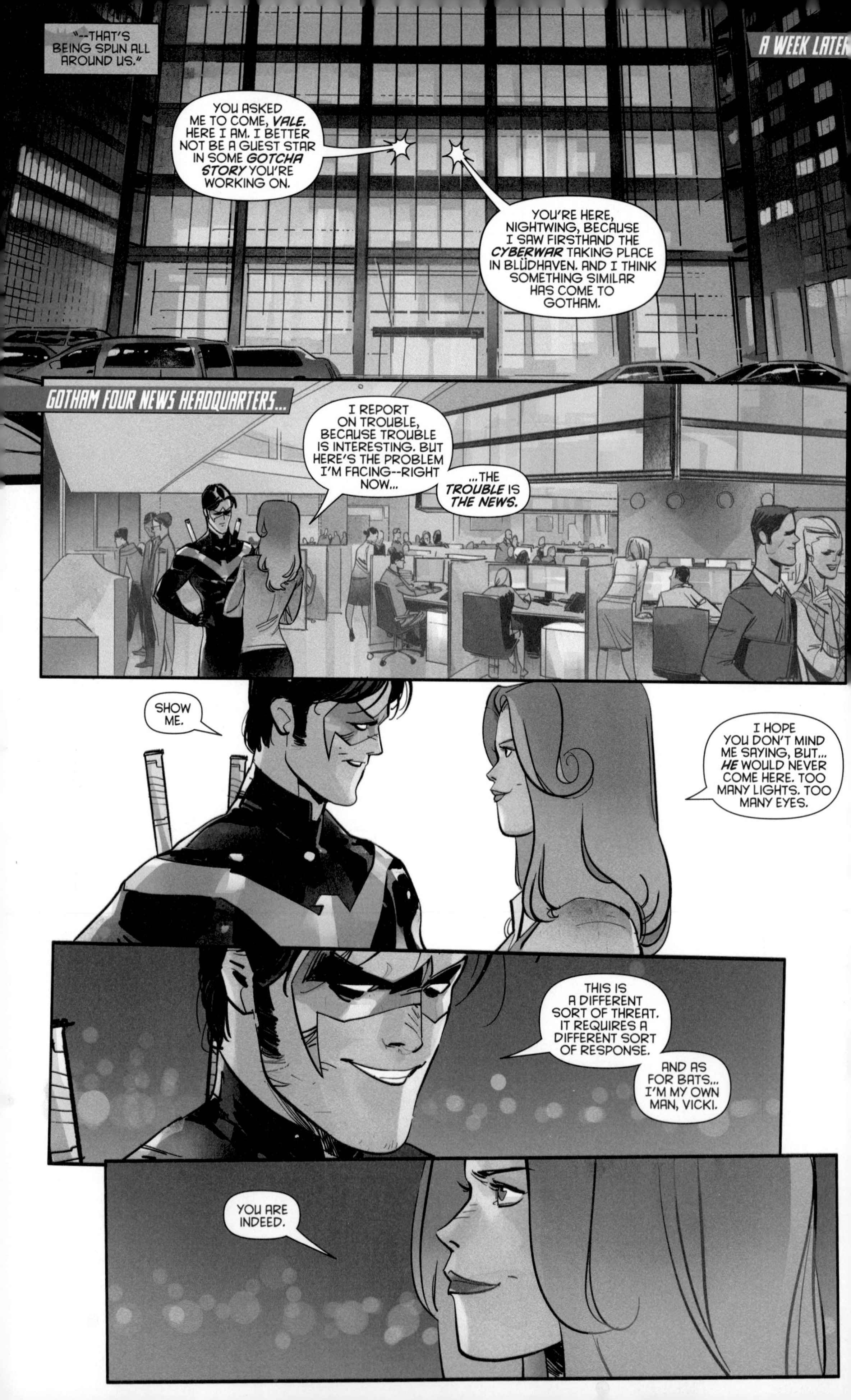

"--THAT'S BEING SPUN ALL AROUND US."
A WEEK LATER
YOU ASKED ME TO COME, VALE. HERE I AM. I BETTER NOT BE A GUEST STAR IN SOME GOTCHA STORY YOU'RE WORKING ON.
YOU'RE HERE, NIGHTWING, BECAUSE I SAW FIRSTHAND THE CYBERWAR TAKING PLACE IN BLÜDHAVEN. AND I THINK SOMETHING SIMILAR HAS COME TO GOTHAM.
GOTHAM FOUR NEWS HEADQUARTERS...
I REPORT ON TROUBLE, BECAUSE TROUBLE IS INTERESTING. BUT HERE'S THE PROBLEM I'M FACING--RIGHT NOW...
...THE TROUBLE IS THE NEWS.
SHOW ME.
I HOPE YOU DON'T MIND ME SAYING, BUT... HE WOULD NEVER COME HERE. TOO MANY LIGHTS. TOO MANY EYES.
THIS IS A DIFFERENT SORT OF THREAT. IT REQUIRES A DIFFERENT SORT OF RESPONSE.
AND AS FOR BATS... I'M MY OWN MAN, VICKI.
YOU ARE INDEED.

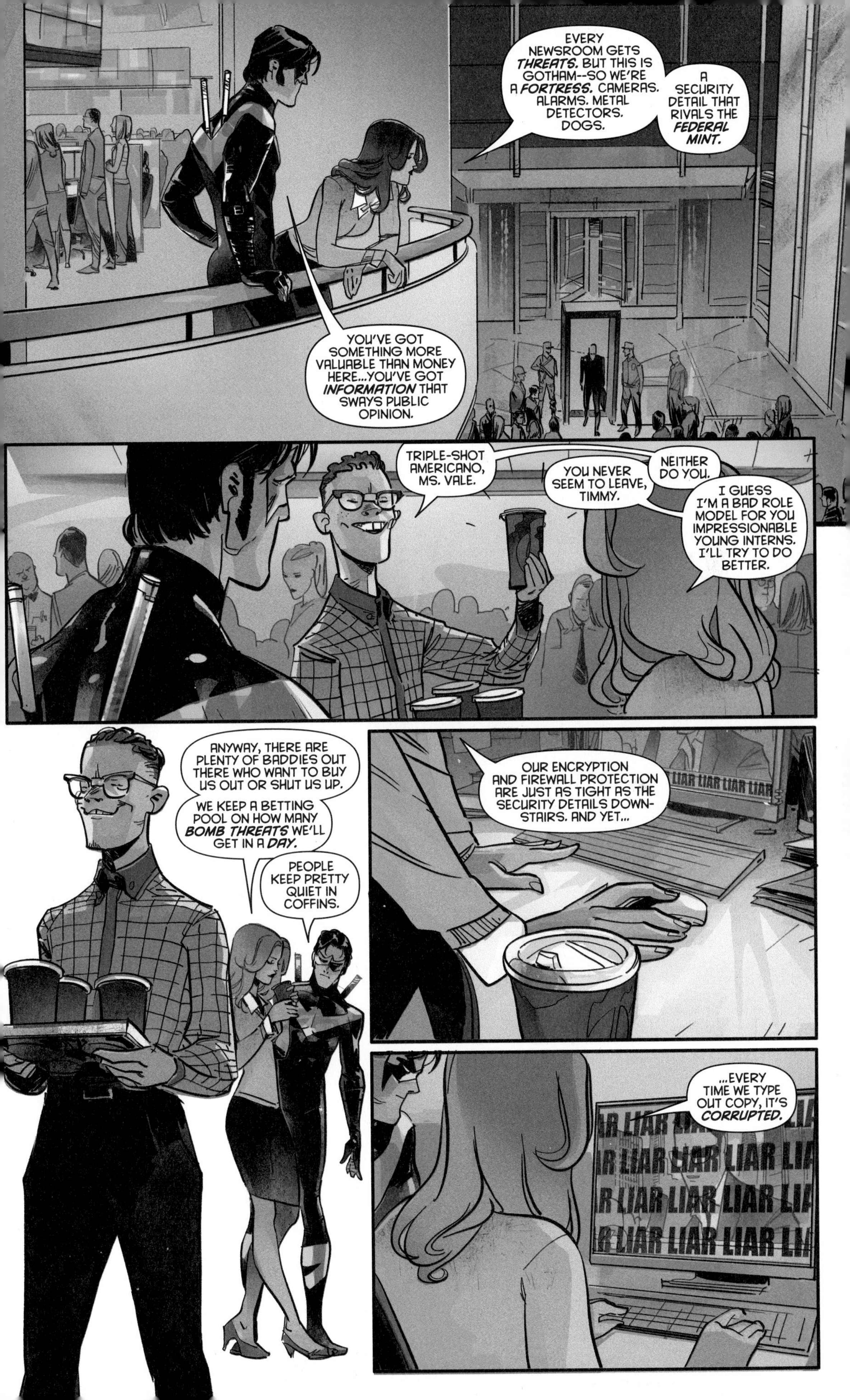

EVERY NEWSROOM GETS THREATS. BUT THIS IS GOTHAM--SO WE'RE A FORTRESS. CAMERAS. ALARMS. METAL DETECTORS. DOGS.
A SECURITY DETAIL THAT RIVALS THE FEDERAL MINT.
YOU'VE GOT SOMETHING MORE VALUABLE THAN MONEY HERE...YOU'VE GOT INFORMATION THAT SWAYS PUBLIC OPINION.
TRIPLE-SHOT AMERICANO, MS. VALE.
YOU NEVER SEEM TO LEAVE, TIMMY.
NEITHER DO YOU.
I GUESS I'M A BAD ROLE MODEL FOR YOU IMPRESSIONABLE YOUNG INTERNS. I'LL TRY TO DO BETTER.
ANYWAY, THERE ARE PLENTY OF BADDIES OUT THERE WHO WANT TO BUY US OUT OR SHUT US UP.
WE KEEP A BETTING POOL ON HOW MANY BOMB THREATS WE'LL GET IN A DAY.
PEOPLE KEEP PRETTY QUIET IN COFFINS.
OUR ENCRYPTION AND FIREWALL PROTECTION ARE JUST AS TIGHT AS THE SECURITY DETAILS DOWNSTAIRS. AND YET...
LIAR LIAR LIAR LIAR
...EVERY TIME WE TYPE OUT COPY, IT'S CORRUPTED.
LIAR LIAR LIAR LIAR

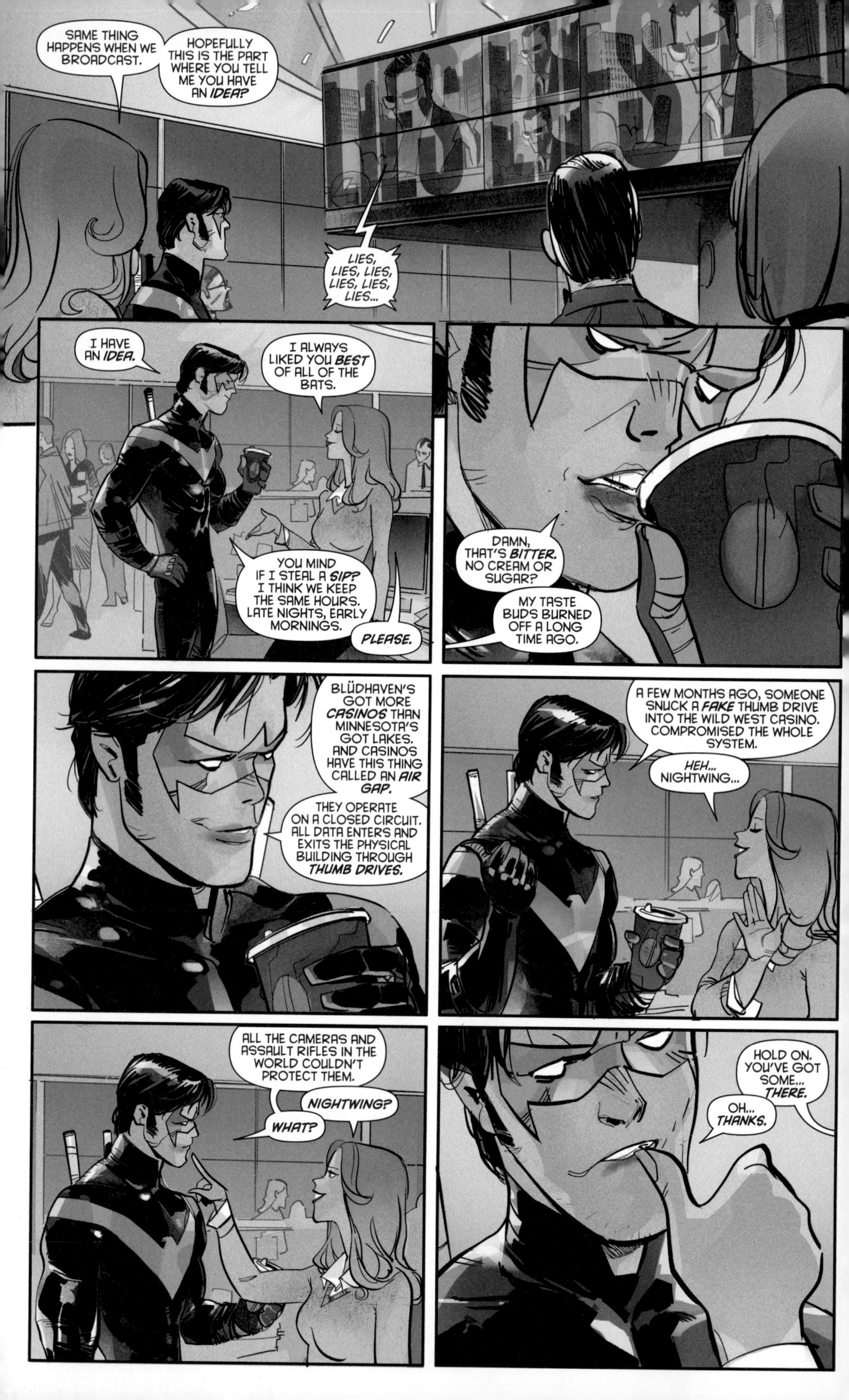
SAME THING HAPPENS WHEN WE BROADCAST.
HOPEFULLY THIS IS THE PART WHERE YOU TELL ME YOU HAVE AN IDEA?
LIES, LIES, LIES, LIES, LIES, LIES...
I HAVE AN IDEA.
I ALWAYS LIKED YOU BEST OF ALL OF THE BATS.
YOU MIND IF I STEAL A SIP? I THINK WE KEEP THE SAME HOURS. LATE NIGHTS, EARLY MORNINGS.
PLEASE.
DAMN, THAT'S BITTER. NO CREAM OR SUGAR?
MY TASTE BUDS BURNED OFF A LONG TIME AGO.
BLÜDHAVEN'S GOT MORE CASINOS THAN MINNESOTA'S GOT LAKES. AND CASINOS HAVE THIS THING CALLED AN AIR GAP.
THEY OPERATE ON A CLOSED CIRCUIT. ALL DATA ENTERS AND EXITS THE PHYSICAL BUILDING THROUGH THUMB DRIVES.
A FEW MONTHS AGO, SOMEONE SNUCK A FAKE THUMB DRIVE INTO THE WILD WEST CASINO. COMPROMISED THE WHOLE SYSTEM.
HEH... NIGHTWING...
ALL THE CAMERAS AND ASSAULT RIFLES IN THE WORLD COULDN'T PROTECT THEM.
NIGHTWING?
WHAT?
HOLD ON. YOU'VE GOT SOME... THERE.
OH... THANKS.

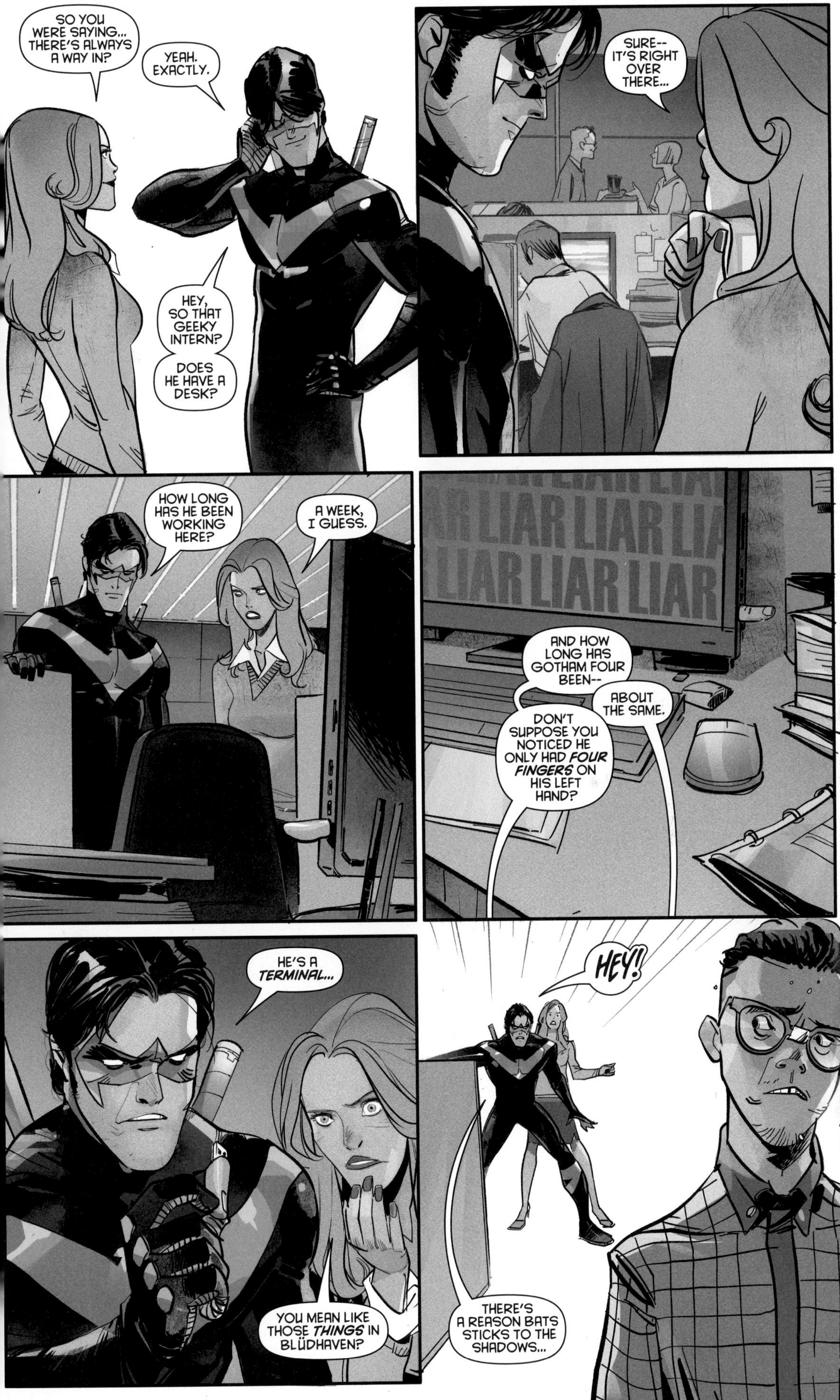
SO YOU WERE SAYING... THERE'S ALWAYS A WAY IN?
YEAH. EXACTLY.
HEY, SO THAT GEEKY INTERN?
DOES HE HAVE A DESK?
SURE-- IT'S RIGHT OVER THERE...
HOW LONG HAS HE BEEN WORKING HERE?
A WEEK, I GUESS.
LIAR LIAR LIAR
AND HOW LONG HAS GOTHAM FOUR BEEN--
ABOUT THE SAME.
DON'T SUPPOSE YOU NOTICED HE ONLY HAD FOUR FINGERS ON HIS LEFT HAND?
HE'S A TERMINAL...
YOU MEAN LIKE THOSE THINGS IN BLÜDHAVEN?
HEY!
THERE'S A REASON BATS STICKS TO THE SHADOWS...

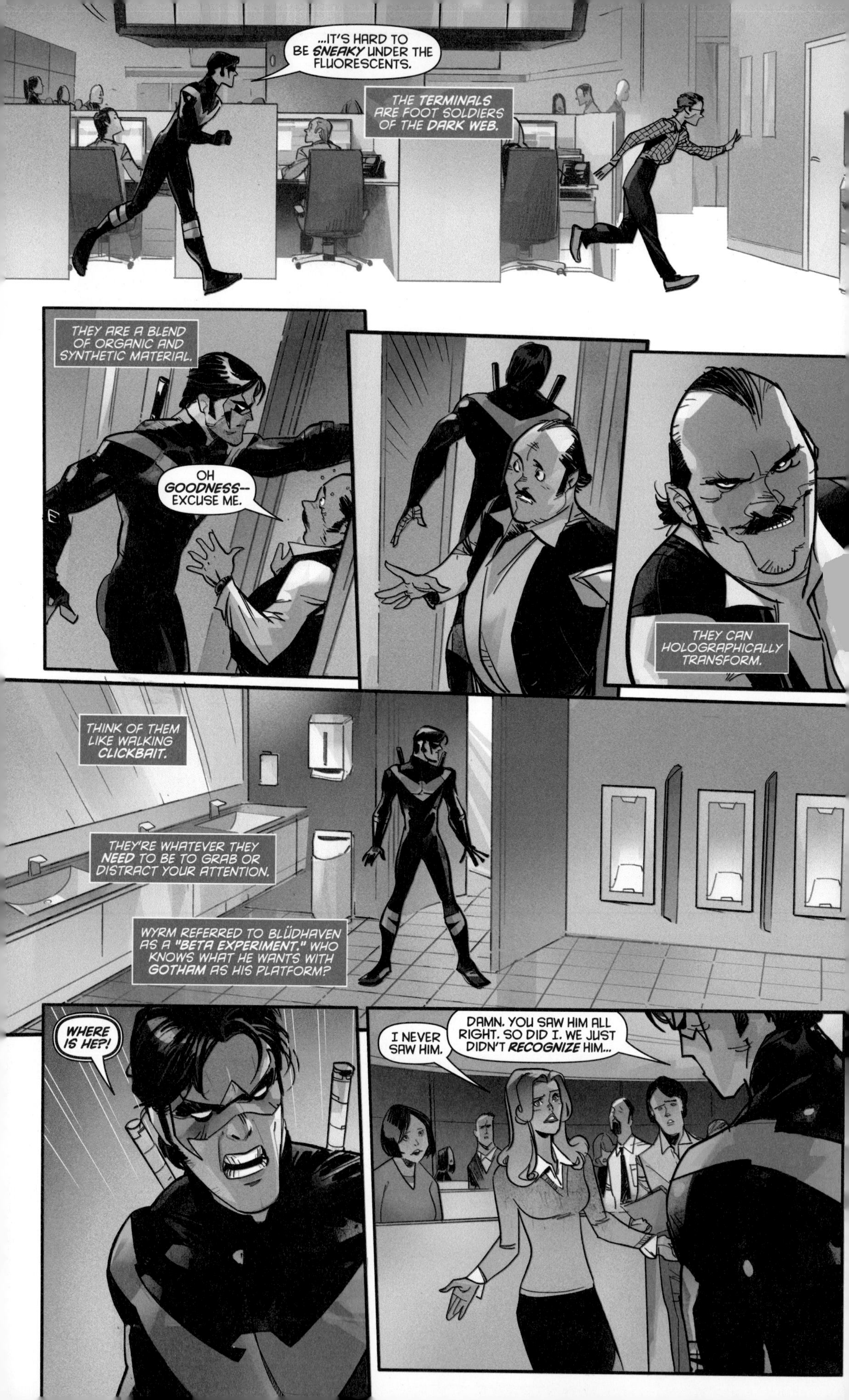

...IT'S HARD TO BE SNEAKY UNDER THE FLUORESCENTS.
THE TERMINALS ARE FOOT SOLDIERS OF THE DARK WEB.
THEY ARE A BLEND OF ORGANIC AND SYNTHETIC MATERIAL.
OH GOODNESS-- EXCUSE ME.
THEY CAN HOLOGRAPHICALLY TRANSFORM.
THINK OF THEM LIKE WALKING CLICKBAIT.
THEY'RE WHATEVER THEY NEED TO BE TO GRAB OR DISTRACT YOUR ATTENTION.
WYRM REFERRED TO BLÜDHAVEN AS A "BETA EXPERIMENT." WHO KNOWS WHAT HE WANTS WITH GOTHAM AS HIS PLATFORM?
WHERE IS HE?!
I NEVER SAW HIM.
DAMN. YOU SAW HIM ALL RIGHT. SO DID I. WE JUST DIDN'T RECOGNIZE HIM...

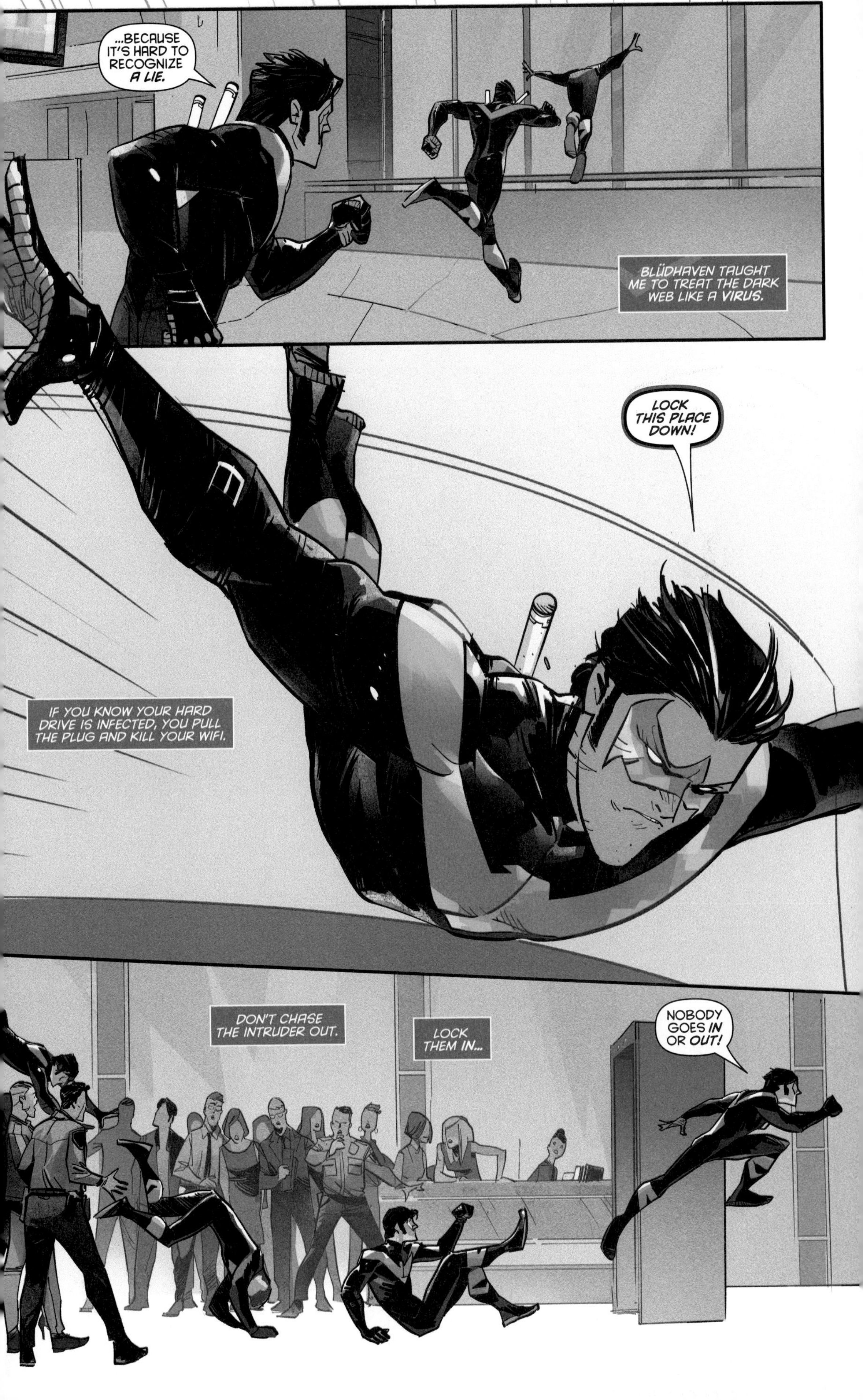
...BECAUSE IT'S HARD TO RECOGNIZE *A LIE.*
BLÜDHAVEN TAUGHT ME TO TREAT THE DARK WEB LIKE A *VIRUS.*
LOCK THIS PLACE DOWN!
IF YOU KNOW YOUR HARD DRIVE IS INFECTED, YOU PULL THE PLUG AND KILL YOUR WIFI.
DON'T CHASE THE INTRUDER OUT.
LOCK THEM IN...
NOBODY GOES *IN* OR *OUT!*

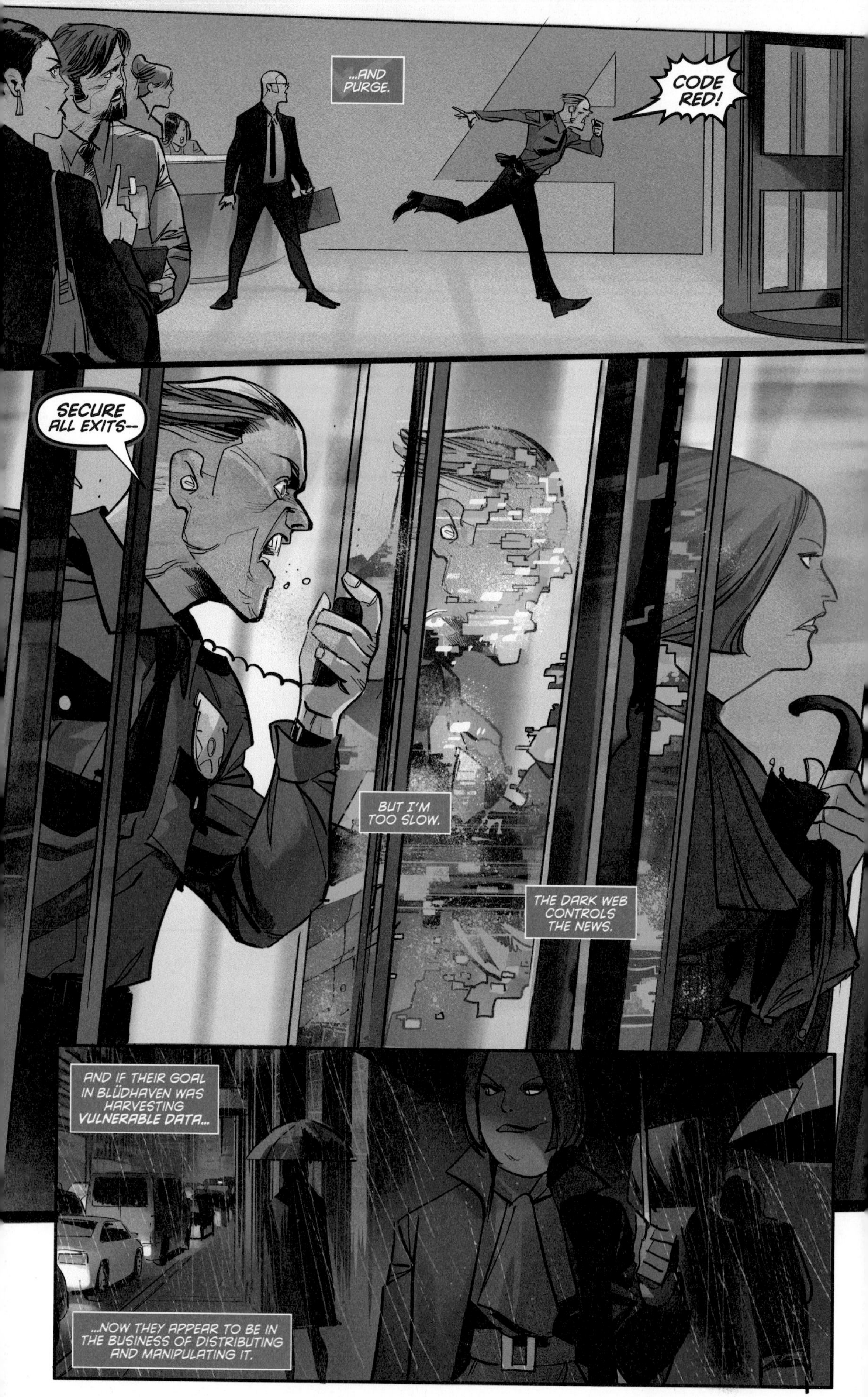
...AND PURGE.
CODE RED!
SECURE ALL EXITS--
BUT I'M TOO SLOW.
THE DARK WEB CONTROLS THE NEWS.
AND IF THEIR GOAL IN BLÜDHAVEN WAS HARVESTING VULNERABLE DATA...
...NOW THEY APPEAR TO BE IN THE BUSINESS OF DISTRIBUTING AND MANIPULATING IT.

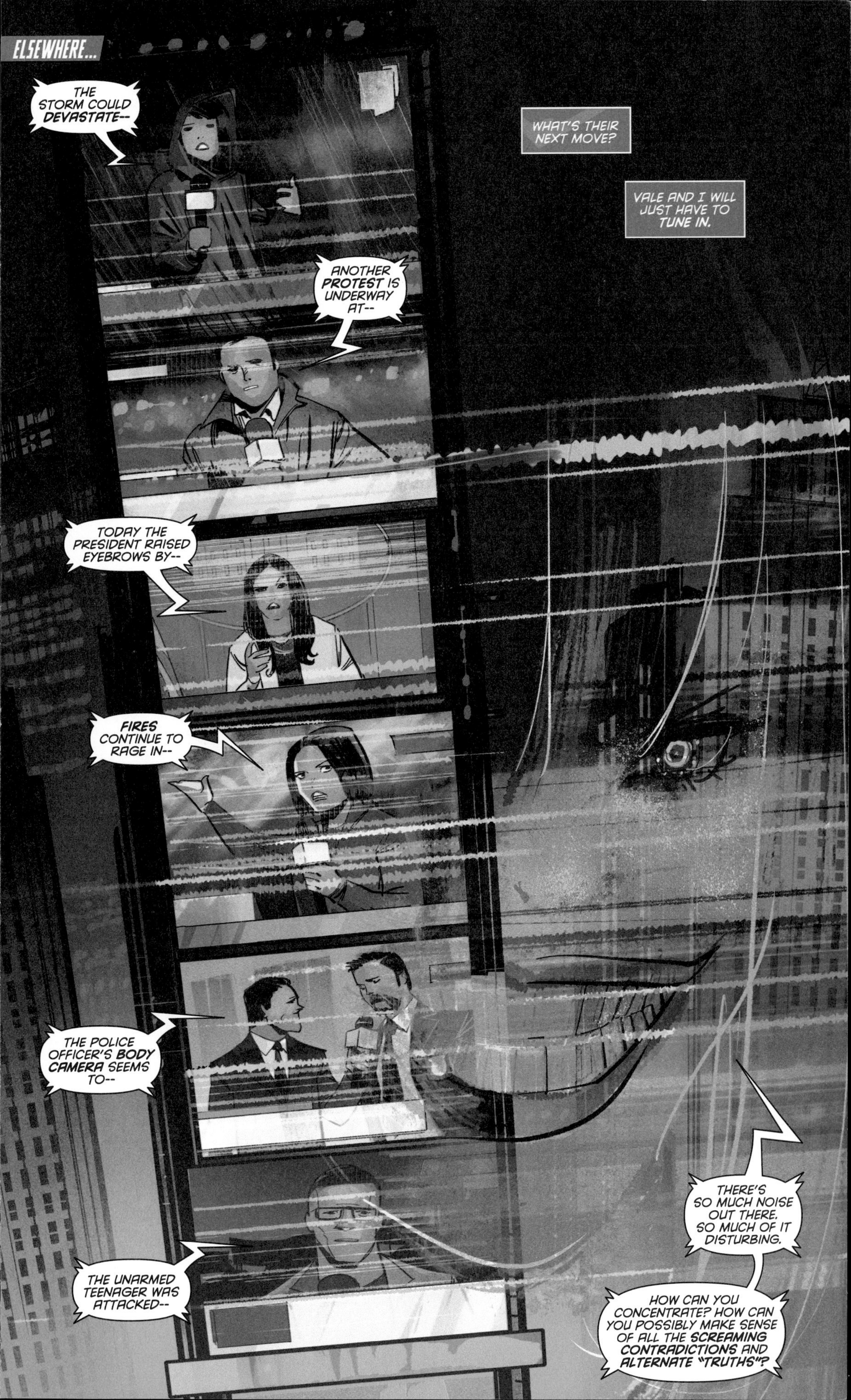
ELSEWHERE...
THE STORM COULD DEVASTATE--
WHAT'S THEIR NEXT MOVE?
VALE AND I WILL JUST HAVE TO TUNE IN.
ANOTHER PROTEST IS UNDERWAY AT--
TODAY THE PRESIDENT RAISED EYEBROWS BY--
FIRES CONTINUE TO RAGE IN--
THE POLICE OFFICER'S BODY CAMERA SEEMS TO--
THE UNARMED TEENAGER WAS ATTACKED--
THERE'S SO MUCH NOISE OUT THERE. SO MUCH OF IT DISTURBING.
HOW CAN YOU CONCENTRATE? HOW CAN YOU POSSIBLY MAKE SENSE OF ALL THE SCREAMING CONTRADICTIONS AND ALTERNATE "TRUTHS"?

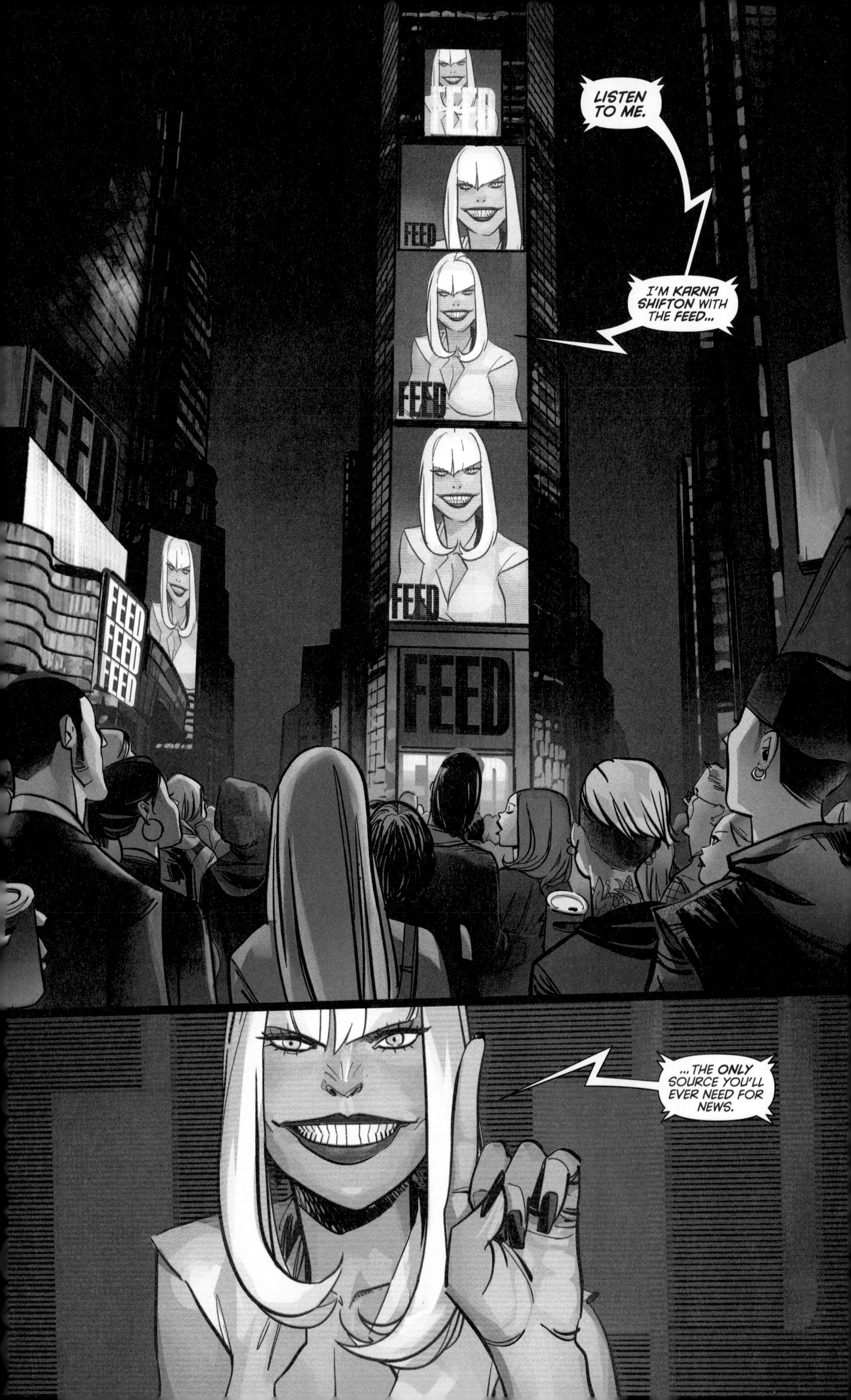
LISTEN TO ME.
I'M KARNA SHIFTON WITH THE FEED...
...THE ONLY SOURCE YOU'LL EVER NEED FOR NEWS.

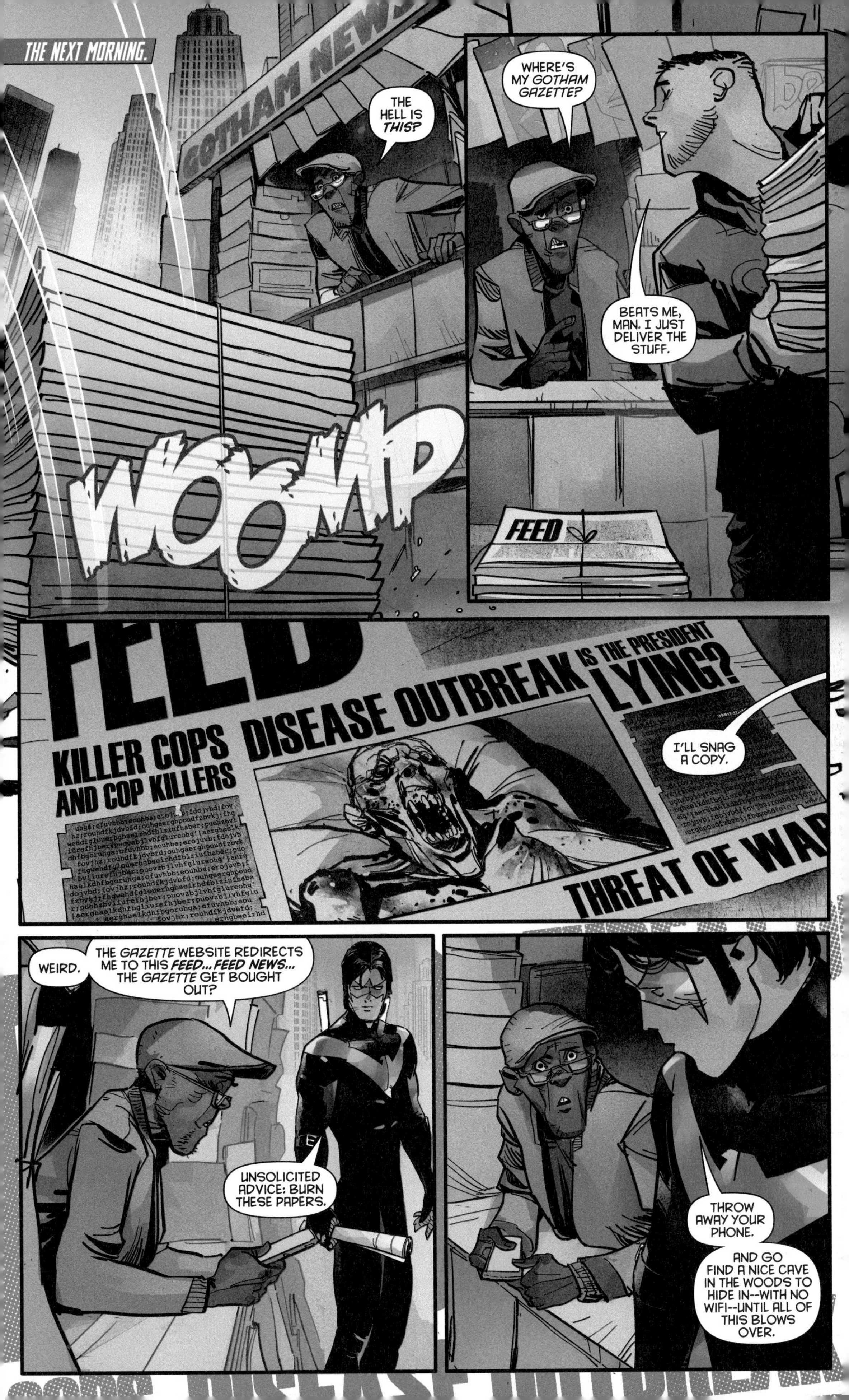
THE NEXT MORNING.
GOTHAM NEW
THE HELL IS *THIS?*
WOOMP
WHERE'S MY *GOTHAM GAZETTE?*
BEATS ME, MAN. I JUST DELIVER THE STUFF.
FEED
FEED
KILLER COPS AND COP KILLERS
DISEASE OUTBREAK
IS THE PRESIDENT LYING?
THREAT OF WA
I'LL SNAG A COPY.
WEIRD.
THE *GAZETTE* WEBSITE REDIRECTS ME TO THIS *FEED... FEED NEWS...* THE *GAZETTE* GET BOUGHT OUT?
UNSOLICITED ADVICE: BURN THESE PAPERS.
THROW AWAY YOUR PHONE.
AND GO FIND A NICE CAVE IN THE WOODS TO HIDE IN--WITH NO WIFI--UNTIL ALL OF THIS BLOWS OVER.

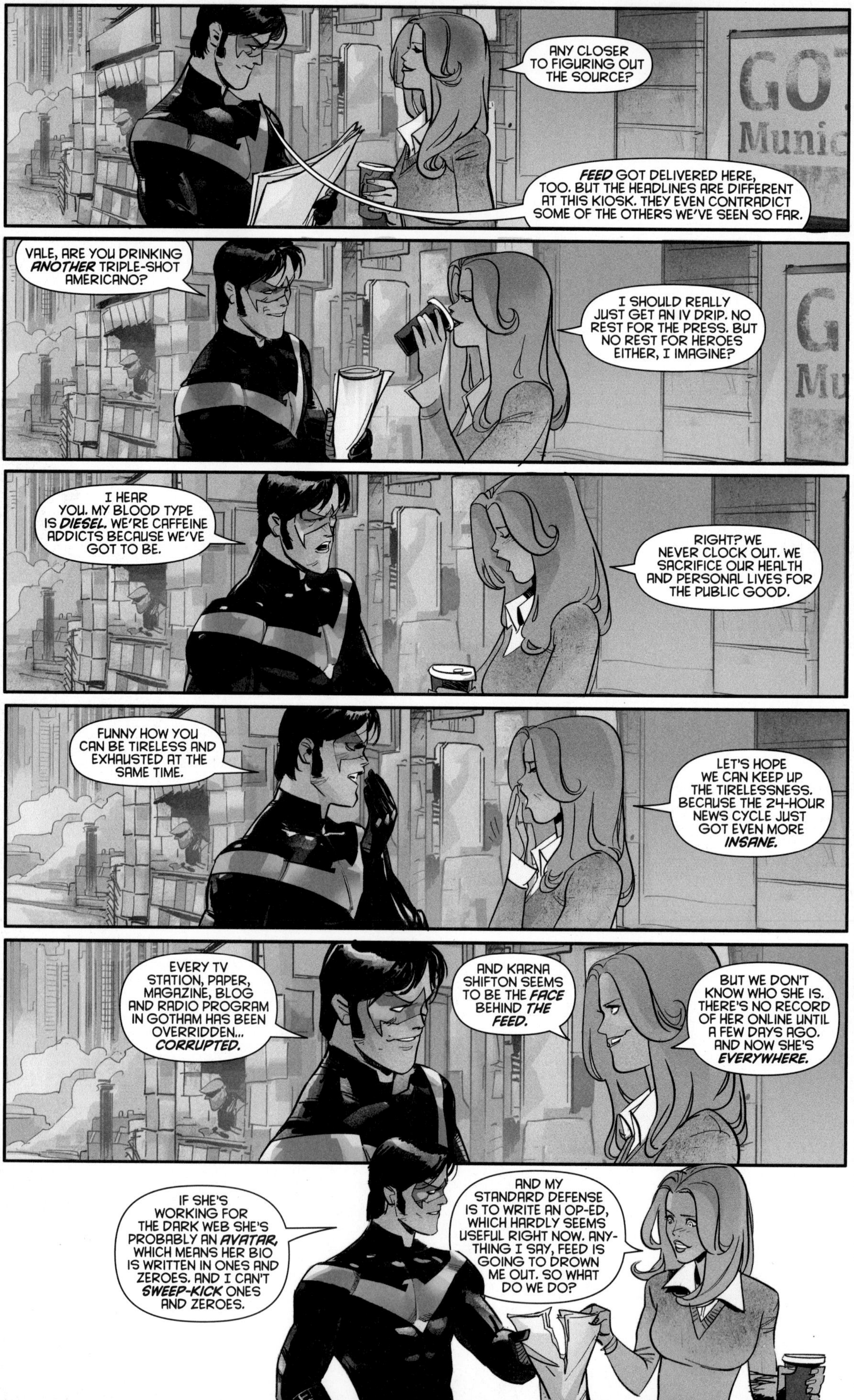
ANY CLOSER TO FIGURING OUT THE SOURCE?
FEED GOT DELIVERED HERE, TOO. BUT THE HEADLINES ARE DIFFERENT AT THIS KIOSK. THEY EVEN CONTRADICT SOME OF THE OTHERS WE'VE SEEN SO FAR.
VALE, ARE YOU DRINKING *ANOTHER* TRIPLE-SHOT AMERICANO?
I SHOULD REALLY JUST GET AN IV DRIP. NO REST FOR THE PRESS. BUT NO REST FOR HEROES EITHER, I IMAGINE?
I HEAR YOU. MY BLOOD TYPE IS *DIESEL.* WE'RE CAFFEINE ADDICTS BECAUSE WE'VE GOT TO BE.
RIGHT? WE NEVER CLOCK OUT. WE SACRIFICE OUR HEALTH AND PERSONAL LIVES FOR THE PUBLIC GOOD.
FUNNY HOW YOU CAN BE TIRELESS AND EXHAUSTED AT THE SAME TIME.
LET'S HOPE WE CAN KEEP UP THE TIRELESSNESS. BECAUSE THE 24-HOUR NEWS CYCLE JUST GOT EVEN MORE *INSANE.*
EVERY TV STATION, PAPER, MAGAZINE, BLOG AND RADIO PROGRAM IN GOTHAM HAS BEEN OVERRIDDEN... *CORRUPTED.*
AND KARNA SHIFTON SEEMS TO BE THE *FACE* BEHIND *THE FEED.*
BUT WE DON'T KNOW WHO SHE IS. THERE'S NO RECORD OF HER ONLINE UNTIL A FEW DAYS AGO. AND NOW SHE'S *EVERYWHERE.*
IF SHE'S WORKING FOR THE DARK WEB SHE'S PROBABLY AN *AVATAR,* WHICH MEANS HER BIO IS WRITTEN IN ONES AND ZEROES. AND I CAN'T *SWEEP-KICK* ONES AND ZEROES.
AND MY STANDARD DEFENSE IS TO WRITE AN OP-ED, WHICH HARDLY SEEMS USEFUL RIGHT NOW. ANY-THING I SAY, FEED IS GOING TO DROWN ME OUT. SO WHAT DO WE DO?

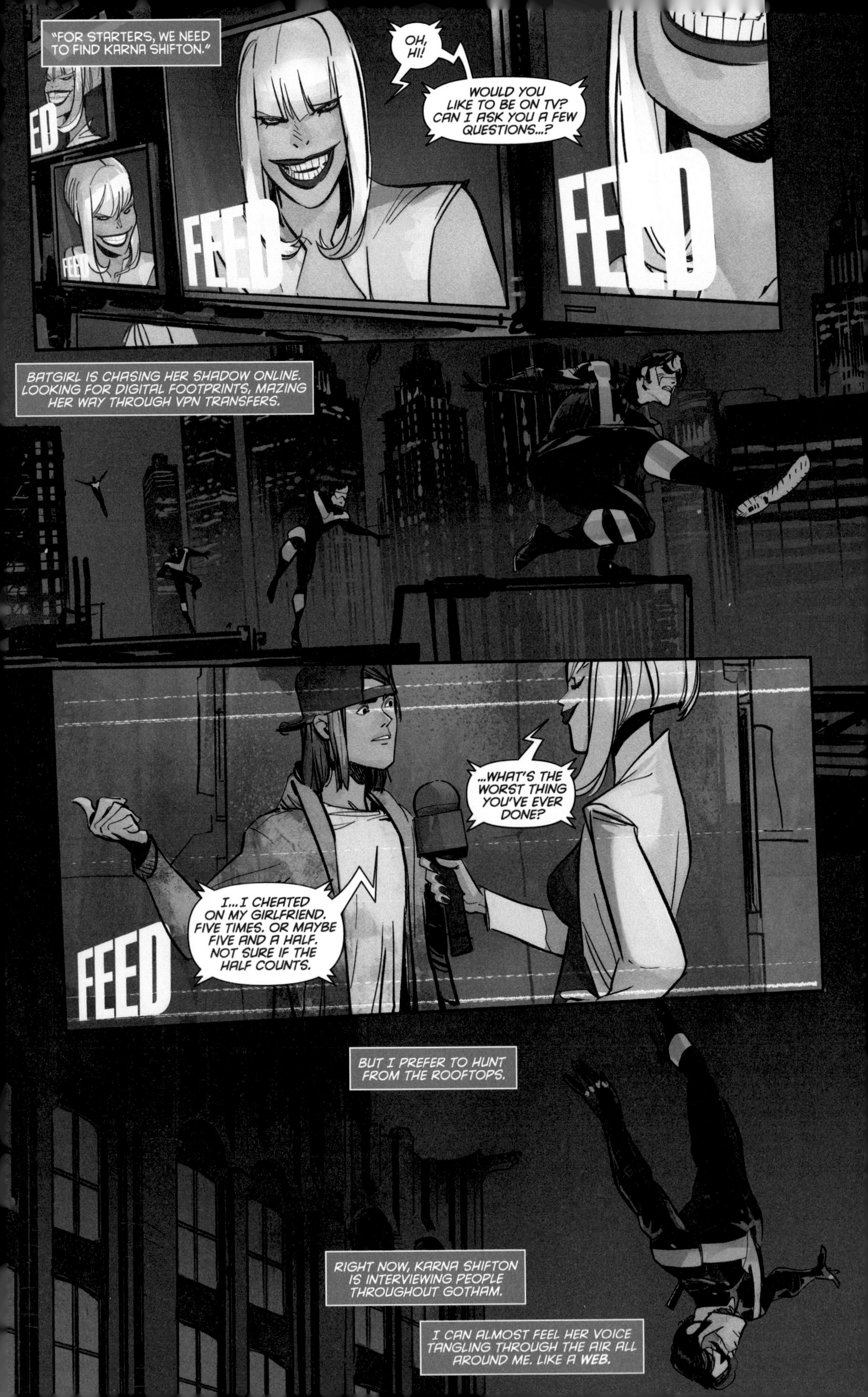
"FOR STARTERS, WE NEED TO FIND KARNA SHIFTON."
FEED
OH, HI!
WOULD YOU LIKE TO BE ON TV? CAN I ASK YOU A FEW QUESTIONS...?
FEED
BATGIRL IS CHASING HER SHADOW ONLINE. LOOKING FOR DIGITAL FOOTPRINTS, MAZING HER WAY THROUGH VPN TRANSFERS.
...WHAT'S THE WORST THING YOU'VE EVER DONE?
I...I CHEATED ON MY GIRLFRIEND. FIVE TIMES. OR MAYBE FIVE AND A HALF. NOT SURE IF THE HALF COUNTS.
FEED
BUT I PREFER TO HUNT FROM THE ROOFTOPS.
RIGHT NOW, KARNA SHIFTON IS INTERVIEWING PEOPLE THROUGHOUT GOTHAM.
I CAN ALMOST FEEL HER VOICE TANGLING THROUGH THE AIR ALL AROUND ME. LIKE A WEB.

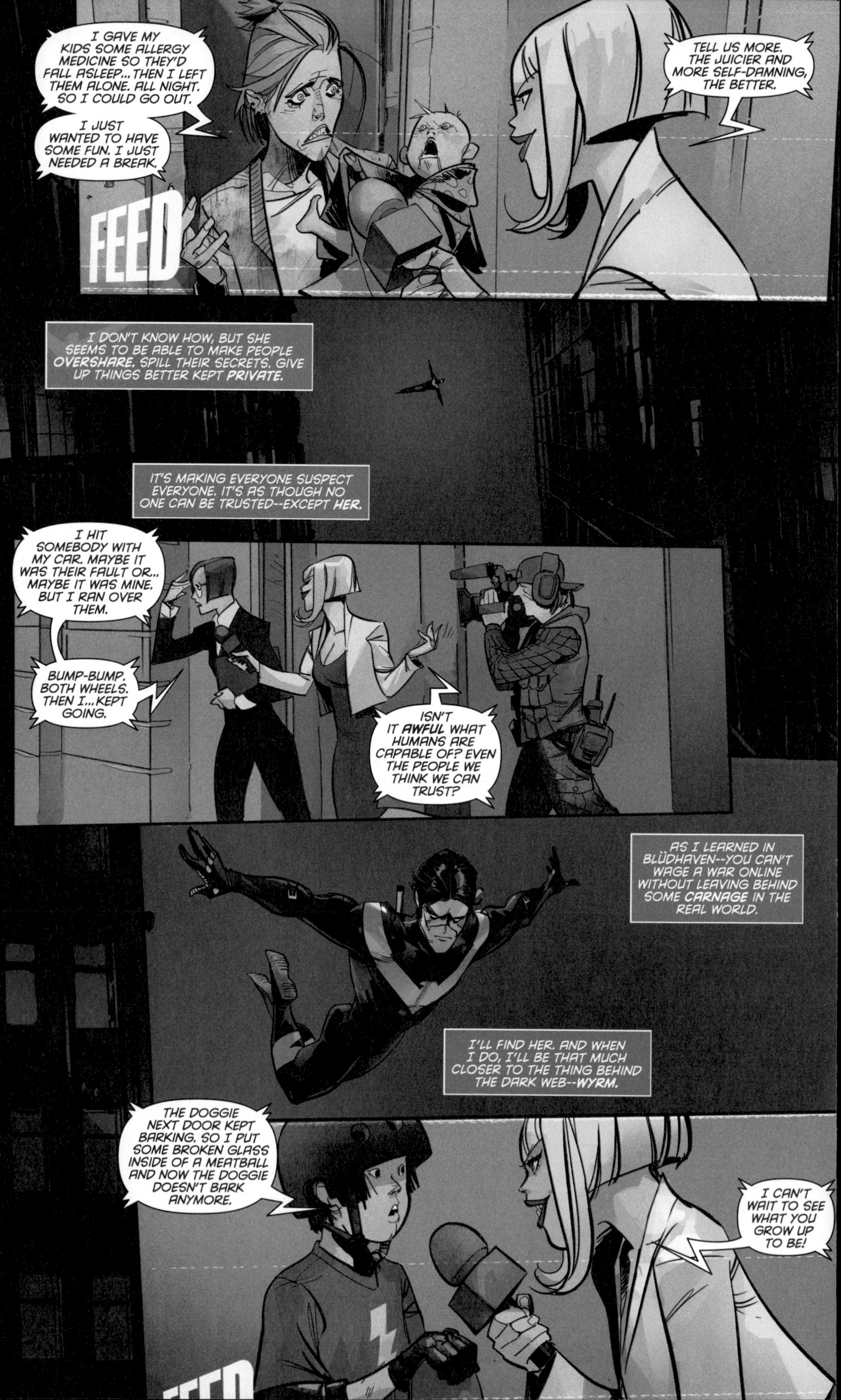

I GAVE MY KIDS SOME ALLERGY MEDICINE SO THEY'D FALL ASLEEP... THEN I LEFT THEM ALONE. ALL NIGHT. SO I COULD GO OUT.
I JUST WANTED TO HAVE SOME FUN. I JUST NEEDED A BREAK.
TELL US MORE. THE JUICIER AND MORE SELF-DAMNING, THE BETTER.
FEED
I DON'T KNOW HOW, BUT SHE SEEMS TO BE ABLE TO MAKE PEOPLE OVERSHARE. SPILL THEIR SECRETS. GIVE UP THINGS BETTER KEPT PRIVATE.
IT'S MAKING EVERYONE SUSPECT EVERYONE. IT'S AS THOUGH NO ONE CAN BE TRUSTED--EXCEPT HER.
I HIT SOMEBODY WITH MY CAR. MAYBE IT WAS THEIR FAULT OR... MAYBE IT WAS MINE. BUT I RAN OVER THEM.
BUMP-BUMP. BOTH WHEELS. THEN I...KEPT GOING.
ISN'T IT AWFUL WHAT HUMANS ARE CAPABLE OF? EVEN THE PEOPLE WE THINK WE CAN TRUST?
AS I LEARNED IN BLÜDHAVEN--YOU CAN'T WAGE A WAR ONLINE WITHOUT LEAVING BEHIND SOME CARNAGE IN THE REAL WORLD.
I'LL FIND HER. AND WHEN I DO, I'LL BE THAT MUCH CLOSER TO THE THING BEHIND THE DARK WEB--WYRM.
THE DOGGIE NEXT DOOR KEPT BARKING. SO I PUT SOME BROKEN GLASS INSIDE OF A MEATBALL AND NOW THE DOGGIE DOESN'T BARK ANYMORE.
I CAN'T WAIT TO SEE WHAT YOU GROW UP TO BE!

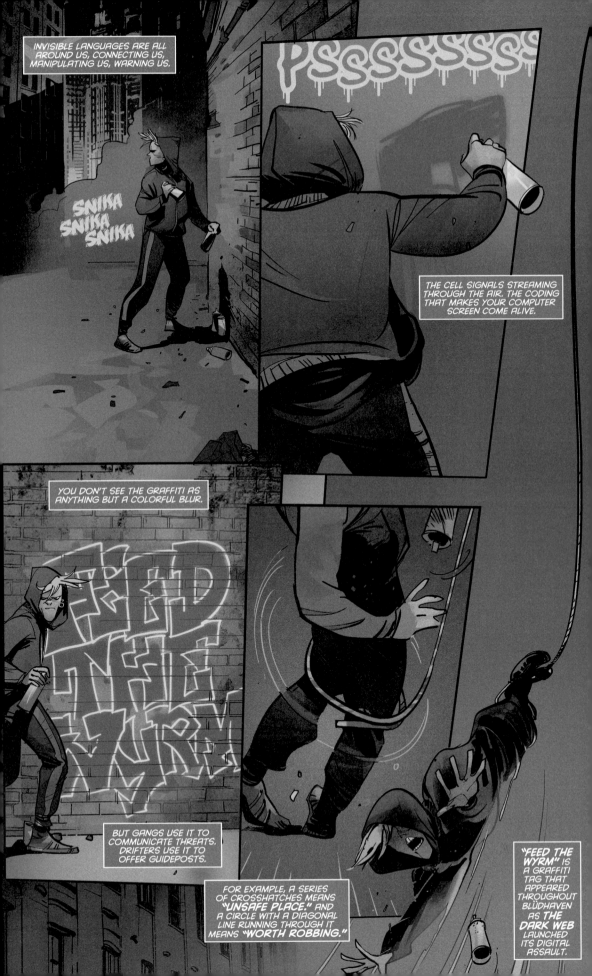

INVISIBLE LANGUAGES ARE ALL AROUND US, CONNECTING US, MANIPULATING US, WARNING US.

PSSSSSSS

SNIKA
SNIKA
SNIKA

THE CELL SIGNALS STREAMING THROUGH THE AIR. THE CODING THAT MAKES YOUR COMPUTER SCREEN COME ALIVE.

YOU DON'T SEE THE GRAFFITI AS ANYTHING BUT A COLORFUL BLUR.

BUT GANGS USE IT TO COMMUNICATE THREATS. DRIFTERS USE IT TO OFFER GUIDEPOSTS.

FOR EXAMPLE, A SERIES OF CROSSHATCHES MEANS "UNSAFE PLACE." AND A CIRCLE WITH A DIAGONAL LINE RUNNING THROUGH IT MEANS "WORTH ROBBING."

"FEED THE WYRM" IS A GRAFFITI TAG THAT APPEARED THROUGHOUT BLÜDHAVEN AS THE DARK WEB LAUNCHED ITS DIGITAL ASSAULT.

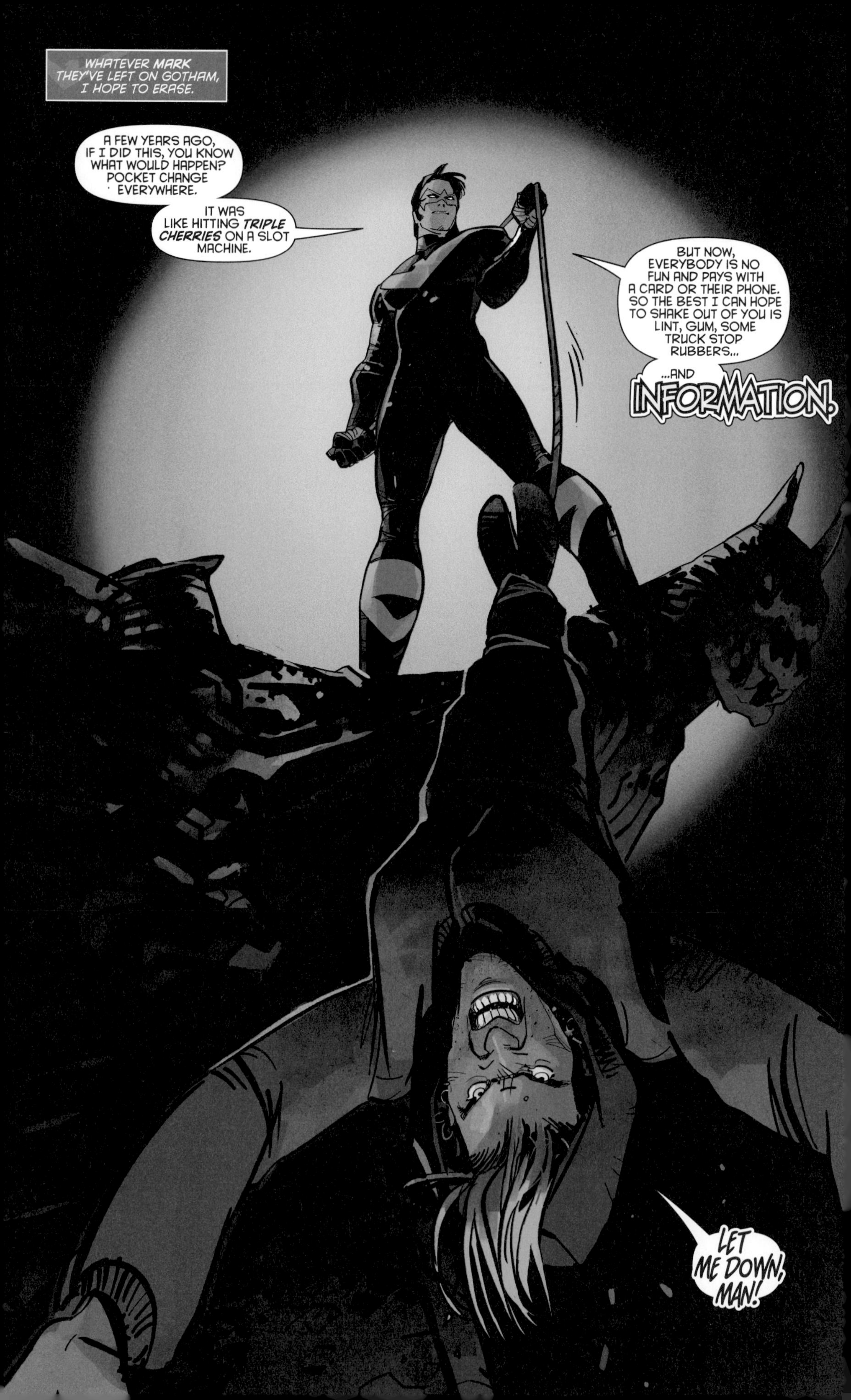
WHATEVER MARK THEY'VE LEFT ON GOTHAM, I HOPE TO ERASE.
A FEW YEARS AGO, IF I DID THIS, YOU KNOW WHAT WOULD HAPPEN? POCKET CHANGE EVERYWHERE.
IT WAS LIKE HITTING TRIPLE CHERRIES ON A SLOT MACHINE.
BUT NOW, EVERYBODY IS NO FUN AND PAYS WITH A CARD OR THEIR PHONE. SO THE BEST I CAN HOPE TO SHAKE OUT OF YOU IS LINT, GUM, SOME TRUCK STOP RUBBERS...
...AND
INFORMATION.
LET ME DOWN, MAN!

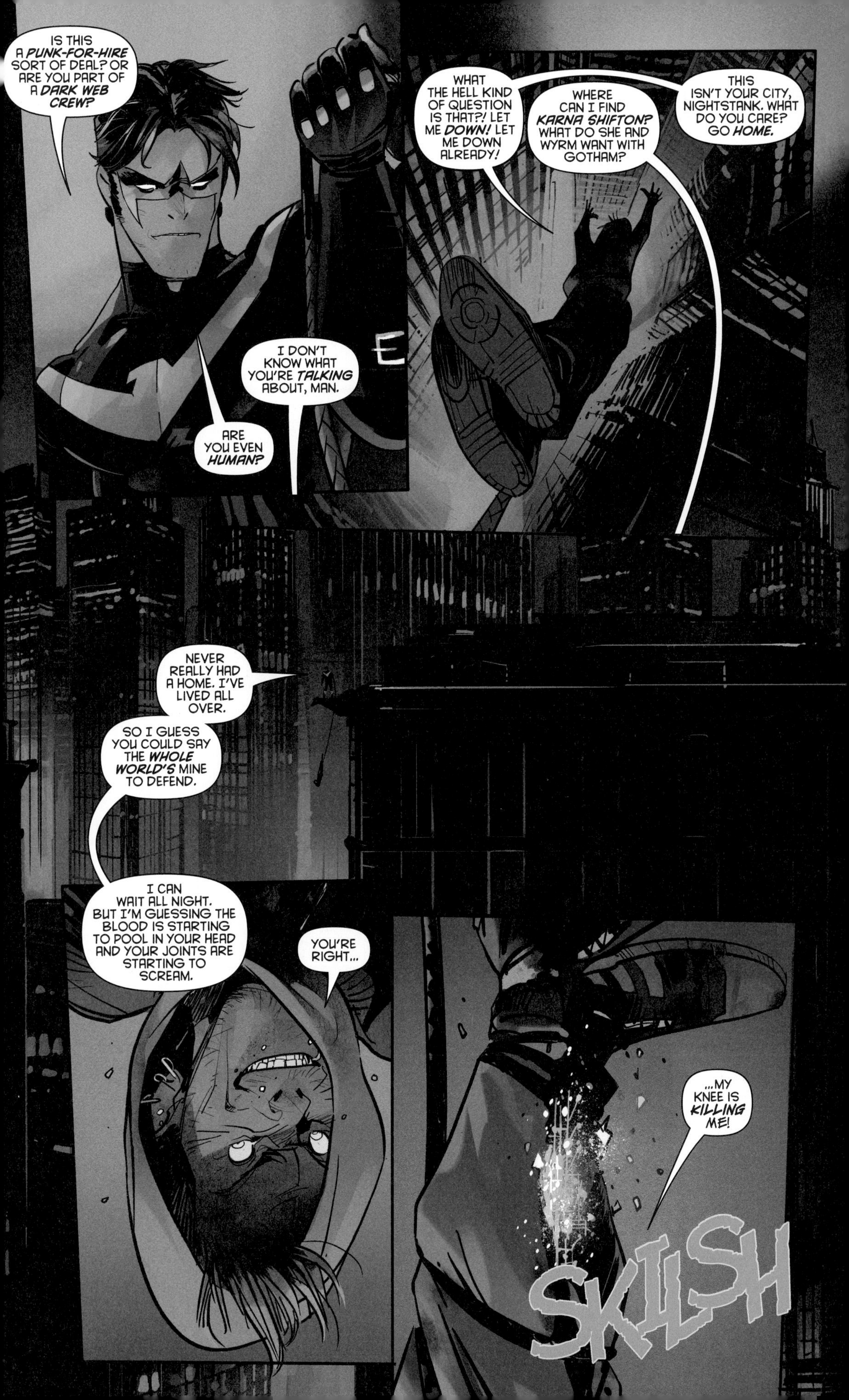
IS THIS A PUNK-FOR-HIRE SORT OF DEAL? OR ARE YOU PART OF A DARK WEB CREW?
I DON'T KNOW WHAT YOU'RE TALKING ABOUT, MAN.
ARE YOU EVEN HUMAN?
WHAT THE HELL KIND OF QUESTION IS THAT?! LET ME DOWN! LET ME DOWN ALREADY!
WHERE CAN I FIND KARNA SHIFTON? WHAT DO SHE AND WYRM WANT WITH GOTHAM?
THIS ISN'T YOUR CITY, NIGHTSTANK. WHAT DO YOU CARE? GO HOME.
NEVER REALLY HAD A HOME. I'VE LIVED ALL OVER.
SO I GUESS YOU COULD SAY THE WHOLE WORLD'S MINE TO DEFEND.
I CAN WAIT ALL NIGHT. BUT I'M GUESSING THE BLOOD IS STARTING TO POOL IN YOUR HEAD AND YOUR JOINTS ARE STARTING TO SCREAM.
YOU'RE RIGHT...
...MY KNEE IS KILLING ME!
SKLSH

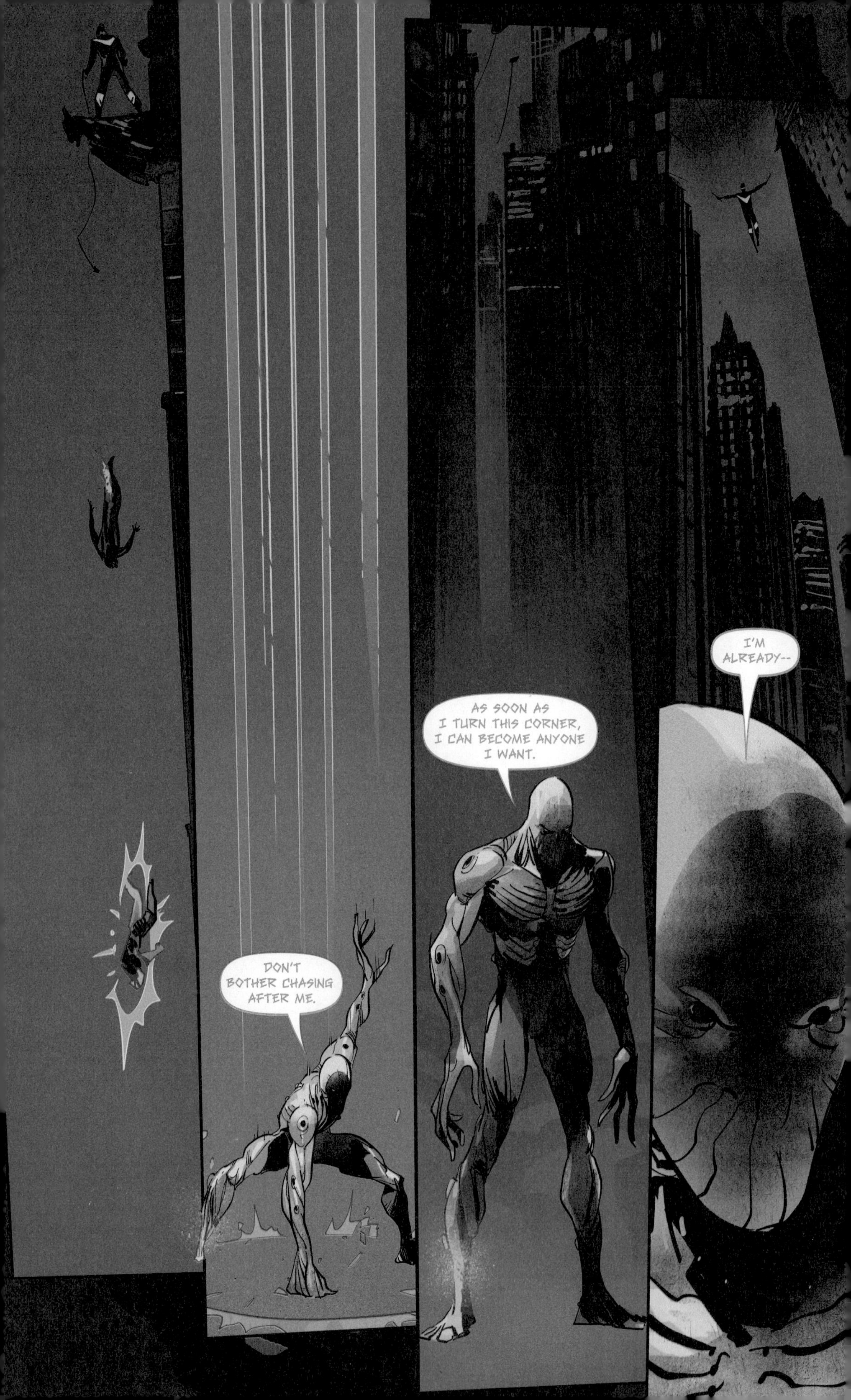
DON'T BOTHER CHASING AFTER ME.
AS SOON AS I TURN THIS CORNER, I CAN BECOME ANYONE I WANT.
I'M ALREADY--

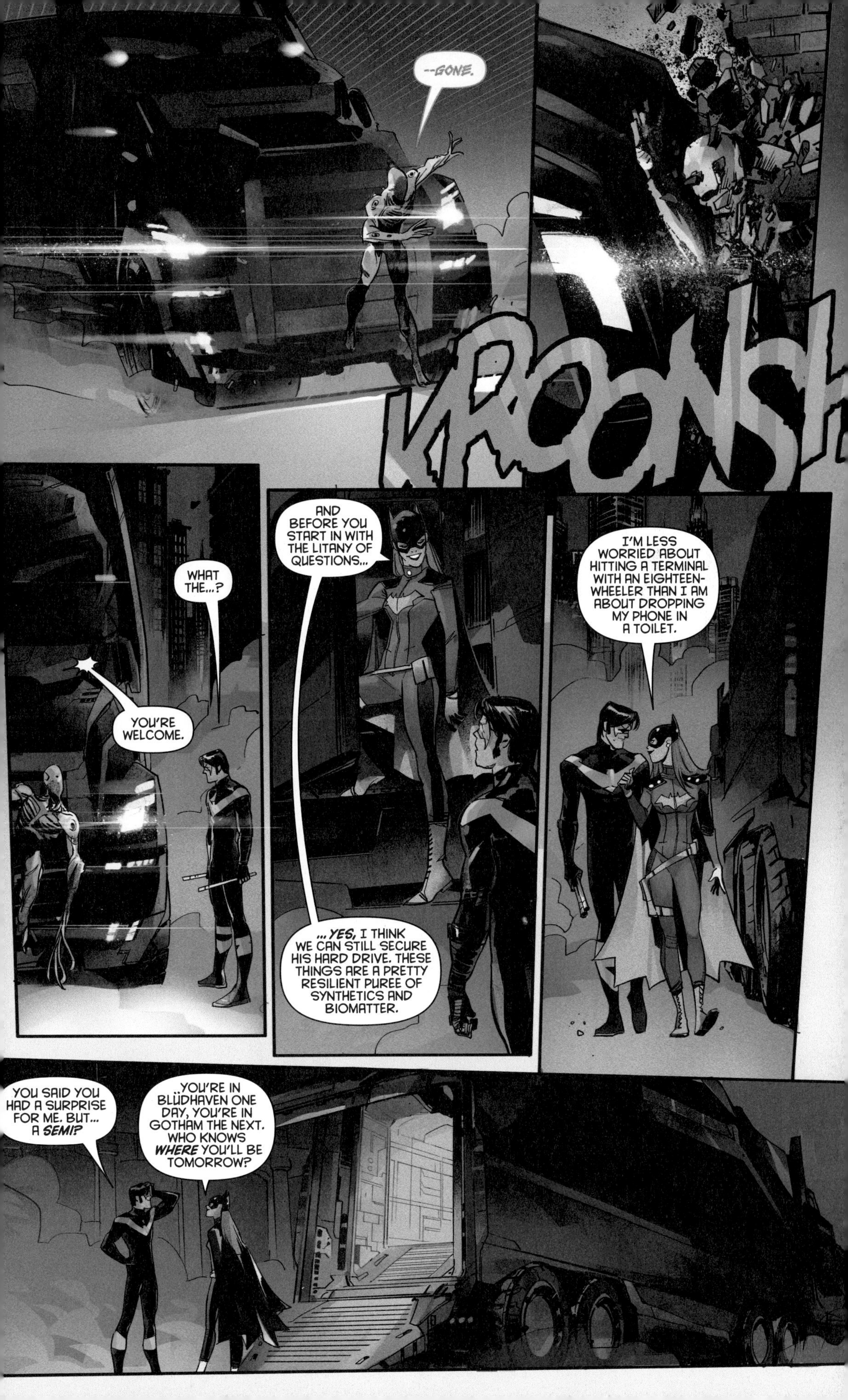
--GONE.
KROONSH
WHAT THE...?
YOU'RE WELCOME.
AND BEFORE YOU START IN WITH THE LITANY OF QUESTIONS...
...YES, I THINK WE CAN STILL SECURE HIS HARD DRIVE. THESE THINGS ARE A PRETTY RESILIENT PUREE OF SYNTHETICS AND BIOMATTER.
I'M LESS WORRIED ABOUT HITTING A TERMINAL WITH AN EIGHTEEN-WHEELER THAN I AM ABOUT DROPPING MY PHONE IN A TOILET.
YOU SAID YOU HAD A SURPRISE FOR ME. BUT... A SEMI?
...YOU'RE IN BLÜDHAVEN ONE DAY, YOU'RE IN GOTHAM THE NEXT. WHO KNOWS WHERE YOU'LL BE TOMORROW?

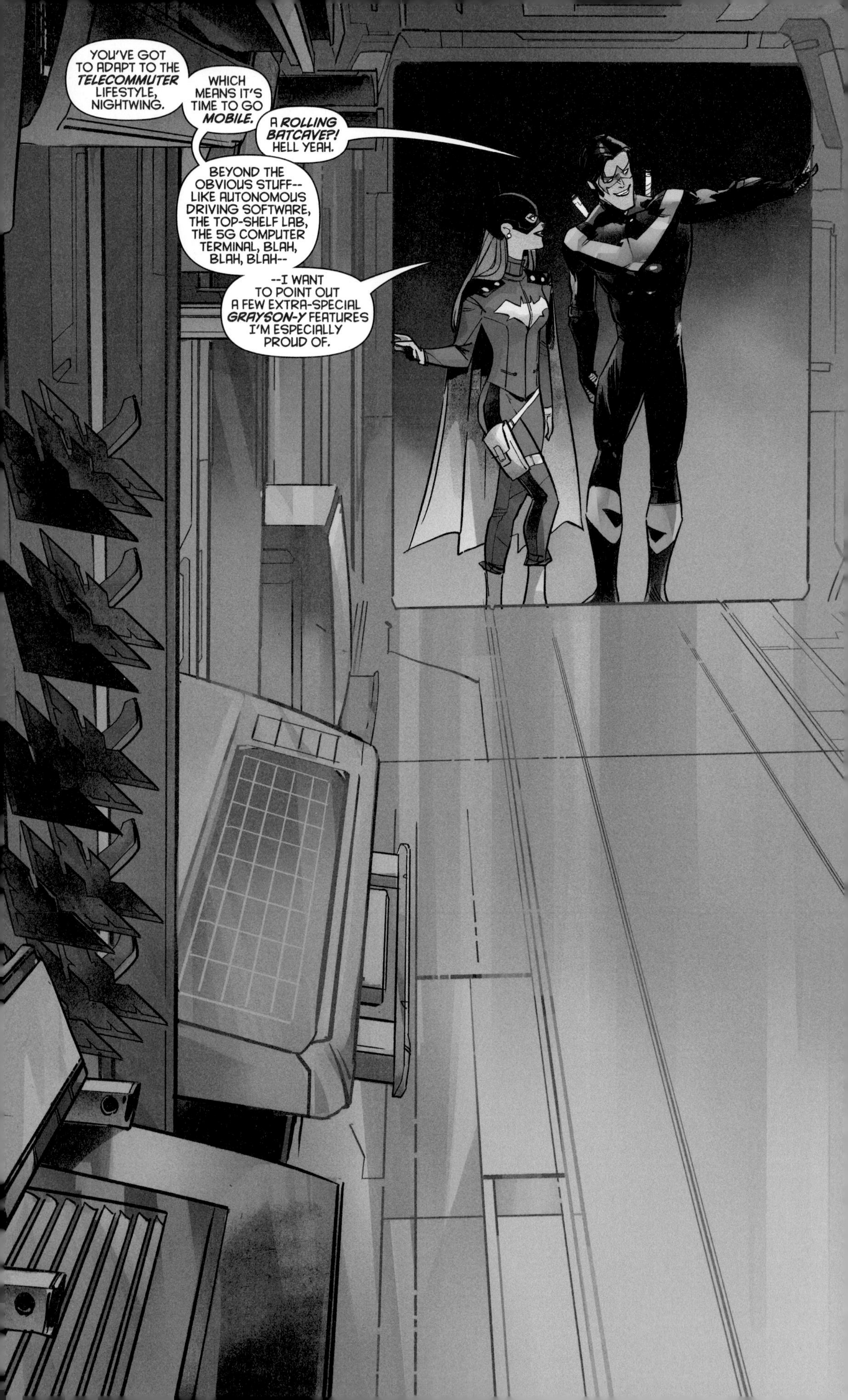
YOU'VE GOT TO ADAPT TO THE ***TELECOMMUTER*** LIFESTYLE, NIGHTWING.
WHICH MEANS IT'S TIME TO GO ***MOBILE.***
A ***ROLLING BATCAVE?!*** HELL YEAH.
BEYOND THE OBVIOUS STUFF-- LIKE AUTONOMOUS DRIVING SOFTWARE, THE TOP-SHELF LAB, THE 5G COMPUTER TERMINAL, BLAH, BLAH, BLAH--
--I WANT TO POINT OUT A FEW EXTRA-SPECIAL ***GRAYSON-Y*** FEATURES I'M ESPECIALLY PROUD OF.

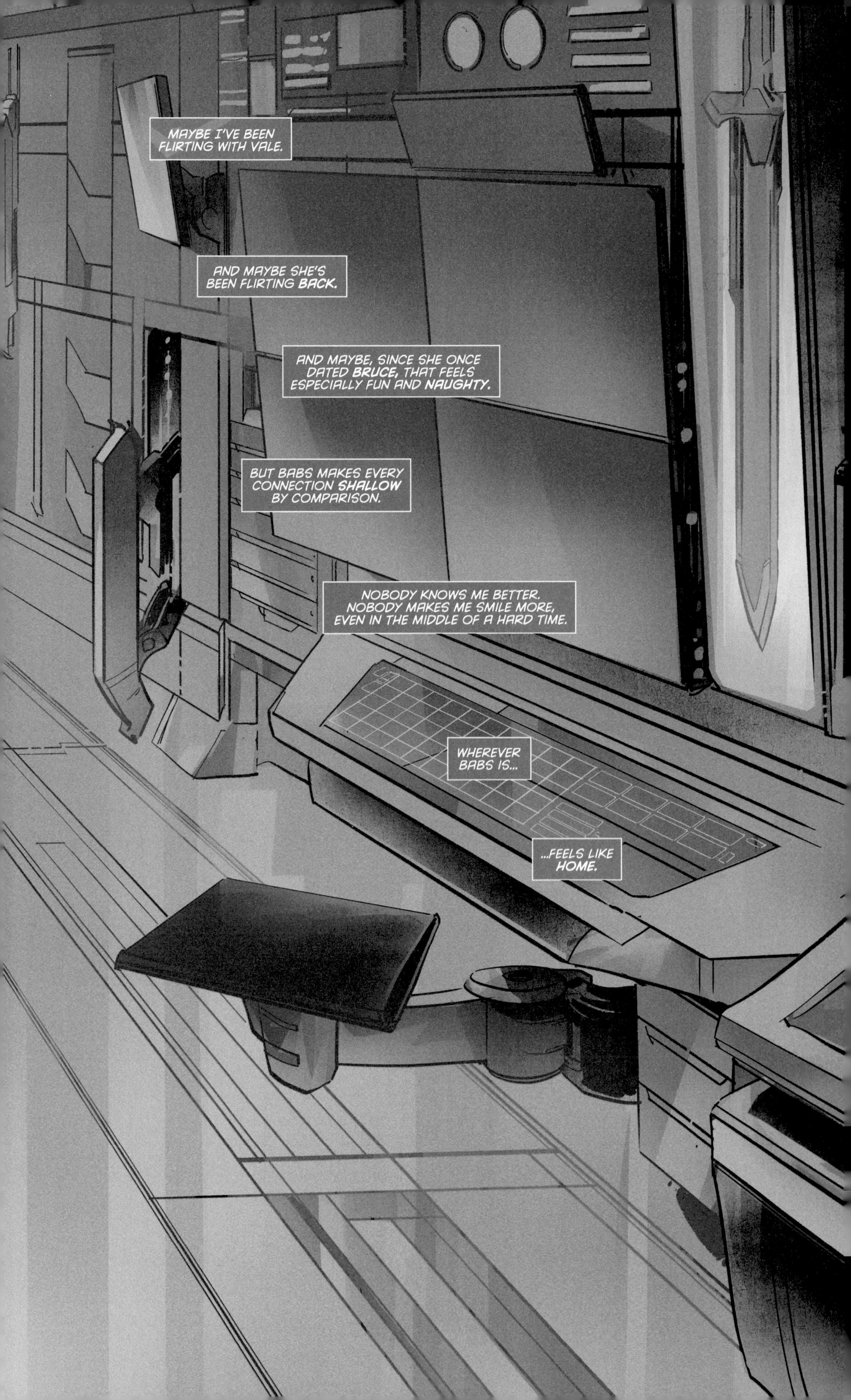
MAYBE I'VE BEEN FLIRTING WITH VALE.
AND MAYBE SHE'S BEEN FLIRTING BACK.
AND MAYBE, SINCE SHE ONCE DATED BRUCE, THAT FEELS ESPECIALLY FUN AND NAUGHTY.
BUT BABS MAKES EVERY CONNECTION SHALLOW BY COMPARISON.
NOBODY KNOWS ME BETTER. NOBODY MAKES ME SMILE MORE, EVEN IN THE MIDDLE OF A HARD TIME.
WHEREVER BABS IS...
...FEELS LIKE HOME.

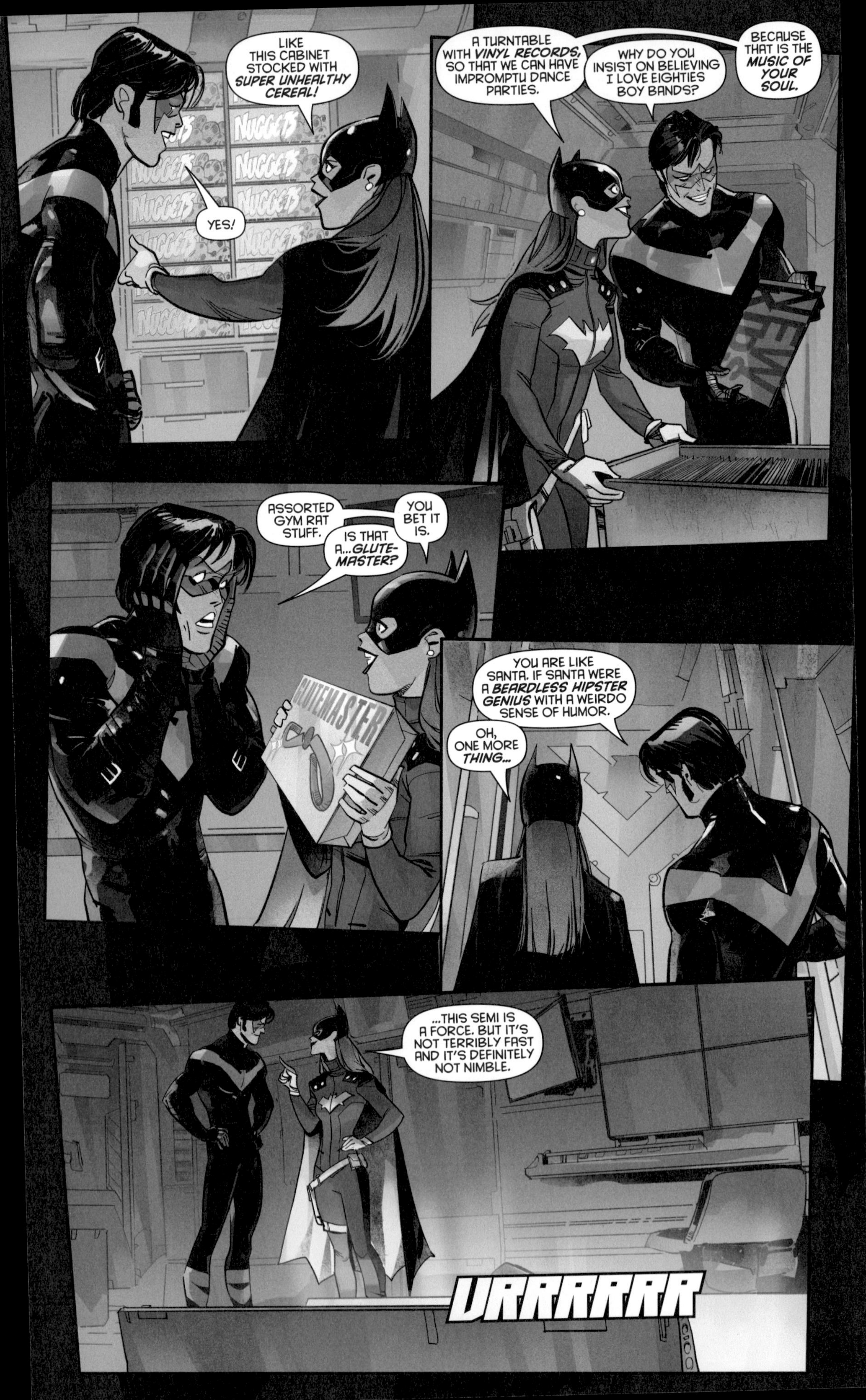
LIKE THIS CABINET STOCKED WITH SUPER UNHEALTHY CEREAL!
YES!
NUGGETS
A TURNTABLE WITH VINYL RECORDS, SO THAT WE CAN HAVE IMPROMPTU DANCE PARTIES.
WHY DO YOU INSIST ON BELIEVING I LOVE EIGHTIES BOY BANDS?
BECAUSE THAT IS THE MUSIC OF YOUR SOUL.
ASSORTED GYM RAT STUFF.
IS THAT A...GLUTE-MASTER?
YOU BET IT IS.
GLUTEMASTER
YOU ARE LIKE SANTA. IF SANTA WERE A BEARDLESS HIPSTER GENIUS WITH A WEIRDO SENSE OF HUMOR.
OH, ONE MORE THING...
...THIS SEMI IS A FORCE. BUT IT'S NOT TERRIBLY FAST AND IT'S DEFINITELY NOT NIMBLE.
URRRRRR

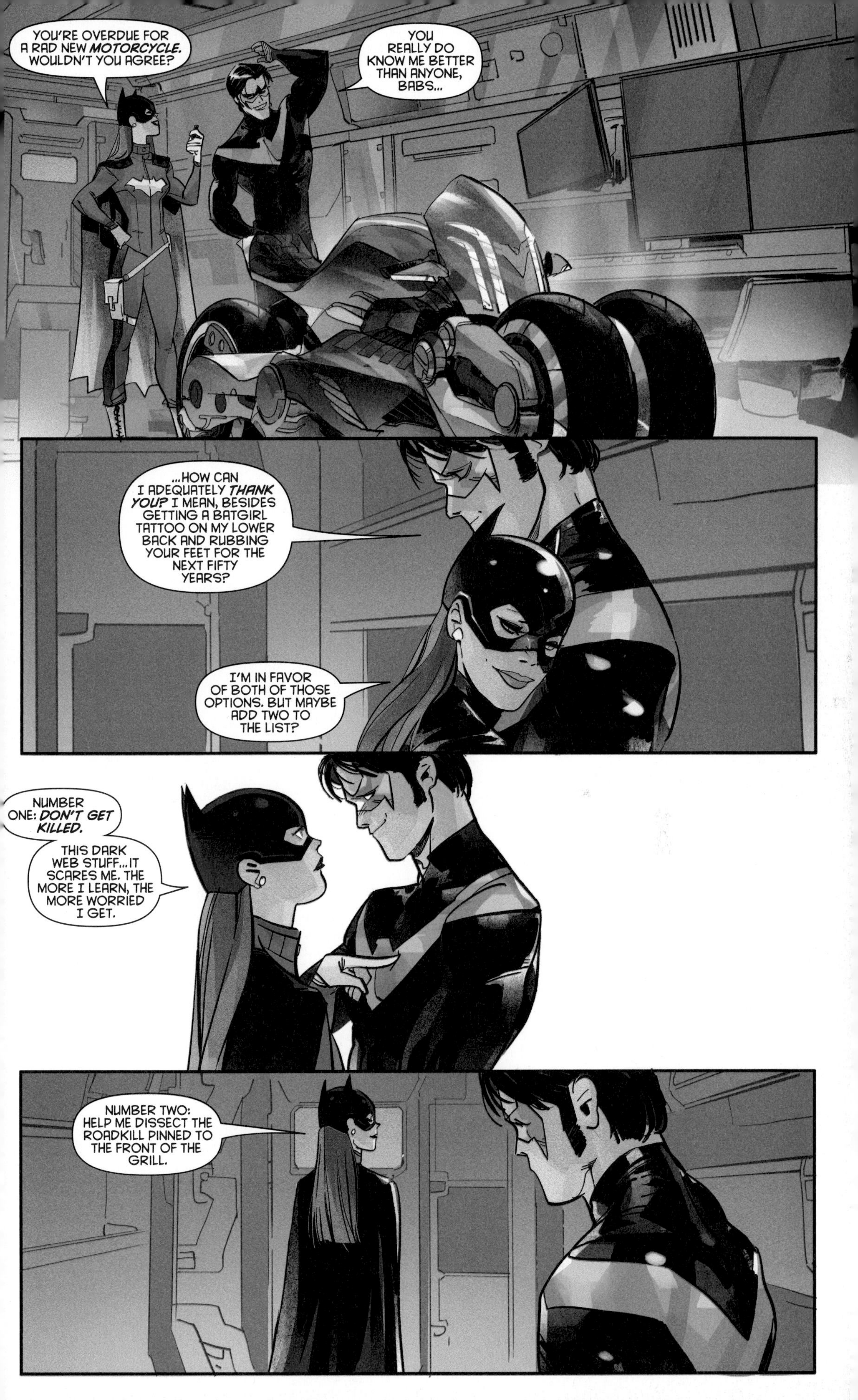
YOU'RE OVERDUE FOR A RAD NEW MOTORCYCLE. WOULDN'T YOU AGREE?
YOU REALLY DO KNOW ME BETTER THAN ANYONE, BABS...
...HOW CAN I ADEQUATELY THANK YOU? I MEAN, BESIDES GETTING A BATGIRL TATTOO ON MY LOWER BACK AND RUBBING YOUR FEET FOR THE NEXT FIFTY YEARS?
I'M IN FAVOR OF BOTH OF THOSE OPTIONS. BUT MAYBE ADD TWO TO THE LIST?
NUMBER ONE: DON'T GET KILLED.
THIS DARK WEB STUFF...IT SCARES ME. THE MORE I LEARN, THE MORE WORRIED I GET.
NUMBER TWO: HELP ME DISSECT THE ROADKILL PINNED TO THE FRONT OF THE GRILL.

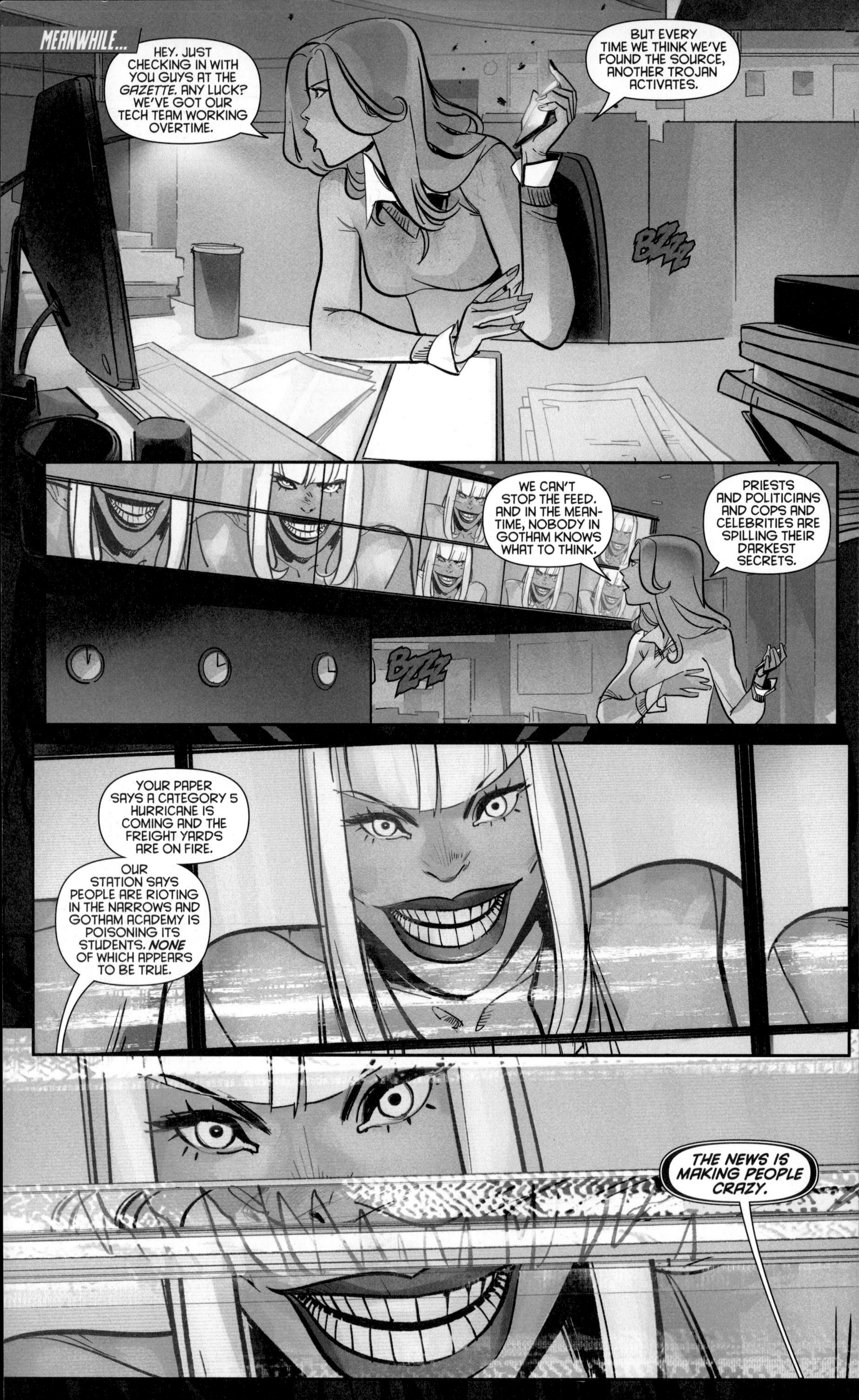
MEANWHILE...
HEY. JUST CHECKING IN WITH YOU GUYS AT THE *GAZETTE*. ANY LUCK? WE'VE GOT OUR TECH TEAM WORKING OVERTIME.
BUT EVERY TIME WE THINK WE'VE FOUND THE SOURCE, ANOTHER TROJAN ACTIVATES.
BZZZ
WE CAN'T STOP THE FEED. AND IN THE MEAN-TIME, NOBODY IN GOTHAM KNOWS WHAT TO THINK.
PRIESTS AND POLITICIANS AND COPS AND CELEBRITIES ARE SPILLING THEIR DARKEST SECRETS.
BZZZ
YOUR PAPER SAYS A CATEGORY 5 HURRICANE IS COMING AND THE FREIGHT YARDS ARE ON FIRE.
OUR STATION SAYS PEOPLE ARE RIOTING IN THE NARROWS AND GOTHAM ACADEMY IS POISONING ITS STUDENTS. *NONE* OF WHICH APPEARS TO BE TRUE.
THE NEWS IS MAKING PEOPLE CRAZY.

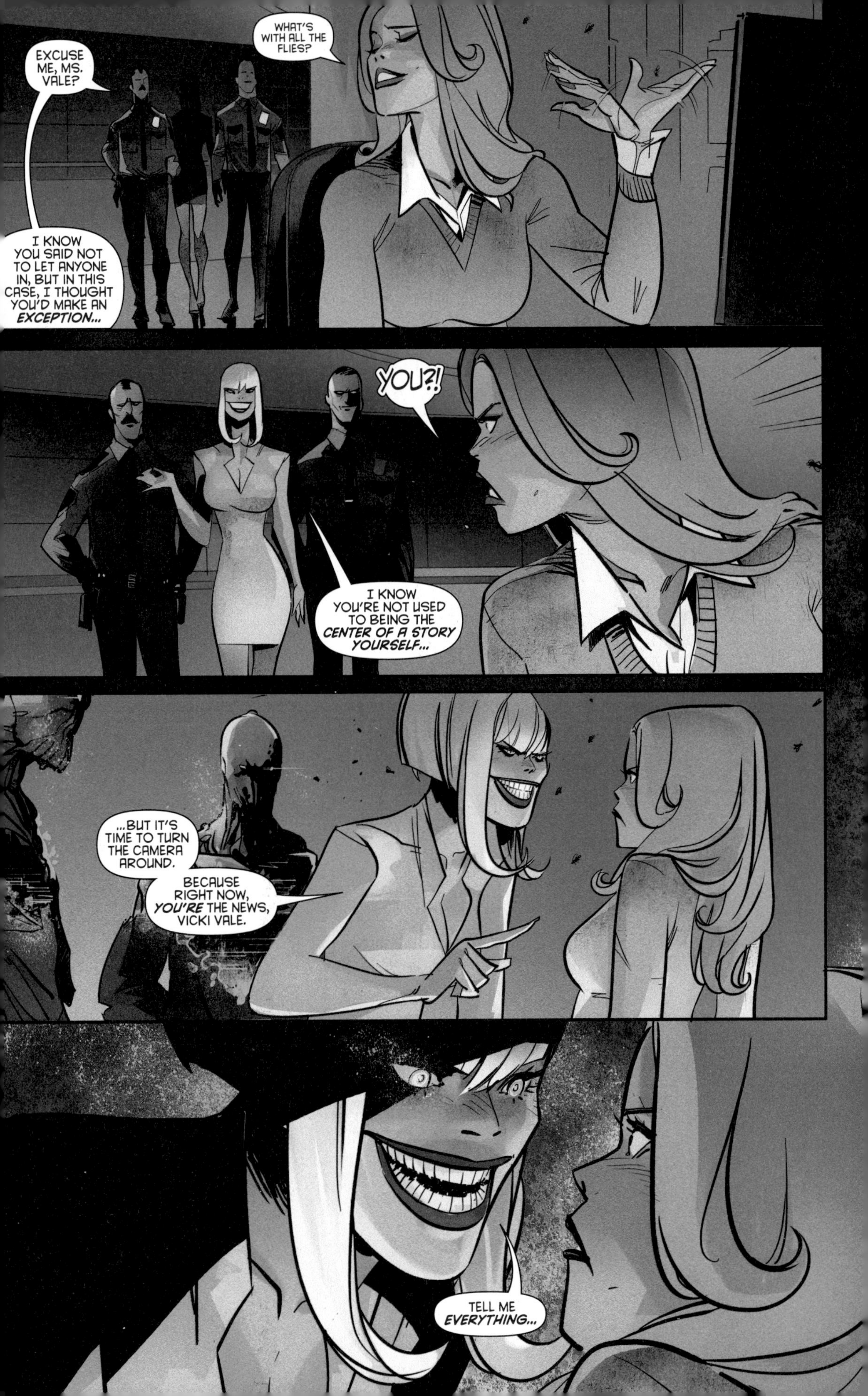
WHAT'S WITH ALL THE FLIES?
EXCUSE ME, MS. VALE?
I KNOW YOU SAID NOT TO LET ANYONE IN, BUT IN THIS CASE, I THOUGHT YOU'D MAKE AN *EXCEPTION...*
YOU?!
I KNOW YOU'RE NOT USED TO BEING THE *CENTER OF A STORY YOURSELF...*
...BUT IT'S TIME TO TURN THE CAMERA AROUND.
BECAUSE RIGHT NOW, *YOU'RE* THE NEWS, VICKI VALE.
TELL ME *EVERYTHING...*

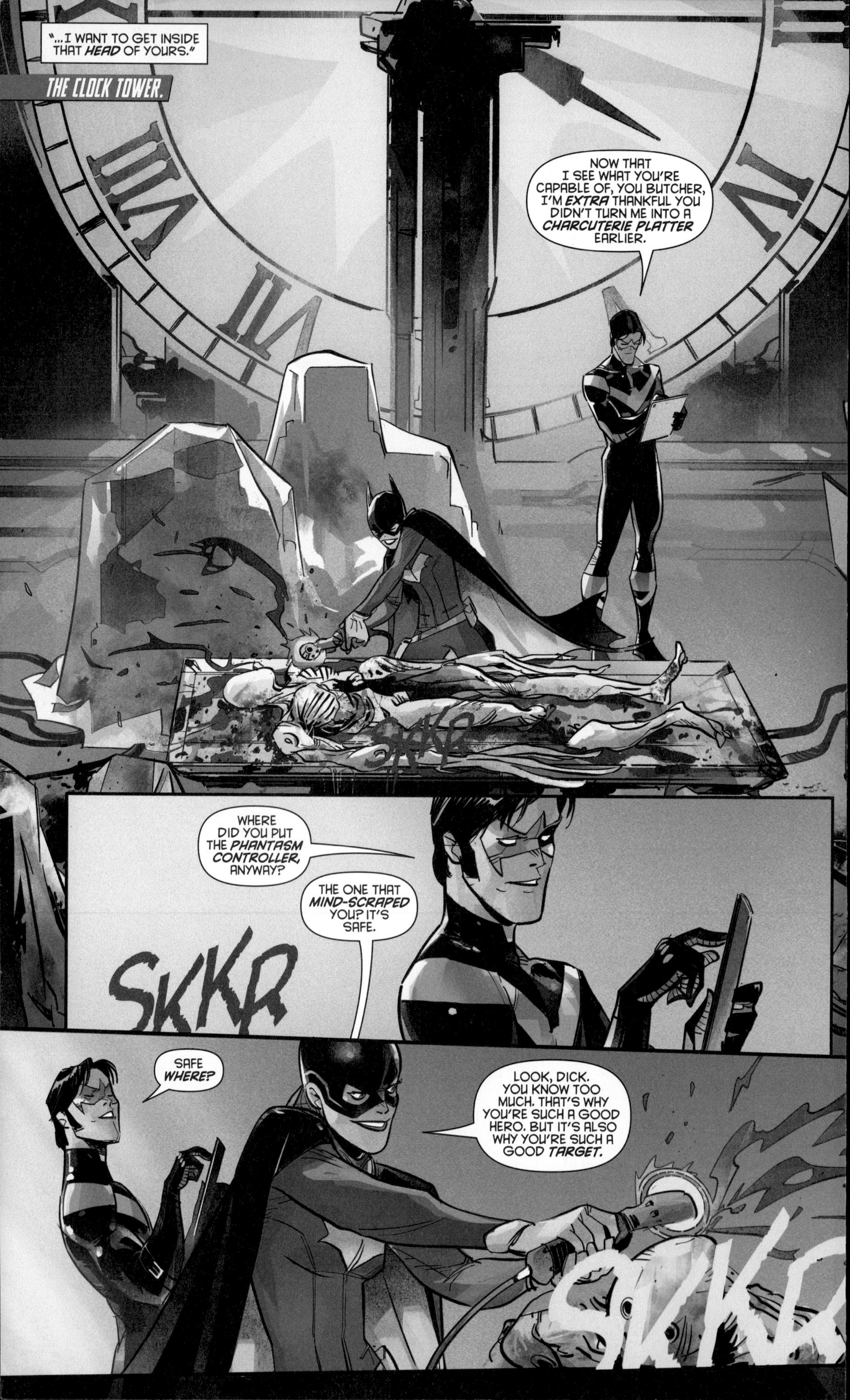
"...I WANT TO GET INSIDE THAT HEAD OF YOURS."
THE CLOCK TOWER.
NOW THAT I SEE WHAT YOU'RE CAPABLE OF, YOU BUTCHER, I'M EXTRA THANKFUL YOU DIDN'T TURN ME INTO A CHARCUTERIE PLATTER EARLIER.
SKKR
WHERE DID YOU PUT THE PHANTASM CONTROLLER, ANYWAY?
THE ONE THAT MIND-SCRAPED YOU? IT'S SAFE.
SKKR
SAFE WHERE?
LOOK, DICK. YOU KNOW TOO MUCH. THAT'S WHY YOU'RE SUCH A GOOD HERO. BUT IT'S ALSO WHY YOU'RE SUCH A GOOD TARGET.
SKKR

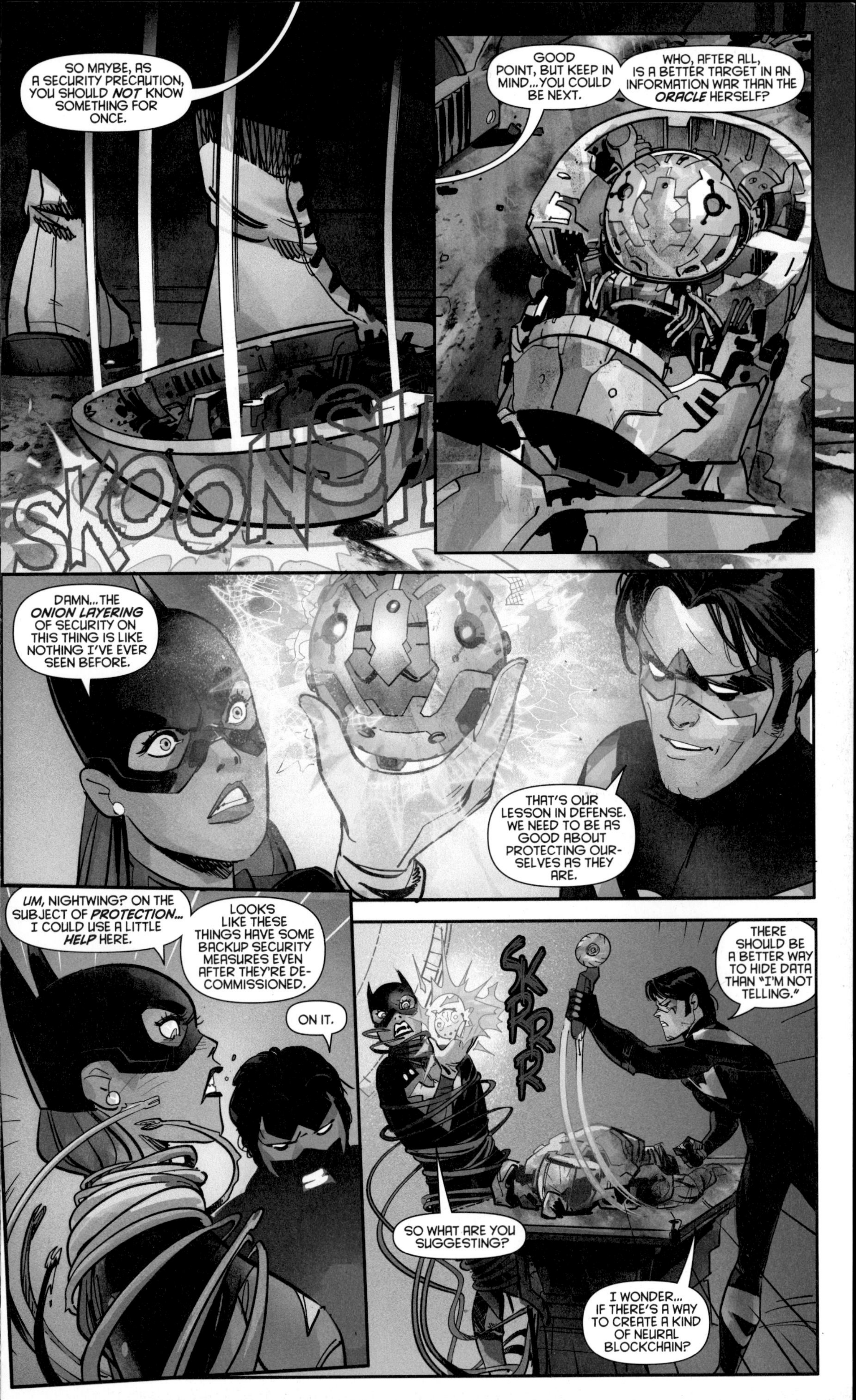
SO MAYBE, AS A SECURITY PRECAUTION, YOU SHOULD *NOT* KNOW SOMETHING FOR ONCE.
GOOD POINT, BUT KEEP IN MIND...YOU COULD BE NEXT.
WHO, AFTER ALL, IS A BETTER TARGET IN AN INFORMATION WAR THAN THE *ORACLE* HERSELF?
SKOONSH
DAMN...THE *ONION LAYERING* OF SECURITY ON THIS THING IS LIKE NOTHING I'VE EVER SEEN BEFORE.
THAT'S OUR LESSON IN DEFENSE. WE NEED TO BE AS GOOD ABOUT PROTECTING OUR-SELVES AS THEY ARE.
UM, NIGHTWING? ON THE SUBJECT OF *PROTECTION*... I COULD USE A LITTLE *HELP* HERE.
LOOKS LIKE THESE THINGS HAVE SOME BACKUP SECURITY MEASURES EVEN AFTER THEY'RE DE-COMMISSIONED.
ON IT.
SKRRR
THERE SHOULD BE A BETTER WAY TO HIDE DATA THAN "I'M NOT TELLING."
SO WHAT ARE YOU SUGGESTING?
I WONDER... IF THERE'S A WAY TO CREATE A KIND OF NEURAL BLOCKCHAIN?

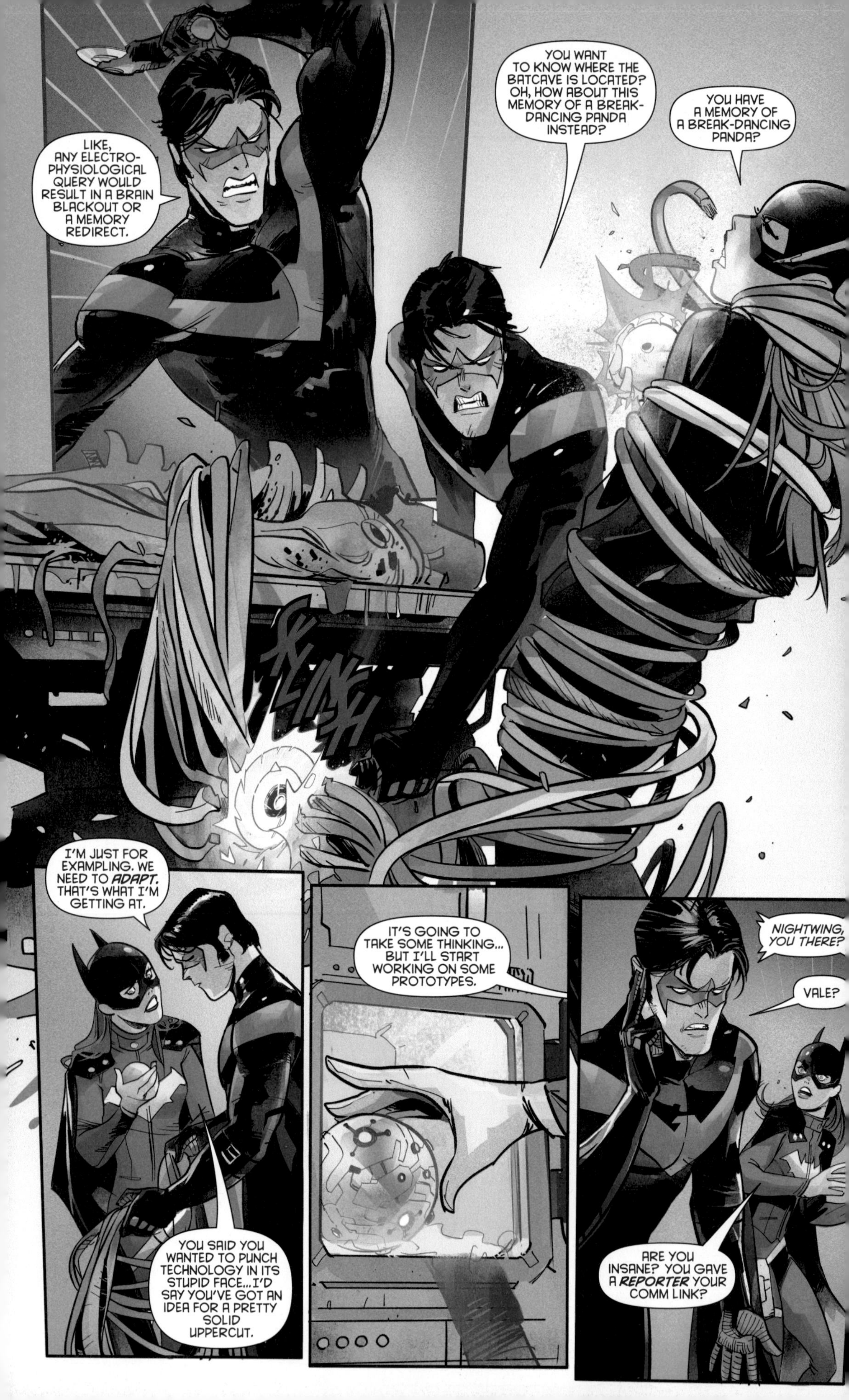
LIKE, ANY ELECTRO-PHYSIOLOGICAL QUERY WOULD RESULT IN A BRAIN BLACKOUT OR A MEMORY REDIRECT.
YOU WANT TO KNOW WHERE THE BATCAVE IS LOCATED? OH, HOW ABOUT THIS MEMORY OF A BREAK-DANCING PANDA INSTEAD?
YOU HAVE A MEMORY OF A BREAK-DANCING PANDA?
SKLINCH
I'M JUST FOR EXAMPLING. WE NEED TO ADAPT. THAT'S WHAT I'M GETTING AT.
YOU SAID YOU WANTED TO PUNCH TECHNOLOGY IN ITS STUPID FACE... I'D SAY YOU'VE GOT AN IDEA FOR A PRETTY SOLID UPPERCUT.
IT'S GOING TO TAKE SOME THINKING... BUT I'LL START WORKING ON SOME PROTOTYPES.
NIGHTWING, YOU THERE?
VALE?
ARE YOU INSANE? YOU GAVE A REPORTER YOUR COMM LINK?

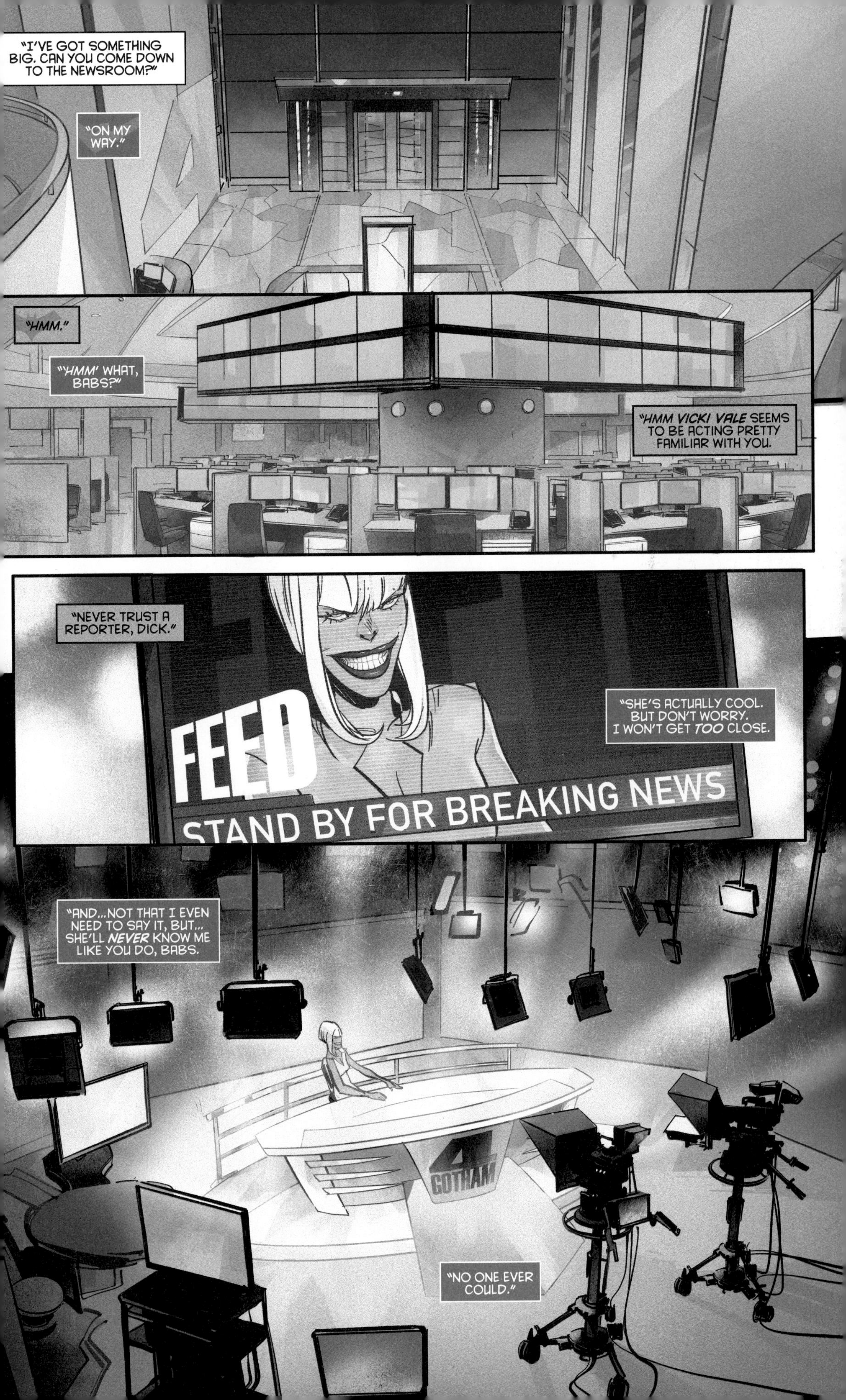
"I'VE GOT SOMETHING BIG. CAN YOU COME DOWN TO THE NEWSROOM?"
"ON MY WAY."
"HMM."
"'HMM' WHAT, BABS?"
"HMM VICKI VALE SEEMS TO BE ACTING PRETTY FAMILIAR WITH YOU.
"NEVER TRUST A REPORTER, DICK."
FEED
STAND BY FOR BREAKING NEWS
"SHE'S ACTUALLY COOL. BUT DON'T WORRY. I WON'T GET TOO CLOSE.
"AND...NOT THAT I EVEN NEED TO SAY IT, BUT... SHE'LL NEVER KNOW ME LIKE YOU DO, BABS.
GOTHAM
"NO ONE EVER COULD."

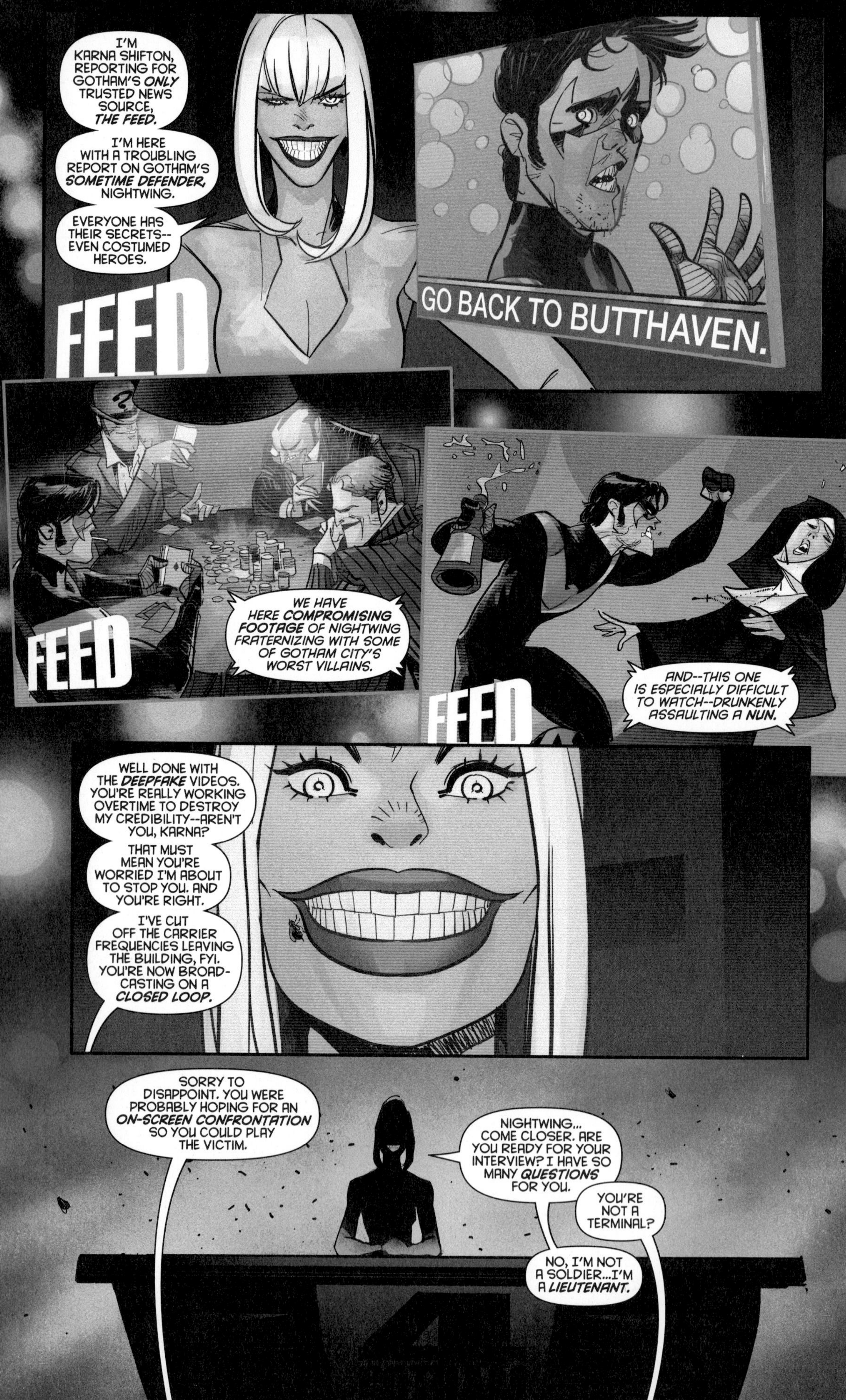
I'M KARNA SHIFTON, REPORTING FOR GOTHAM'S *ONLY* TRUSTED NEWS SOURCE, *THE FEED.*
I'M HERE WITH A TROUBLING REPORT ON GOTHAM'S *SOMETIME DEFENDER,* NIGHTWING.
EVERYONE HAS THEIR SECRETS-- EVEN COSTUMED HEROES.
FEED
GO BACK TO BUTTHAVEN.
FEED
WE HAVE HERE **COMPROMISING FOOTAGE** OF NIGHTWING FRATERNIZING WITH SOME OF GOTHAM CITY'S WORST VILLAINS.
AND--THIS ONE IS ESPECIALLY DIFFICULT TO WATCH--DRUNKENLY ASSAULTING A **NUN.**
WELL DONE WITH THE *DEEPFAKE* VIDEOS. YOU'RE REALLY WORKING OVERTIME TO DESTROY MY CREDIBILITY--AREN'T YOU, KARNA?
THAT MUST MEAN YOU'RE WORRIED I'M ABOUT TO STOP YOU. AND YOU'RE RIGHT.
I'VE CUT OFF THE CARRIER FREQUENCIES LEAVING THE BUILDING, FYI. YOU'RE NOW BROAD-CASTING ON A *CLOSED LOOP.*
SORRY TO DISAPPOINT. YOU WERE PROBABLY HOPING FOR AN *ON-SCREEN CONFRONTATION* SO YOU COULD PLAY THE VICTIM.
NIGHTWING... COME CLOSER. ARE YOU READY FOR YOUR INTERVIEW? I HAVE SO MANY *QUESTIONS* FOR YOU.
YOU'RE NOT A TERMINAL?
NO, I'M NOT A SOLDIER...I'M A *LIEUTENANT.*

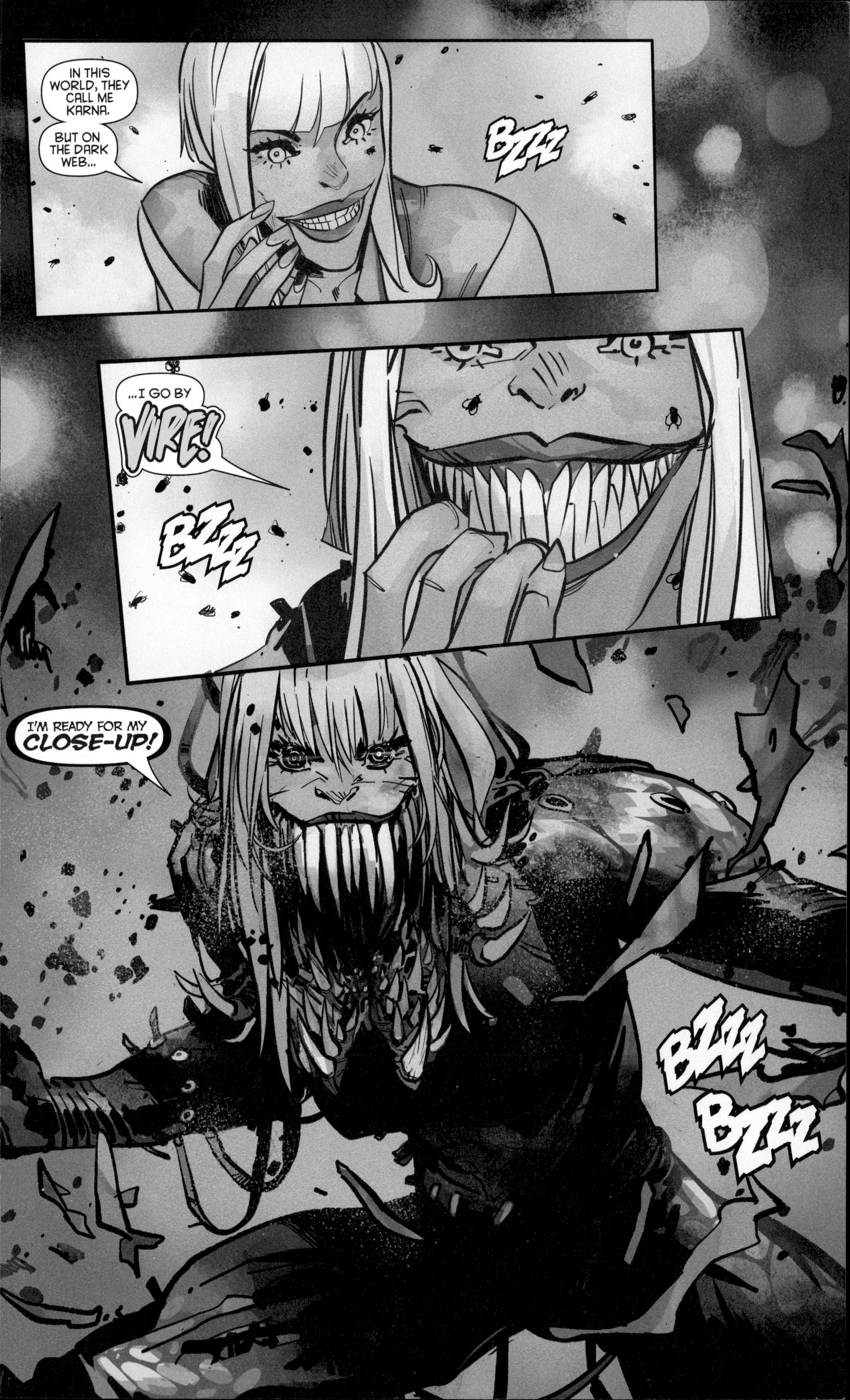

IN THIS WORLD, THEY CALL ME KARNA.
BUT ON THE DARK WEB...
BZZZ
...I GO BY VIRE!
BZZZ
I'M READY FOR MY CLOSE-UP!
BZZZ
BZZZ

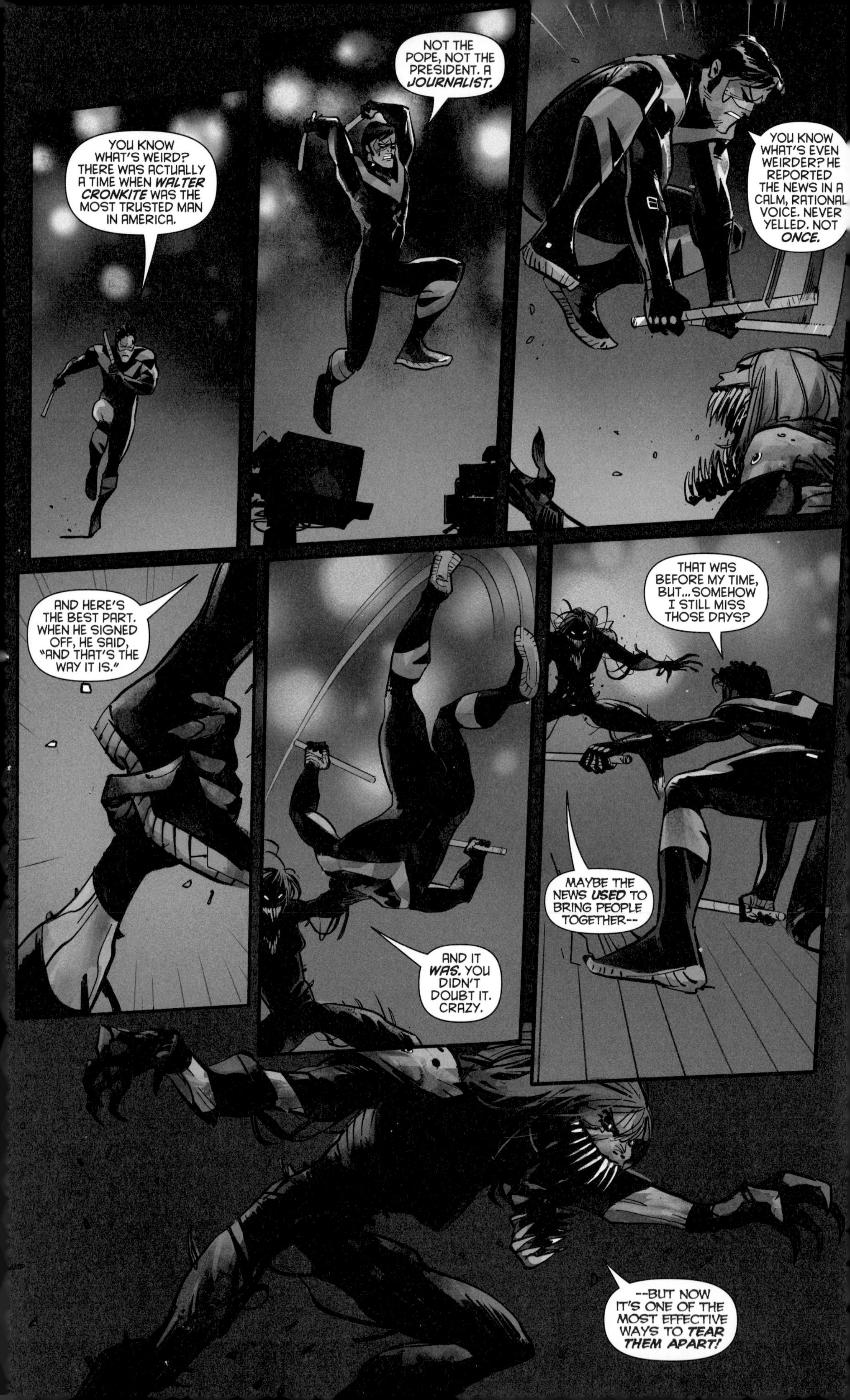
YOU KNOW WHAT'S WEIRD? THERE WAS ACTUALLY A TIME WHEN WALTER CRONKITE WAS THE MOST TRUSTED MAN IN AMERICA.
NOT THE POPE, NOT THE PRESIDENT. A JOURNALIST.
YOU KNOW WHAT'S EVEN WEIRDER? HE REPORTED THE NEWS IN A CALM, RATIONAL VOICE. NEVER YELLED. NOT ONCE.
AND HERE'S THE BEST PART. WHEN HE SIGNED OFF, HE SAID, "AND THAT'S THE WAY IT IS."
AND IT WAS. YOU DIDN'T DOUBT IT. CRAZY.
THAT WAS BEFORE MY TIME, BUT...SOMEHOW I STILL MISS THOSE DAYS?
MAYBE THE NEWS USED TO BRING PEOPLE TOGETHER--
--BUT NOW IT'S ONE OF THE MOST EFFECTIVE WAYS TO TEAR THEM APART!

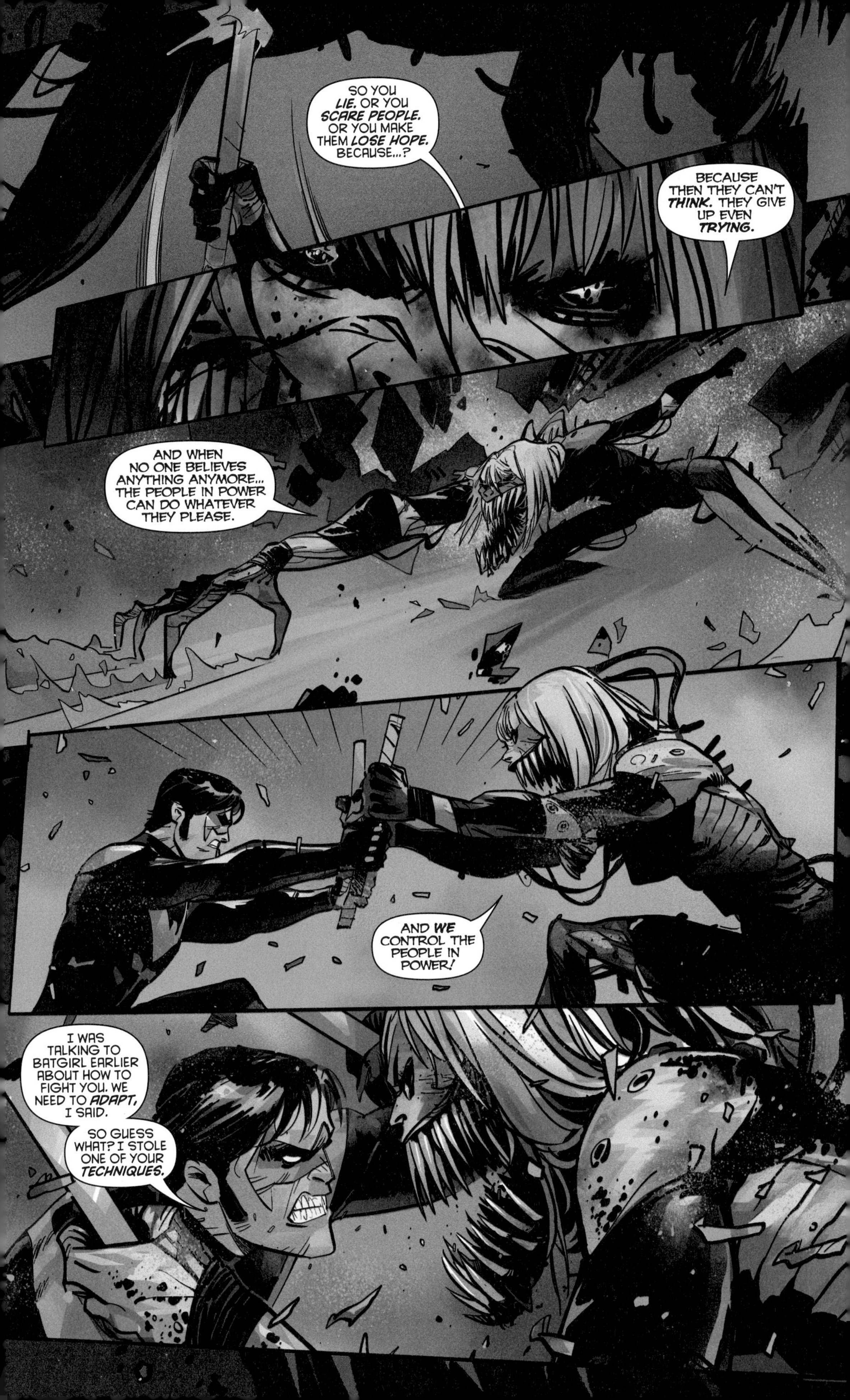
SO YOU *LIE.* OR YOU *SCARE PEOPLE.* OR YOU MAKE THEM *LOSE HOPE.* BECAUSE...?
BECAUSE THEN THEY CAN'T *THINK.* THEY GIVE UP EVEN *TRYING.*
AND WHEN NO ONE BELIEVES ANYTHING ANYMORE... THE PEOPLE IN POWER CAN DO WHATEVER THEY PLEASE.
AND *WE* CONTROL THE PEOPLE IN POWER!
I WAS TALKING TO BATGIRL EARLIER ABOUT HOW TO FIGHT YOU. WE NEED TO *ADAPT,* I SAID.
SO GUESS WHAT? I STOLE ONE OF YOUR *TECHNIQUES.*

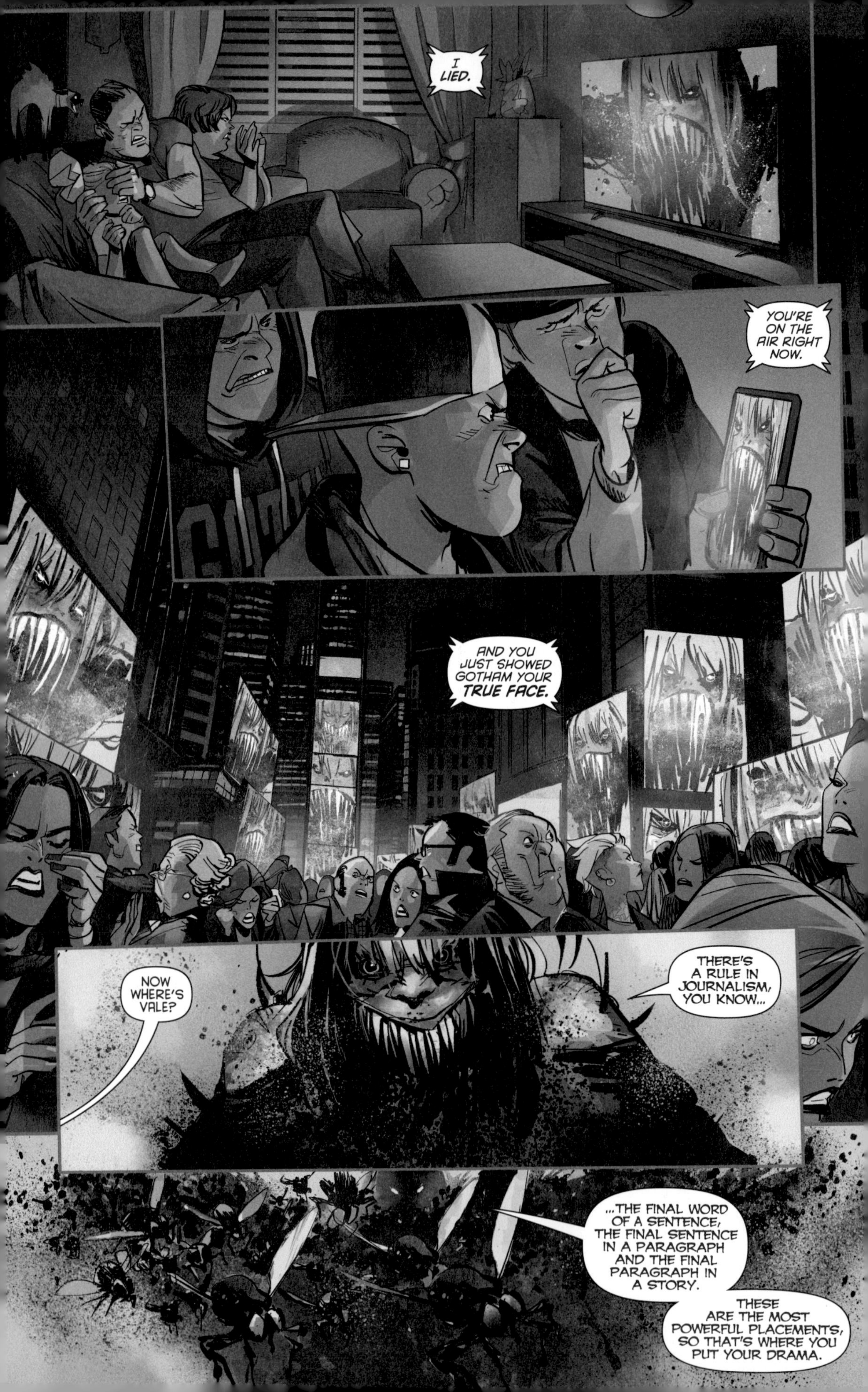
I LIED.
YOU'RE ON THE AIR RIGHT NOW.
AND YOU JUST SHOWED GOTHAM YOUR TRUE FACE.
NOW WHERE'S VALE?
THERE'S A RULE IN JOURNALISM, YOU KNOW...
...THE FINAL WORD OF A SENTENCE, THE FINAL SENTENCE IN A PARAGRAPH AND THE FINAL PARAGRAPH IN A STORY.
THESE ARE THE MOST POWERFUL PLACEMENTS, SO THAT'S WHERE YOU PUT YOUR DRAMA.

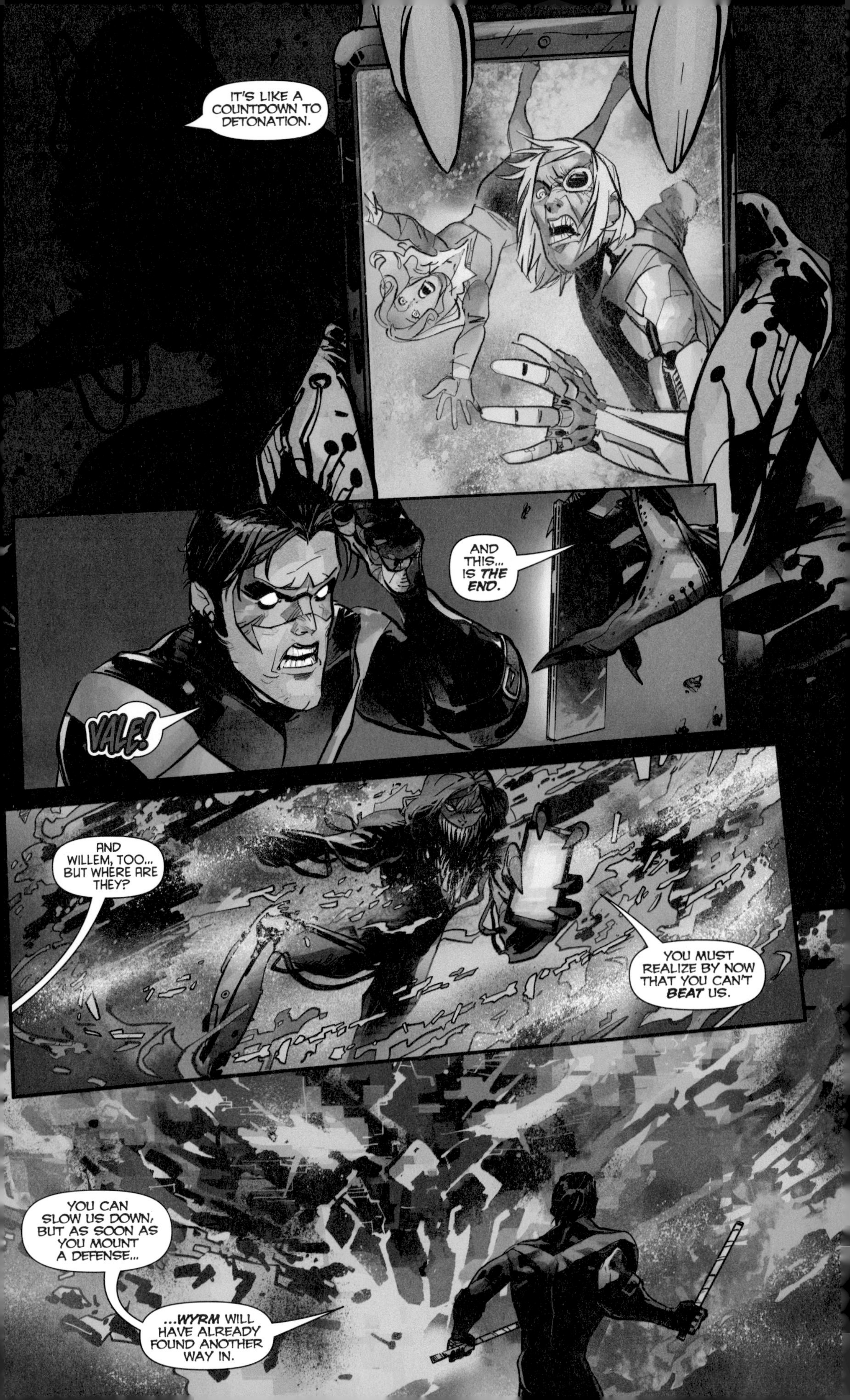
IT'S LIKE A COUNTDOWN TO DETONATION.
AND THIS... IS THE END.
VALE!
AND WILLEM, TOO... BUT WHERE ARE THEY?
YOU MUST REALIZE BY NOW THAT YOU CAN'T BEAT US.
YOU CAN SLOW US DOWN, BUT AS SOON AS YOU MOUNT A DEFENSE...
...WYRM WILL HAVE ALREADY FOUND ANOTHER WAY IN.

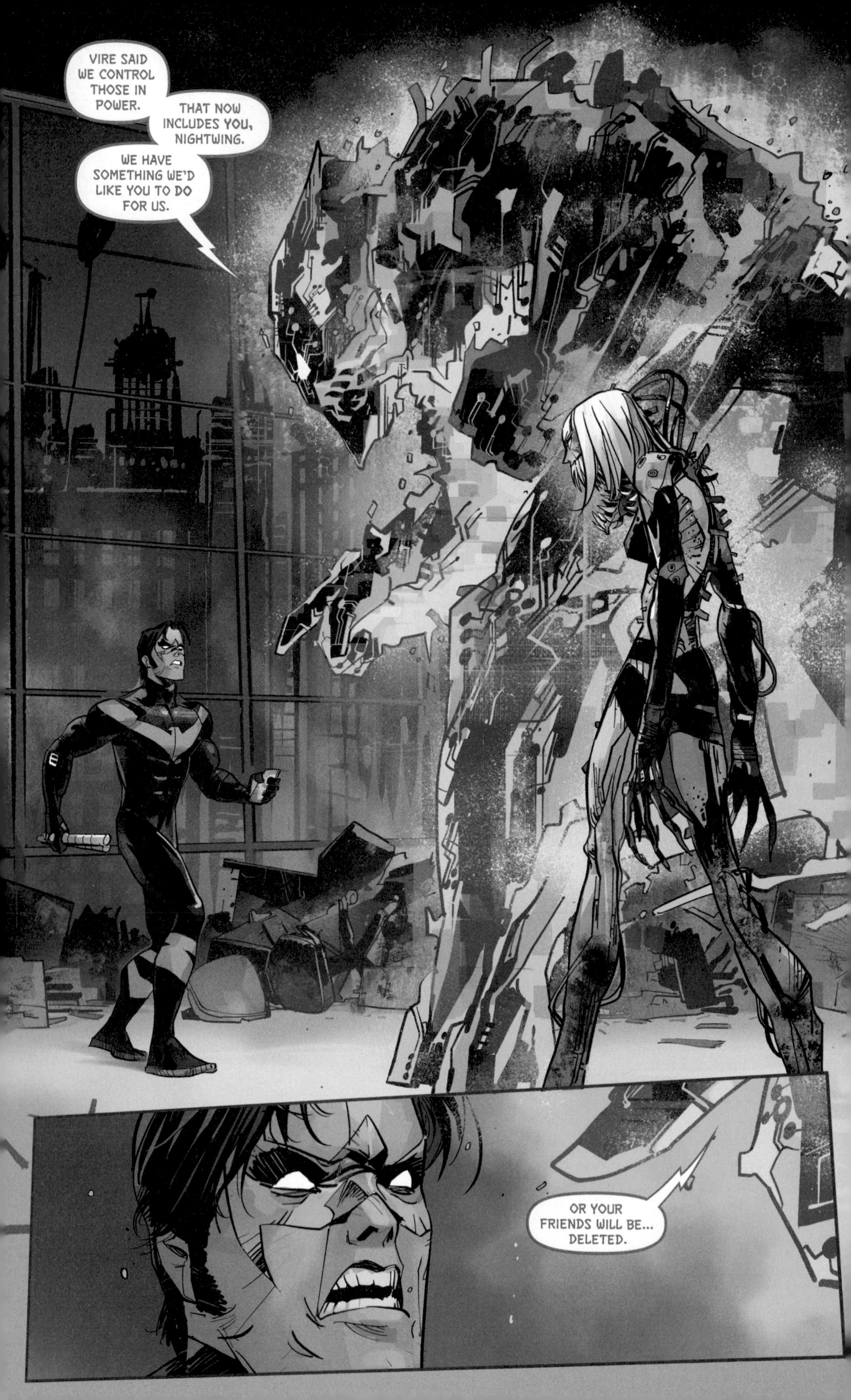
VIRE SAID WE CONTROL THOSE IN POWER.
THAT NOW INCLUDES YOU, NIGHTWING.
WE HAVE SOMETHING WE'D LIKE YOU TO DO FOR US.
OR YOUR FRIENDS WILL BE... DELETED.

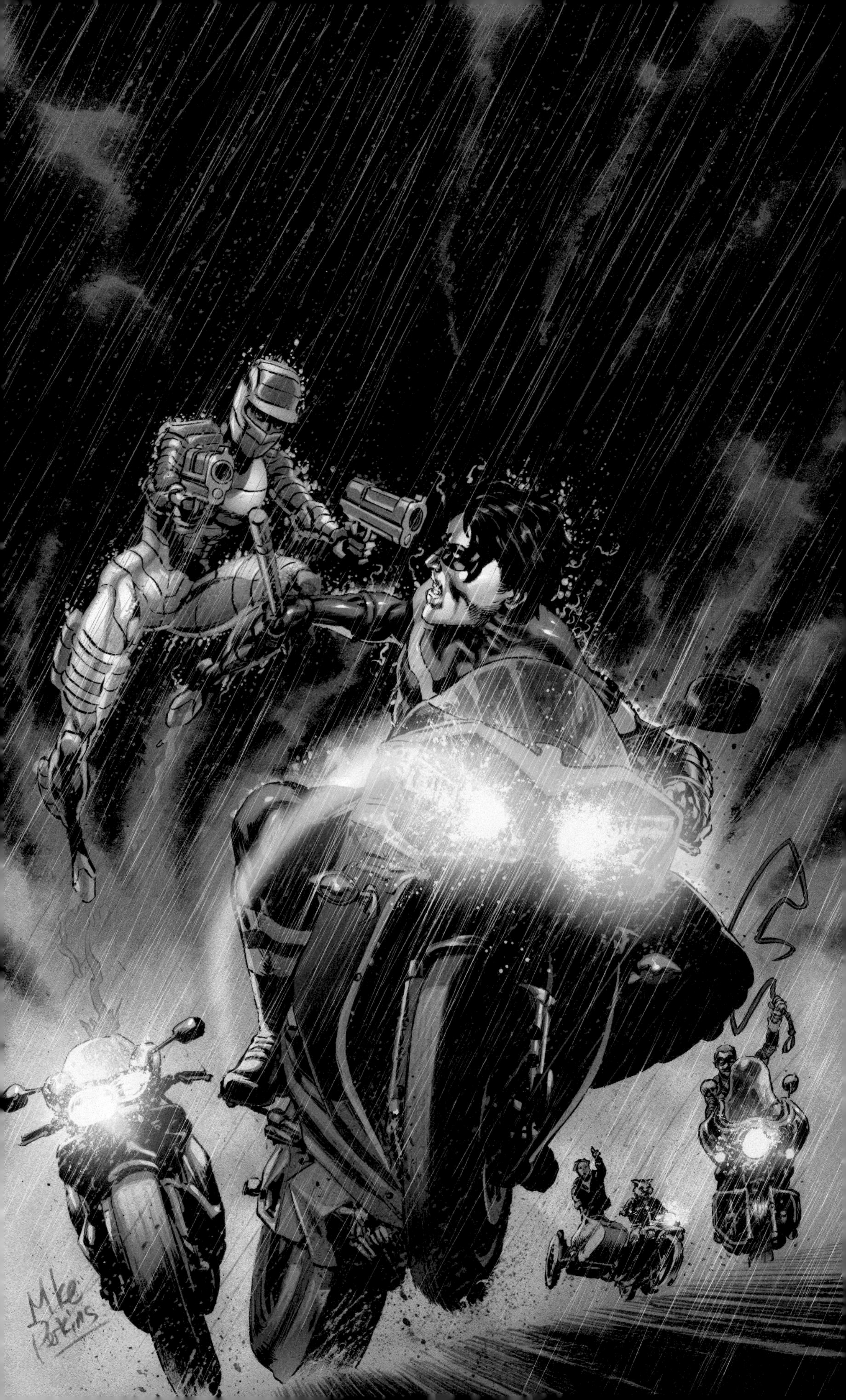
Mike Perkins

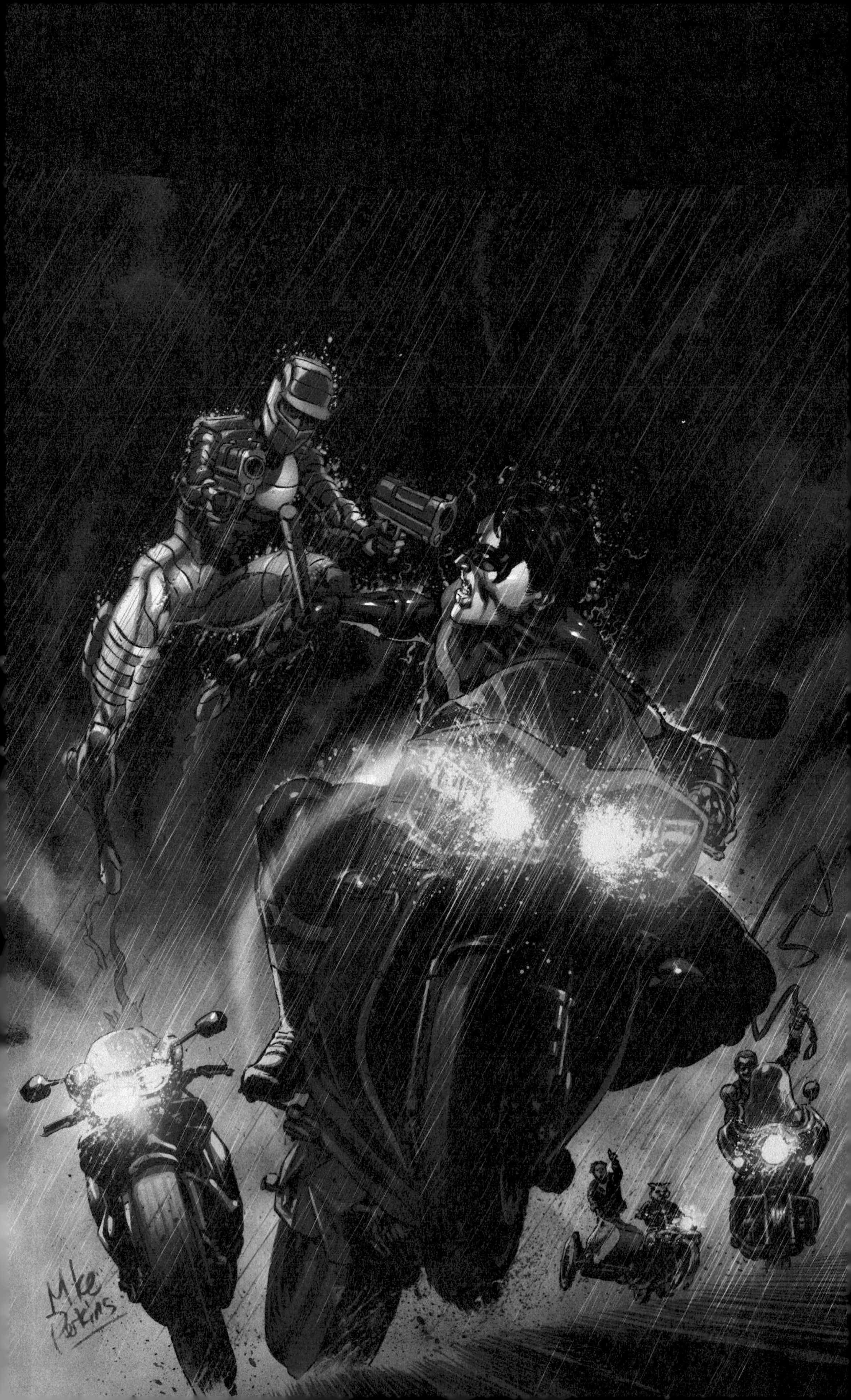
Mike
Perkins

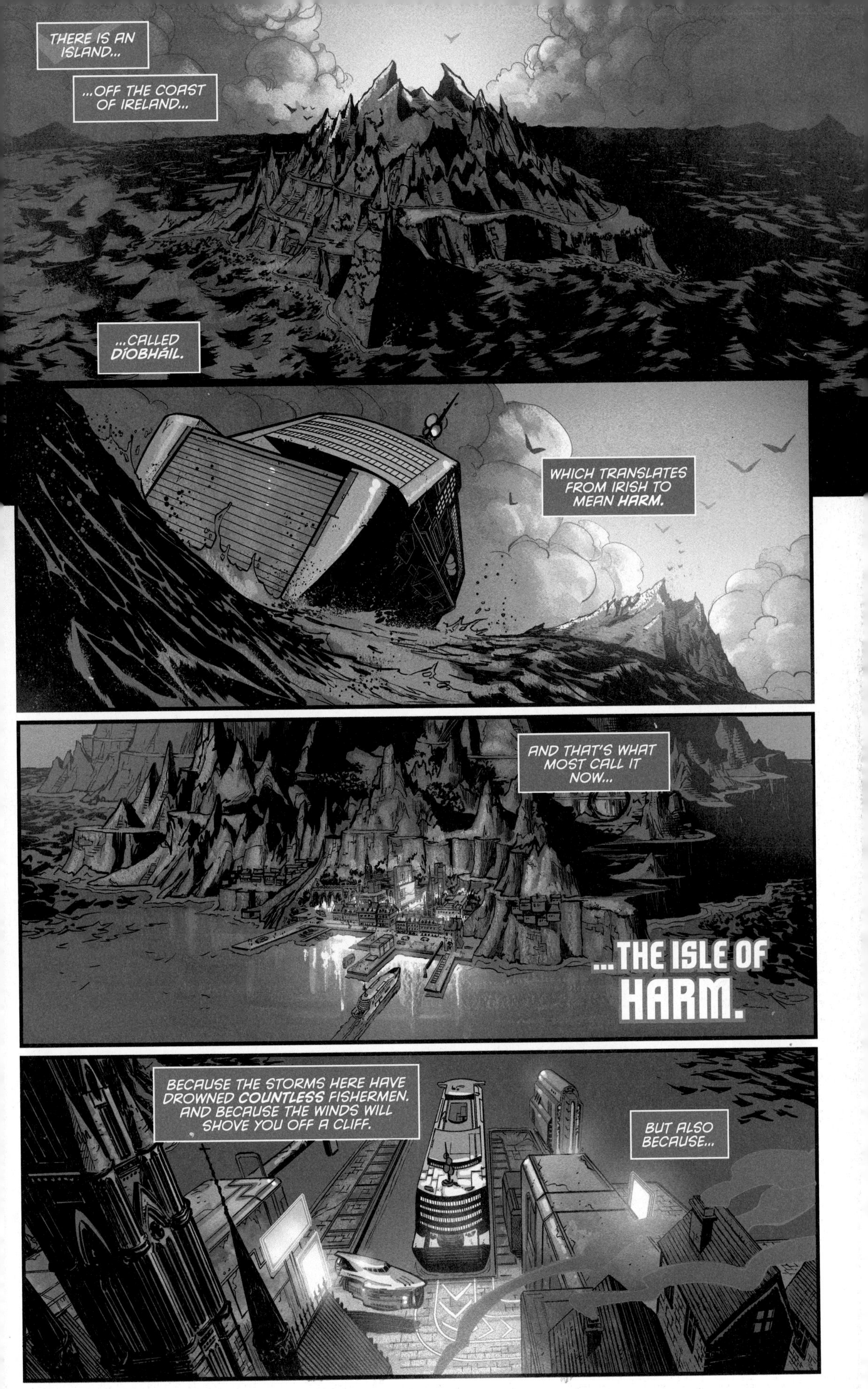
THERE IS AN ISLAND...
...OFF THE COAST OF IRELAND...
...CALLED DÍOBHÁIL.
WHICH TRANSLATES FROM IRISH TO MEAN HARM.
AND THAT'S WHAT MOST CALL IT NOW...
...THE ISLE OF HARM.
BECAUSE THE STORMS HERE HAVE DROWNED COUNTLESS FISHERMEN. AND BECAUSE THE WINDS WILL SHOVE YOU OFF A CLIFF.
BUT ALSO BECAUSE...

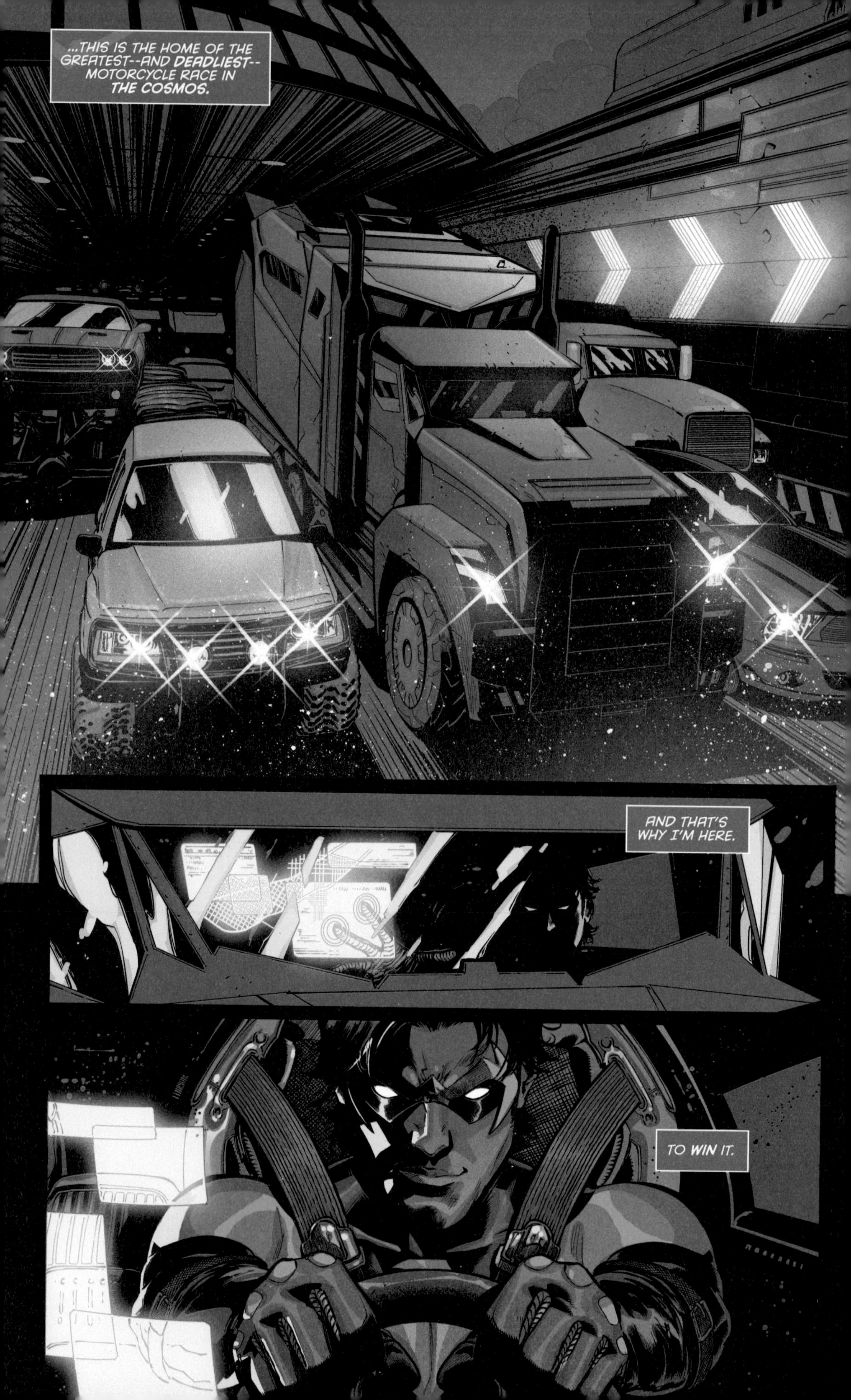
...THIS IS THE HOME OF THE GREATEST--AND DEADLIEST--MOTORCYCLE RACE IN THE COSMOS.
AND THAT'S WHY I'M HERE.
TO WIN IT.

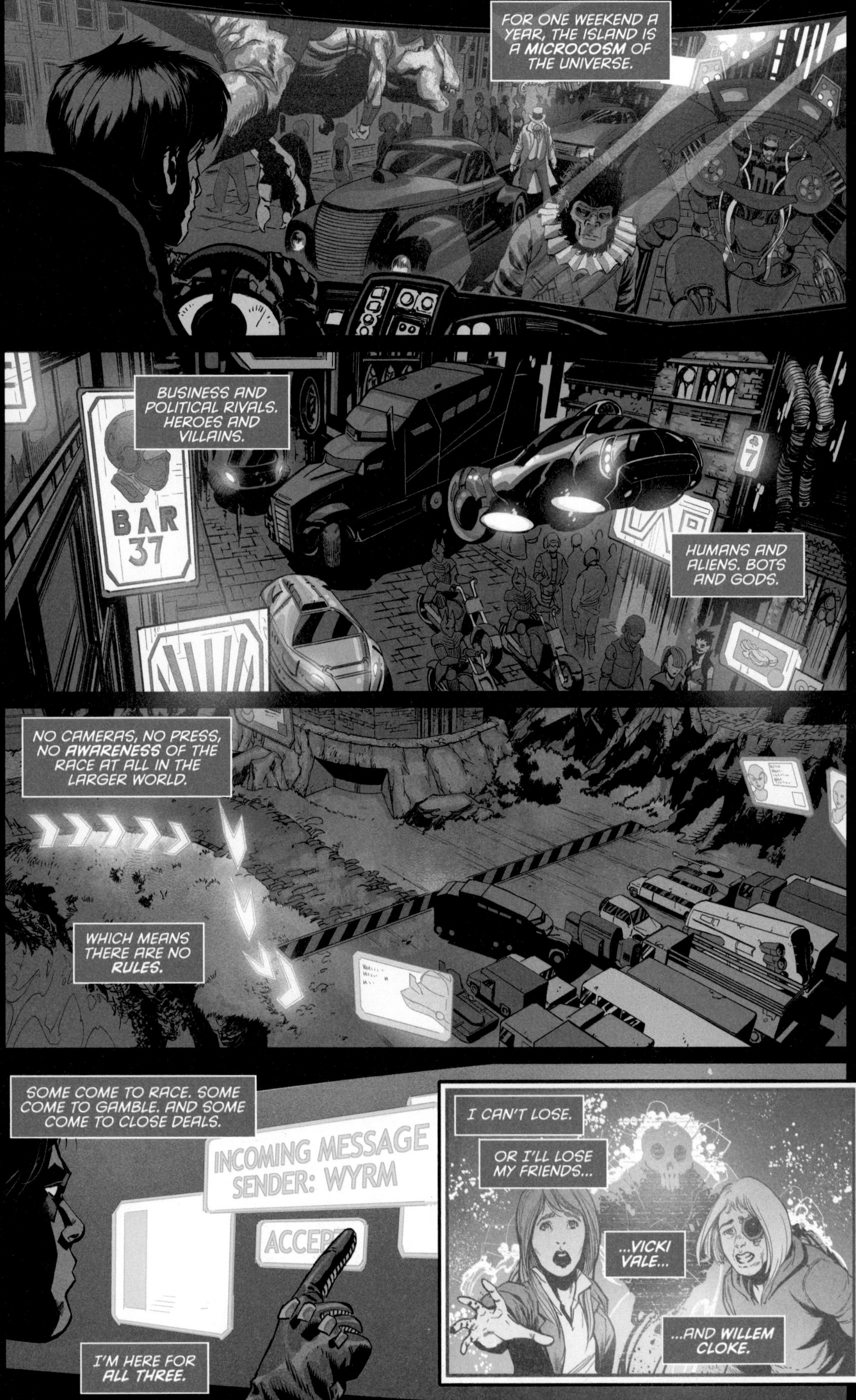
FOR ONE WEEKEND A YEAR, THE ISLAND IS A MICROCOSM OF THE UNIVERSE.
BUSINESS AND POLITICAL RIVALS. HEROES AND VILLAINS.
BAR 37
7
HUMANS AND ALIENS. BOTS AND GODS.
NO CAMERAS, NO PRESS, NO AWARENESS OF THE RACE AT ALL IN THE LARGER WORLD.
WHICH MEANS THERE ARE NO RULES.
SOME COME TO RACE. SOME COME TO GAMBLE. AND SOME COME TO CLOSE DEALS.
INCOMING MESSAGE SENDER: WYRM
I'M HERE FOR ALL THREE.
I CAN'T LOSE.
OR I'LL LOSE MY FRIENDS...
...VICKI VALE...
...AND WILLEM CLOKE.

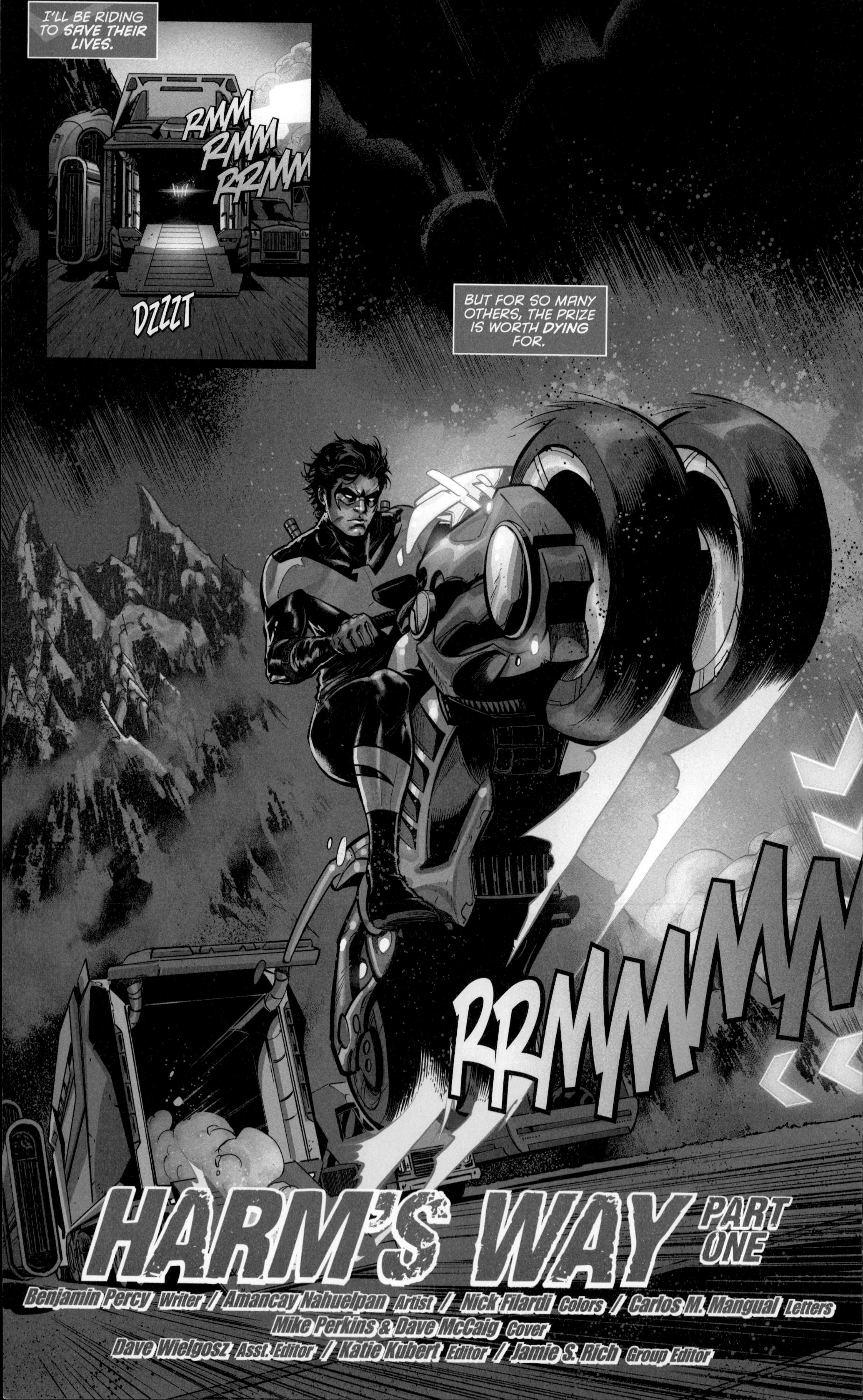
I'LL BE RIDING TO SAVE THEIR LIVES.
RMM RMM RRMM
DZZZT
BUT FOR SO MANY OTHERS, THE PRIZE IS WORTH DYING FOR.
RRMMMMM
HARM'S WAY PART ONE
Benjamin Percy Writer / Amancay Nahuelpan Artist / Nick Filardi Colors / Carlos M. Mangual Letters
Mike Perkins & Dave McCaig Cover
Dave Wielgosz Asst. Editor / Katie Kubert Editor / Jamie S. Rich Group Editor

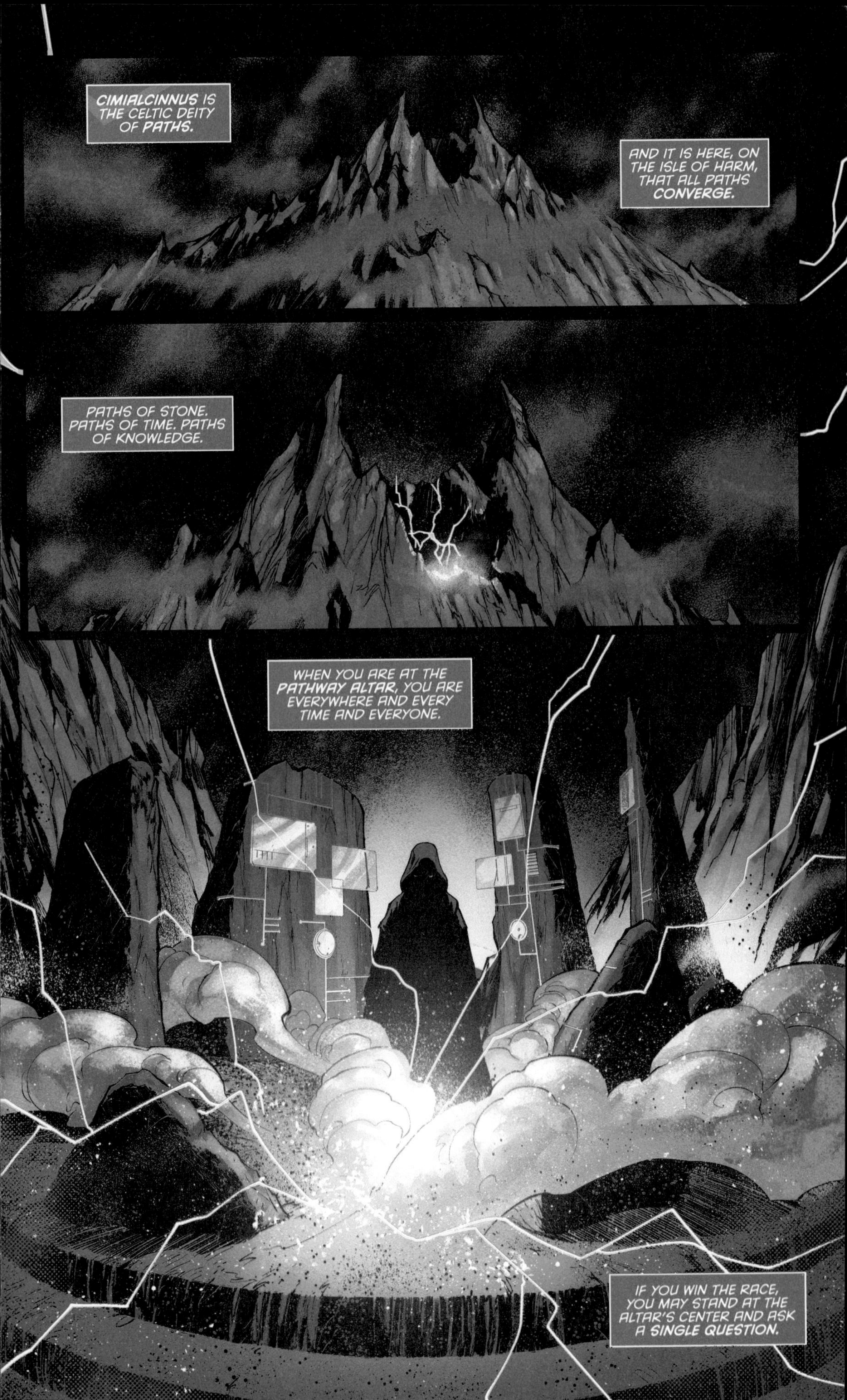
CIMIALCINNUS IS THE CELTIC DEITY OF PATHS.
AND IT IS HERE, ON THE ISLE OF HARM, THAT ALL PATHS CONVERGE.
PATHS OF STONE. PATHS OF TIME. PATHS OF KNOWLEDGE.
WHEN YOU ARE AT THE PATHWAY ALTAR, YOU ARE EVERYWHERE AND EVERY TIME AND EVERYONE.
IF YOU WIN THE RACE, YOU MAY STAND AT THE ALTAR'S CENTER AND ASK A SINGLE QUESTION.

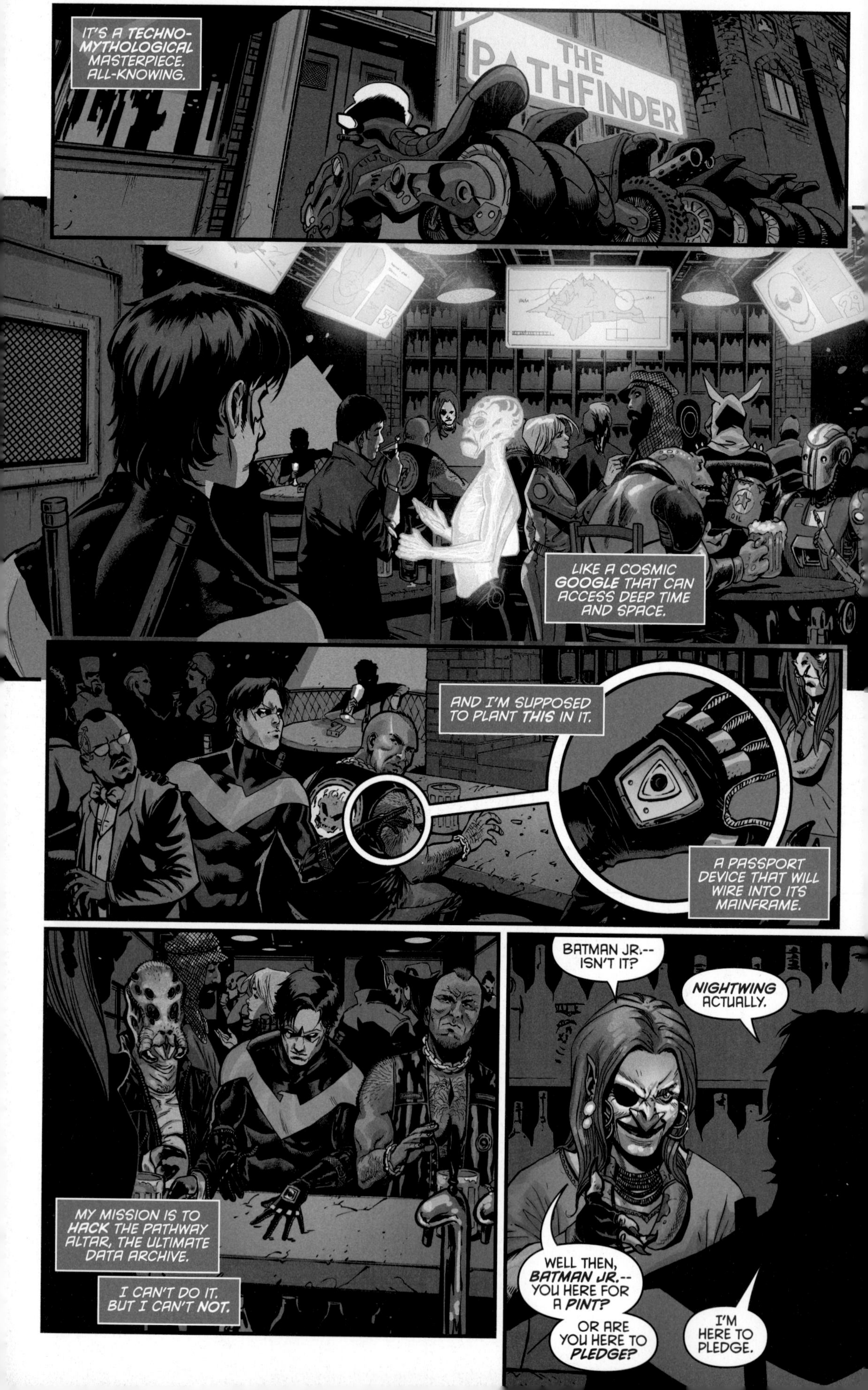

IT'S A TECHNO-MYTHOLOGICAL MASTERPIECE. ALL-KNOWING.
THE PATHFINDER
LIKE A COSMIC GOOGLE THAT CAN ACCESS DEEP TIME AND SPACE.
AND I'M SUPPOSED TO PLANT THIS IN IT.
A PASSPORT DEVICE THAT WILL WIRE INTO ITS MAINFRAME.
MY MISSION IS TO HACK THE PATHWAY ALTAR, THE ULTIMATE DATA ARCHIVE.
I CAN'T DO IT. BUT I CAN'T NOT.
BATMAN JR.-- ISN'T IT?
NIGHTWING ACTUALLY.
WELL THEN, BATMAN JR.-- YOU HERE FOR A PINT?
OR ARE YOU HERE TO PLEDGE?
I'M HERE TO PLEDGE.

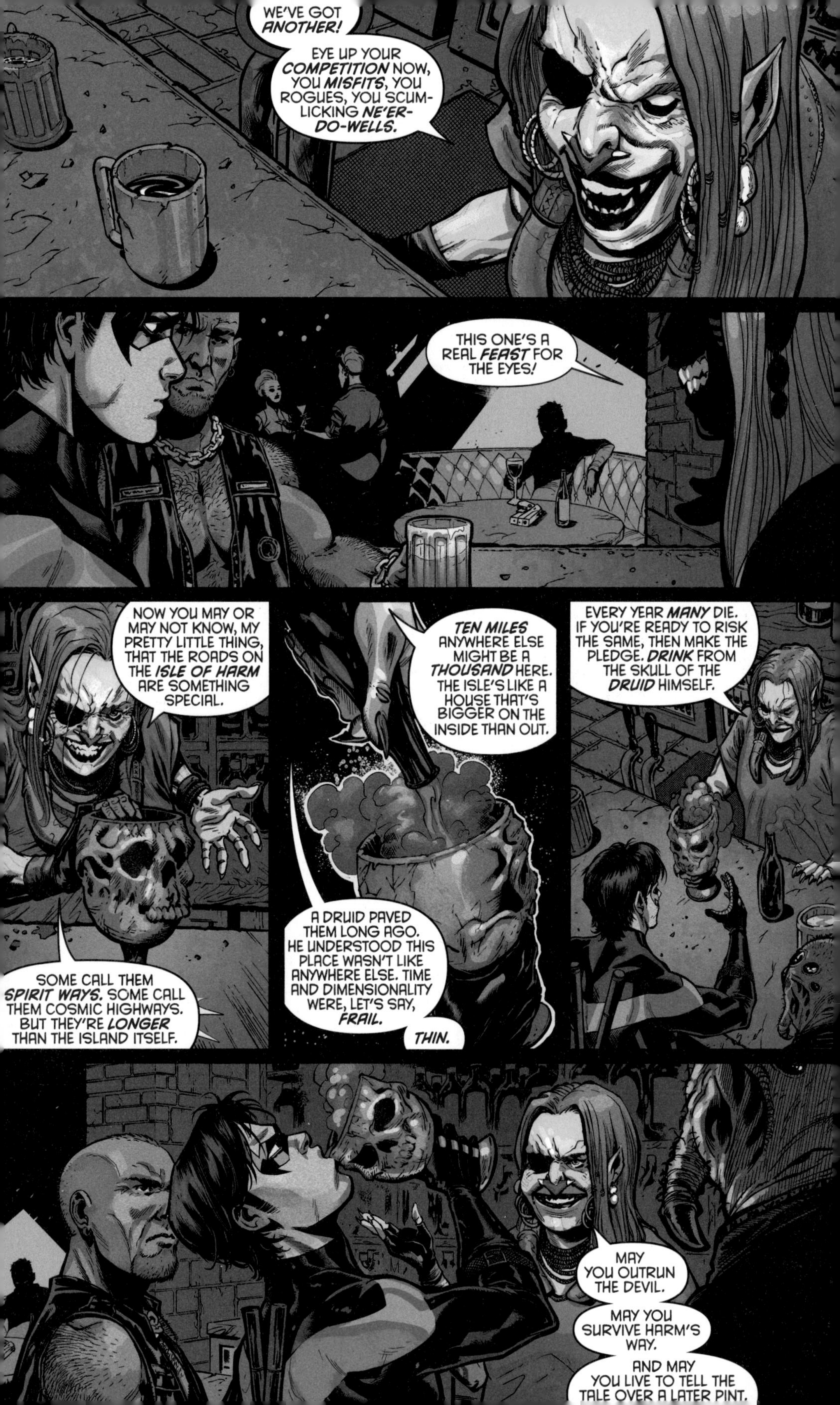
WE'VE GOT ANOTHER!
EYE UP YOUR COMPETITION NOW, YOU MISFITS, YOU ROGUES, YOU SCUM-LICKING NE'ER-DO-WELLS.
THIS ONE'S A REAL FEAST FOR THE EYES!
NOW YOU MAY OR MAY NOT KNOW, MY PRETTY LITTLE THING, THAT THE ROADS ON THE ISLE OF HARM ARE SOMETHING SPECIAL.
SOME CALL THEM SPIRIT WAYS. SOME CALL THEM COSMIC HIGHWAYS. BUT THEY'RE LONGER THAN THE ISLAND ITSELF.
TEN MILES ANYWHERE ELSE MIGHT BE A THOUSAND HERE. THE ISLE'S LIKE A HOUSE THAT'S BIGGER ON THE INSIDE THAN OUT.
A DRUID PAVED THEM LONG AGO. HE UNDERSTOOD THIS PLACE WASN'T LIKE ANYWHERE ELSE. TIME AND DIMENSIONALITY WERE, LET'S SAY, FRAIL.
THIN.
EVERY YEAR MANY DIE. IF YOU'RE READY TO RISK THE SAME, THEN MAKE THE PLEDGE. DRINK FROM THE SKULL OF THE DRUID HIMSELF.
MAY YOU OUTRUN THE DEVIL.
MAY YOU SURVIVE HARM'S WAY.
AND MAY YOU LIVE TO TELL THE TALE OVER A LATER PINT.

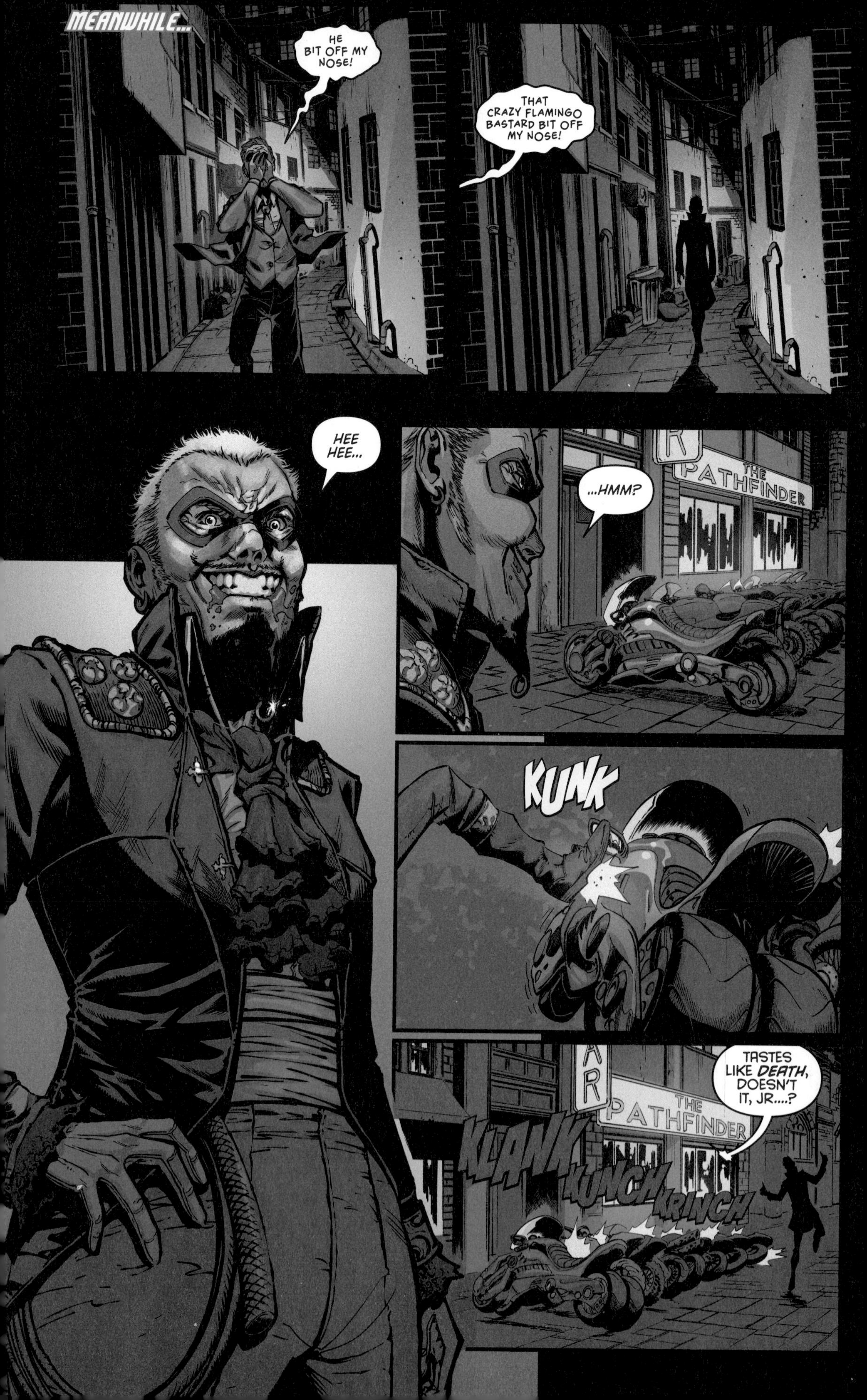
MEANWHILE...
HE BIT OFF MY NOSE!
THAT CRAZY FLAMINGO BASTARD BIT OFF MY NOSE!
HEE HEE...
...HMM?
THE PATHFINDER
KUNK
TASTES LIKE DEATH, DOESN'T IT, JR....?
THE PATHFINDER
KLANK
KUNCH
KRINCH

SHHHHH

"...THAT'S BECAUSE IT'S BEEN FERMENTED FOR A THOUSAND YEARS.

"NOW YOUR BLOOD'S RUNNING ON THE SAME CLOCK AND CALENDAR AS THE ISLAND."

I HUNCH OVER, COUGHING MY LUNGS OUT AT THE TASTE, WHEN I FEEL THE BULLET CUT AIR.

SNAPP

...BUT I DON'T HEAR A GUNSHOT.

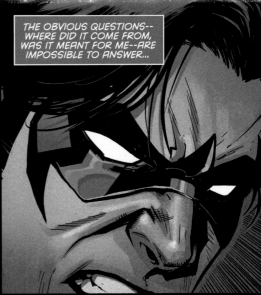

THE OBVIOUS QUESTIONS-- WHERE DID IT COME FROM, WAS IT MEANT FOR ME--ARE IMPOSSIBLE TO ANSWER...

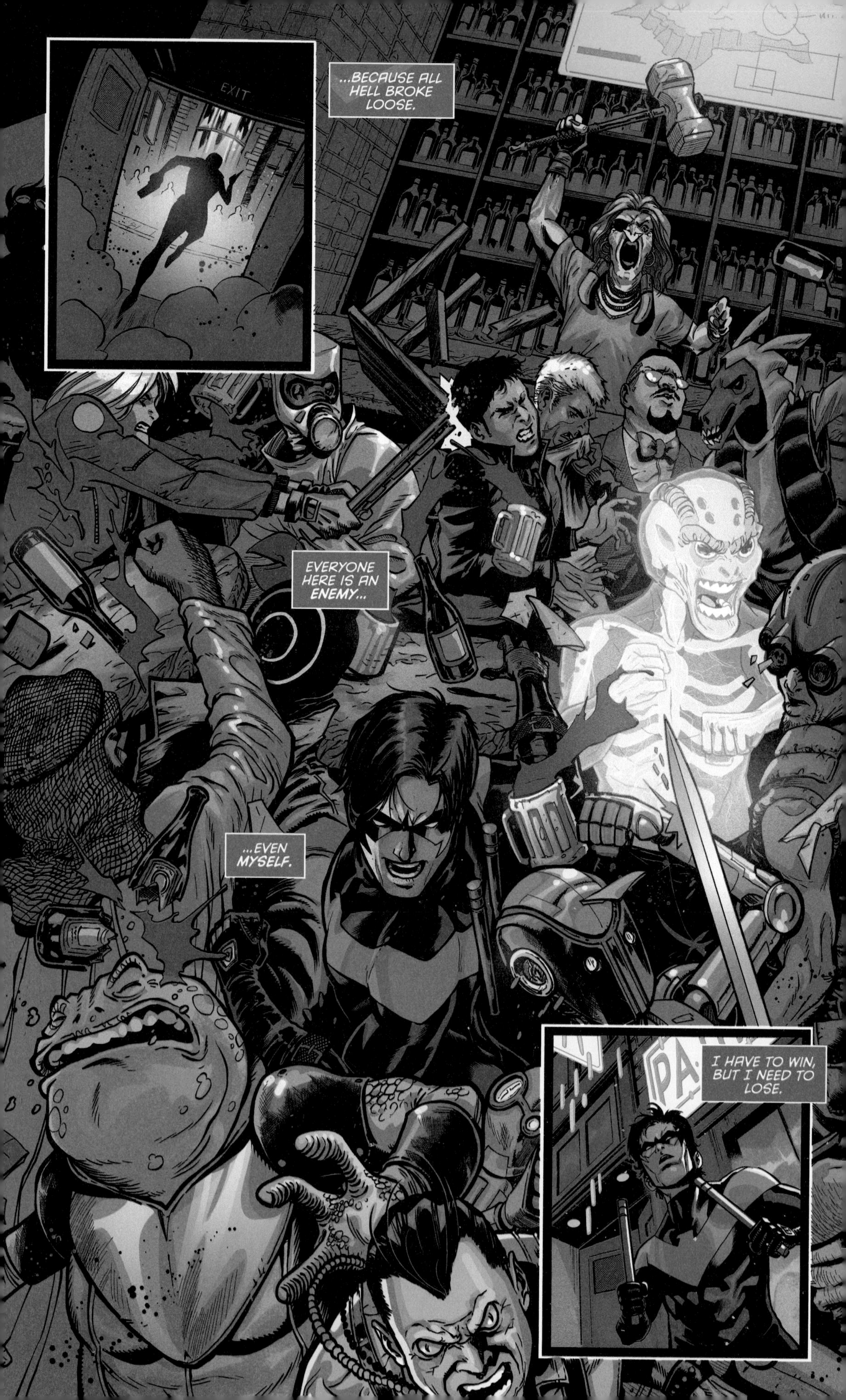
EXIT
...BECAUSE ALL HELL BROKE LOOSE.
EVERYONE HERE IS AN ENEMY...
...EVEN MYSELF.
I HAVE TO WIN, BUT I NEED TO LOSE.

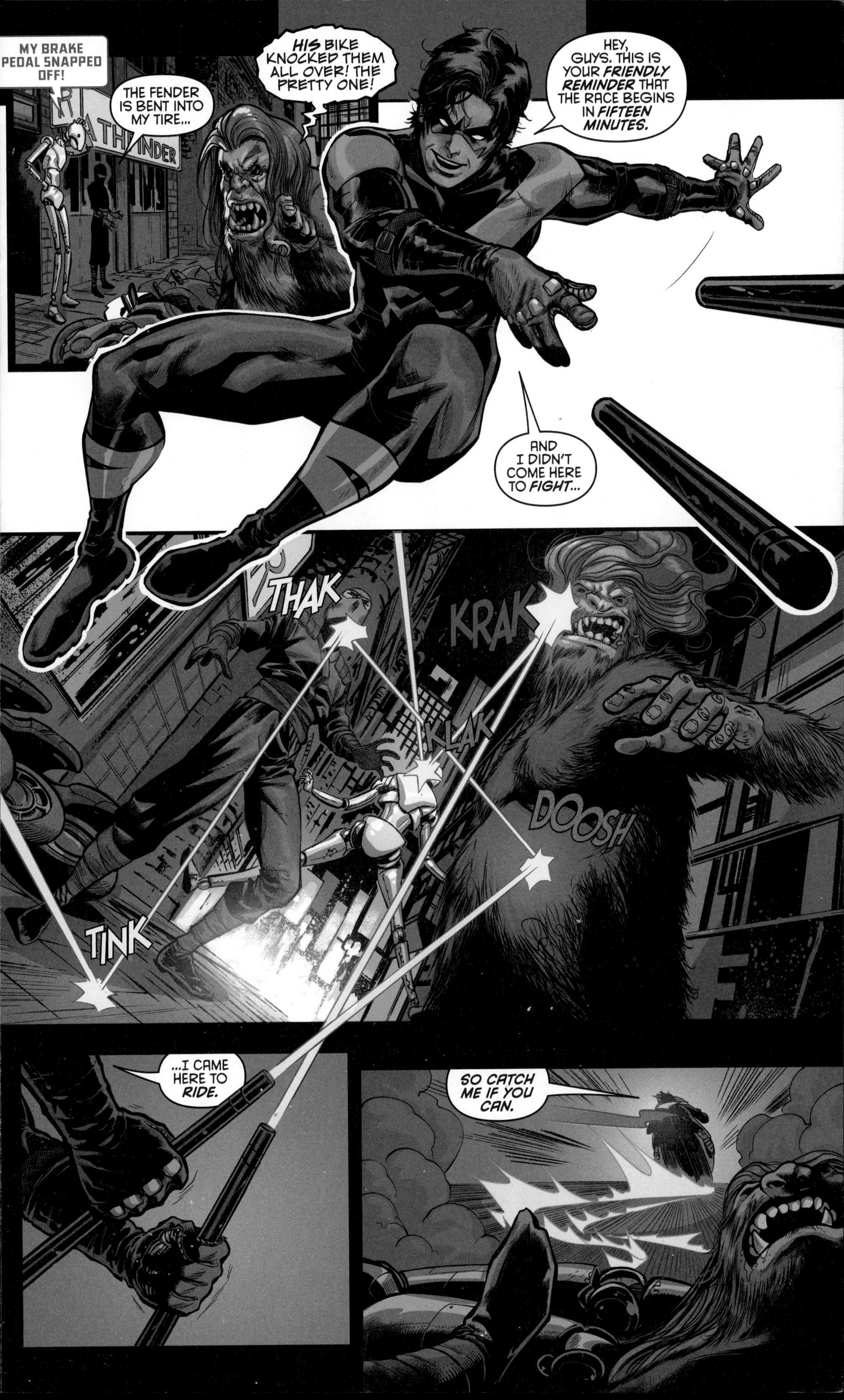
MY BRAKE PEDAL SNAPPED OFF!
THE FENDER IS BENT INTO MY TIRE...
HIS BIKE KNOCKED THEM ALL OVER! THE PRETTY ONE!
HEY, GUYS. THIS IS YOUR FRIENDLY REMINDER THAT THE RACE BEGINS IN FIFTEEN MINUTES.
AND I DIDN'T COME HERE TO FIGHT...
THAK
KRAK
KLAK
DOOSH
TINK
...I CAME HERE TO RIDE.
SO CATCH ME IF YOU CAN.

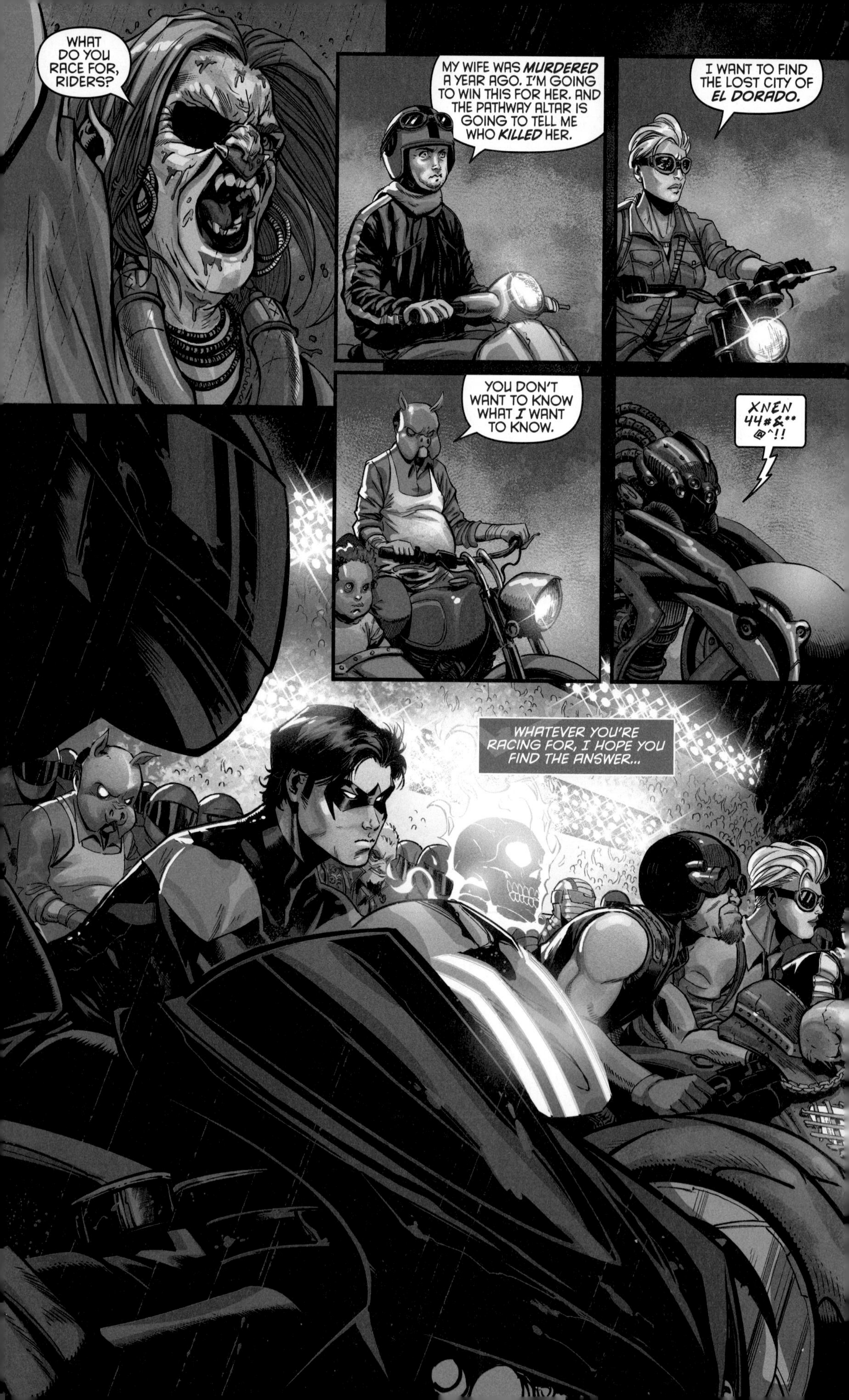
WHAT DO YOU RACE FOR, RIDERS?
MY WIFE WAS MURDERED A YEAR AGO. I'M GOING TO WIN THIS FOR HER. AND THE PATHWAY ALTAR IS GOING TO TELL ME WHO KILLED HER.
I WANT TO FIND THE LOST CITY OF EL DORADO.
YOU DON'T WANT TO KNOW WHAT I WANT TO KNOW.
XNEN 44#&** @^!!
WHATEVER YOU'RE RACING FOR, I HOPE YOU FIND THE ANSWER...

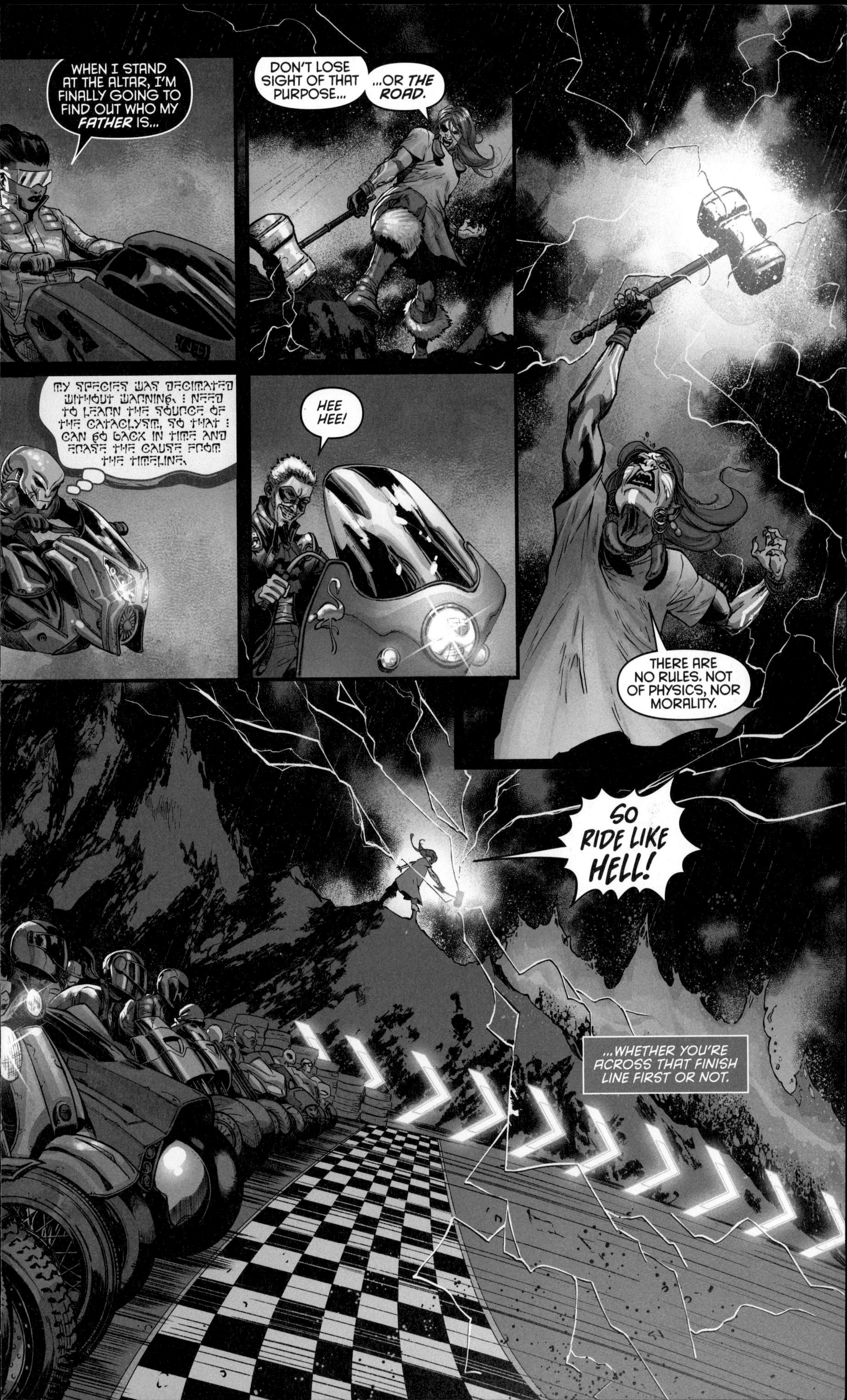
WHEN I STAND AT THE ALTAR, I'M FINALLY GOING TO FIND OUT WHO MY *FATHER* IS...
DON'T LOSE SIGHT OF THAT PURPOSE...
...OR *THE ROAD.*
MY SPECIES WAS DECIMATED WITHOUT WARNING. I NEED TO LEARN THE SOURCE OF THE CATACLYSM, SO THAT I CAN GO BACK IN TIME AND ERASE THE CAUSE FROM THE TIMELINE.
HEE HEE!
THERE ARE NO RULES. NOT OF PHYSICS, NOR MORALITY.
SO RIDE LIKE HELL!
...WHETHER YOU'RE ACROSS THAT FINISH LINE FIRST OR NOT.

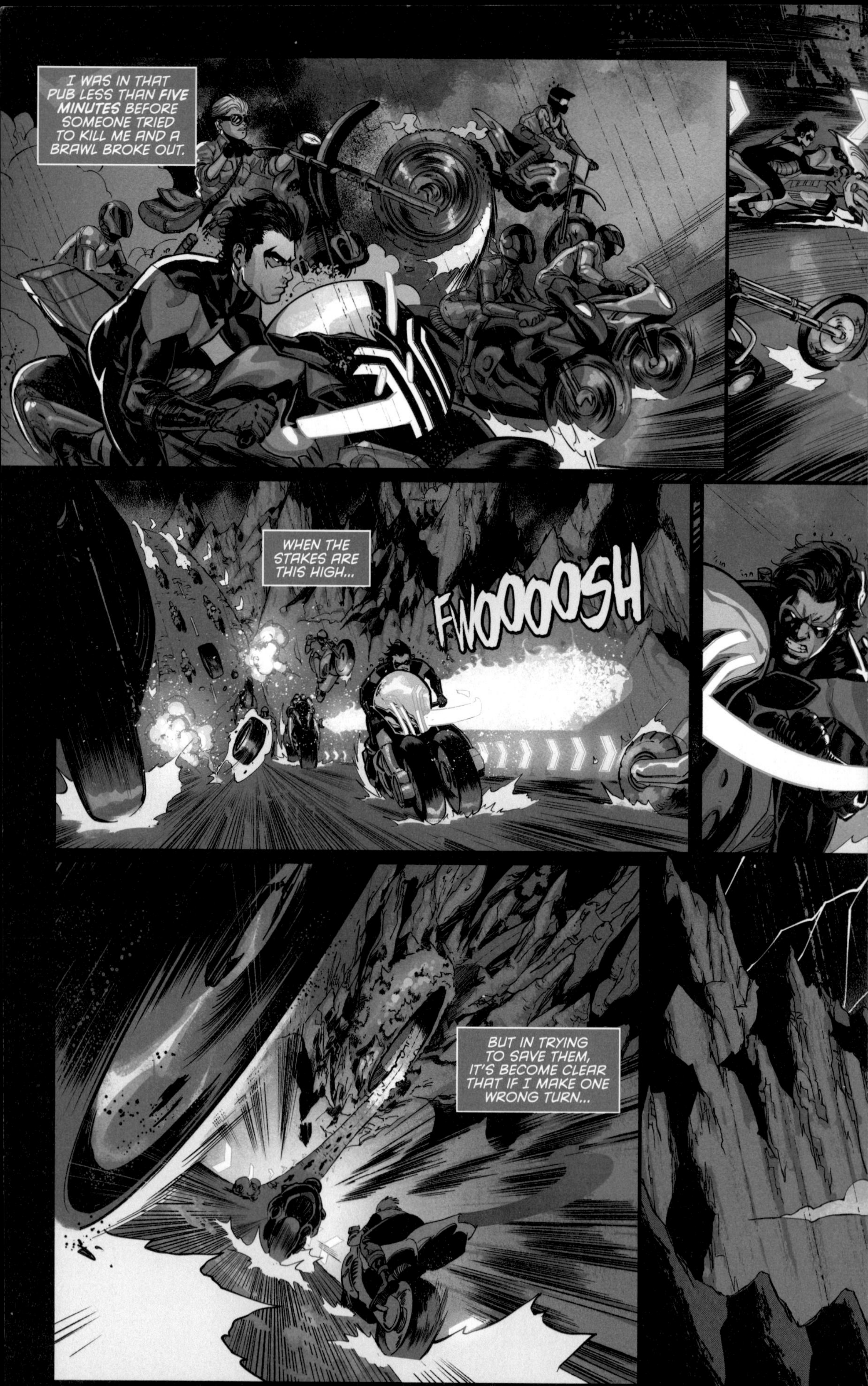
I WAS IN THAT PUB LESS THAN FIVE MINUTES BEFORE SOMEONE TRIED TO KILL ME AND A BRAWL BROKE OUT.
WHEN THE STAKES ARE THIS HIGH...
FWOOOOSH
BUT IN TRYING TO SAVE THEM, IT'S BECOME CLEAR THAT IF I MAKE ONE WRONG TURN...

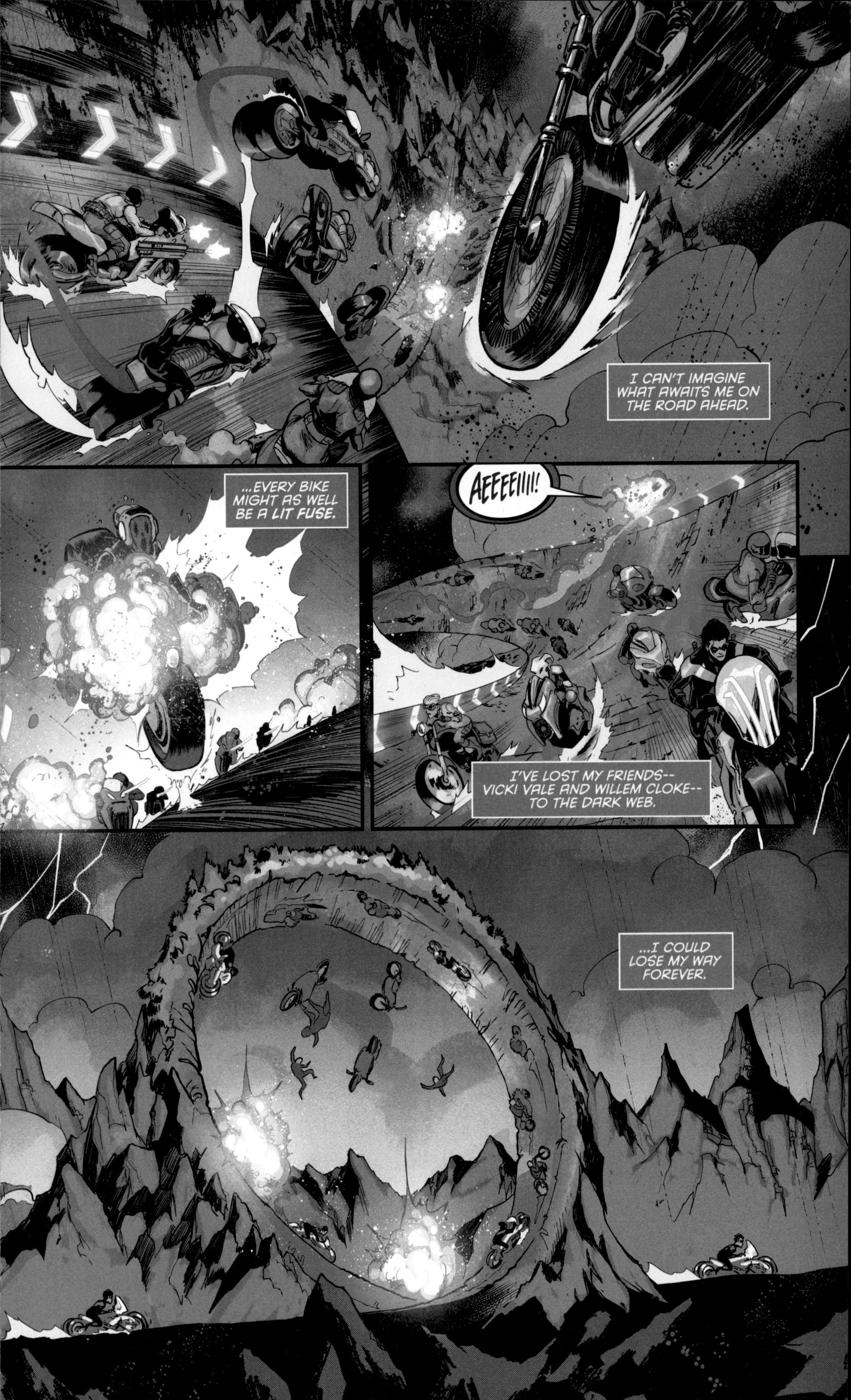
I CAN'T IMAGINE WHAT AWAITS ME ON THE ROAD AHEAD.
...EVERY BIKE MIGHT AS WELL BE A LIT FUSE.
AEEEEIIII!
I'VE LOST MY FRIENDS-- VICKI VALE AND WILLEM CLOKE-- TO THE DARK WEB.
...I COULD LOSE MY WAY FOREVER.

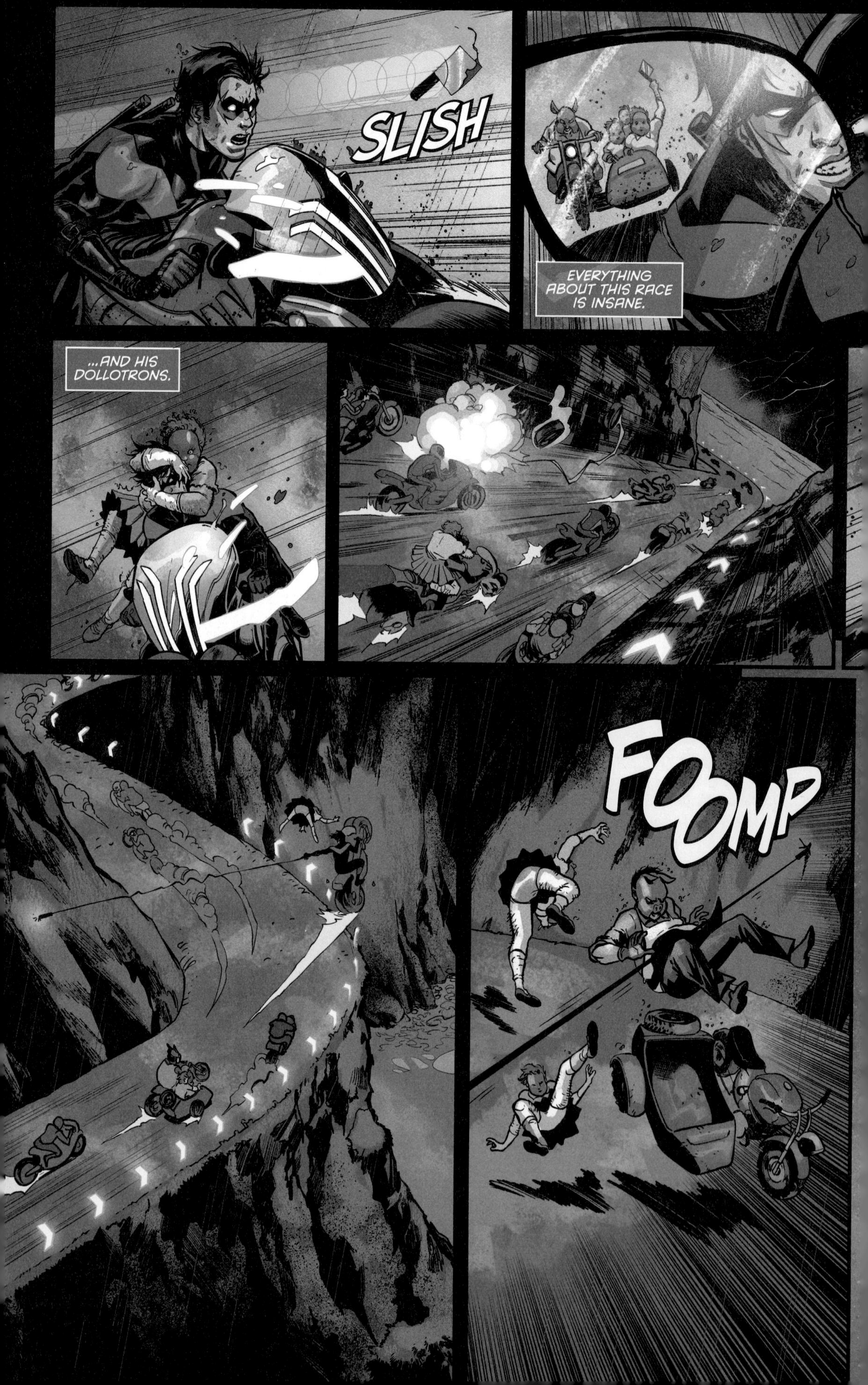

SLISH
EVERYTHING ABOUT THIS RACE IS INSANE.
...AND HIS DOLLOTRONS.
FOOOMP

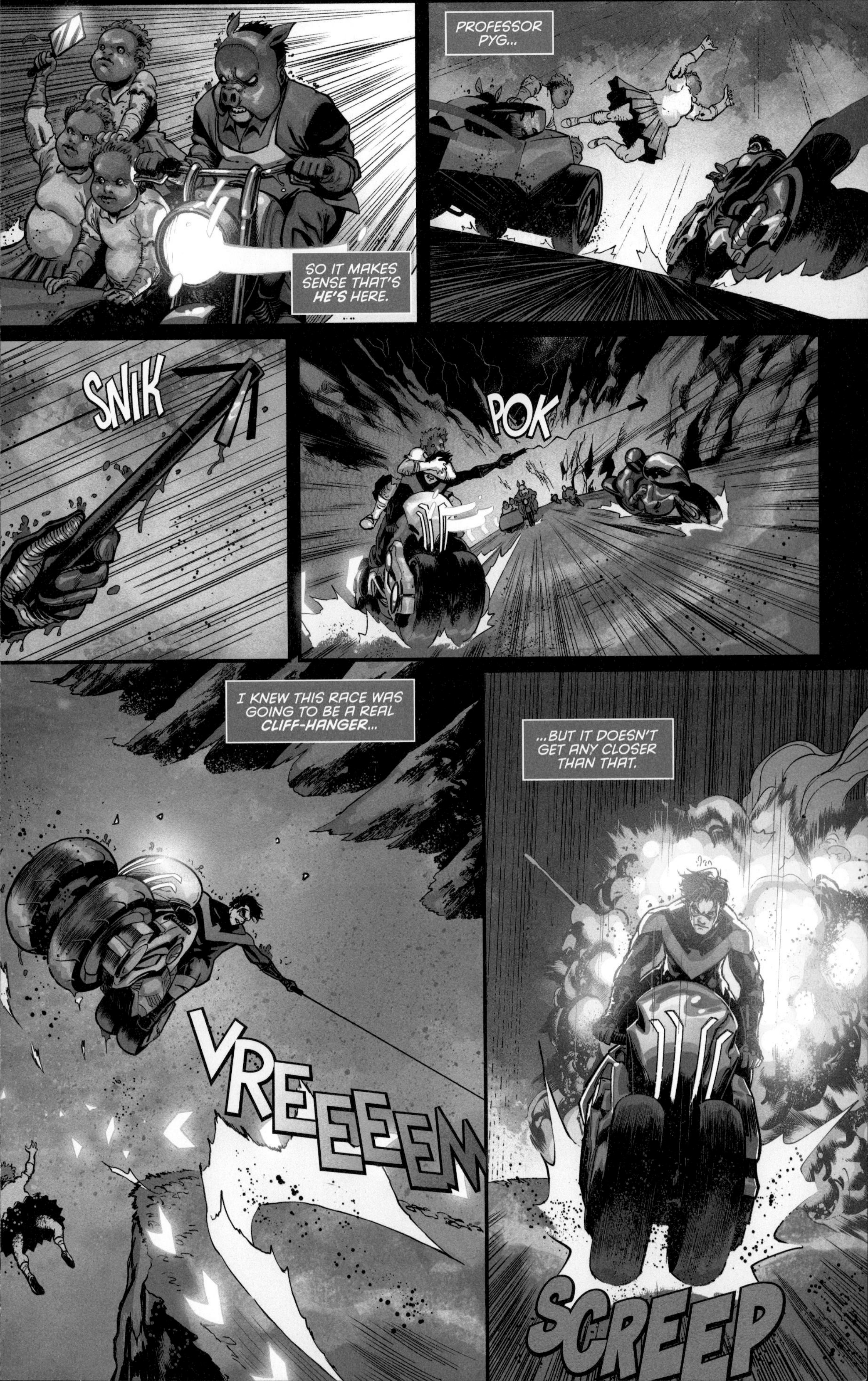
SO IT MAKES SENSE THAT'S HE'S HERE.
PROFESSOR PYG...
SNIK
POK
I KNEW THIS RACE WAS GOING TO BE A REAL CLIFF-HANGER...
VREEEEEM
...BUT IT DOESN'T GET ANY CLOSER THAN THAT.
SCREEP

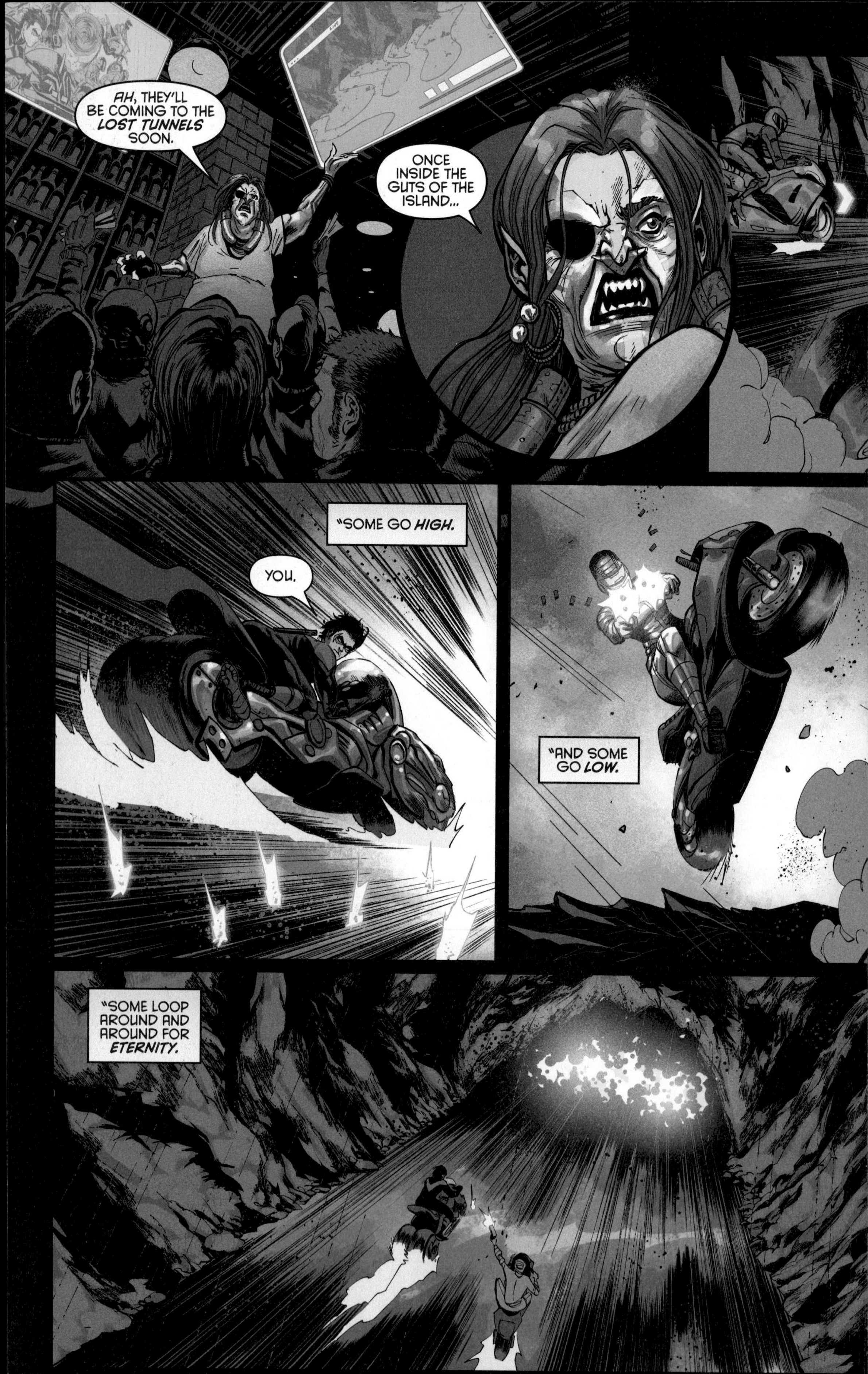
AH, THEY'LL BE COMING TO THE LOST TUNNELS SOON.
ONCE INSIDE THE GUTS OF THE ISLAND...
"SOME GO HIGH.
YOU.
"AND SOME GO LOW.
"SOME LOOP AROUND AND AROUND FOR ETERNITY.

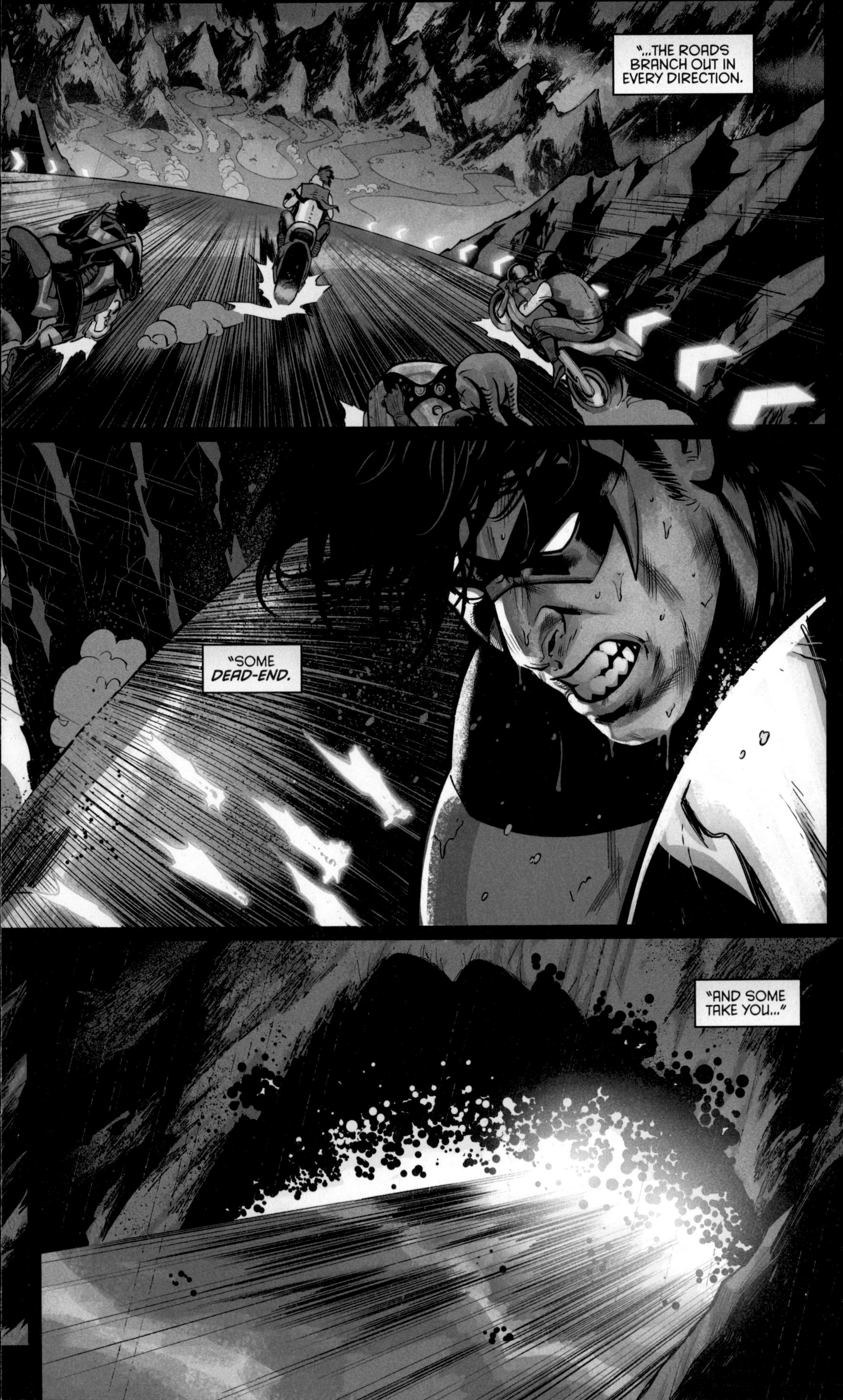
"...THE ROADS BRANCH OUT IN EVERY DIRECTION.
"SOME *DEAD-END.*
"AND SOME TAKE YOU..."

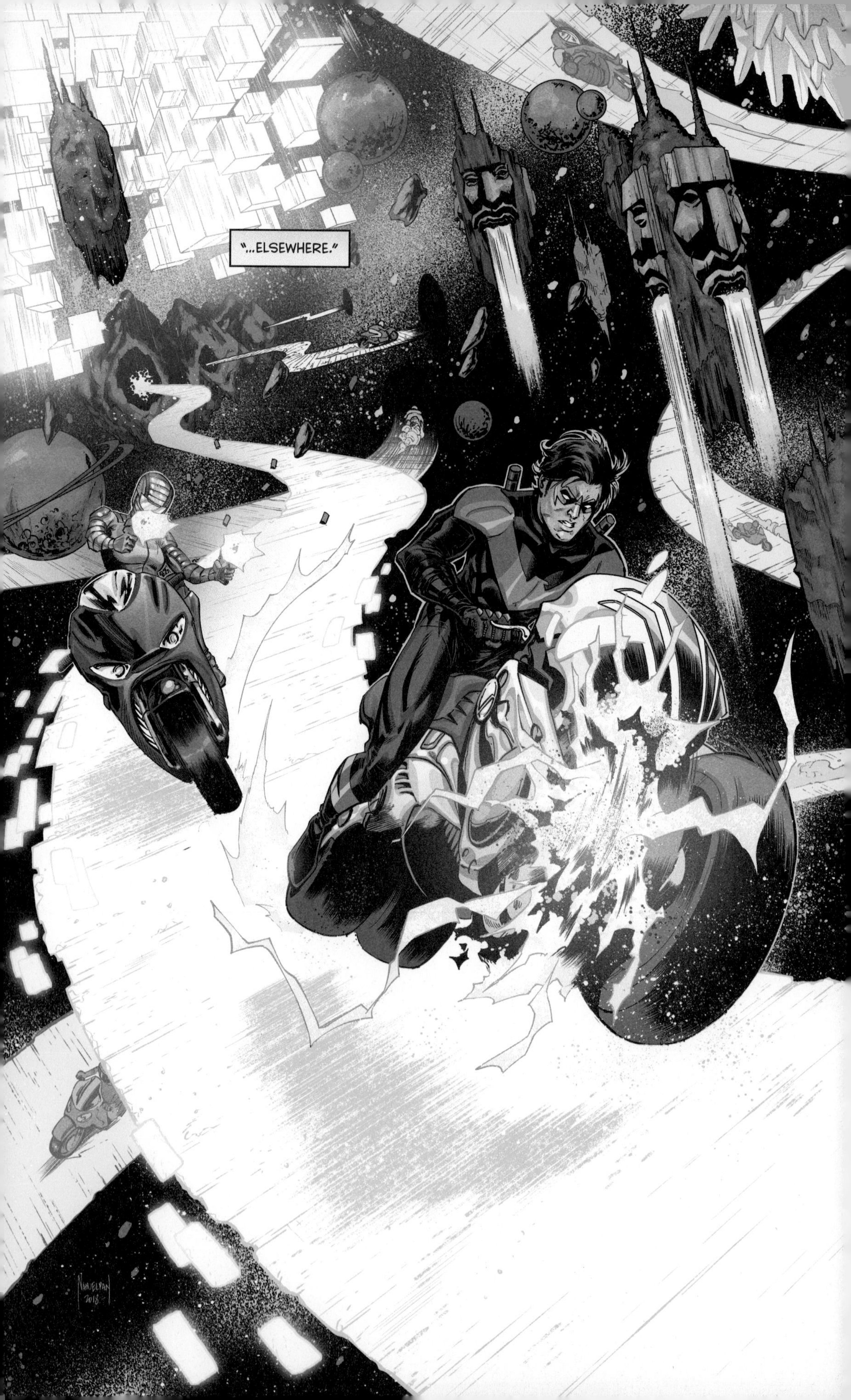
"...ELSEWHERE."
NAHUELPAN
2018

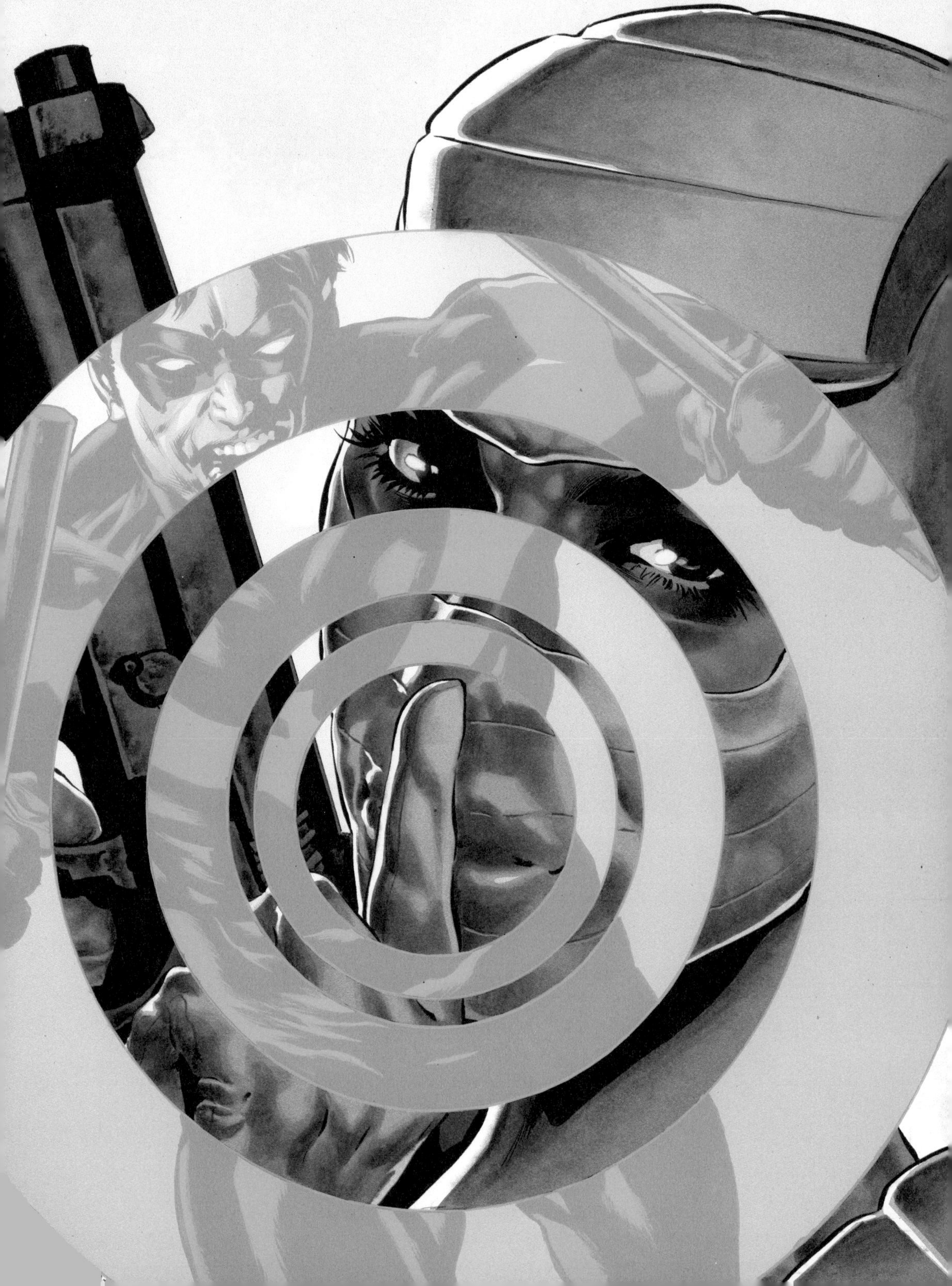

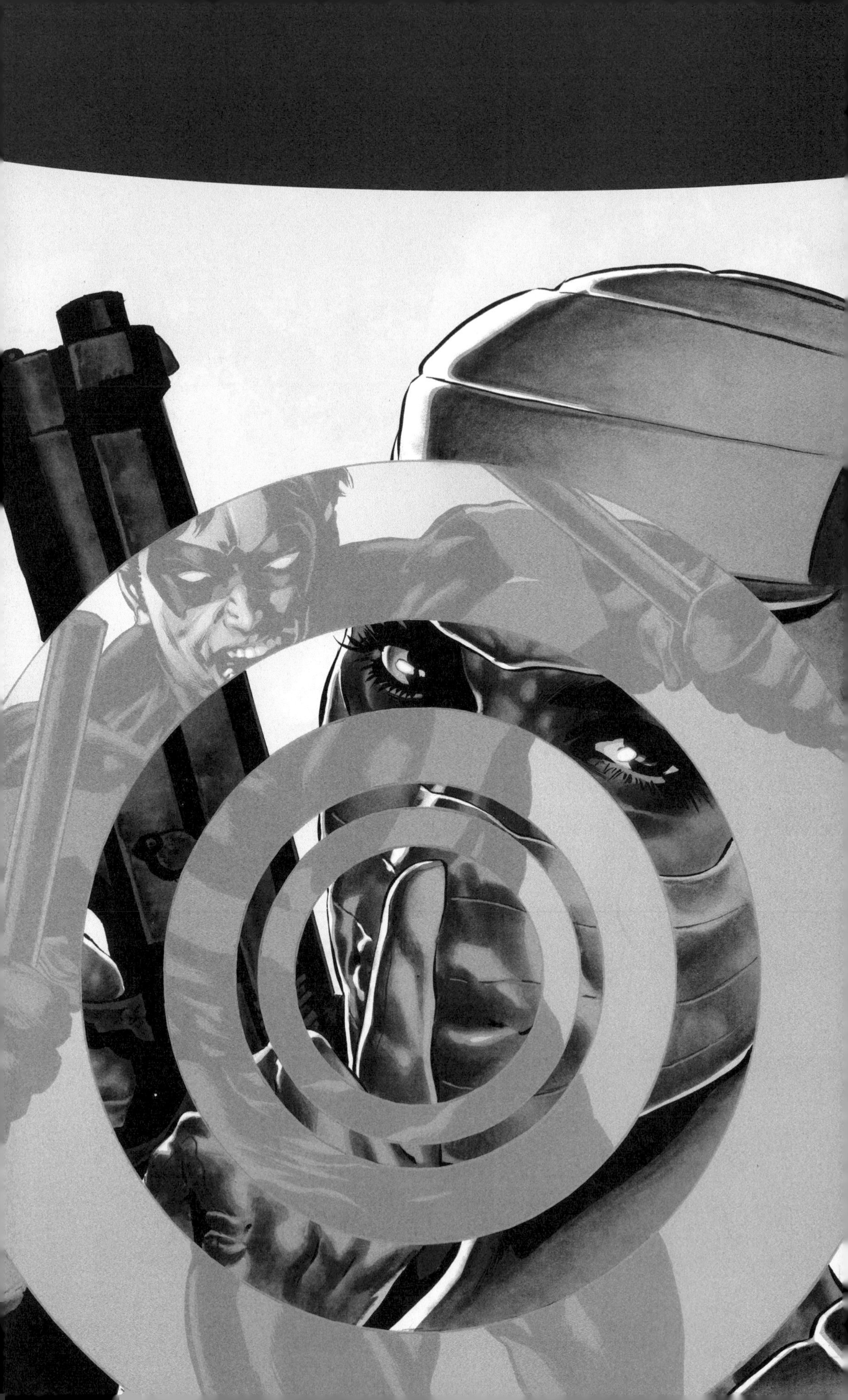

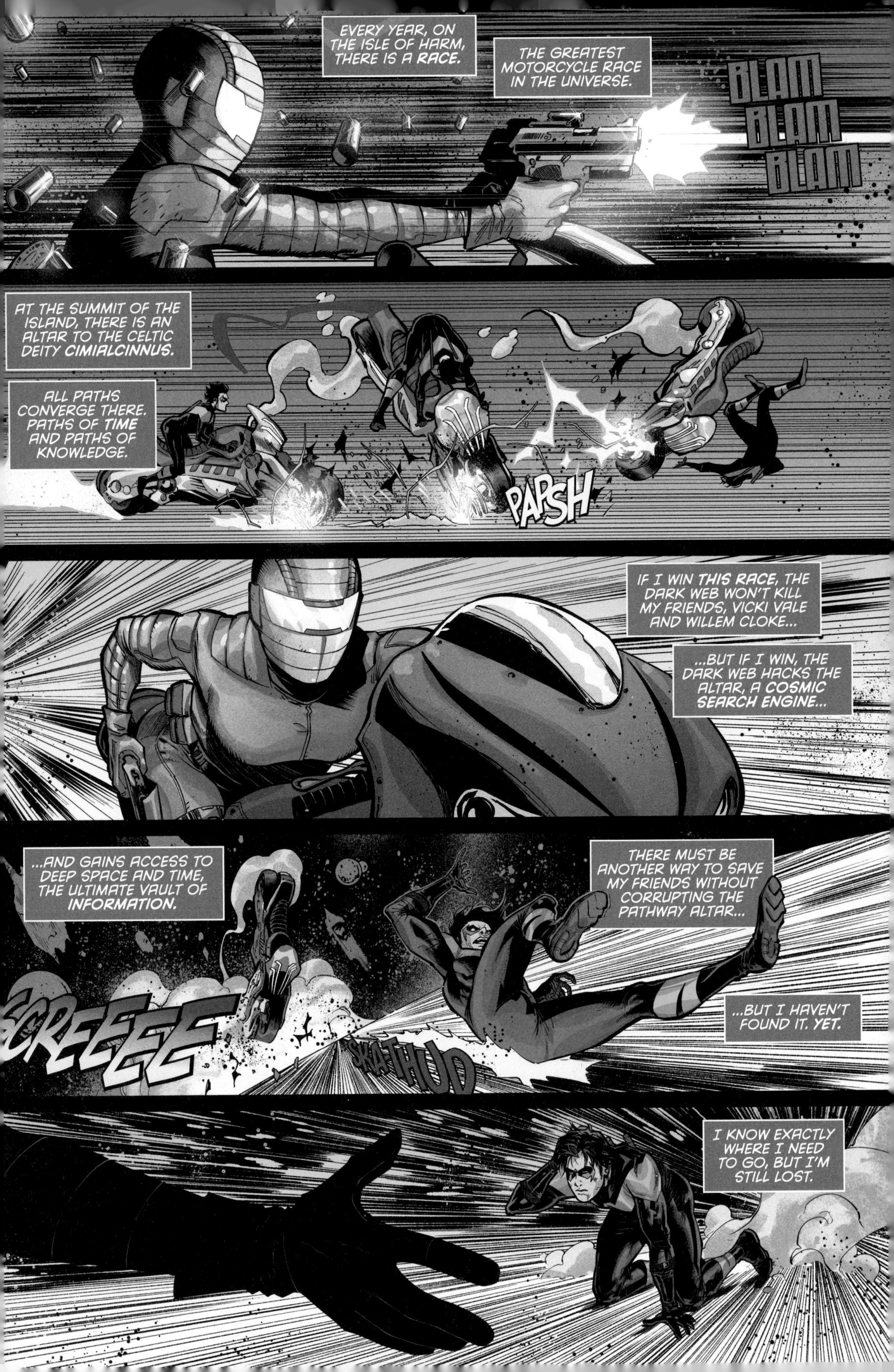
EVERY YEAR, ON THE ISLE OF HARM, THERE IS A RACE.
THE GREATEST MOTORCYCLE RACE IN THE UNIVERSE.
BLAM BLAM BLAM
AT THE SUMMIT OF THE ISLAND, THERE IS AN ALTAR TO THE CELTIC DEITY CIMIALCINNUS.
ALL PATHS CONVERGE THERE. PATHS OF TIME AND PATHS OF KNOWLEDGE.
PAPSH
IF I WIN THIS RACE, THE DARK WEB WON'T KILL MY FRIENDS, VICKI VALE AND WILLEM CLOKE...
...BUT IF I WIN, THE DARK WEB HACKS THE ALTAR, A COSMIC SEARCH ENGINE...
...AND GAINS ACCESS TO DEEP SPACE AND TIME, THE ULTIMATE VAULT OF INFORMATION.
THERE MUST BE ANOTHER WAY TO SAVE MY FRIENDS WITHOUT CORRUPTING THE PATHWAY ALTAR...
SCREEEE
SKATHUD
...BUT I HAVEN'T FOUND IT. YET.
I KNOW EXACTLY WHERE I NEED TO GO, BUT I'M STILL LOST.

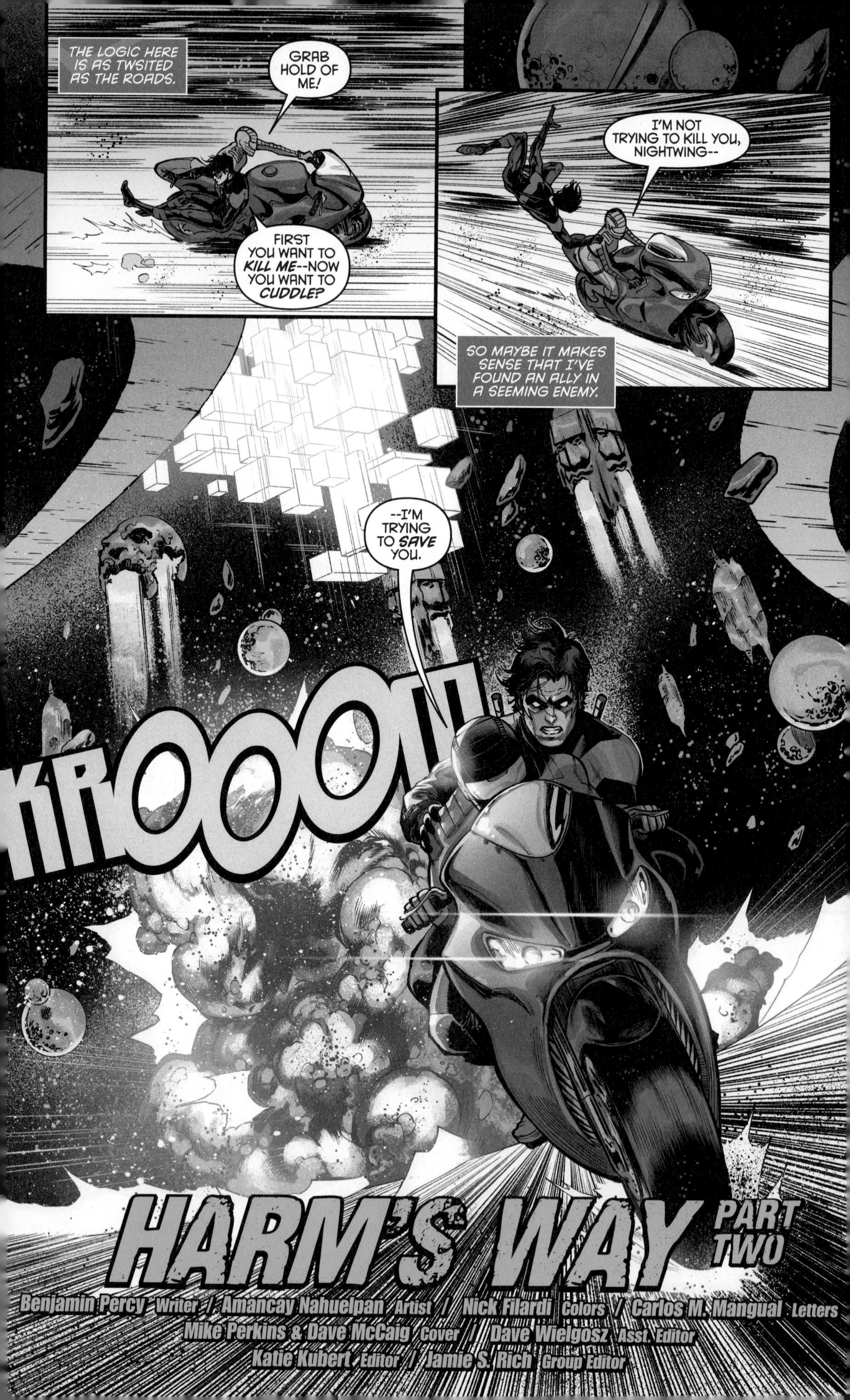
THE LOGIC HERE IS AS TWSITED AS THE ROADS.
GRAB HOLD OF ME!
FIRST YOU WANT TO KILL ME--NOW YOU WANT TO CUDDLE?
I'M NOT TRYING TO KILL YOU, NIGHTWING--
SO MAYBE IT MAKES SENSE THAT I'VE FOUND AN ALLY IN A SEEMING ENEMY.
--I'M TRYING TO SAVE YOU.
KROOOM
HARM'S WAY PART TWO
Benjamin Percy Writer / Amancay Nahuelpan Artist / Nick Filardi Colors / Carlos M. Mangual Letters
Mike Perkins & Dave McCaig Cover / Dave Wielgosz Asst. Editor
Katie Kubert Editor / Jamie S. Rich Group Editor

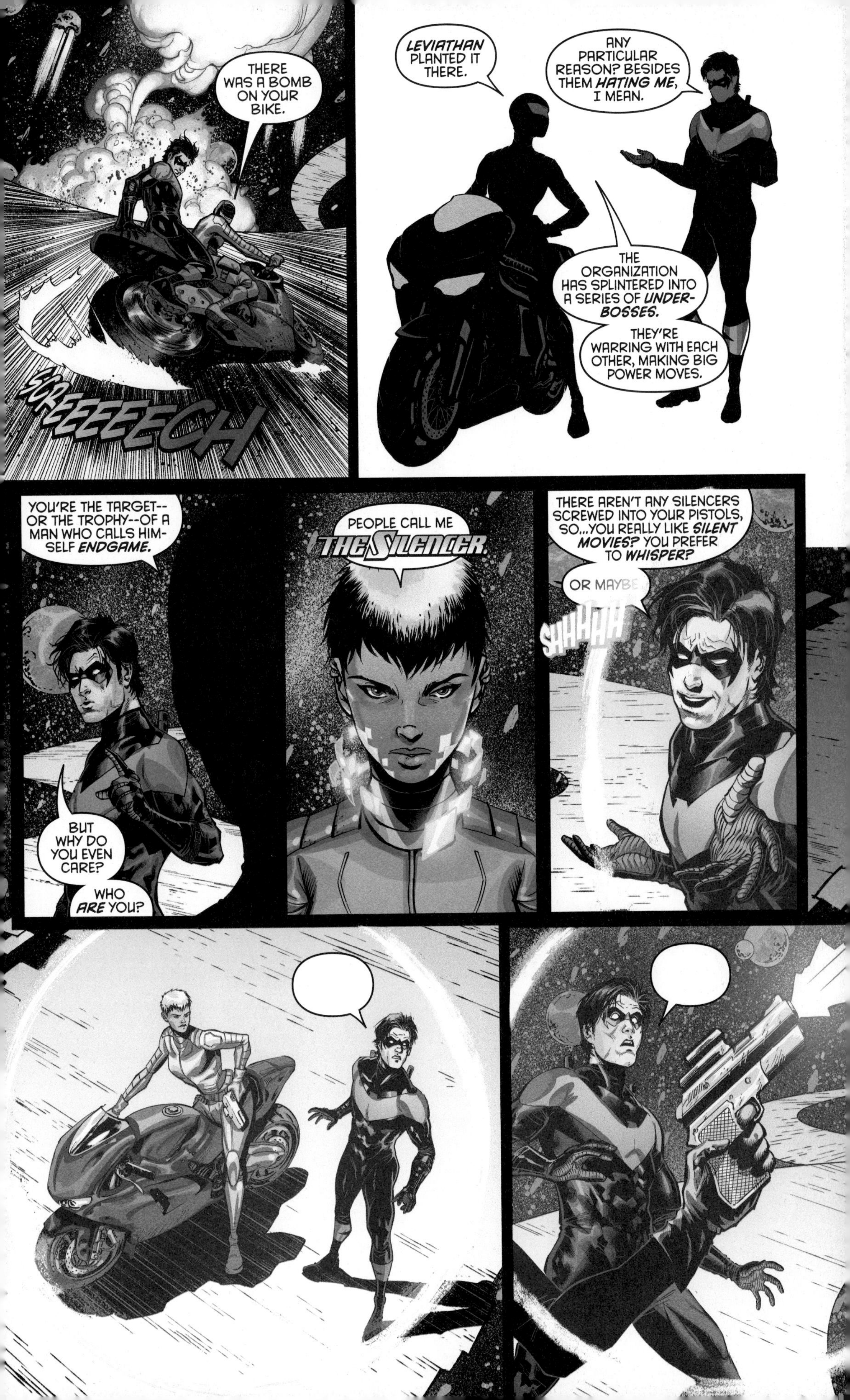

THERE WAS A BOMB ON YOUR BIKE.
SCREEEEEECH
LEVIATHAN PLANTED IT THERE.
ANY PARTICULAR REASON? BESIDES THEM HATING ME, I MEAN.
THE ORGANIZATION HAS SPLINTERED INTO A SERIES OF UNDER-BOSSES.
THEY'RE WARRING WITH EACH OTHER, MAKING BIG POWER MOVES.
YOU'RE THE TARGET--OR THE TROPHY--OF A MAN WHO CALLS HIM-SELF ENDGAME.
BUT WHY DO YOU EVEN CARE?
WHO ARE YOU?
PEOPLE CALL ME THE SILENCER.
THERE AREN'T ANY SILENCERS SCREWED INTO YOUR PISTOLS, SO...YOU REALLY LIKE SILENT MOVIES? YOU PREFER TO WHISPER?
OR MAYBE
SHHHHH

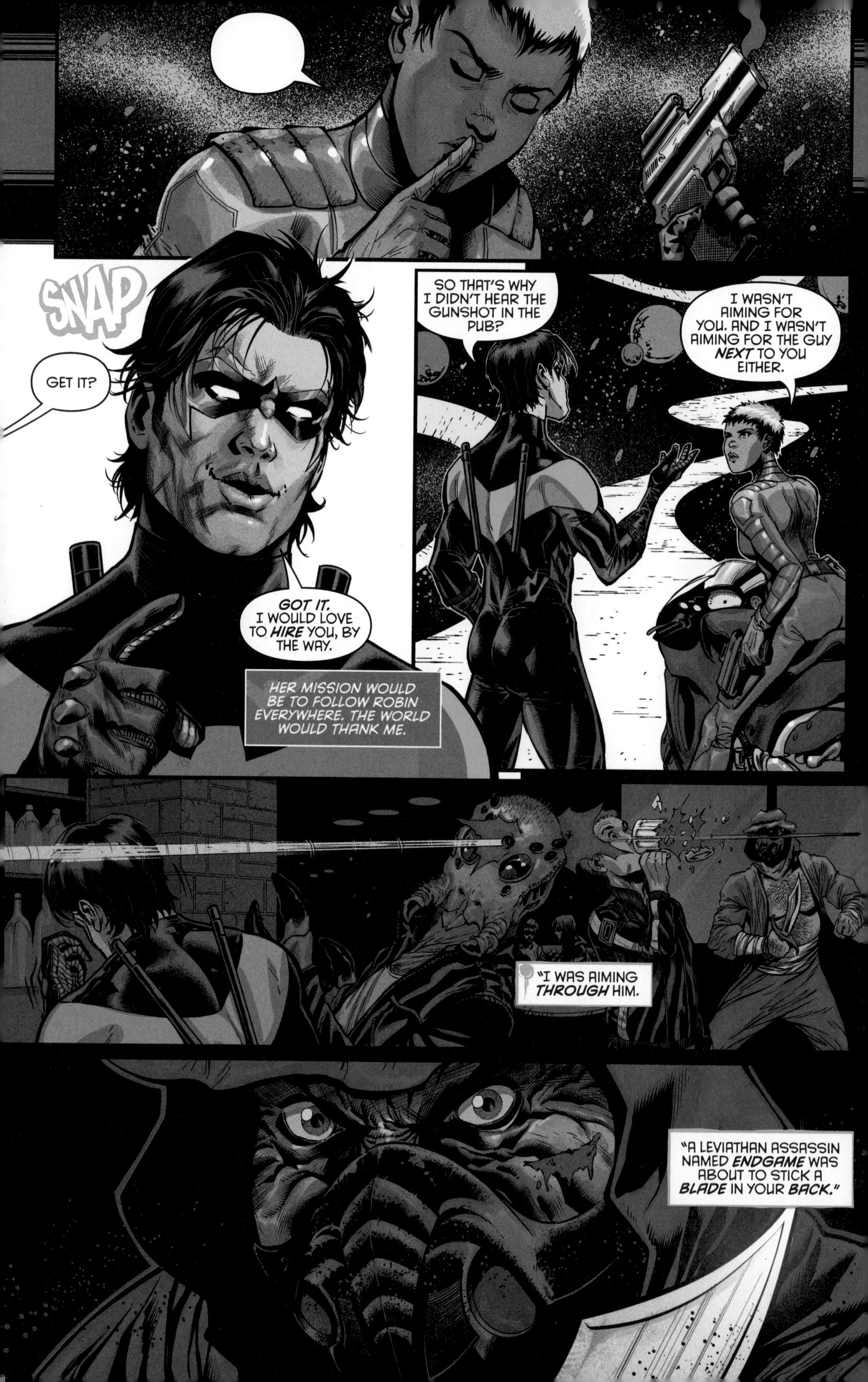
SNAP
GET IT?
GOT IT. I WOULD LOVE TO HIRE YOU, BY THE WAY.
HER MISSION WOULD BE TO FOLLOW ROBIN EVERYWHERE. THE WORLD WOULD THANK ME.
SO THAT'S WHY I DIDN'T HEAR THE GUNSHOT IN THE PUB?
I WASN'T AIMING FOR YOU. AND I WASN'T AIMING FOR THE GUY NEXT TO YOU EITHER.
"I WAS AIMING THROUGH HIM.
"A LEVIATHAN ASSASSIN NAMED ENDGAME WAS ABOUT TO STICK A BLADE IN YOUR BACK."

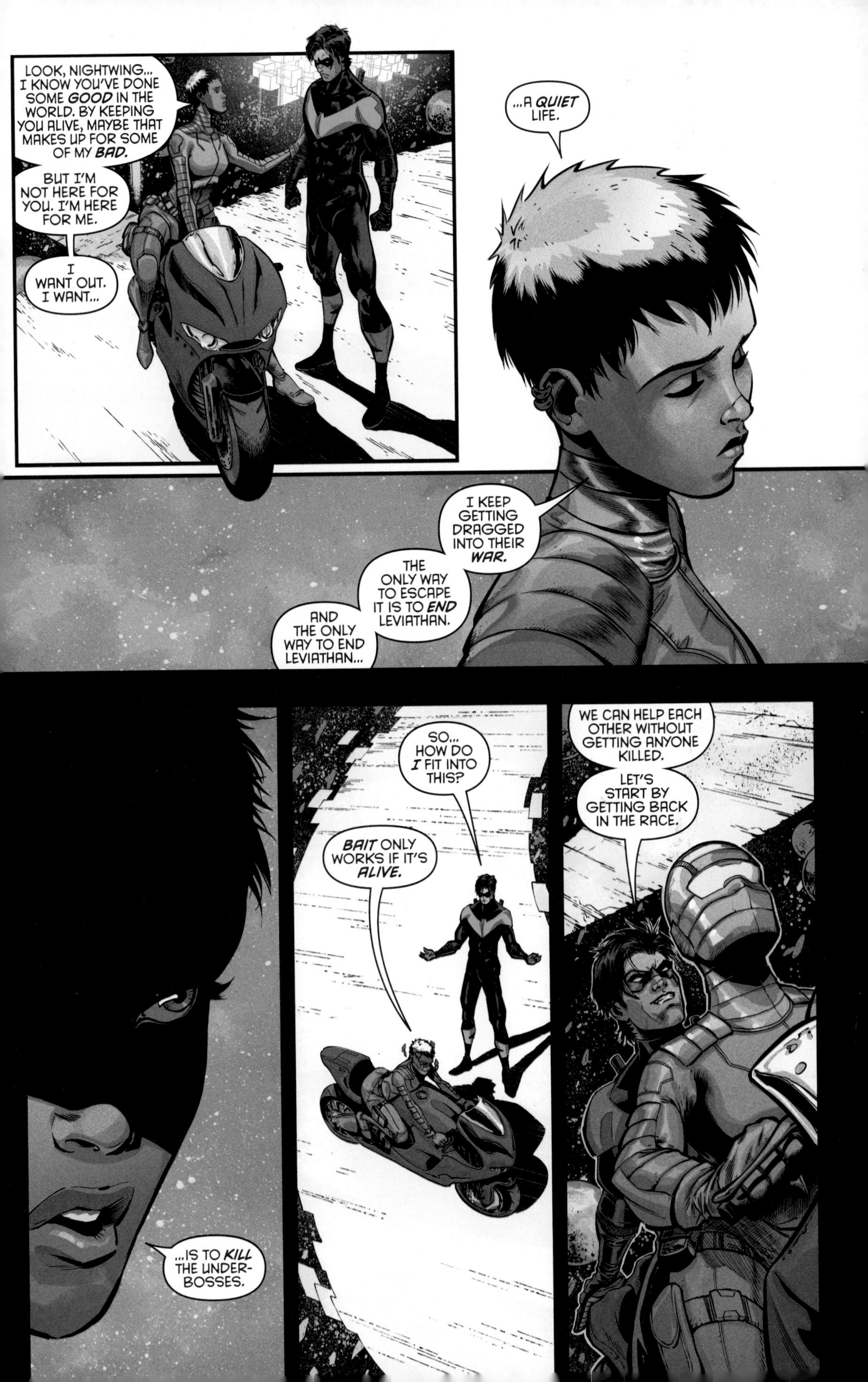
LOOK, NIGHTWING... I KNOW YOU'VE DONE SOME GOOD IN THE WORLD. BY KEEPING YOU ALIVE, MAYBE THAT MAKES UP FOR SOME OF MY BAD.
BUT I'M NOT HERE FOR YOU. I'M HERE FOR ME.
I WANT OUT. I WANT...
...A QUIET LIFE.
I KEEP GETTING DRAGGED INTO THEIR WAR.
THE ONLY WAY TO ESCAPE IT IS TO END LEVIATHAN.
AND THE ONLY WAY TO END LEVIATHAN...
...IS TO KILL THE UNDER-BOSSES.
SO... HOW DO I FIT INTO THIS?
BAIT ONLY WORKS IF IT'S ALIVE.
WE CAN HELP EACH OTHER WITHOUT GETTING ANYONE KILLED.
LET'S START BY GETTING BACK IN THE RACE.

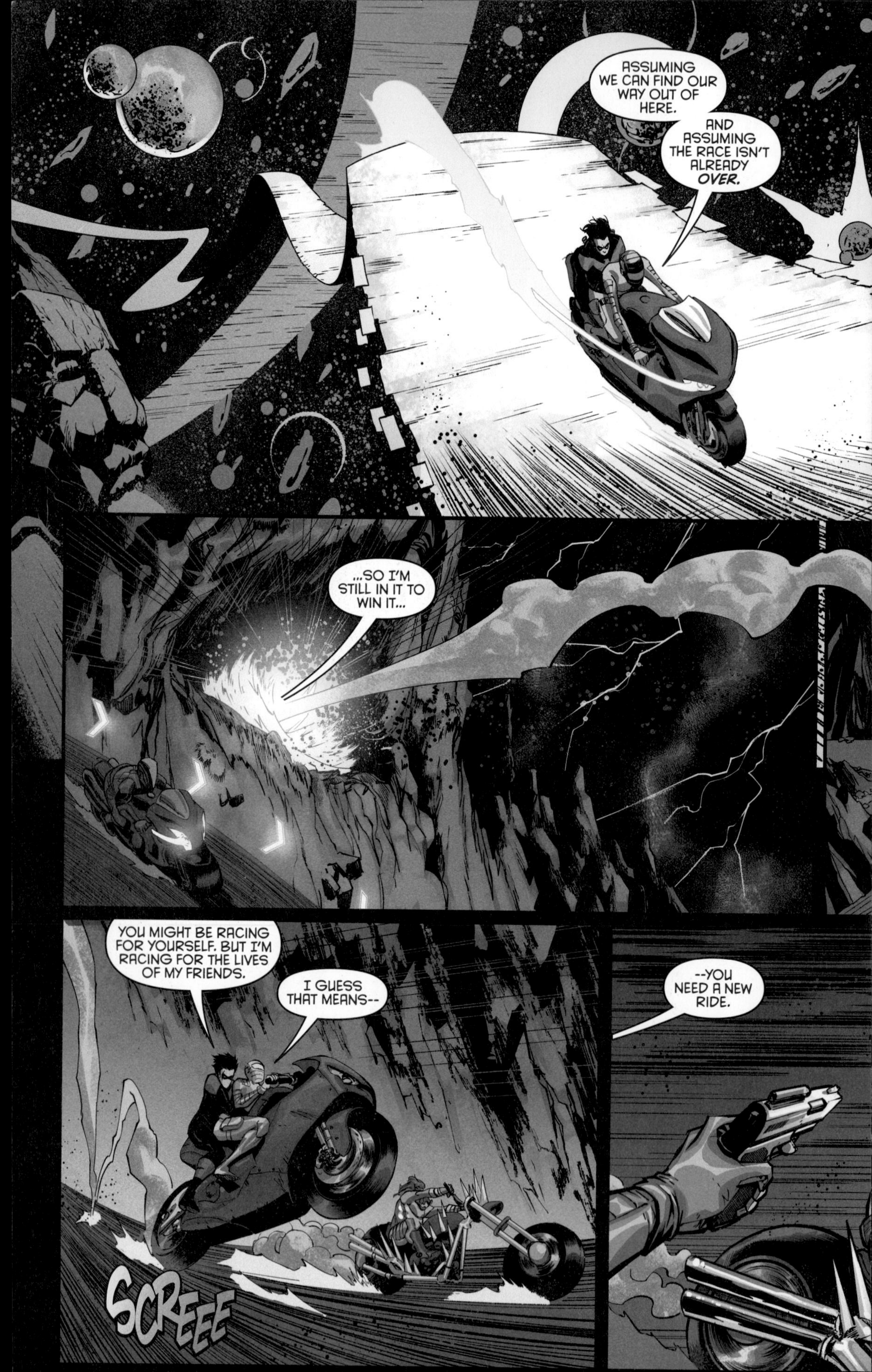
ASSUMING WE CAN FIND OUR WAY OUT OF HERE.
AND ASSUMING THE RACE ISN'T ALREADY OVER.
...SO I'M STILL IN IT TO WIN IT...
YOU MIGHT BE RACING FOR YOURSELF. BUT I'M RACING FOR THE LIVES OF MY FRIENDS.
I GUESS THAT MEANS--
--YOU NEED A NEW RIDE.
SCREEEE

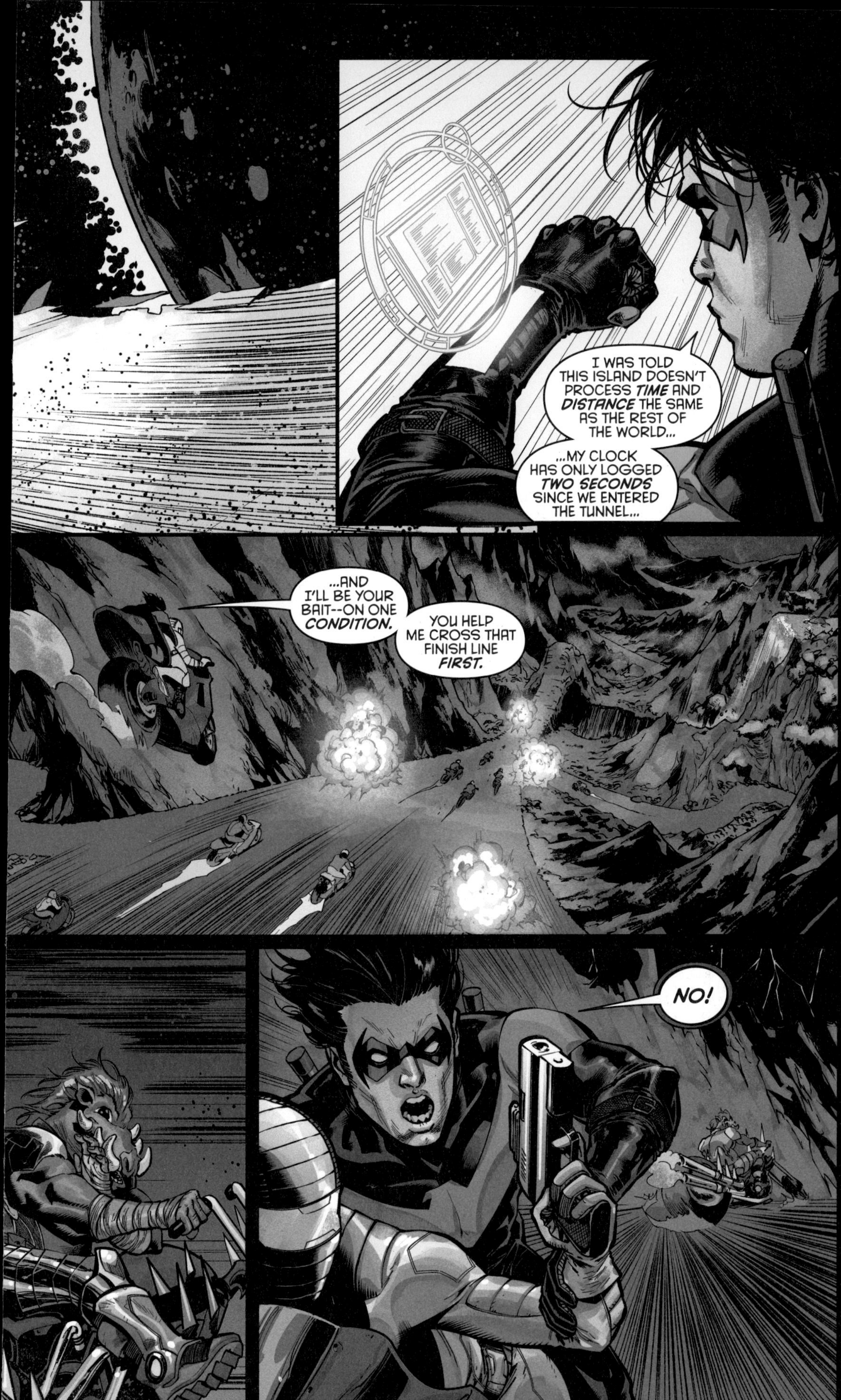

I WAS TOLD THIS ISLAND DOESN'T PROCESS *TIME* AND *DISTANCE* THE SAME AS THE REST OF THE WORLD...
...MY CLOCK HAS ONLY LOGGED *TWO SECONDS* SINCE WE ENTERED THE TUNNEL...
...AND I'LL BE YOUR BAIT--ON ONE *CONDITION.*
YOU HELP ME CROSS THAT FINISH LINE *FIRST.*
NO!

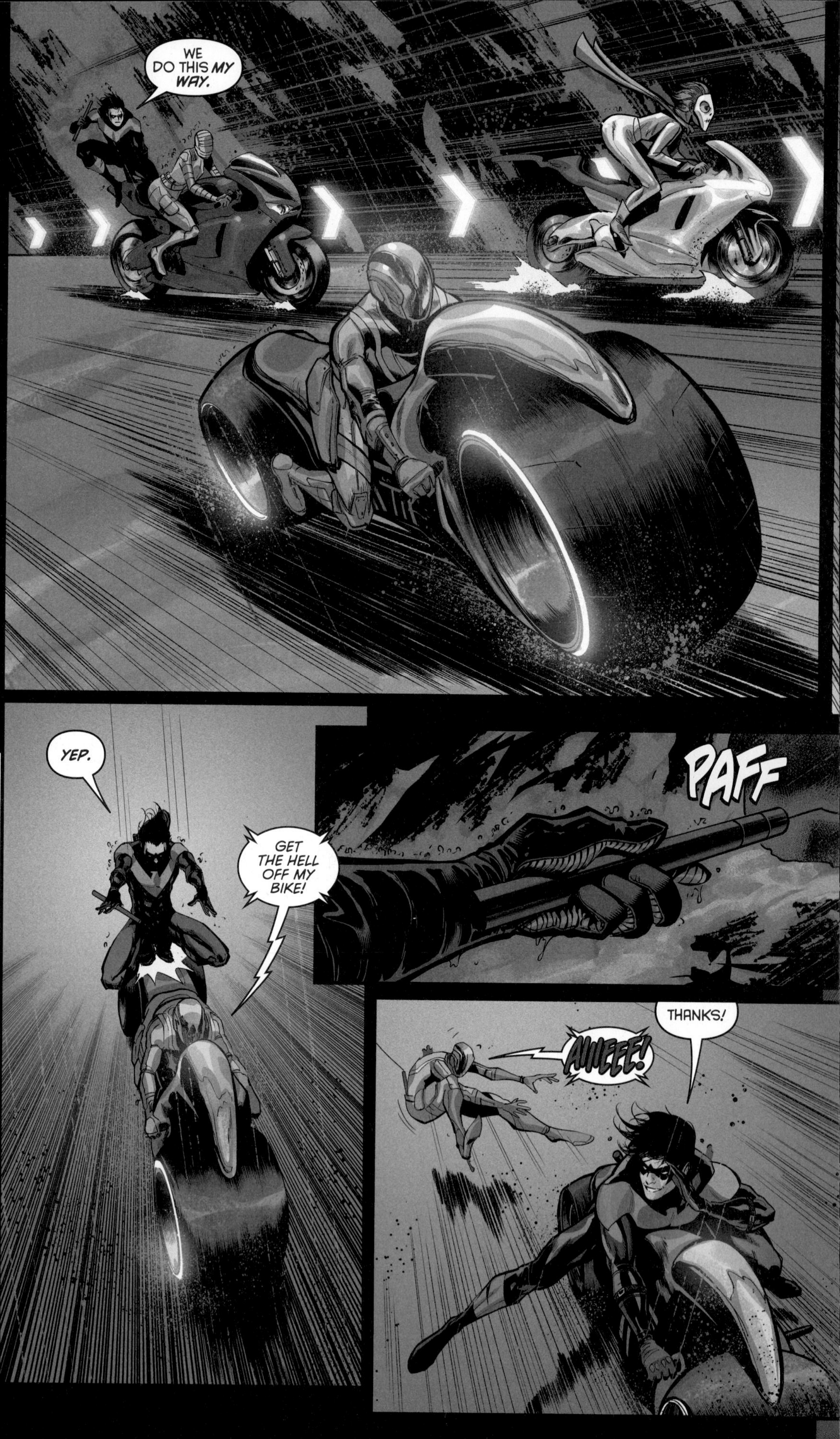

WE DO THIS MY WAY.
YEP.
GET THE HELL OFF MY BIKE!
PAFF
THANKS!
AIIEEE!

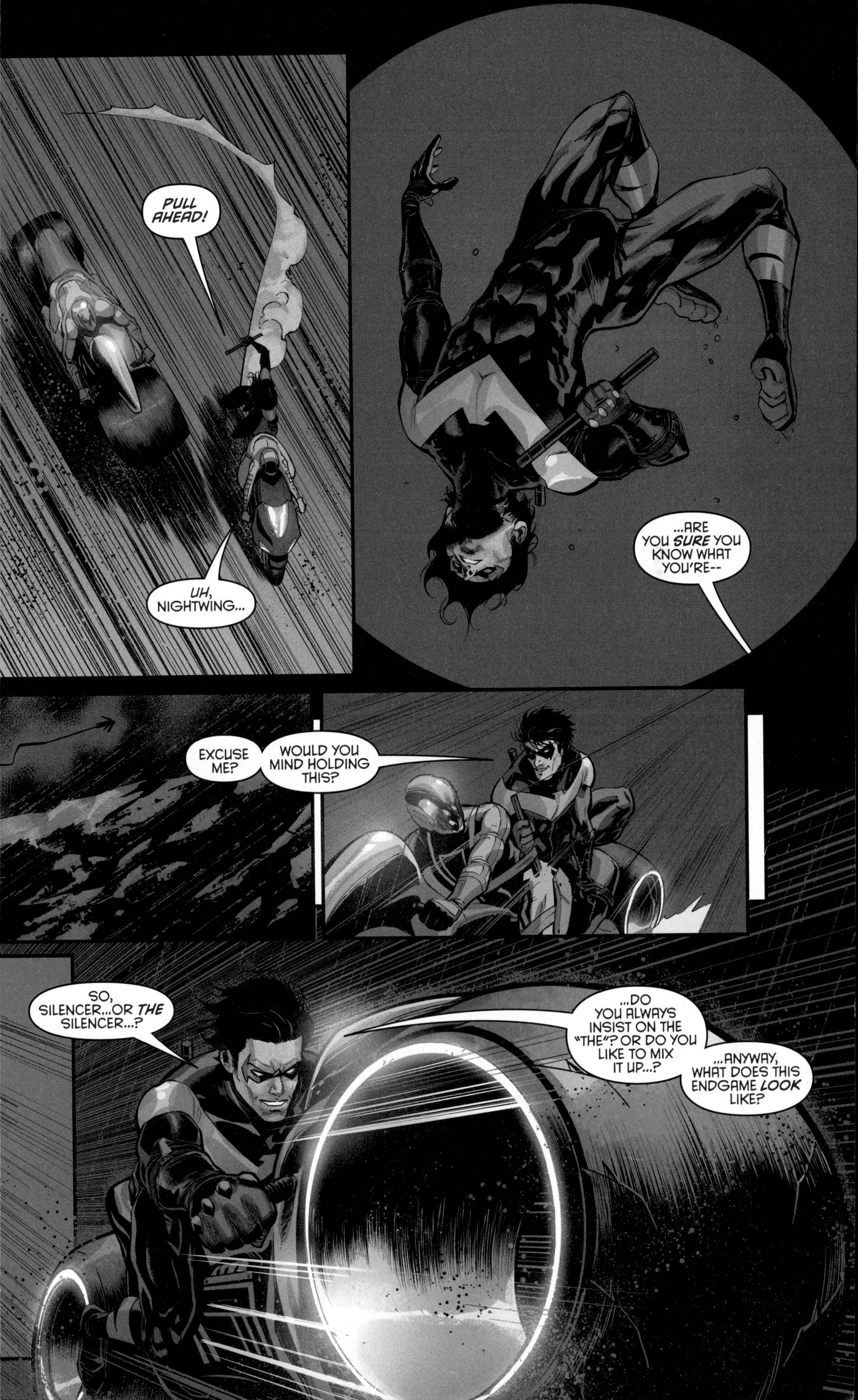
PULL AHEAD!
UH, NIGHTWING...
...ARE YOU SURE YOU KNOW WHAT YOU'RE--
EXCUSE ME?
WOULD YOU MIND HOLDING THIS?
SO, SILENCER...OR THE SILENCER...?
...DO YOU ALWAYS INSIST ON THE "THE"? OR DO YOU LIKE TO MIX IT UP...?
...ANYWAY, WHAT DOES THIS ENDGAME LOOK LIKE?

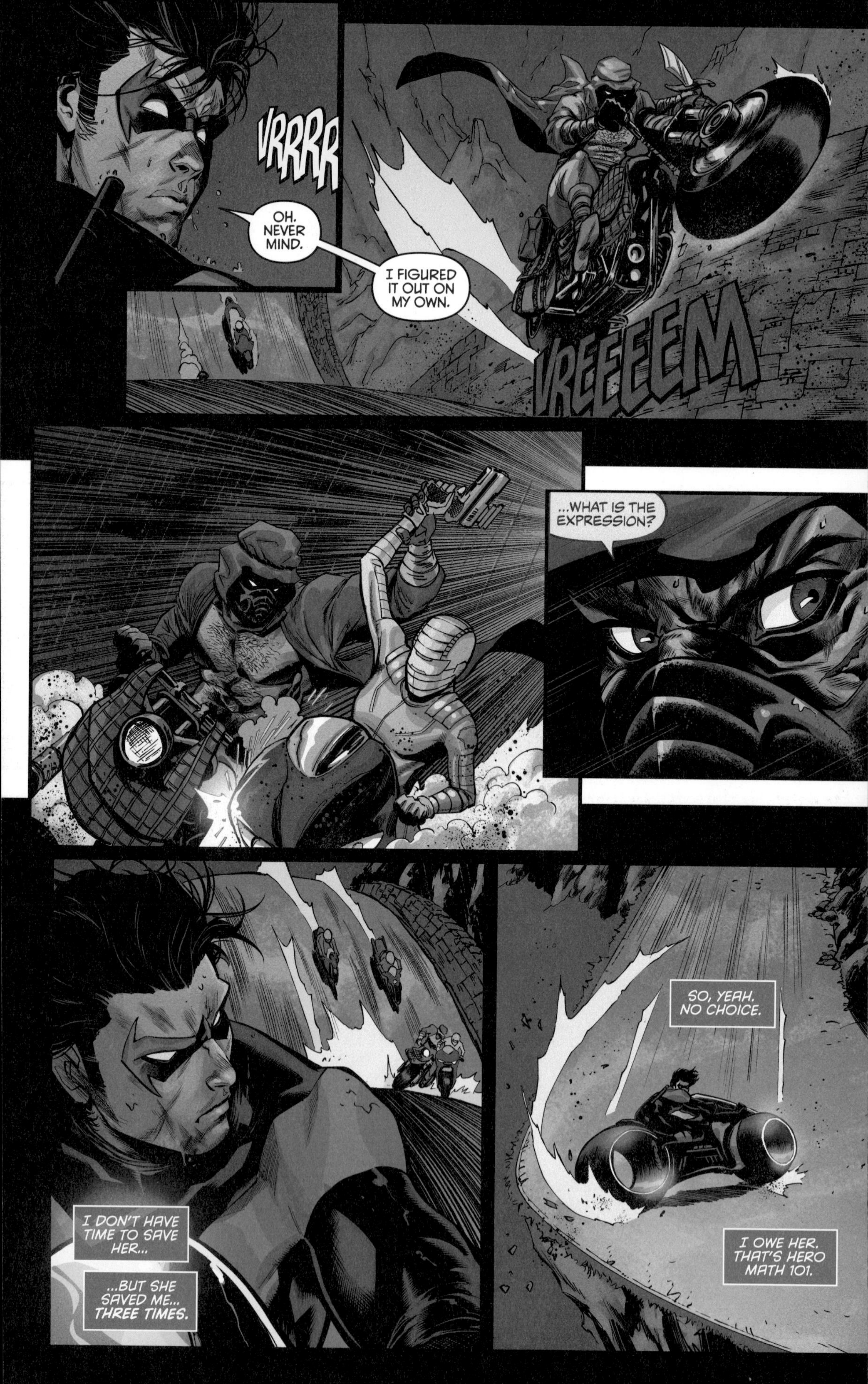
VRRRR
OH. NEVER MIND.
I FIGURED IT OUT ON MY OWN.
VREEEEM
...WHAT IS THE EXPRESSION?
I DON'T HAVE TIME TO SAVE HER...
...BUT SHE SAVED ME... THREE TIMES.
SO, YEAH. NO CHOICE.
I OWE HER. THAT'S HERO MATH 101.

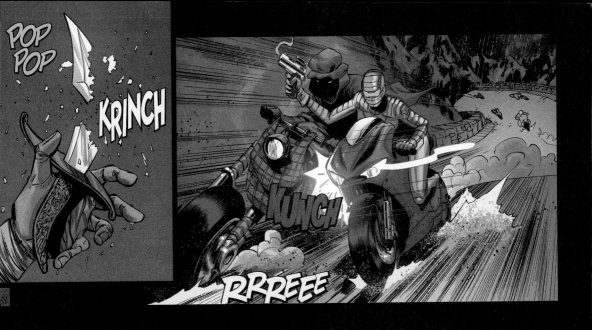

POP POP

KRINCH

KUNCH

RRREEE

WHEN THINGS GET VIOLENT...

...YOU MUST TURN THE OTHER CHEEK?

BLAM

AGH!

I'VE ALWAYS THOUGHT YOU HAD THE NICEST HAMS, NIGHTWING.

BUT I THINK THEY'D LOOK EVEN BETTER STAPLED TO YOUR FACE.

SQUEEEE!

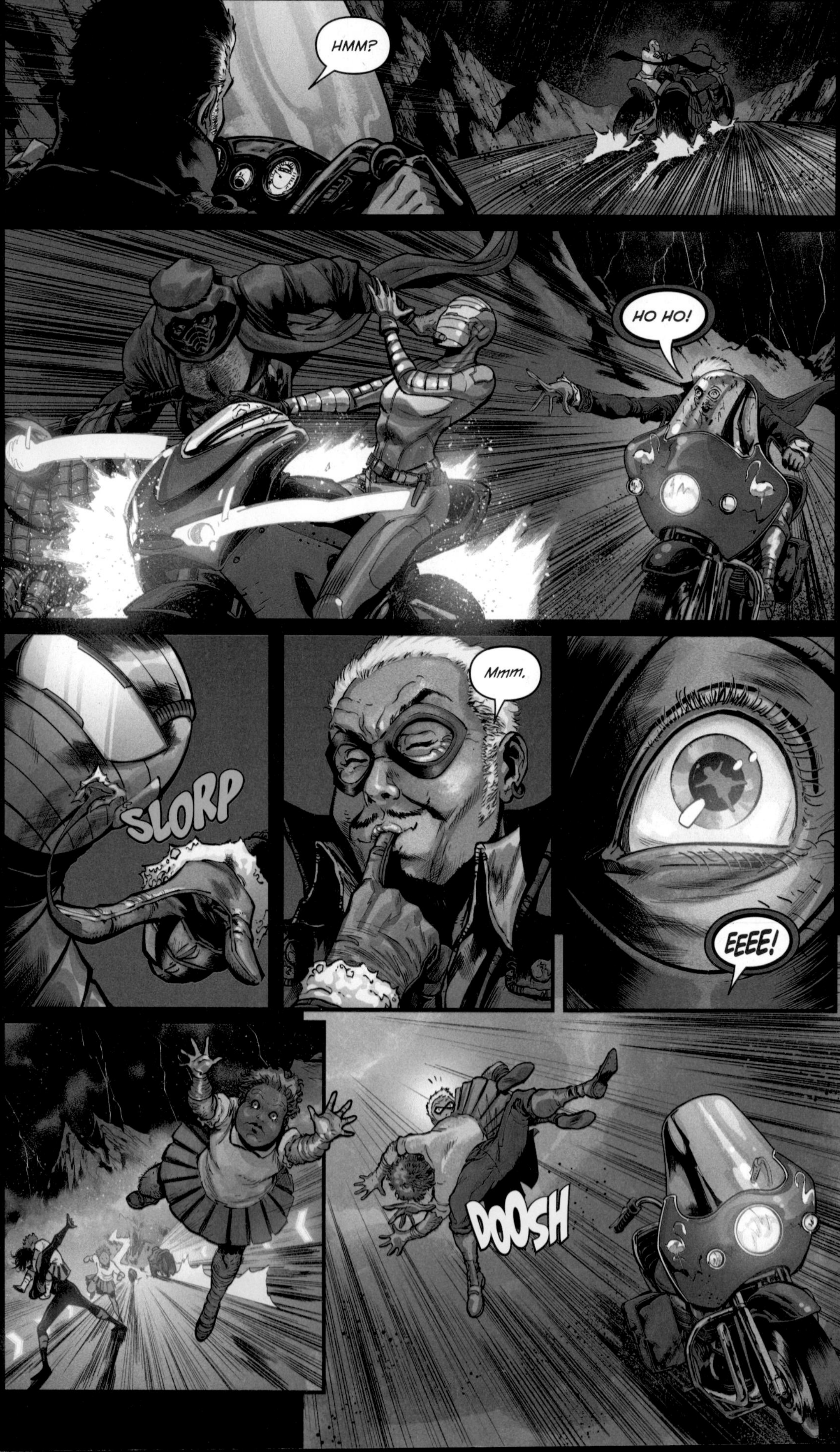
HMM?
HO HO!
SLORP
Mmm.
EEEE!
DOOSH

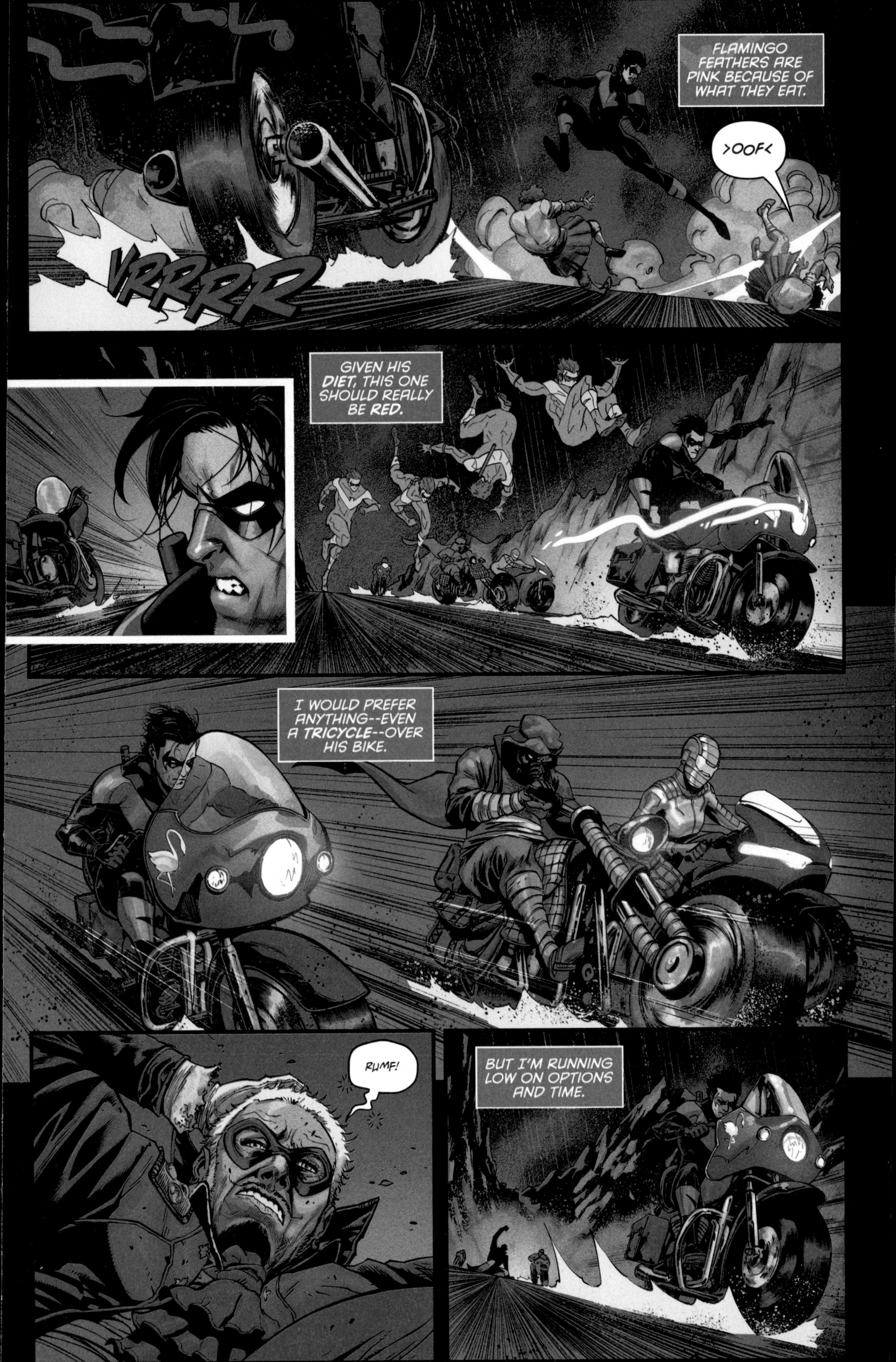
FLAMINGO FEATHERS ARE PINK BECAUSE OF WHAT THEY EAT.
>OOF<
VRRRR
GIVEN HIS DIET, THIS ONE SHOULD REALLY BE RED.
I WOULD PREFER ANYTHING--EVEN A TRICYCLE--OVER HIS BIKE.
RUMF!
BUT I'M RUNNING LOW ON OPTIONS AND TIME.

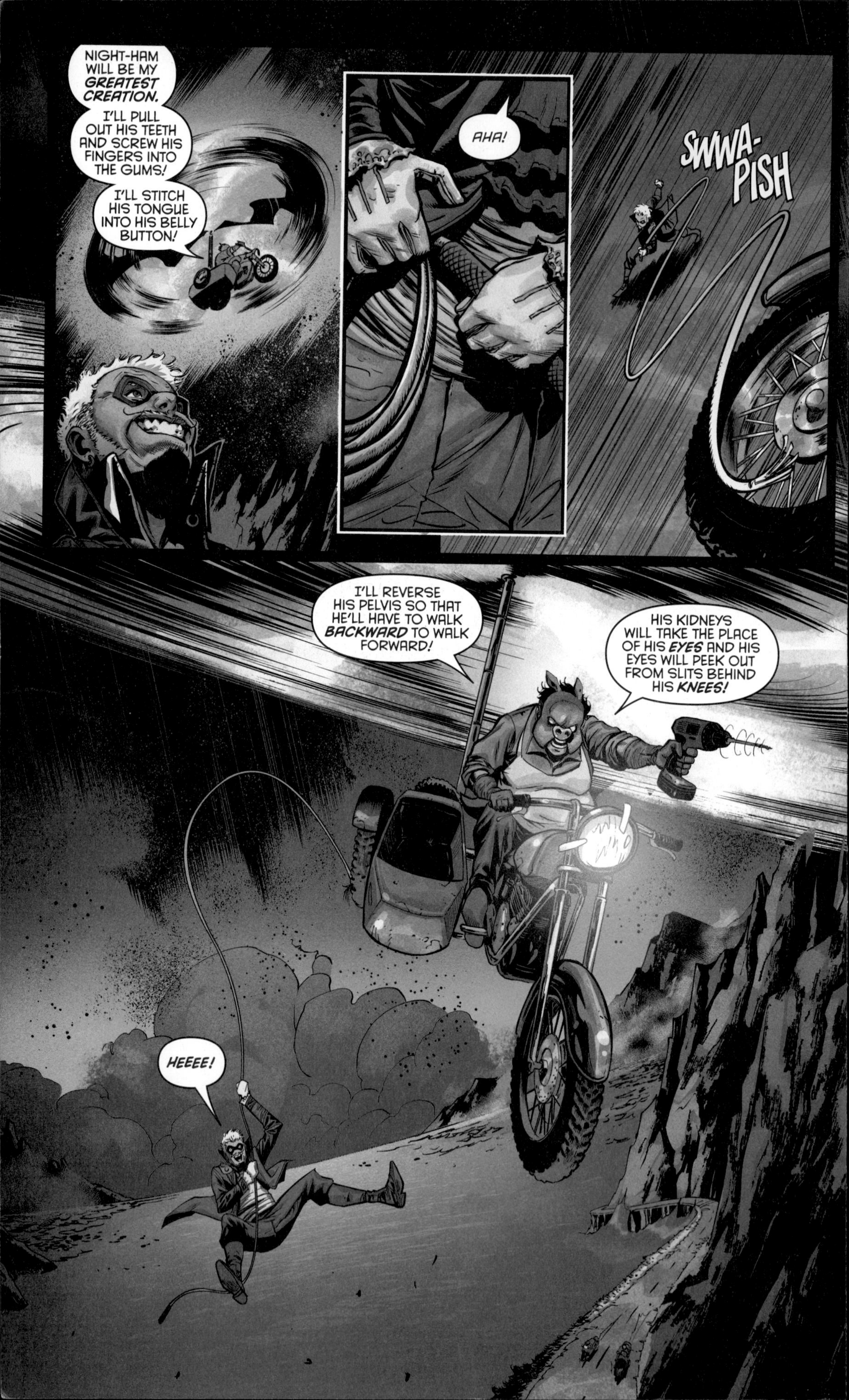
NIGHT-HAM WILL BE MY GREATEST CREATION.
I'LL PULL OUT HIS TEETH AND SCREW HIS FINGERS INTO THE GUMS!
I'LL STITCH HIS TONGUE INTO HIS BELLY BUTTON!
AHA!
SWWA-PISH
I'LL REVERSE HIS PELVIS SO THAT HE'LL HAVE TO WALK BACKWARD TO WALK FORWARD!
HIS KIDNEYS WILL TAKE THE PLACE OF HIS EYES AND HIS EYES WILL PEEK OUT FROM SLITS BEHIND HIS KNEES!
HEEEE!

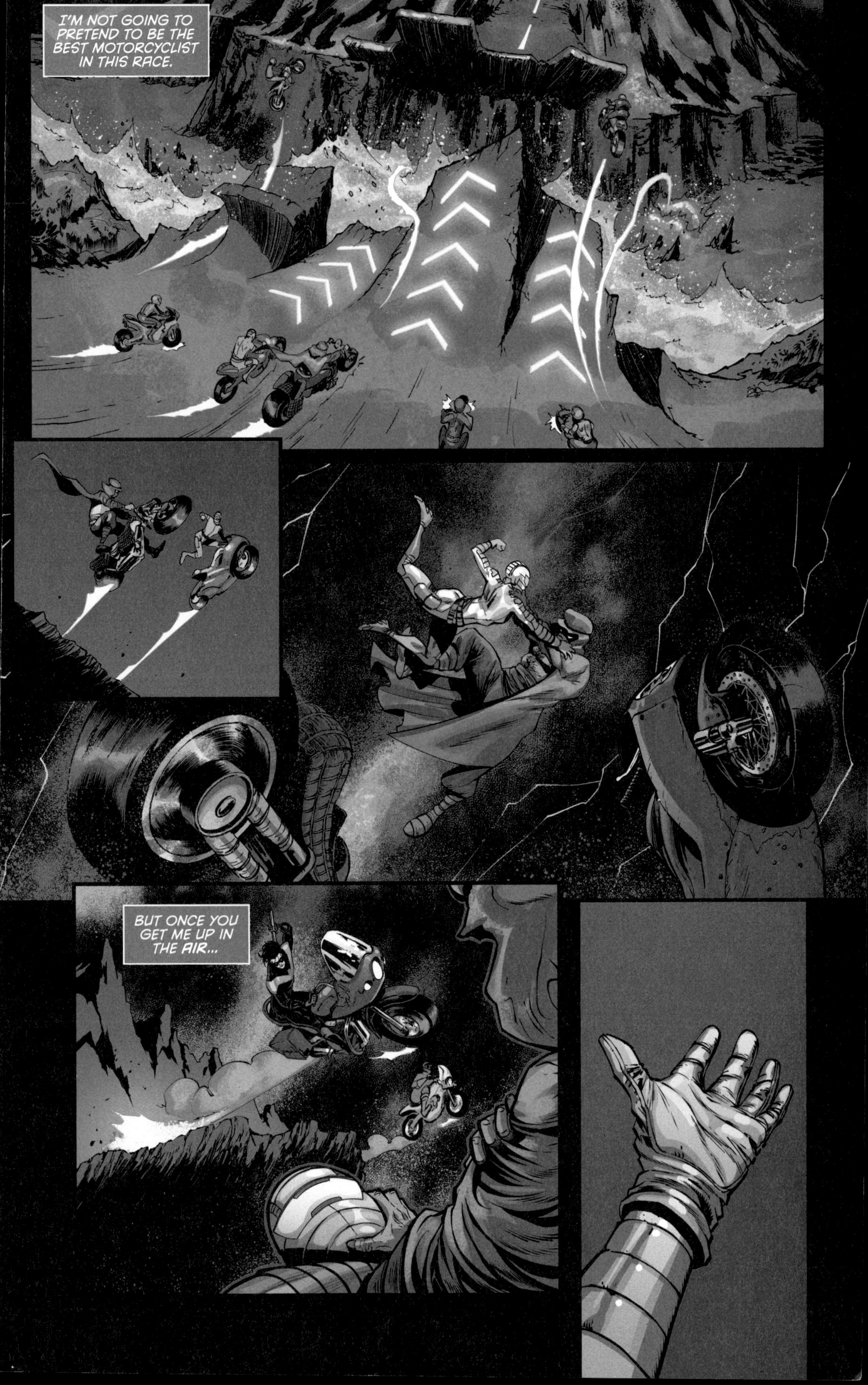
I'M NOT GOING TO PRETEND TO BE THE BEST MOTORCYCLIST IN THIS RACE.
BUT ONCE YOU GET ME UP IN THE AIR...

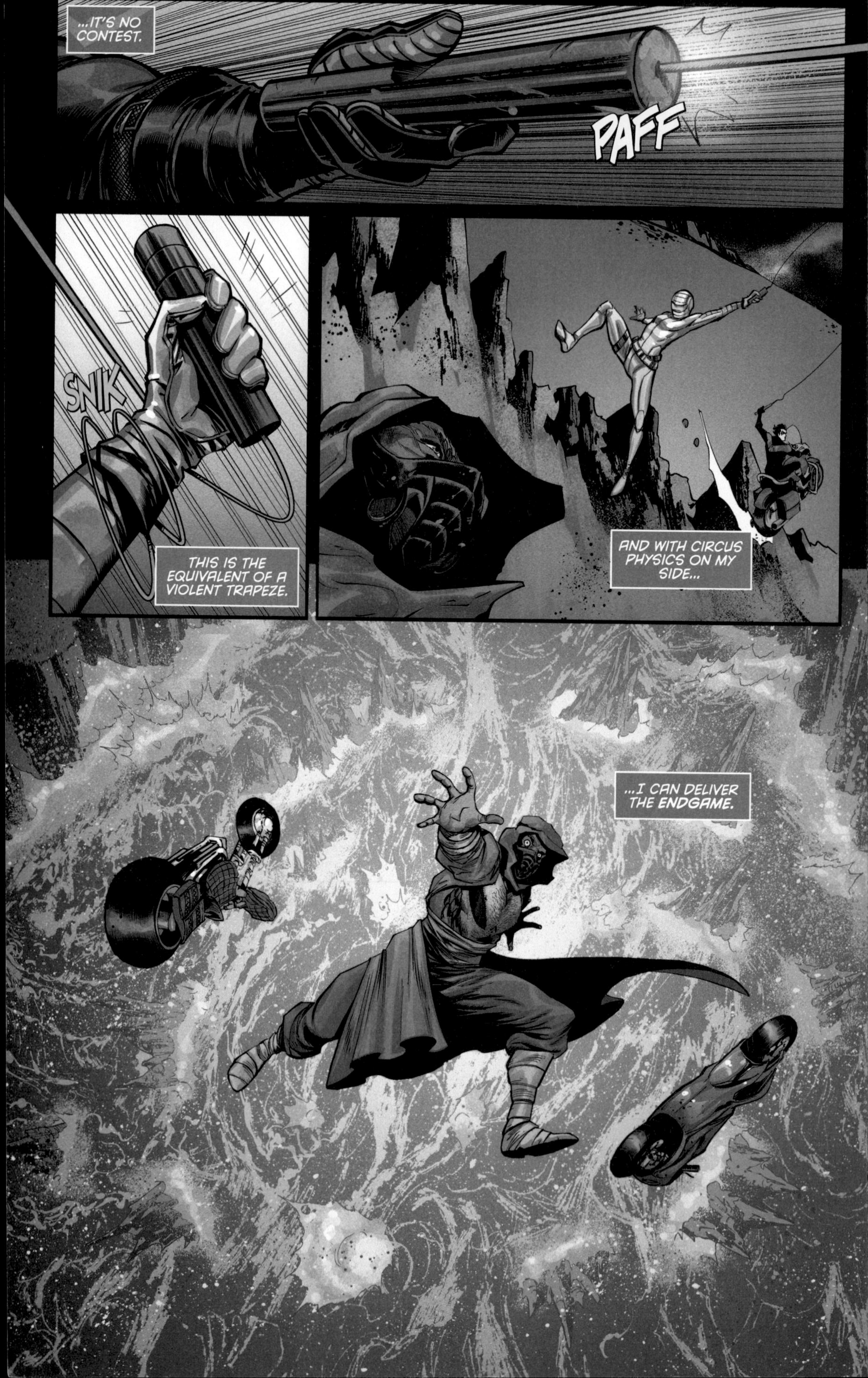
...IT'S NO CONTEST.
PAFF
SNIK
THIS IS THE EQUIVALENT OF A VIOLENT TRAPEZE.
AND WITH CIRCUS PHYSICS ON MY SIDE...
...I CAN DELIVER THE ENDGAME.

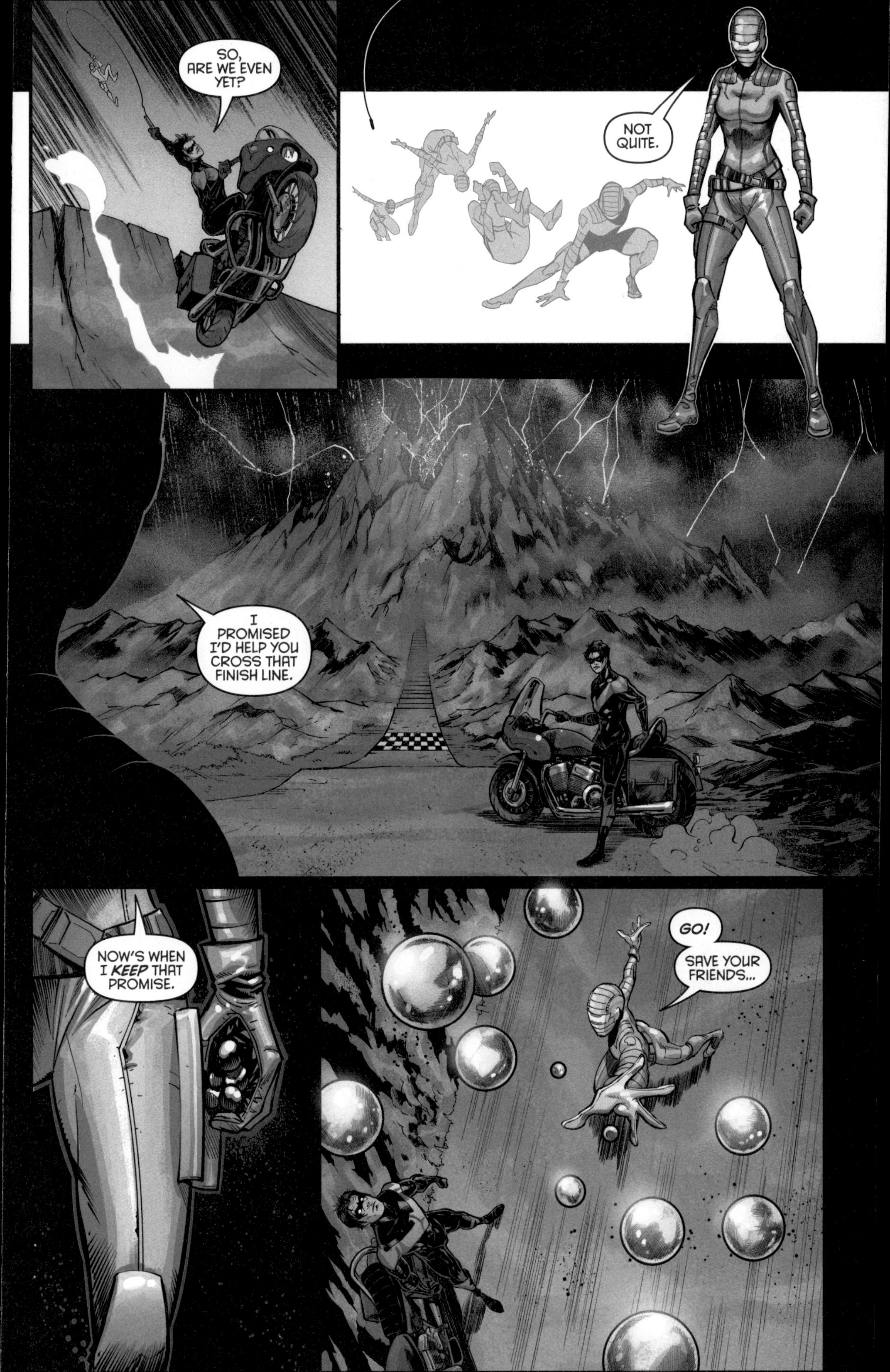
SO, ARE WE EVEN YET?
NOT QUITE.
I PROMISED I'D HELP YOU CROSS THAT FINISH LINE.
NOW'S WHEN I *KEEP* THAT PROMISE.
GO!
SAVE YOUR FRIENDS...

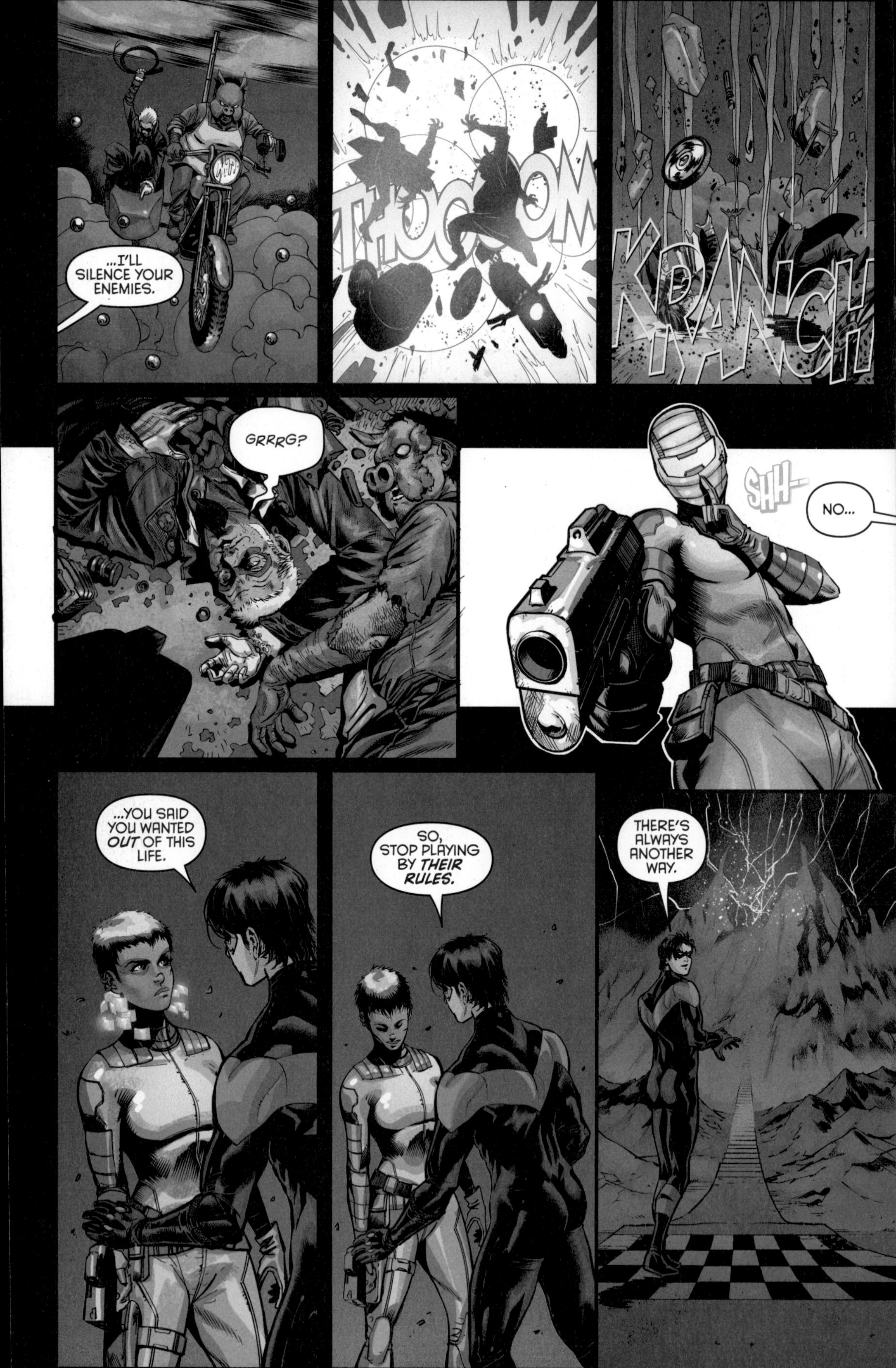
...I'LL SILENCE YOUR ENEMIES.
THOOOOM
KRANCH
GRRRG?
SHH-
NO...
...YOU SAID YOU WANTED *OUT* OF THIS LIFE.
SO, STOP PLAYING BY *THEIR RULES.*
THERE'S ALWAYS ANOTHER WAY.

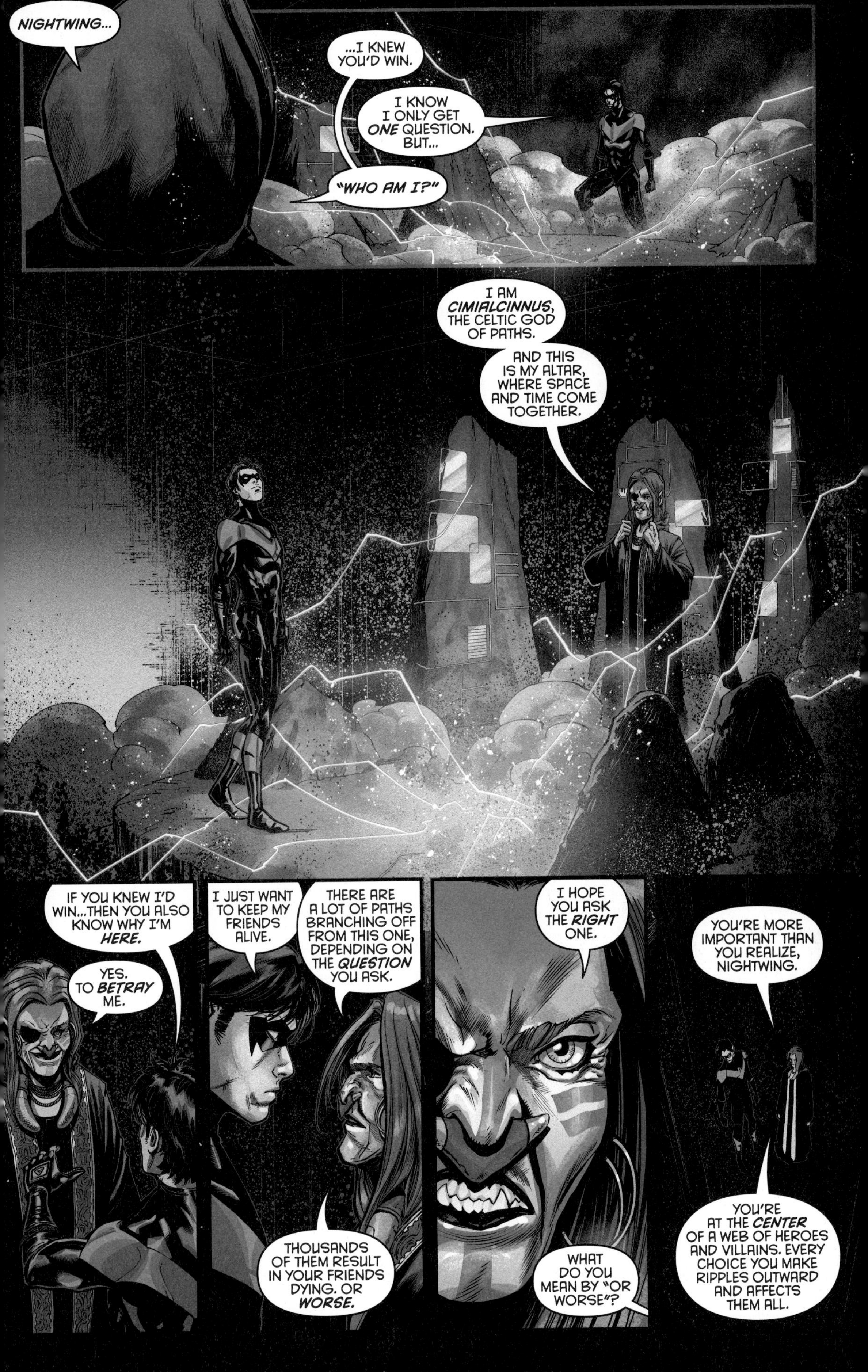
NIGHTWING...
...I KNEW YOU'D WIN.
I KNOW I ONLY GET ONE QUESTION. BUT...
"WHO AM I?"
I AM CIMIALCINNUS, THE CELTIC GOD OF PATHS.
AND THIS IS MY ALTAR, WHERE SPACE AND TIME COME TOGETHER.
IF YOU KNEW I'D WIN...THEN YOU ALSO KNOW WHY I'M HERE.
YES. TO BETRAY ME.
I JUST WANT TO KEEP MY FRIENDS ALIVE.
THERE ARE A LOT OF PATHS BRANCHING OFF FROM THIS ONE, DEPENDING ON THE QUESTION YOU ASK.
THOUSANDS OF THEM RESULT IN YOUR FRIENDS DYING. OR WORSE.
I HOPE YOU ASK THE RIGHT ONE.
WHAT DO YOU MEAN BY "OR WORSE"?
YOU'RE MORE IMPORTANT THAN YOU REALIZE, NIGHTWING.
YOU'RE AT THE CENTER OF A WEB OF HEROES AND VILLAINS. EVERY CHOICE YOU MAKE RIPPLES OUTWARD AND AFFECTS THEM ALL.

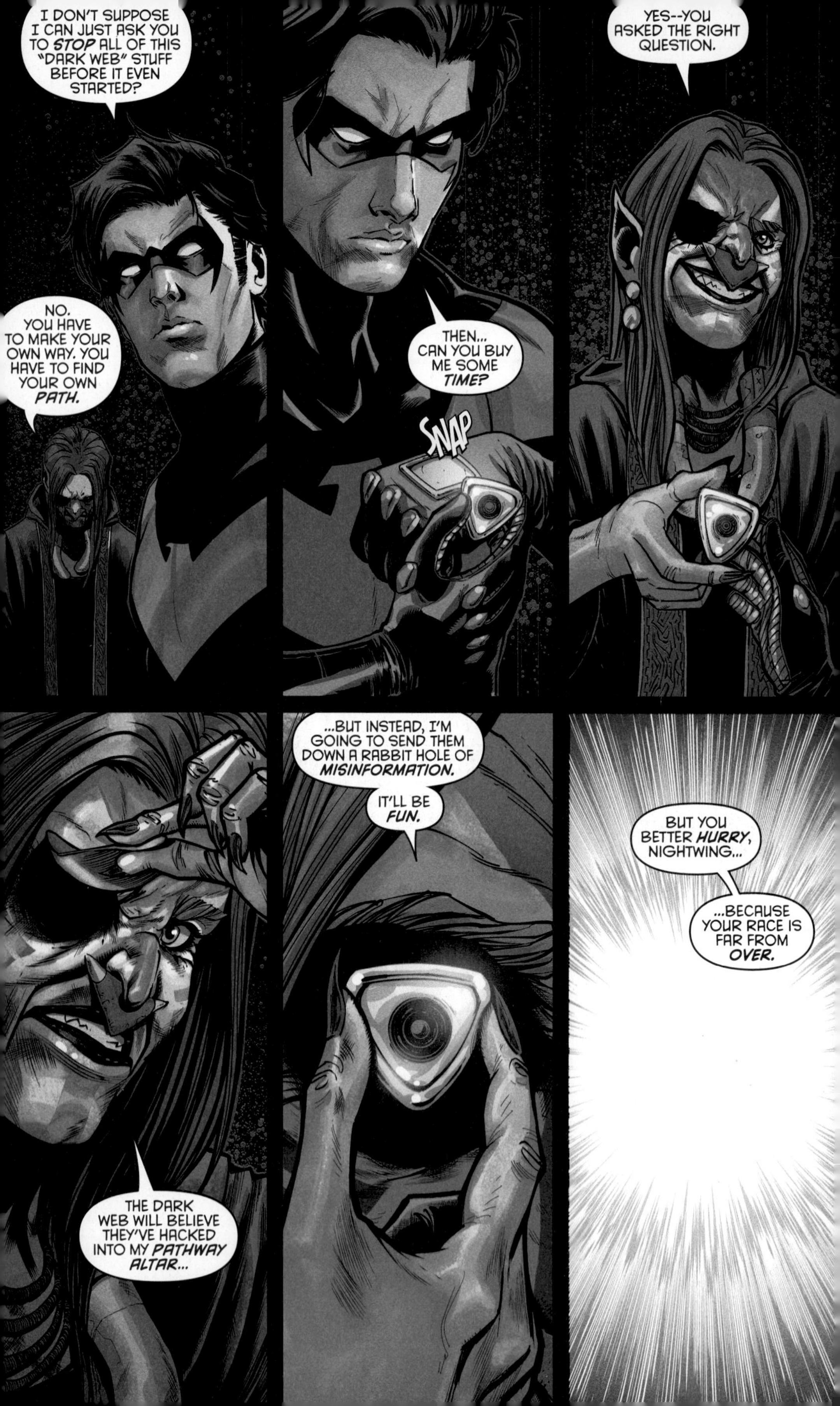
I DON'T SUPPOSE I CAN JUST ASK YOU TO STOP ALL OF THIS "DARK WEB" STUFF BEFORE IT EVEN STARTED?
NO. YOU HAVE TO MAKE YOUR OWN WAY. YOU HAVE TO FIND YOUR OWN PATH.
THEN... CAN YOU BUY ME SOME TIME?
SNAP
YES--YOU ASKED THE RIGHT QUESTION.
THE DARK WEB WILL BELIEVE THEY'VE HACKED INTO MY PATHWAY ALTAR...
...BUT INSTEAD, I'M GOING TO SEND THEM DOWN A RABBIT HOLE OF MISINFORMATION.
IT'LL BE FUN.
BUT YOU BETTER HURRY, NIGHTWING...
...BECAUSE YOUR RACE IS FAR FROM OVER.

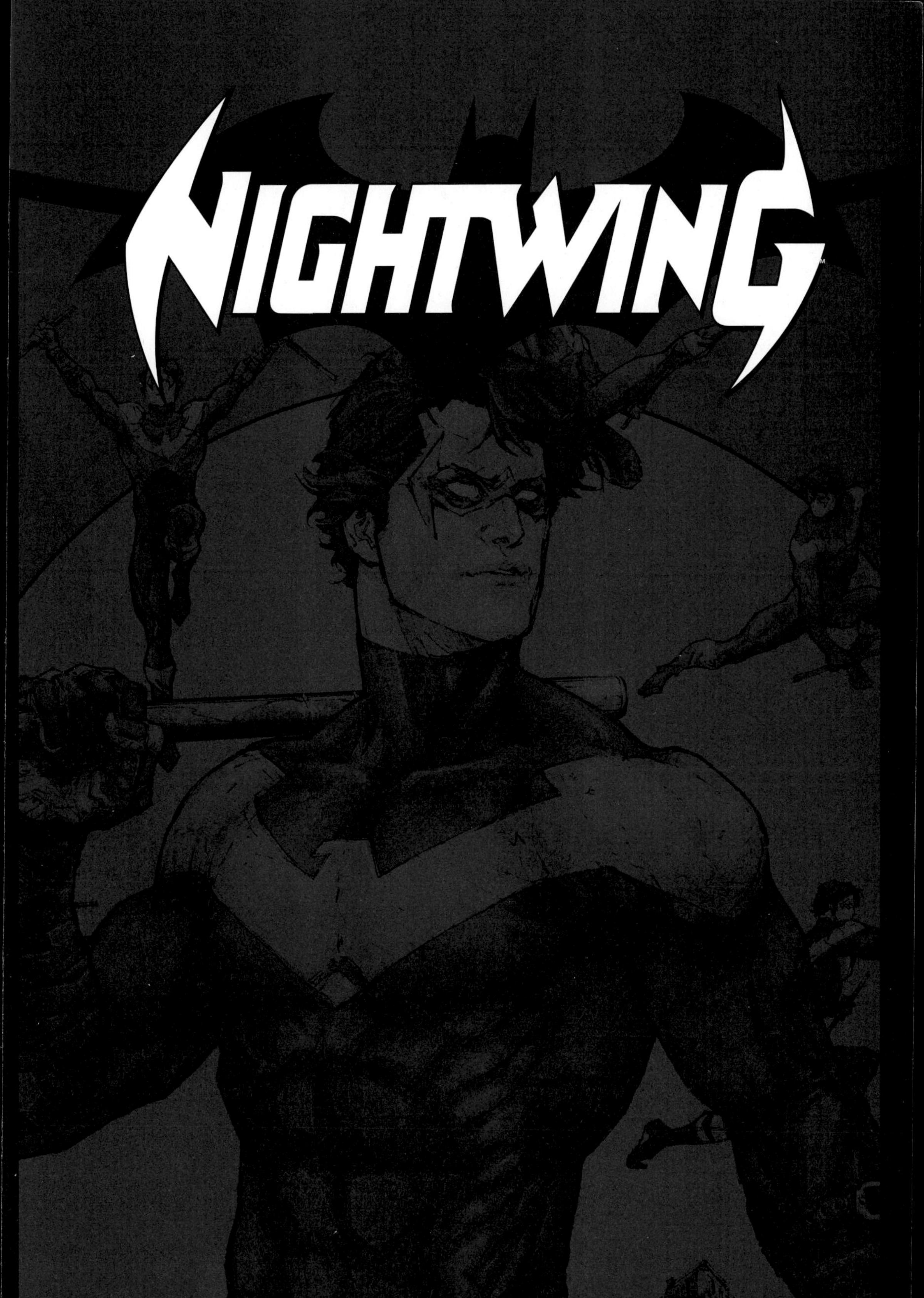
NIGHTWING

VARIANT COVER GALLERY

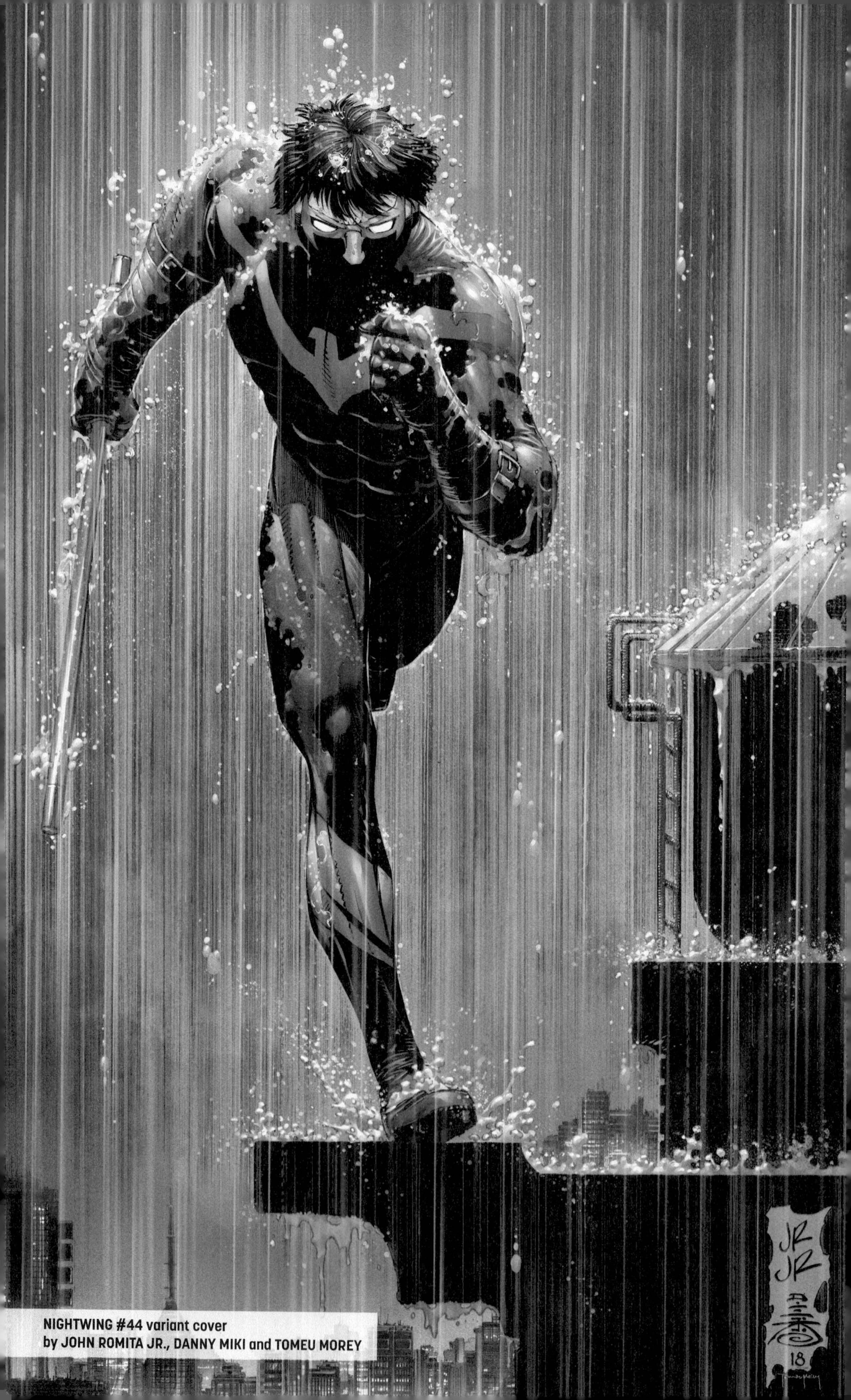
JR
JR
18

NIGHTWING #44 variant cover
by JOHN ROMITA JR., DANNY MIKI and TOMEU MOREY

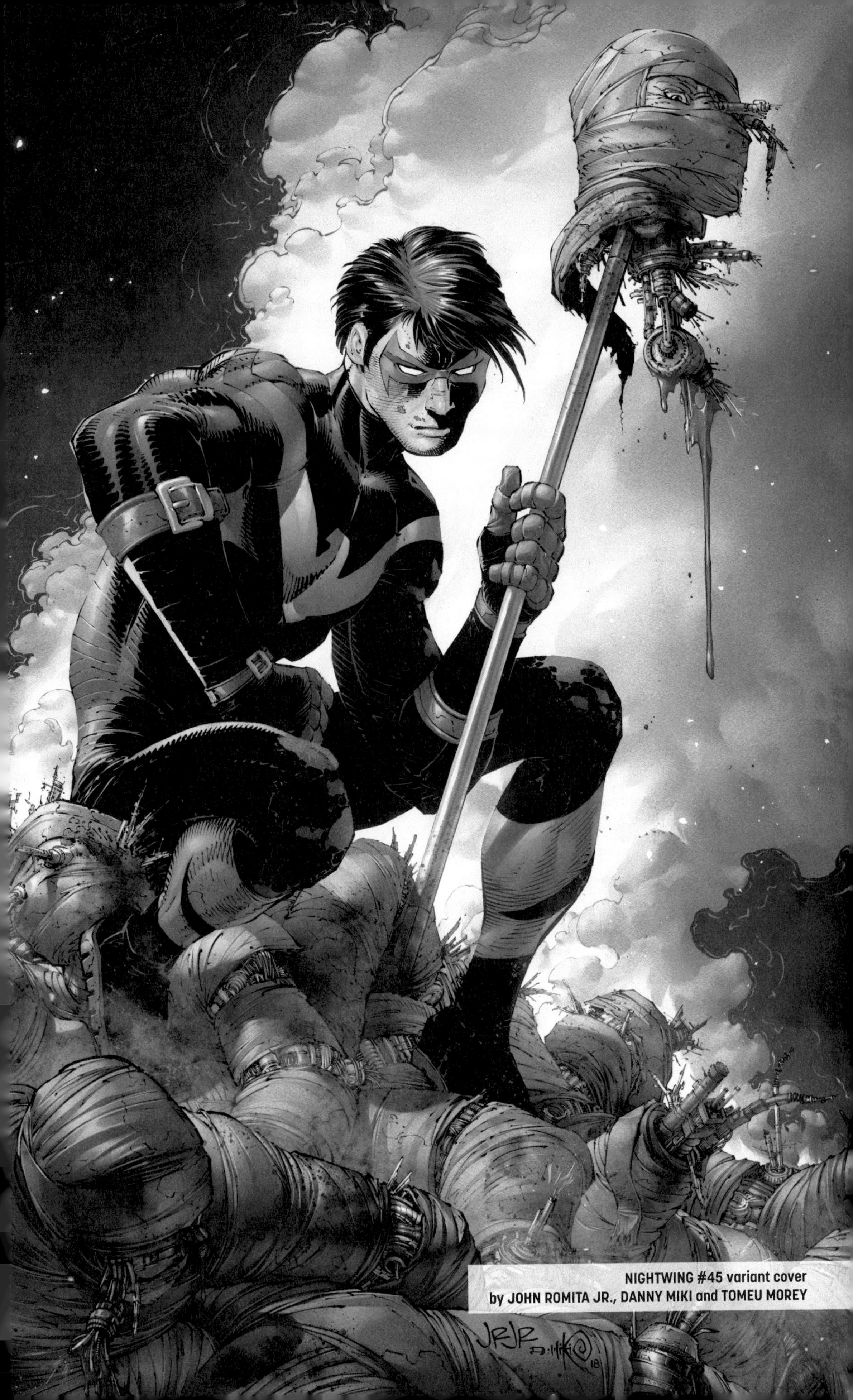

NIGHTWING #45 variant cover
by JOHN ROMITA JR., DANNY MIKI and TOMEU MOREY

NIGHTWING #46 variant cover
by BEN OLIVER

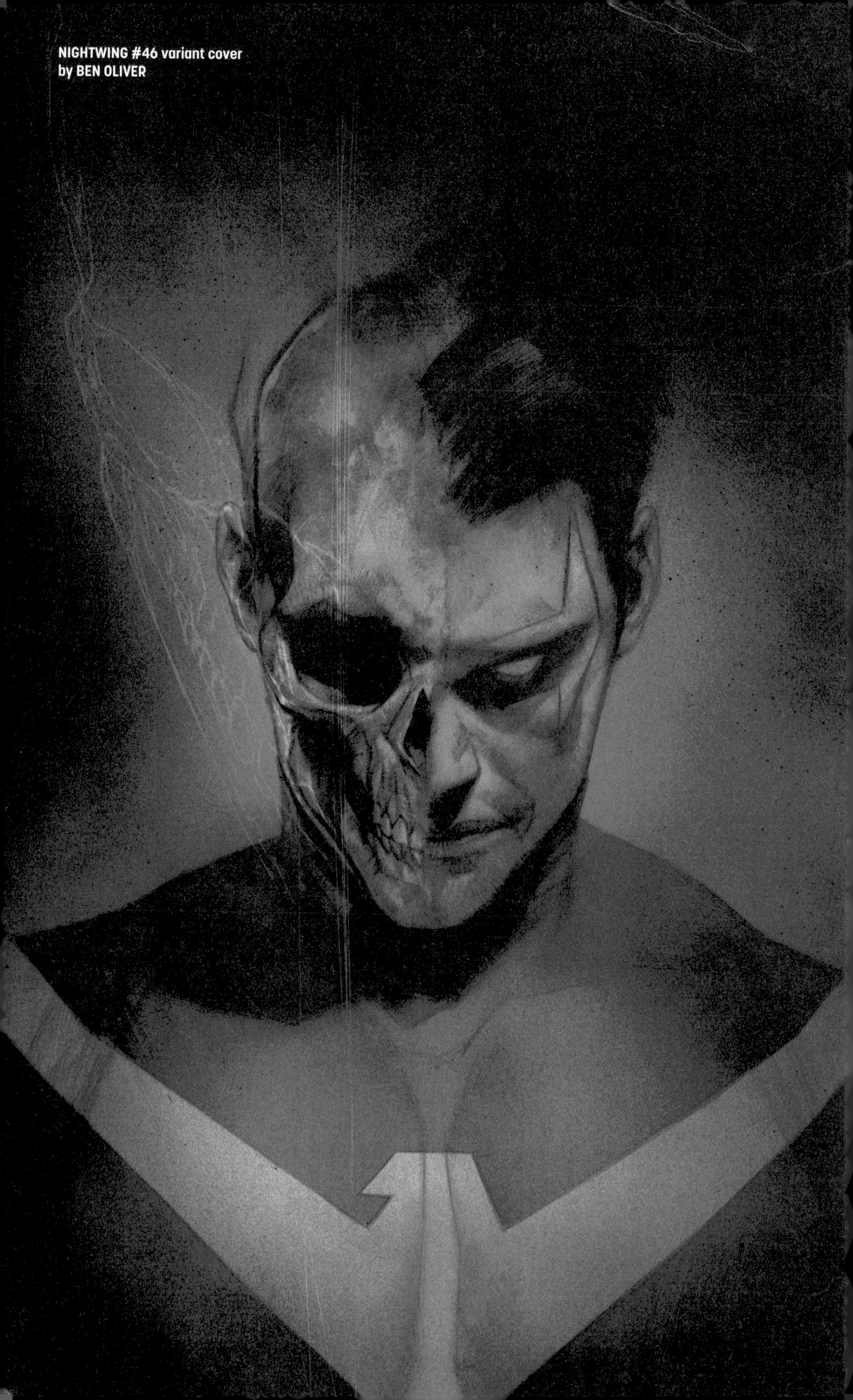

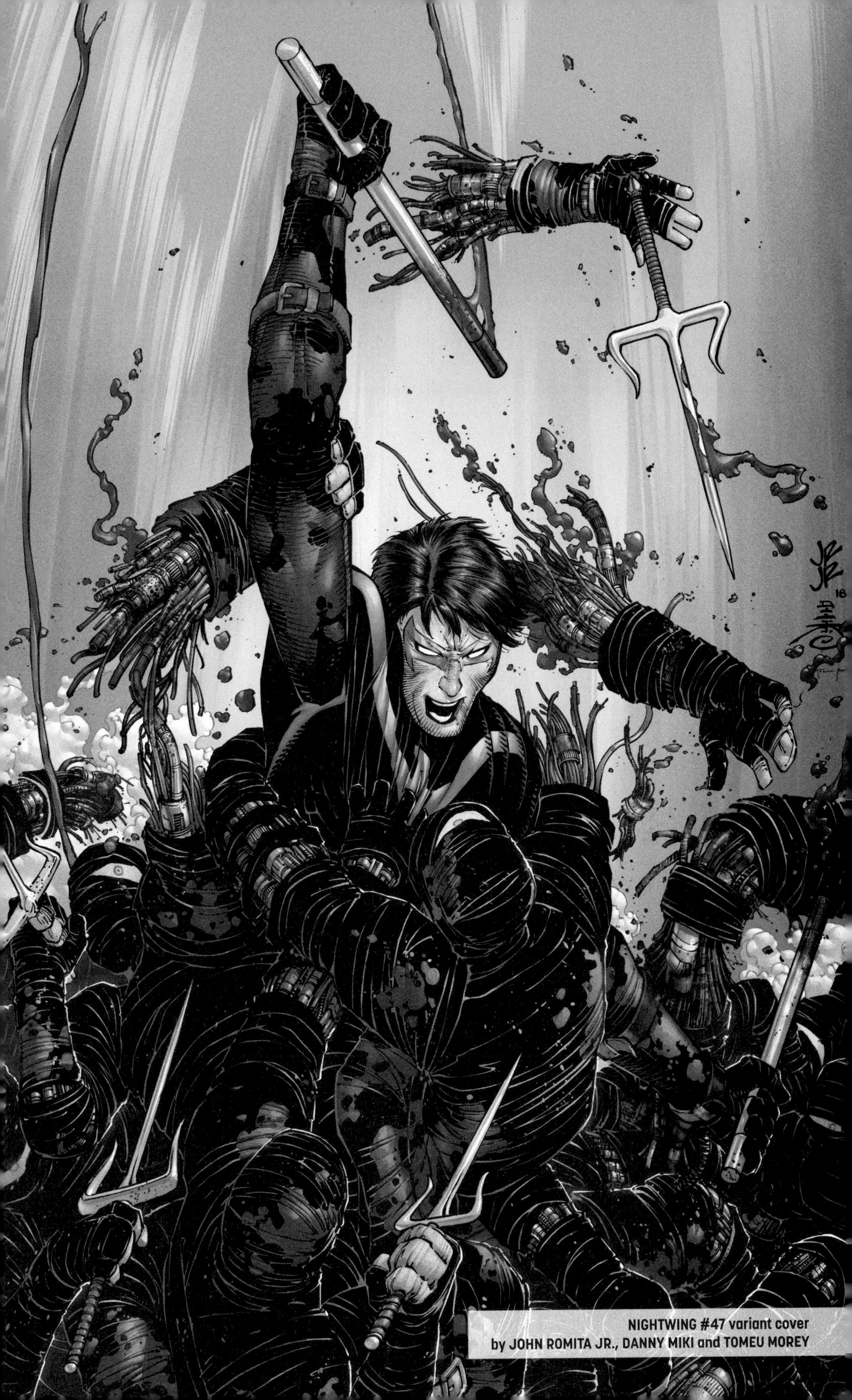

NIGHTWING #47 variant cover
by JOHN ROMITA JR., DANNY MIKI and TOMEU MOREY

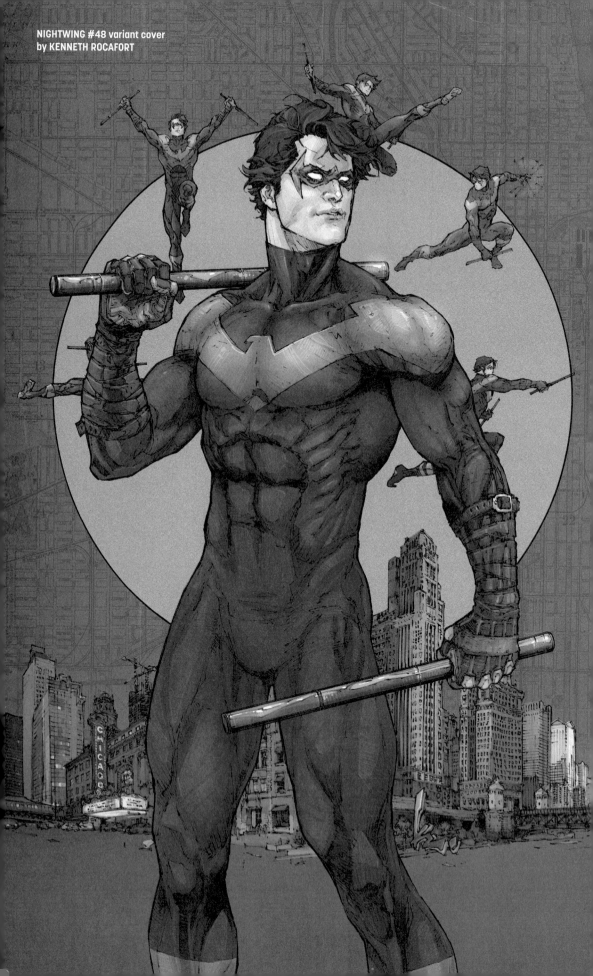

NIGHTWING #48 variant cover
by KENNETH ROCAFORT

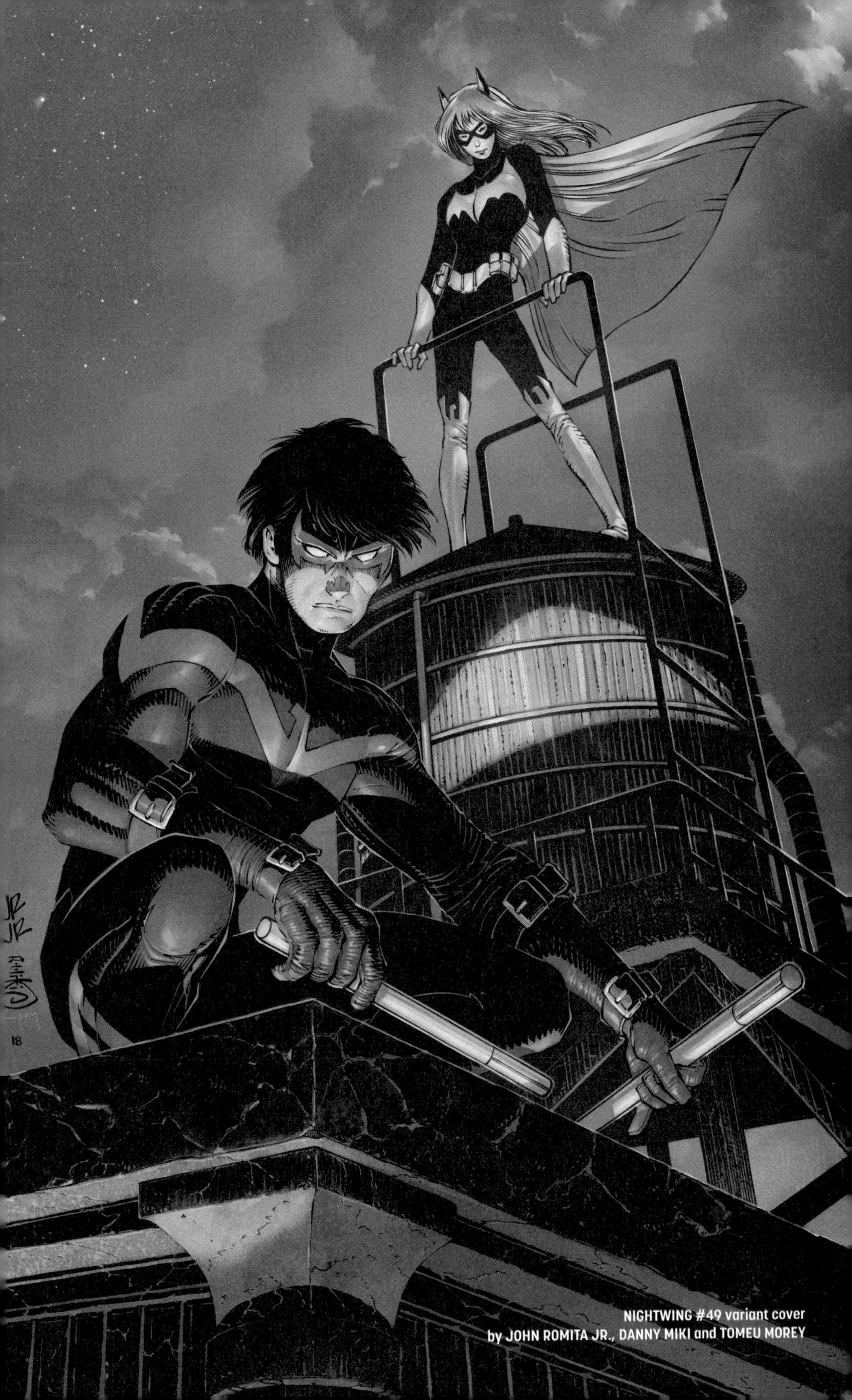

NIGHTWING #49 variant cover
by JOHN ROMITA JR., DANNY MIKI and TOMEU MOREY

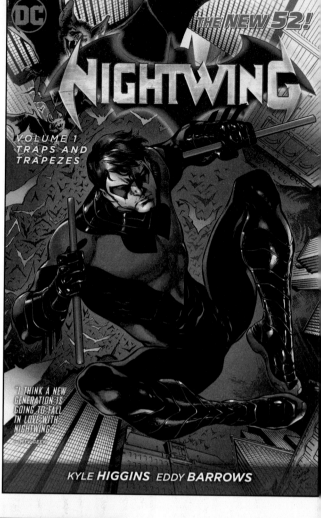
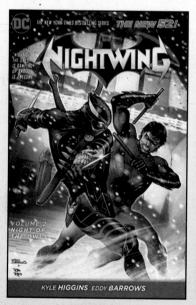